FUNDING FOR LAW

LEGAL EDUCATION RESEARCH & STUDY

LAW SCHOOL FELLOWSHIPS & INTERNSHIPS

GRANTS FOR LEGAL RESEARCH

KAREN CANTRELL AND DENISE WALLEN

ORYX PRESS 1991

Copyright © 1991 by
The Oryx Press
4041 North Central at Indian School Road
Phoenix, Arizona 85012-3397

Published simultaneously in Canada

Printed and Bound in the United States of America

♾ The paper used in this publication meets the minimum requirements of American National Standard for Information Science—Permanence of Paper for Printed Library Materials, ANSI Z39.48, 1984.

Library of Congress Cataloging-in-Publication Data

Cantrell, Karen.
   Funding for law : legal education, research and study / Karen Cantrell and Denise Wallen.
       p.   cm.
   Includes bibliographical references and index.
   ISBN 0-89774-565-5
   1. Law—Study and teaching—United States—Finance—Directories.
2. Law schools—United States—Finance—Directories.   3. Law libraries—United States—Finance—Directories.   I. Wallen, Denise.
II. Title.
KF266.C36   1990
340′.071′173—dc20   90-21456
                                                                        CIP

Table of Contents

Introduction

Funding for Law: Legal Education, Research and Study is designed to facilitate the search for financial support for scholars of the law. This directory includes funding for students and educators; law libraries and law schools; policy analysts; practitioners; and academicians in a wide variety of disciplines including anthropology, economics, history, the humanities, law, political science, philosophy, sociology, and public administration. It lists funding support for work in traditional areas of the law, such as administrative law, civil law, constitutional law, criminal law, environmental law, and international law and support for work in a variety of areas of sociolegal studies including legal anthropology, bioethics, sociology of law, legal history, philosophy of law, law and economics, and law and society.

This directory targets funding for legal education, research, and study. It *does not* include support for advocacy, litigation, or legal services. Further, it does not include contract opportunities, community foundations, or, with few exceptions, geographically restricted funding sources. The directory is primarily focused on the study of or research on the law, broadly defined.

The sources of support were selected for inclusion after reviewing annual reports, award lists, the general literature on funding, program guidelines, and government publications. Potential sources were contacted for current information on program guidelines and areas of funding interest. After review of these materials, those sources most likely to fund legal education, research, or study were determined.

The directory lists nearly 500 sources of support and is designed to provide sufficient detail to steer applicants in the right direction in their search for funding. The funding sources, arranged alphabetically by sponsor, include support offered by private and corporate foundations, corporate direct giving, government agencies, associations and organizations, universities, and professional societies. Program profiles include available information essential to securing support: address, telephone number, program purpose and activities, samples of previously funded projects, eligibility and limitations, fiscal information, application information, deadlines, and any useful additional information. Applicants should, however, confirm all profile contents prior to proposal development. This means that current funding priorities, the availability of funding, and deadlines should be confirmed with the sponsor. It is especially important for applicants interested in East Europe, specifically Germany, to contact potential funding sources to determine up-to-the-minute grant-making programs and policies.

To facilitate the identification of appropriate sources of support, a section on "How to Use this Directory" follows, and a number of useful indexes have been designed and included. A Subject Index of keyword terms allows the user to locate sources of funding in a particular area of law or interest, e.g., aging, administration of justice, bioethics, health policy, natural resources, tax law, or water. It also identifies funding mechanisms and specific types of support, such as fellowships, travel, publication, dissertation and faculty support, or postdoctoral support abroad. A Sponsor Type Index is also included so the user may properly discern corporate and private foundations, associations and organizations, and government agencies. This book concludes with a list of the sponsoring organizations and their addresses and a Selected Bibliography of useful printed and electronic sources.

How to Use This Directory

Funding for Law: Legal Education, Research and Study is composed of a Program Profiles Section, a Subject Index, a Sponsor Type Index, a Listing of Sponsoring Organizations, and a Selected Bibliography.

PROGRAM PROFILES SECTION

Each entry in this section is composed of all or some of the following elements: accession number; sponsoring organization name; department or division name; street address with city, state, zip, country, and telephone number; the program title; for federal programs, the *Catalog of Federal Domestic Assistance* program identification number; a program description which briefly details the purpose of the program; a sample grants statement which lists programs recently funded by the sponsor; a statement of program eligibility/limitations describing any special requirements or restrictions for each program; fiscal information; application information; deadline information; and a statement of any additional, useful information that does not fit into one of the listed categories.

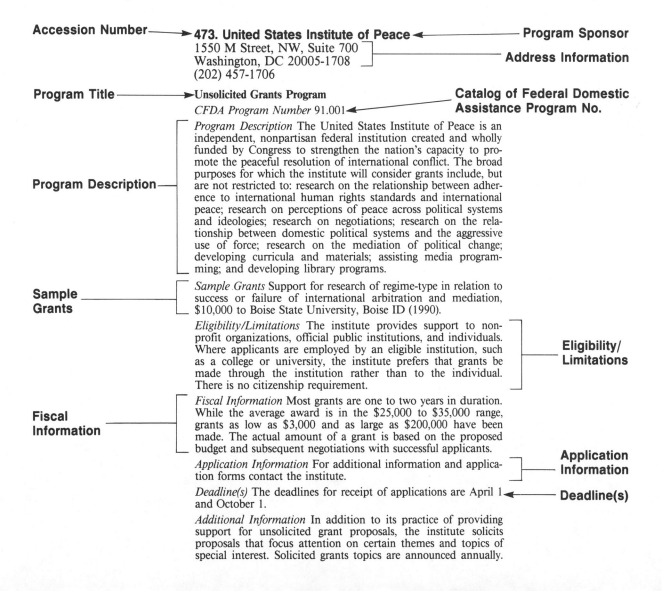

SUBJECT INDEX

The most effective way to access specific funding programs is by searching the Subject Index. Index terms have been assigned to each program. All subject terms are displayed with the applicable program and the program's accession number listed alphabetically under each term.

Subject Term ——————→ **Human Rights** *See Also* **Economic Justice; Social Justice**

J. Roderick MacArthur Foundation, 287
The John Merck Fund, 294
United States Institute of Peace, 473 ◄——— **Sponsor Name & Accession No.**

SPONSOR TYPE INDEX

This index is organized into six different sponsor types with the name of the program sponsor and the program's accession number listed under each type. The six sponsor types are: Corporation; Federal; Foundation; Museum/Library; Nonprofit Organization; and University.

Sponsor Type ——————→ **Nonprofit Organization**

Social Science Research Council, 435-52
The Harry S Truman Library Institute, 467-69
United States Institute of Peace, 472-73 ◄——— **Sponsor Name Accession No.**
W.E. Upjohn Institute for Employment Research, 477
The Urban Institute, 478

LISTING OF SPONSORING ORGANIZATIONS

This index alphabetically lists all sponsors with their addresses.

United States Institute of Peace ◄——— **Sponsoring Organization**
1550 M Street, NW, Suite 700
Washington, DC 20005-1708

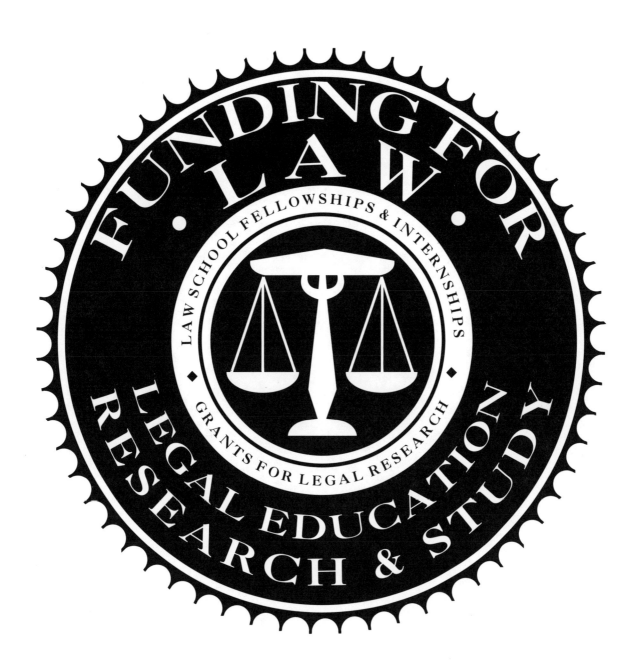

FUNDING FOR LAW

LAW SCHOOL FELLOWSHIPS & INTERNSHIPS

GRANTS FOR LEGAL RESEARCH

LEGAL EDUCATION RESEARCH & STUDY

Program Profiles

1. AARP Andrus Foundation

1909 K Street, NW
Washington, DC 20049
(202) 662-4986

Research Grants to Universities

Program Description These grants support applied research in gerontology (behavioral, social, health sciences, policy planning and practice) aimed at producing information of a practical, usable character which will assist the association, older persons, policy planners and formulators, service providers and practitioners.

Sample Grants Support for a study "Medicare Home Health Coverage: Protecting the Right of Medicare Beneficiaries to a Formal Coverage Determination," Indiana University-Purdue University of Indianapolis, School of Law (1988). Support for a study "Factors Influencing Hospital Patients Preferences in Health Care Decisions within the Process of Assigning a Durable Power of Attorney," Department of Psychiatry and Center on Aging, Georgetown University (1990). Support for a study "The Impact of Statutory Bans on Physician Balance Billing for Services to Medicare Beneficiaries," Brookdale Center on Aging, City University of New York, Hunter College (1990).

Eligibility/Limitations Universities and colleges are eligible to apply.

Fiscal Information A university or college may receive up to $75,000 a year for approved research projects. Purchase or rental of nonexpendable equipment, graduate student research assistants, tuition, fees or stipends are not supported by the grant. Not more than 8 percent of the total grant funds may be used for overhead.

Application Information Application guidelines are available on request.

Deadline(s) The foundation has semiannual deadlines, January 1, June 1.

2. ABA IOLTA Clearinghouse

750 North Lake Shore Drive
Chicago, IL 60611
(312) 988-5748

IOLTA Programs

Program Description IOLTA (Interest on Lawyers Trust Accounts) programs operate in all states except Indiana, the District of Columbia, and Puerto Rico. IOLTA programs fund legal services, pro bono work, law-related education, administration of justice programs, and scholarships and loans. Contact your state bar association for information about IOLTA programs in your area, or contact the IOLTA Clearinghouse of the ABA for a list of IOLTA programs in the United States and its territories.

3. Administrative Conference of the United States

2120 L Street, NW, Suite 500
Washington, DC 20037
(202) 254-7020

Grants

Program Description The Administrative Conference of the United States has a broad charter to look at federal administrative procedures and recommend improvements. The conference supports studies on a wide range of topics in the administrative process/administrative law fields. The principal areas of research in 1989 were alternative dispute resolution, bank regulatory procedures, government ethics laws, international trade procedures, and the federal health care system.

Sample Grants In 1989 research included: evaluation of choice of forum in government contract litigation; study of pro bono practice by government attorneys; a review of procedures for deciding antidumping and countervailing duty cases; a study of the National Labor Relations Board's use of informal rule making to establish bargaining units; and a study of judicial remands of cases to administrative agencies.

Eligibility/Limitations Grant recipients are usually law professors.

Fiscal Information Grants range from $5,000 to $12,000 for up to 18 months of study.

Application Information Specific interest lists are distributed periodically in the *Commerce Business Daily*. There are no formally published guidelines. Contact the conference for application information.

Deadline(s) No deadlines are published.

4. Aetna Life & Casualty Foundation

Corporate Public Involvement Department
151 Farmington Avenue
Hartford, CT 06156
(203) 273-3340

Contributions Program

Program Description The Aetna Life and Casualty Company and Aetna Life & Casualty Foundation, Inc., are able to help communities meet their needs through grants and investment programs, partnerships with community organizations and encouragement of employees' volunteer activities. The foundation's national grants program focuses on organizations that pursue innovative work in education and youth employment, urban revitalization, civil justice system reform, and leadership development. Within the program category of civil justice system reform the foundation will consider support for organizations that research, quantify and document civil justice system issues. The foundation is particularly interested in programs that result in effective changes in the cost, efficiency, and predictability of the civil justice system. The foundation's overall priorities target the young and disadvantaged, the needs of urban communities, and programs that help disadvantaged persons attain economic and social self-sufficiency. In addition, the foundation looks for programs that have measurable results and offer opportunities to leverage its resources with those of other funders.

Sample Grants To the Yale Law School, New Haven, CT, for a civil liability program, $13,000 (1989). To support the Institute for Civil Justice, Santa Monica, CA, $200,000 (1989). To support the National Center for State Courts, Williamsburg, VA, $30,000 (1989).

Eligibility/Limitations The foundation will not make grants to: individuals; organizations not designated 501(c)(3) tax-exempt public charities by the Internal Revenue Service; capital or endowment campaigns; fund-raising dinners or special events; or the sponsorship of conferences.

Fiscal Information The foundation awarded over $9 million in grants in 1989.

Application Information The foundation requires that all grant applicants submit a preliminary proposal. The proposal must include: a description of the organization and its history and purpose; documentation of 501(c)(3) public charity status; a description of the project for which funds are requested; a summary of the program or organization budget; and the amount requested. The foundation staff will review this information and determine if the organization and its project are consistent with foundation priorities. Once the foundation staff gives a positive response, a formal proposal will be requested.

Deadline(s) The foundation staff will acknowledge receipt of your proposal within three weeks.

Additional Information In addition to a national grants program, the foundation also operates local grants programs through selected Aetna field offices across the country. If the foundation staff thinks your organization's needs may be more appropriately served by manager-referred programs, proposals may be referred to the nearest field office for review.

5. The Ahmanson Foundation

9215 Wilshire Boulevard
Beverly Hills, CA 90210
(213) 278-0770

Program Description The foundation emphasizes support of the arts and humanities, education, medicine and health, and support for a broad range of social welfare programs.

Eligibility/Limitations Grants are provided only to nonprofit organizations classified as tax-exempt under Section 501(c)(3) of the Internal Revenue Code of 1954 and treated as other than a private foundation under Section 509(a) of the Code. Grants are made primarily to organizations in Southern California with an emphasis on the Los Angeles area. The foundation occasionally makes a few selected grants to organizations located outside of this geographic area; proposals are invited. The foundation does not make grants to individuals or for continuing support, annual campaigns, deficit financing, professorships, internships, individual scholarships, fellowships or exchange programs, film productions, or loans. The foundation offers support for building funds, capital compaigns, endowment funds, equipment, matching funds, renovation projects, scholarship funds to institutions, and special projects.

Fiscal Information Grants awarded in 1988 totaled over $13.7 million.

Application Information Organizations seeking funding should initially submit a brief proposal letter which describes the goals and activities of the organization and its specific need for funding. The proposal letter should include brief budgetary information related to the request, the funding plan, a financial statement, and other commitments received for support. If the proposal is within the scope of the foundation's activities and resources permit consideration of the request, a review will be made. If necessary, additional information will be requested.

Deadline(s) The foundation has no application deadlines.

6. Alcoa Foundation

1501 Alcoa Building
Pittsburgh, PA 15219-1850
(412) 553-2348

Grants

Program Description The Alcoa Foundation was established in 1952 to help people and programs in communities where Aluminum Company of America (Alcoa) operates facilities and to contribute to worthwhile projects and organizations that benefit the public at large. Grants are made for educational, cultural, health and welfare, civic and community development, and youth organization purposes at the discretion of the foundation directors.

Sample Grants Fellowship support to The Dickinson School of Law, Carlisle, PA (1988). Law Library Fellowship support to Georgetown University, Washington, DC (1988). Support of international tax program to Harvard Law School, Cambridge, MA (1989). Support to Institute for Law and Economics, University of Pennsylvania, Philadelphia, PA (1989).

Eligibility/Limitations Priority consideration is given to programs and activities or organizations and educational institutions in or near communities where Alcoa plants or offices are located. Attention also is given to certain national and international organizations. Only those organizations classified as "public" charities and tax-exempt under Section 501(c)(3) of the Internal Revenue Code will be considered. In general, the foundation does not consider the following for funding: organizations and causes in states or countries where Alcoa does not have a location; individuals; endowment funds; trips or tours; tickets or tables for benefit purposes; or advertising.

Fiscal Information In 1989 Alcoa awarded grants totaling over $5 million.

Application Information Address grant requests to a specific project or need. All requests for funding must be in writing. The foundation prefers that you do not send a letter of inquiry; include a proposal with your initial letter. All requests for funding will be acknowledged upon receipt. The foundation does not have a special application form; requests should be in letter format, including or attaching the following: a description of the project; its purpose and objective; in the case of research, the procedure to be followed; an itemized budget for the project, including income and expense; list of other corporate and foundation donors; copy of your 501(c)(3) tax-exempt declaration ruling from the Internal Revenue Service; audited financial statement; and the amount of money requested.

Deadline(s) Grant applications are accepted year-round, and there is no deadline for submitting a request.

7. American Anthropological Association

Congressional Fellowship Program
1703 New Hampshire Avenue, NW
Washington, DC 20009
(202) 232-8800

Congressional Fellowship Program

Program Description This program is a professional-level internship program that places anthropologists on the staffs of senators, representatives, and congressional committees. Its goals are to enhance the understanding of Congress and the policy-making process within the discipline, assist Congress by having highly qualified anthropologists serve temporarily on personal and committee staffs, and provide practical experience in congressional politics to anthropologists.

Eligibility/Limitations Candidates must have a Ph.D. in anthropology or be fellows of the association. Doctoral candidates who will deposit their dissertations by July 1 and be assured by October 1 that the doctorate will be awarded are also eligible. Applicants must demonstrate exceptional competence in the field, strong interest in the application of anthropology to policy issues, excellence in written and spoken communications, and the ability to work effectively with a broad range of people.

Fiscal Information A stipend of $25,000 is awarded to each fellow.

Application Information Applications will consist of five parts: (1) curriculum vitae; (2) names, addresses, and telephone numbers of at least three references familiar with the professional interests and competence of the applicant; (3) a 1500- to 2500-word paper that convincingly relates a research interest to a specific policy area (applicants are not limited to issues currently before the Congress); (4) a 250- to 500-word summary that conveys the scope and significance of the larger work in terms that are meaningful to a nonanthropologist; and (5) a personal statement of 250-500 words describing future professional goals and how these goals relate to the fellowship program.

Deadline(s) Applications must be received by February 15. Awards will be announced by April 30.

8. American Antiquarian Society
185 Salisbury Street
Worcester, MA 01609-1634
(508) 752-5813 or (508) 755-5221

Frances Hiatt Fellowships

Program Description The American Antiquarian Society, to encourage imaginative and productive research in its unparalleled library collections in early American history and culture, awards to qualified scholars a number of short- and long-term visiting research fellowships. The Frances Hiatt fellowships provide short-term support to graduate students engaged in research for doctoral dissertations in any field of American history and culture.

Eligibility/Limitations Recipients are expected to be in regular and continuous residence at the society's library during the period of the grant.

Fiscal Information The awards carry stipends of $800 per month for one or two months' study at the society.

Application Information Application materials are available from the Associate Director for Research and Publication.

Deadline(s) Completed applications must be received by January 31.

Additional Information AAS and The Newberry Library in Chicago encourage scholars whose research can be strengthened and enriched through residence at both libraries to make application jointly to both institutions' short-term fellowship programs. Scholars seeking short-term fellowships at both institutions may make application using either the AAS or the Newberry form. Applicants for joint consideration must hold the Ph.D. or have completed all requirements for it except the dissertation. Each library's selection committee will judge joint applications independently. Applicants must meet each institution's deadlines to be considered for awards by both libraries.

9. American Antiquarian Society
185 Salisbury Street
Worcester, MA 01609-1634
(508) 752-5813 or (508) 755-5221

National Endowment for the Humanities Fellowships

Program Description The American Antiquarian Society, to encourage imaginative and productive research in its unparalleled library collections in early American history and culture, awards to qualified scholars a number of short- and long-term visiting research fellowships. These fellowships offer long-term support for scholarly research and writing in any field of early American history and culture.

Sample Grants Support for research on "Where's Mine? Debt Litigation in Post-Revolutionary Massachusetts" (1987).

Eligibility/Limitations Fellowships are not awarded to degree candidates or for study leading to advanced degrees, nor are they granted to foreign nationals unless they have been residents in the United States for at least three years preceding the award.

NEH fellows must devote full time to their study and may not accept teaching assignments or undertake any other major activities during the tenure of the award. Also, they may not hold any other major fellowships, except sabbaticals or other grants from their own institutions. Fellows are expected to be in regular and continuous residence at the society's library during the period of the grant.

Fiscal Information At least two fellowships tenable for from six to twelve months; the maximum available stipend is $27,500.

Application Information Application materials are available from the Associate Director for Research and Publication.

Deadline(s) Completed applications must be received by January 31.

Additional Information AAS and The Newberry Library in Chicago encourage scholars whose research can be strengthened and enriched through residence at both libraries to make application jointly to both institutions' short-term fellowship programs. Scholars seeking short-term fellowships at both institutions may make application using either the AAS or the Newberry form. Applicants for joint consideration must hold the Ph.D. or have completed all requirements for it except the dissertation. Each library's selection committee will judge joint applications independently. Applicants must meet each institution's deadlines to be considered for awards by both libraries.

10. American Antiquarian Society
185 Salisbury Street
Worcester, MA 01609-1634
(508) 752-5813 or (508) 755-5221

Kate B. and Hall J. Peterson Fellowships

Program Description The American Antiquarian Society, to encourage imaginative and productive research in its unparalleled library collections in early American history and culture, awards to qualified scholars a number of short- and long-term visiting research fellowships. Peterson fellowships provide short-term support for scholarly research and writing in any field of early American history and culture through 1876.

Eligibility/Limitations Individuals, including foreign nationals and persons at work on dissertations, are eligible to apply. Recipients are expected to be in regular and continuous residence at the society's library during the period of the grant.

Fiscal Information Fellowships vary in duration from one to three months and carry monthly stipends of $800.

Application Information Application materials are available from the Associate Director for Research and Publications.

Deadline(s) Completed applications must be received by January 31.

Additional Information AAS and The Newberry Library in Chicago encourage scholars whose research can be strengthened and enriched through residence at both libraries to make application jointly to both institutions' short-term fellowship programs. Scholars seeking short-term fellowships at both institutions may make application using either the AAS or the Newberry form. Applicants for joint consideration must hold the Ph.D. or have completed all requirements for it except the dissertation. Each library's selection committee will judge joint applications independently. Applicants must meet each institution's deadlines to be considered for awards by both libraries.

11. American Antiquarian Society
185 Salisbury Street
Worcester, MA 01609-1634
(508) 752-5813 or (508) 755-5221

Research Associates

Program Description Scholars who hold sabbaticals or fellowships from other grant-making agencies and who wish to spend at least four weeks researching in the society's collections may make application to be designated a Research Associate. Research Associates may be granted the privileges accorded the society's own fellows, including access to a carrel and participation in the society's seminars and colloquia.

Fiscal Information Research Associates will be paid no stipend by AAS.

Application Information Scholars interested in applying should write the Associate Director for Research and Publication, enclosing a current curriculum vitae, listing the names of two scholarly references, and giving particulars of the sabbatical or fellowship held or to be held, the subject of research, and the dates of proposed residence at the society.

Deadline(s) Applications for designation as a Research Associate may be made at any time.

12. American Association for State and Local History

172 Second Avenue North, Suite 102
Nashville, TN 37201
(615) 255-2971

Grants-in-Aid

Program Description This program supports research that fosters understanding of the history and culture of states, regions, localities, and communities. Projects may draw upon any of the disciplines in the humanities—including anthropology, archaeology, architectural and art history, folklore, language and literature, and relevant social sciences—as well as history. Research must be original, culminating in new knowledge or new interpretation or both. Collecting research materials, compiling information, cataloguing, transcribing, historical editing, and other such projects are eligible, but should focus on historical inquiry rather than documentation. Projects using oral history, material culture, or other nontraditional sources research using written or printed sources, are encouraged. Research into the technical aspects of work in any of the various kinds of historical organizations is not eligible, nor is pedagogical or curricular research, nor are projects that are not strictly research. The proposed work must be intended for publication in some form.

Eligibility/Limitations These grants are open to both individuals and institutions, including historical organizations and museums of any size, as well as to colleges and universities. Ineligible are students whose research projects are part of the requirements for a degree.

Fiscal Information Grants vary in size up to a maximum of $5,000 each and can cover any aspect of a qualified research project, such as travel to conduct research, duplication of materials for use in the project, costs of clerical, secretarial, or research assistance, and costs entailed in preparing a manuscript for submission to a publisher, but not the costs of publication itself. An award cannot be used for the purchase of equipment or to pay indirect costs. Assistance with salaries of project principles is not generally allowed, except in cases of individual applicants who can demonstrate need caused by lack of release time, unemployment, or other circumstances. An award cannot be used by an institution or organization to offset the salary of a regular employee, although it can be used to pay a consultant, research assistant, or other support staff hired on a temporary basis.

Application Information Application information is available on request; specify individual or institutional application.

Deadline(s) The deadline for receipt of applications is June 1.

13. American Association of Law Libraries

53 West Jackson Boulevard, Suite 940
Chicago, IL 60604
(312) 939-4764

Scholarships

Program Description Each year the American Association of Law Libraries offers scholarships to students who plan to pursue a career in law librarianship.

Eligibility/Limitations Eligible applicants are: graduates of accredited law schools who are degree candidates in an accredited library school; library school graduates who are in the process of working towards a law degree in an accredited law school, with no more than 36 semester (54 quarter) credit hours of study remaining before qualifying for the law degree, and who have meaningful law library experience; college graduates with meaningful law library experience who are degree candidates in an accredited library school; and law librarians for a course related to law librarianship.

Fiscal Information Amount of award varies.

Application Information For scholarship applications and further details write to the association's scholarships committee.

Deadline(s) Applications must be received by April 1.

Additional Information Two scholarships, each in the amount of $3,500, will be awarded to members of a minority group who are college graduates with library experience who are working toward an advanced degree which would further their library careers.

14. American Association of University Women Educational Foundation

2401 Virginia Avenue, NW
Washington, DC 20037
(202) 728-7630

American Fellowships—Dissertation Fellowships

Program Description Dissertation fellowships are available for women in any field who will complete all required course work and examinations for the doctorate, except the dissertation defense by November 30. It is expected that the fellowship will be used for the final year of doctoral work and that the degree will be received at the end of the fellowship year.

Sample Grants Support for research on "Questioning Child Witnesses," State University of New York at Buffalo (1989).

Eligibility/Limitations Women who are citizens of the United States or hold permanent resident status are eligible to apply for the final year of doctoral work. There are no restrictions as to place of study.

Fiscal Information Awards are for $12,500 for a 12-month period beginning July 1. Fellows are expected to devote full time to their projects during the fellowship year.

Application Information Application forms are available to individuals only from the AAUW Educational Foundation Programs Office by written request from August 1 to November 1. No telephone requests will be honored.

Deadline(s) Final date for postmark of completed applications is November 15.

15. American Association of University Women Educational Foundation

2401 Virginia Avenue, NW
Washington, DC 20037
(202) 728-7630

American Fellowships—Postdoctoral

Program Description Postdoctoral fellowships are available to women who hold a doctoral degree and wish to pursue research.

Eligibility/Limitations Women who are citizens of the United States or hold permanent resident status and who have achieved distinction or promise of distinction in their fields are eligible to apply. There are no restrictions as to an applicant's age or place of study. Postdoctoral fellowships are not awarded for the revision of the dissertation or for tuition for additional course work. Preference is given to women who have held the doctorate at least three years. Fellows are expected to devote full time to their projects during the fellowship year.

Fiscal Information Postdoctoral fellowships carry an award of $20,000.

Application Information Application forms are available to individuals between August 1 and November 1 only from the AAUW Educational Foundation Programs Office by written request. No telephone requests will be honored.

Deadline(s) The final date for postmark of completed applications is November 15.

Additional Information Additional research and project grants for AAUW members are available. Contact the Programs Office for additional information.

16. American Association of University Women Educational Foundation
2401 Virginia Avenue, NW
Washington, DC 20037
(202) 728-7630

Career Development Grants

Program Description These grants are awarded to women pursuing course work to prepare for reentry into the work force, career advancement, or a career change.

Eligibility/Limitations Applicants must be U.S. citizens or permanent residents, hold a baccalaureate degree, and have completed their most recent degree no later than June 30, 1985. Course work must be prerequisite for a professional employment plan. Preference is given to applicants seeking to enter nontraditional career fields.

Fiscal Information These grants are $500 to $5,000 each.

Application Information Applications are available from August 1 to December 15.

Deadline(s) Application postmark deadline is January 1.

17. American Bar Association
Commission on College & University Nonprofessional
  Legal Studies
750 North Lake Shore Drive
Chicago, IL 60611
(312) 988-5725

Mini-Grants

Program Description The purpose of this grant program is to stimulate projects designed to enhance undergraduate education about law, the legal process and law's role in society, utilizing a liberal arts approach.

Eligibility/Limitations Eligible applicants include faculty members (full- or part-time), at accredited two-year and four-year colleges and universities that grant an undergraduate liberal arts degree (A.A., A.S., B.A., B.S.).

Fiscal Information Awards up to $1,200 are available. Indirect costs and equipment costs will not be paid. Requests for faculty salary or stipends are discouraged.

Application Information Submit a brief proposal that describes: the need for the project proposed; law-related themes/topics to be addressed; criteria for success, including how the project's benefits might be extended to other campuses. The proposal should not exceed three pages. Include also the project director's curriculum vitae and a one-page budget that identifies and explains key expenditure items. Submit four copies of the proposal, budget, and curriculum vitae.

Deadline(s) The postmark deadline is March 15.

18. American Bar Foundation
750 North Lake Shore Drive
Chicago, IL 60611
(312) 988-6500

Affiliated Scholars

Program Description The foundation draws on the expertise of scholars at other institutions to undertake studies, to help with project development, and occasionally to serve with a foundation-based team on major, long-term research undertakings. The foundation also maintains continuing relationships with scholars who have initiated projects at the foundation and then assumed posts at other institutions.

Application Information Contact the foundation for additional information.

19. American Bar Foundation
750 North Lake Shore Drive
Chicago, IL 60611
(312) 988-6500

Doctoral Dissertation Fellowships in Law and Social Science

Program Description The purposes of this program are to encourage original and significant research on law and legal institutions and to make a contribution to the intellectual life of the foundation. Proposed research must be in the general area of sociolegal studies or in social scientific approaches to law, the legal profession, or legal institutions. The dissertation must address critical issues in the field and show promise of major contribution to social scientific understanding of law and legal processes.

Eligibility/Limitations Applicants must be candidates for Ph.D. degrees in the social sciences. They must have completed all doctoral requirements except the dissertation by September 1.

Fiscal Information Fellows will receive a stipend of $12,000 for 12 months. By mutual arrangement, doctoral fellows may earn additional income by working up to 10 hours per week for research fellows, although this is entirely optional and employment is not guaranteed. Expenses for research are negotiable on a case by case basis. Doctoral fellows have access to the computing and word-processing facilities of the ABF. Moving expenses up to $1,000 may be reimbursed on application. The fellowships are to be held in residence at the ABF and appointments are full-time.

Application Information Applications must include: transcripts of undergraduate and graduate record; three letters of reference, preferably including at least one letter from a supervisor of the dissertation; GREs, if available; short sample of written work; and a dissertation prospectus or proposal with an outline of the substance and methods of the intended research.

Deadline(s) Applications must be received no later than January 16.

20. American Bar Foundation
750 North Lake Shore Drive
Chicago, IL 60611
(312) 988-6500

Summer Research Fellowships in Law and Social Science for Minority Undergraduate Students

Program Description The American Bar Foundation sponsors a program of summer research fellowships to acquaint minority undergraduate students with research, and research careers in the field of law and social science.

Eligibility/Limitations Eligible groups are American Indians, Blacks, Mexicans, and Puerto Ricans. Candidates must be American citizens or lawful permanent residents. Applications will be considered only from sophomores and juniors with a grade point average of at least 3.0 (on a 4.0 scale) who are planning an academic major in one of the social science disciplines.

Fiscal Information Successful applicants will work at the foundation's offices in Chicago, Illinois, for 35 hours a week for a period of 10 weeks. Each student will receive a stipend of $3,000.

Application Information Applicants must provide the following: a completed application form; a personal statement; official transcripts of all academic courses completed at the time of application; and one letter of recommendation from a faculty member familiar with the student's work.

Deadline(s) Completed applications are due no later than March 15.

21. American Bar Foundation
750 North Lake Shore Drive
Chicago, IL 60611
(312) 988-6500

Visiting Research Fellows

Program Description The Visiting Research Fellows Program was developed by the foundation as a way of introducing new points of view and special expertise to the foundation's permanent staff. It offers selected scholars an opportunity to work in the research atmosphere of the foundation, away from the demands of teaching and committee work.

Application Information Contact the foundation for additional information.

22. American Conservation Association, Inc.
30 Rockefeller Plaza, Room 5402
New York, NY 10112
(212) 649-5822

Grants

Program Description The association's grant-making activities are directed toward information and action projects that increase public understanding and awareness of conservation issues.

Eligibility/Limitations Grants are not made to individuals.

Fiscal Information The association awarded over $1.6 million in grants in 1988.

Application Information The association does not have a formal application form.

Deadline(s) Proposals are accepted at any time.

23. American Council of Learned Societies
228 East 45th Street
New York, NY 10017-3398
(212) 697-1505

Dissertation Fellowships in East European Studies

Program Description Fellowships are offered for research and training in the social sciences and humanities relating to Albania, Bulgaria, Czechoslovakia, Germany, Hungary, Poland, Romania, and Yugoslavia. In awarding these grants, consideration is given to the scholarly merit of the proposal, its importance to the development of East European studies, and the scholarly potential, accomplishments, and financial need of the applicant. The fellowships are not intended to support research within East Europe.

Sample Grants Fellowship support for a graduate student in political science, "Communism and Legality" (1989).

Eligibility/Limitations Doctoral candidates may apply for support of dissertation research and writing to be undertaken at any university or institution outside of East Europe.

Fiscal Information The maximum stipend is $12,000 plus expenses per year. Reapplication for a second year, if necessary, is encouraged.

Application Information General inquiries and requests for application forms should be addressed to the Office of Fellowships and Grants. In requesting application forms the prospective applicant should state the highest academic degree held and the date the degree was received, country of citizenship or permanent legal residence, academic or other position, field of specialization, proposed subject of research or study, and the period of time for which support is requested.

Deadline(s) The deadline for receipt of applications is November 15.

24. American Council of Learned Societies
228 East 45th Street
New York, NY 10017-3398
(212) 697-1505

Fellowships

Program Description The general programs of the American Council of Learned Societies support postdoctoral research in the humanities. The following fields of specialization are included: philosophy (including the philosophy of law and science), aesthetics, philology, languages, literature and linguistics, archaeology, art history and musicology, history (including the history of science, law, and religions), cultural anthropology, and folklore. Proposals with a predominantly humanistic emphasis in economics, geography, political science, psychology, sociology, and the natural sciences will also be considered.

Sample Grants Fellowship support for a project, "History of Women Lawyers in Modern America, 1860 to the Present" (1988). Fellowship support for a project, "Breaking the Codes—Interpretations of Female Criminality in 19th Century Paris" (1988). Fellowship support for a project, "Law and the Conditions of Freedom in the American Family: Husbands and Wives, 1835-1900" (1989). Fellowship support for a project, "Defining and Criminalizing the Status of the Jew: the Practice of Law under Vichy and Occupied France" (1989). Fellowship support for a project, "History of the United States Supreme Court during the period of 1921-30, when William Howard Taft was Chief Justice" (1990).

Eligibility/Limitations Fellows must devote a minimum of six continuous months (to a maximum of 12) to full-time work on their projects. Applicants must be citizens and permanent residents of the United States, hold the doctorate or its equivalent (scholarly maturity as demonstrated by professional experience and publications) as of the deadline that has been set. The conditions of the awards should make them of particular interest to scholars whose teaching loads restrict time for research, those whose normal places of work are remote from repositories of research materials, and those independent scholars who have no institutional support for their research and writing.

Fiscal Information Awards do not exceed $15,000 and are intended primarily as salary replacement for the provision of free time for research. The ACLS Fellowship stipend, plus any sabbatical salary and minor grants, may not exceed the candidates normal salary for the period.

Application Information General inquiries and requests for application forms should be addressed to the Office of Fellowships and Grants. In requesting application forms the prospective applicant should state the highest academic degree held and the date the degree was received, country of citizenship or permanent legal residence, academic or other position, field of specialization, proposed subject of research or study, and the period of time for which support is requested.

Deadline(s) The deadline for receipt of applications is October 1.

25. American Council of Learned Societies
228 East 45th Street
New York, NY 10017-3398
(212) 697-1505

Fellowships for Advanced Graduate Training in East European Studies

Program Description Fellowships are offered for research and training in the social sciences and humanities relating to Albania, Bulgaria, Czechoslovakia, Germany, Hungary, Poland, Romania, and Yugoslavia. In awarding these grants, consideration is given to the scholarly merit of the proposal, its importance to the development of East European studies, and the scholarly potential, accomplishments, and financial need of the applicant.

The fellowships are not intended to support research within East Europe.

Eligibility/Limitations Graduate students currently enrolled in a degree program who will have completed at least two academic years of work toward the doctorate by June 30 are eligible to apply. The work to be supported must be done at a university or research institute outside of East Europe, except that brief trips to East Europe of up to two months, especially for advanced language training, may be supported when they are part of a coherent overall program.

Fiscal Information The fellowship carries a stipend of up to $10,000 plus expenses for a program of course work and training in any aspect of East European studies or in any discipline in which the applicant is preparing to qualify for writing a dissertation on East Europe.

Application Information General inquiries and requests for application forms should be addressed to the Office of Fellowships and Grants. In requesting application forms the prospective applicant should state the highest academic degree held and the date the degree was received, country of citizenship or permanent legal residence, academic or other position, field of specialization, proposed subject of research or study, and the period of time for which support is requested.

Deadline(s) The deadline for receipt of applications is November 15.

26. American Council of Learned Societies
228 East 45th Street
New York, NY 10017-3398
(212) 697-1505

Fellowships for Dissertation Research Abroad

Program Description These fellowships are offered to enable doctoral degree candidates to undertake a period of dissertation research outside the United States in any country with the exception of the People's Republic of China. The dissertation must be related to China, although it may be comparative in nature, and the research may be in any discipline of the humanities and social sciences or interdisciplinary.

Eligibility/Limitations Applicants must be regular Ph.D. candidates who expect to complete all requirements for the doctorate except the dissertation by June 30 of the award year. There are no citizenship restrictions, but foreign nationals must be enrolled as full-time Ph.D. candidates in U.S. institutions.

Fiscal Information Stipends include funds up to $20,000 for full-year programs for maintenance, transportation, and research expenses.

Application Information General inquiries and requests for application forms should be addressed to the Office of Fellowships and Grants. In requesting application forms the prospective applicant should state the highest academic degree held and the date the degree was received, country of citizenship or permanent legal residence, academic or other position, field of specialization, proposed subject of research or study, and the period of time for which support is requested.

Deadline(s) Applications must be received by November 15.

27. American Council of Learned Societies
228 East 45th Street
New York, NY 10017-3398
(212) 697-1505

Fellowships for Postdoctoral Research

Program Description Grants are offered to support original research on Chinese culture or society, including research designed to synthesize or reinterpret the applicant's past research to produce an original overview of scholarship on any topic or problem of importance in the study of China. Awards will be made on the basis of the quality and scholarly importance of the proposed research, its importance to the development of scholarship on China, and its contribution to knowledge of other

areas or disciplines. This program is not intended to support research within the People's Republic of China.

Sample Grants Fellowship support for an assistant professor of history, "Rulership and the Law in Early Imperial China" (1989). Fellowship support for a lecturer in East Asian languages and culture, "Justice and Power in Late Imperial China—The Murder of Magistrate Li" (1990).

Eligibility/Limitations Applicants for postdoctoral research or study must be citizens and permanent residents of the United States and hold the doctorate or expect to receive it in the current academic year.

Fiscal Information Fellowships are generally awarded for six months to one year of full-time research. Stipends, which are adjusted according to need, are generally set at one-half the applicant's academic salary, not including fringe benefits, less other outside support, up to a maximum of $25,000. Normally the cost of travel to Asia for less than six months of research cannot be covered.

Application Information General inquiries and requests for application forms should be addressed to the Office of Fellowships and Grants. In requesting application forms the prospective applicant should state the highest academic degree held and the date the degree was received, country of citizenship or permanent legal residence, academic or other position, field of specialization, proposed subject of research or study, and the period of time for which support is requested.

Deadline(s) Applications must be received by November 15.

28. American Council of Learned Societies
228 East 45th Street
New York, NY 10017-3398
(212) 697-1505

Fellowships for Postdoctoral Research in East European Studies

Program Description Fellowships are offered for research and training in the social sciences and humanities relating to Albania, Bulgaria, Czechoslovakia, Germany, Hungary, Poland, Romania, and Yugoslavia. In awarding these grants, consideration is given to the scholarly merit of the proposal, its importance to the development of East European studies, and the scholarly potential, accomplishments, and financial need of the applicant. The fellowships are not intended to support research within East Europe.

Eligibility/Limitations Tenured scholars may apply for fellowships to undertake a period of at least six consecutive months of full-time research. In special circumstances untenured scholars or younger independent scholars without an academic appointment may apply for support.

Fiscal Information Awards range up to $25,000 maximum. The fellowships are intended primarily as salary replacement to provide free time for research; the funds may be used to supplement sabbatical salaries or awards from other sources, provided they would intensify or extend the contemplated research.

Application Information General inquiries and requests for application forms should be addressed to the Office of Fellowships and Grants. In requesting application forms the prospective applicant should state the highest academic degree held and the date the degree was received, country of citizenship or permanent legal residence, academic or other position, field of specialization, proposed subject of research or study, and the period of time for which support is requested.

Deadline(s) The deadline for receipt of applications is November 15.

29. American Council of Learned Societies
228 East 45th Street
New York, NY 10017-3398
(212) 697-1505

Fellowships for Recent Recipients of the Ph.D.

Program Description The general programs of the American Council of Learned Societies support postdoctoral research in the humanities. The following fields of specialization are included: philosophy (including the philosophy of law and science), aesthetics, philology, languages, literature and linguistics, archaeology, art history and musicology, history (including the history of science, law, and religions), cultural anthropology, and folklore. Proposals with a predominantly humanistic emphasis in economics, geography, political science, psychology, sociology, and the natural sciences will also be considered.

Sample Grants Fellowship support to an associate professor of political science for a project, "The Amendable Constitution—A Theory of Constitution-Making" (1988). Fellowship support to an assistant professor of economics for a project, "The Rise of the Fair Trade Laws: a Legal and Historical Perspective" (1989). Fellowship support to an assistant professor of history for a project, "Immigration Law, Elite Ideology and Religious Exclusion in World War II-era Brazil" (1990).

Eligibility/Limitations These research awards are limited to scholars whose Ph.D. degree has been conferred in the year of and not more than two calendar years prior to the competition to engage in research. Proposals for dissertation revision, as well as those for work on other projects, are appropriate. Fellows must devote a minimum of six continuous months (to a maximum of 12) to full-time work on their proposals. Applicants must be citizens and permanent residents of the United States.

Fiscal Information Fellowships do not exceed $10,000 and are intended primarily as salary replacement for the provision of free time for research. The stipend, plus any sabbatical salary and minor grants, may not exceed the candidate's normal salary for the period.

Application Information General inquiries and requests for application forms should be addressed to the Office of Fellowships and Grants. In requesting application forms the prospective applicant should state the highest academic degree held and the date the degree was received, country of citizenship or permanent legal residence, academic or other position, field of specialization, proposed subject of research or study and the period of time for which support is requested.

Deadline(s) The deadline for receipt of applications is October 1.

30. American Council of Learned Societies
228 East 45th Street
New York, NY 10017-3398
(212) 697-1505

Grants-in-Aid

Program Description The general programs of the American Council of Learned Societies support postdoctoral research in the humanities. The following fields of specialization are included: philosophy (including the philosophy of law and science), aesthetics, philology, languages, literature and linguistics, archaeology, art history and musicology, history (including the history of science, law, and religions), cultural anthropology, and folklore. Proposals with a predominantly humanistic emphasis in economics, geography, political science, psychology, sociology, and the natural sciences will also be considered. ACLS Grants-in-Aid are designed to assist scholars with the expenses of specific programs of research in progress

Sample Grants Fellowship support for a professor of legal history, "Roscoe Pound and Karl Llewellyn—American Jurisprudence in Transition, 1927-1962" (1988). Fellowship support for a professor of government, "Attorneys in 19th Century Native American Litigation" (1988). Fellowship support for a professor of economics, "The Law and Economics of Bicultural Treaties" (1989). Fellowship support for an associate professor of political

science, "Men's Law, Women's Lives—the Future of Women-centered Jurisprudence" (1990).

Eligibility/Limitations Applicants must be citizens and permanent residents of the United States and hold the doctorate or its equivalent.

Fiscal Information Stipends will not exceed $3,000 and should be expended within one year after acceptance. Awards for living expenses at home to relieve the applicant of the necessity of teaching beyond the conventional academic year will be made only in exceptional cases. Allowable expenses may include personal travel and maintenance away from home while gaining access to materials, research or clerical assistance and reproduction or purchase of materials. Grants are not ordinarily made for the purchase of personal computers, books, or other nonexpendible materials.

Application Information General inquiries and requests for application forms should be addressed to the Office of Fellowships and Grants. In requesting application forms the prospective applicant should state the highest academic degree held and the date the degree was received, country of citizenship or permanent legal residence, academic or other position, field of specialization, proposed subject of research or study, and the period of time for which support is requested.

Deadline(s) The deadline for receipt of applications is December 14.

31. American Defense Institute
Fellowship Program Director
214 Massachusetts Avenue, NE, P.O. Box 2497
Washington, DC 20013-2497
(202) 544-4704

Fellowship in National Defense Studies

Program Description The American Defense Institute, a nonpartisan, educational organization dedicated to the study, analysis, and dissemination of research in national security and foreign policy issues, invites application for a fellowship in national defense studies. Selected applicants will spend one year in Washington to pursue independent research, to interact with high-level national security policymakers and to work directly in policy agencies on Capitol Hill.

Eligibility/Limitations Applicants must be candidates at the master's or doctoral levels nearing degree completion in one of the following areas: political science, history, international relations, international law, or economics. Candidates should have a record of outstanding academic achievement and specific research designs for which support is desired. Evidence of leadership potential and demonstrated interest in and knowledge of national security issues is required. Applicants must also be U.S. citizens.

Fiscal Information The fellowship carries a stipend of from $13,000 to $15,000.

Application Information Application materials and additional information are available from the address listed above.

Deadline(s) The deadline for completed applications is February 15.

32. American Express Philanthropic Program
American Express Plaza Tower
New York, NY 10285-4710
(212) 640-5661

Philanthropic Program

Program Description The foundation concentrates its efforts on those areas where real and lasting impact can be attained, harnessing talent and resources from the company to evaluate and address local needs. The Philanthropic Program is committed to programs in the areas of community service, education and employment, and culture.

Eligibility/Limitations Applicant organizations must be recognized by the Internal Revenue Service as having 501(c)(3) charitable status. The foundation does not award grants to individuals, to religious, veterans, labor or fraternal organizations, or to political candidates.

Fiscal Information 1989 grants by the program totaled $23 million.

Application Information Applicants may request an application form or receive more information by contacting the foundation.

Deadline(s) Applications are accepted at any time.

33. American Historical Association
400 A Street, SE
Washington, DC 20003
(202) 544-2422

The Littleton-Griswold Research Grant

Program Description The American Historical Association is accepting applications for the Littleton-Griswold Grant for research in American legal history and the field of law and society. The grants are intended to further research in progress and may be used for travel to a library or archive, for microfilms, photographs, photocopying—a list of purposes that is meant to be merely illustrative, not exhaustive. Preference will be given to those with specific research needs, such as the completion of a project or completion of a discrete segment thereof.

Sample Grants Prize for "The Fisherman's Problems: Ecology and the Law in California Fisherees, 1850-1980" (1987).

Eligibility/Limitations Only members of the association are eligible.

Fiscal Information Two or more grants not exceeding $1,000 each are awarded annually.

Application Information Application forms and guidelines are available from the association.

Deadline(s) The deadline for application is February 1.

Additional Information The association offers other fellowships and research grants. Contact the association for additional information.

34. American Indian Graduate Center
4520 Montgomery Boulevard, NE
Albuquerque, NM 87109
(505) 881-4584

Graduate Fellowship Program for American Indians

Program Description The American Indian Graduate Center (AIGC), formerly American Indian Scholarships, Inc., was established in 1960 in response to the growing number of Indian college graduates who wanted to continue their education at the master's, doctorate, and professional degree level and needed financial support. American Indians were, and continue to be, the least represented of all minority groups in the country in medicine, business, law, the sciences, and other fields requiring advanced degrees. AIGC was founded to help open the doors to graduate education for American Indians and to help tribes obtain the educated Indian professionals they need to become more self-sufficient and exercise their rights of self-determination.

Eligibility/Limitations To be considered for an AIGC fellowship, an applicant must be: a member of a federally recognized American Indian tribe or Alaska native group; at least one-fourth degree Indian or Alaska Native; enrolled full time at an accredited graduate school. The BIA has identified six areas of study which AIGC must give some preference to in the review and award process. These are: health, business, law, education, natural resources, and engineering. Applicants in other areas are definitely eligible and are encouraged to apply.

Fiscal Information Awards range from $250 to a maximum of $10,000 for the nine-month academic year. Awards are based

on each applicant's unmet financial need as verified by the applicant's college financial aid office. Since AIGC is a supplemental program, applicants must apply in a timely manner for campus-based aid at the college they are attending to be considered for aid. Failure to apply will disqualify an applicant from consideration.

Application Information Application packets are sent out only upon individual request. There is no application fee. Individuals who are eligible should request the application packet from the address listed above.

Deadline(s) Deadline for summer term is April 15; deadline for the academic year is June 1. Late applications will be considered only if there are funds available after awarding all on-time eligible applicants.

Additional Information AIGC fellowship awards are generally not awarded for the summer term. The few exceptions are: if the applicant will be completing all degree requirements in the summer; if the applicant was an AIGC recipient as a third-year law student in the previous academic year and will be studying for the summer bar examination; or if the applicant was an AIGC fellow in the previous academic year and in one of the professional fields requiring summer attendance (i.e., medicine, dentistry, veterinary science, etc.).

35. American Institute of Indian Studies
1130 East 59th Street
Chicago, IL 60637
(312) 702-8638

Fellowships for Scholarly Development

Program Description The American Institute of Indian Studies (AIIS) is a cooperative, nonprofit organization of 40 American colleges and universities with a special interest in Indian studies. It is designed to support the advancement of knowledge and understanding of India primarily through research conducted in that country by American scholars. The AIIS offers a variety of fellowships for research in India. Fellowships for scholarly development are awarded to established scholars who have not previously specialized in Indian studies, and to established professionals who have not previously worked or studied in India. Proposals in this category should have a substantial research or project component and the anticipated results should be clearly defined.

Eligibility/Limitations U.S. citizens are eligible for AIIS grants. Resident aliens who are engaged in research or teaching at American colleges or universities are also eligible. No individual will be awarded grants in this category more than once.

Fiscal Information Award periods are short term (up to four months) and long term (six to ten months).

Application Information Application forms and additional information are available from AIIS.

Deadline(s) The deadline for submitting applications is July 1.

36. American Institute of Indian Studies
1130 East 59th Street
Chicago, IL 60637
(312) 702-8638

Junior Fellowships

Program Description The American Institute of Indian Studies (AIIS) is a cooperative, nonprofit organization of 40 American colleges and universities with a special interest in Indian studies. It is designed to support the advancement of knowledge and understanding of India primarily through research conducted in that country by American scholars. The AIIS offers a variety of fellowships for research in India. Junior fellowships are awarded to graduate students specializing in Indian aspects of academic disciplines.

Eligibility/Limitations Graduate students specializing in Indian aspects of academic disciplines for dissertation research are eligible to apply. Junior fellows will have formal affiliation with Indian universities and Indian research supervisors.

Fiscal Information Awards are for a period of nine to twelve months.

Application Information Application forms and additional information are available from AIIS.

Deadline(s) The deadline for submitting applications is July 1.

37. American Institute of Indian Studies
1130 East 59th Street
Chicago, IL 60637
(312) 702-8638

Senior Research Fellowships

Program Description The American Institute of Indian Studies (AIIS) is a cooperative, nonprofit organization of 40 American colleges and universities with a special interest in Indian studies. It is designed to support the advancement of knowledge and understanding of India primarily through research conducted in that country by American scholars. The AIIS offers a variety of fellowships for research in India. Senior Research Fellowships are awarded to academic specialists in Indian studies.

Eligibility/Limitations Applicants must possess the Ph.D. or its equivalent. While in India, each Senior Research fellow will be formally affiliated with an Indian university.

Fiscal Information Award periods range from six to ten months.

Application Information Application forms and additional information are available from AIIS.

Deadline(s) The deadline for submitting applications is July 1.

38. American Institute of Indian Studies
1130 East 59th Street
Chicago, IL 60637
(312) 702-8638

Short-Term Fellowships

Program Description The American Institute of Indian Studies (AIIS) is a cooperative, nonprofit organization of 40 American colleges and universities with a special interest in Indian studies. It is designed to support the advancement of knowledge and understanding of India primarily through research conducted in that country by American scholars. The AIIS offers a variety of fellowships for research in India. Short-term fellowships are awarded to academic specialists in Indian studies.

Eligibility/Limitations Applicants must possess the Ph.D. or its equivalent. While in India, short-term fellows will be formally affiliated with an Indian university.

Fiscal Information Award periods are for up to four months.

Application Information Application forms and additional information are available from AIIS.

Deadline(s) The deadline for submitting applications is July 1.

39. American Institute of Indian Studies
1130 East 59th Street
Chicago, IL 60637
(312) 702-8638

Translation Projects

Program Description The American Institute of Indian Studies (AIIS) is a cooperative, nonprofit organization of 40 American colleges and universities with a special interest in Indian studies. It is designed to support the advancement of knowledge and understanding of India primarily through research conducted in that country by American scholars. The AIIS, the Smithsonian Institution, and the National Endowment for the Humanities have established a cooperative program to support translations of Indian texts into English.

Application Information Application forms and additional information are available from AIIS. Please signify your interest in this grant when requesting application materials.

Deadline(s) The deadline for submitting applications is July 1.

40. American Institute of Pakistan Studies
Wake Forest University
P.O. Box 7568
Winston-Salem, NC 27109
(919) 761-5449 or 761-5453

Fellowships

Program Description Fellowships are awarded to support research on Pakistan by scholars and advanced graduate students engaged in research on Pakistan in ancient, medieval and modern times, in any field of the humanities or social sciences. Topics by specialists in other countries or areas which include research on Pakistan in a comparative perspective are also encouraged. Such topics as rural development, agriculture, local government, economic problems, and demography, as well as broader historical and cultural subjects, are suggestive of suitable projects. Acceptable subjects are not, however, limited to these.

Eligibility/Limitations Applicants must be citizens of the United States. Fellowships are offered in several categories including predoctoral research, postdoctoral study, library service, and professional development. Graduate student applicants must have fulfilled all residence, language, and preliminary examination requirements for the doctorate. In addition, their dissertation projects must have the approval of their faculty. Postdoctoral applicants are expected to be members in good standing of educational or research institutions in the United States and to submit a suitable research project or program of study. The AIPS grant is not designed to be a supplement to any other funding or research in Pakistan and applications requesting a continuation of support in Pakistan following an award by another agency will not be considered.

Fiscal Information Because major support for the institute's activities is derived from Pakistani currency, support is provided in terms of air transportation, maintenance, and travel allowances in Pakistan, paid in local currency. The amount paid for maintenance will depend upon whether the fellow is a predoctoral or a postdoctoral fellow. A rental allowance is also provided. A small contribution is made toward excess baggage, research materials in Pakistan, and internal travel. International travel is paid only for the fellow and not for dependents. Grantees who are not affiliated with supporting institutions are required to pay an administrative fee in United States currency to partially defray the costs of processing their applications. All awards are subject to confirmation by the Government of Pakistan.

Application Information Packets of application materials for grants are available from the director of the institute.

Deadline(s) Application for grants should not be made later than January 1.

Additional Information Special Project Grants in archaeology, anthropology, and other social sciences funded by the Smithsonian Institution are available. In addition to normal review procedures, these grants are subject to additional approval by the Smithsonian Institution. The deadline for these grants is January 1.

41. American Jewish Archives
Administrative Director
3101 Clifton Avenue
Cincinnati, OH 45220
(513) 221-1875

Fellowships

Program Description The American Jewish Archives support fellowships for research and writing at the archives.

Eligibility/Limitations Fellowships are available to doctoral candidates and postdoctoral scholars.

Fiscal Information The stipend varies from $1,000 to $4,000.

Application Information Contact the archives for application guidelines and additional information.

Deadline(s) The application deadline is April 1.

42. American Philosophical Society
104 South Fifth Street
Philadelphia, PA 19106-3387
(215) 627-0706

General Research Grants

Program Description The American Philosophical Society makes grants towards the cost of scholarly research in all areas of knowledge except those in which support by government or corporate enterprise is more appropriate and regularly available. "Scholarly research," as the term is used here, covers most kinds of scholarly inquiry by individuals. It does not include journalistic or other writing for general readership; the preparation of textbooks, casebooks, anthologies, or other materials for classroom use by students; or the work of creative and performing artists.

Sample Grants For a study of "American Law and the Chinese on the Trans-Mississippi West Frontier," $2,500 (1988). For a study of the "Supreme Court and Judicial Leadership," $1,850 (1988).

Eligibility/Limitations Applicants are normally expected to have a doctorate, but applications will be considered from persons who display equivalent scholarly preparation and achievement. Grants are rarely made to persons who have had the doctorate less than a year; and never for predoctoral study or research. Applications may be made by residents of the United States, by American citizens on the staffs of foreign institutions, and by foreign nationals whose research can only or best be carried on in the United States. Applicants expecting to use materials or conduct interviews in a foreign language must possess the necessary competence in the language or languages involved. It is the society's long-standing practice to encourage research by younger and less well-established scholars.

Fiscal Information The maximum grant that will be made is $4,000, and this amount will be approved only in exceptional cases. The maximum grant for a full professor is $3,000. The grant will pay for: living costs while away from home (the per diem is $40); microfilms, photostats, photographs and the like, which will shorten the grantee's stay away from home, or enable more efficient and accurate work; consumable supplies; and necessary foreign and domestic travel.

Application Information For application forms briefly describe your project and proposed budget in a letter to the Committee on Research.

Deadline(s) Deadlines are February 1, April 1, August 1, October 1, and December 1.

43. American Philosophical Society
104 South Fifth Street
Philadelphia, PA 19106-3387
(215) 627-0706

Phillips Grants on North American Indians

Program Description The American Philosophical Society makes these grants for research on North American linguistics and ethnohistory.

Eligibility/Limitations These grants are available for graduate students, as well as postdoctoral candidates.

Fiscal Information Awards average $1,300.

Application Information For application forms briefly describe your project and proposed budget in a letter to the Committee on Research.

Deadline(s) Deadlines are February 1, April 1, August 1, October 1, and December 1.

44. American Philosophical Society
104 South Fifth Street
Philadelphia, PA 19106-3387
(215) 627-0706

Henry M. Phillips Grants in Jurisprudence

Program Description These grants support postdoctoral research in jurisprudence.

Sample Grants Grants supported the following research projects: organized interests before the senate—confirmation and rejection of nominations to the Supreme Court; the life of Oliver Ellsworth; the Nuremberg trials and contemporary international law; the Black Hand on trial—Salonika and Belgrade; rural communities in France and French Canada during the 18th and early 19th century.

Eligibility/Limitations Postdoctoral scholars in appropriate disciplines are eligible to apply.

Fiscal Information The maximum size of grants is $4,000 ($3,000 for full professors). Eligible expenses are generally limited to: necessary travel, $40 per diem toward cost of room and meals, and photocopying or microfilming. If expenses exceed the limit, please indicate those items and the amount requested from the society.

Application Information Application forms and additional information are available from the society.

Deadline(s) The deadline for application and all supporting material is December 1.

45. The American Research Center in Egypt
New York University
50 Washington Square South
New York, NY 10003
(212) 998-8890

ARCE Fellowships

Program Description The American Research Center in Egypt, Inc., founded in 1948, promotes research in Egypt and on Egypt from earliest times to the present. The broad aims of ARCE are to obtain a fresh and more profound knowledge of Egypt and the Near East through scholarly research; train American specialists in Near Eastern studies in academic disciplines which require familiarity with Egypt; disseminate knowledge of Egypt and thus understanding of the whole Near East; and promote American Egyptian cultural relations. In pursuit of these goals, ARCE supports a Research Fellowship Program to enable American scholars and students to conduct research in all periods and in all phases of Egyptian civilization.

Eligibility/Limitations Awards are open to all qualified candidates without regard to sex, race, and religion. Because under certain circumstances non-U.S. nationality results in funding problems, it is advisable to contact the U.S. office for further clarification if there is a doubt about status.

Fiscal Information Most fellows receive a monthly stipend commensurate with academic status and number of accompanying dependents plus round-trip air transportation for recipients only. Monthly stipends range from $1,000 to $2,750, commensurate with academic status. Stipends are normally for from three to twelve months duration.

Application Information Contact the center for information, applications, and brochures.

Deadline(s) Applications, letters of recommendation, and filing fees must be received by November 30.

46. American Research Institute in Turkey

University Museum
33rd and Spruce Streets
Philadelphia, PA 19105
(215) 898-3474

Fellowships

Program Description These awards support scholars and advanced graduate students engaged in research in Turkey in ancient, medieval, or modern times, in any field of the humanities and social sciences.

Sample Grants Support for research on records of 17th-century lawcourts in eastern Anatolia as a source of economic, social and administrative history. Support for research on big city crime.

Eligibility/Limitations Student applicants must have fulfilled all requirements for the doctorate except the dissertation. Applicants are expected to be members in good standing of educational institutions in the United States or Canada.

Fiscal Information Although grants for travel and maintenance for up to one year will be considered, preference will be given to projects of shorter duration (generally no less than two months). Grants are made only for research to be carried out in Turkey and to defray costs of transportation to and from Turkey.

Application Information To be considered, applicants must follow the form and specifications given on an instruction sheet available from the institute.

Deadline(s) Completed application forms and letters of recommendation must be submitted before November 15.

Additional Information Turkish law requires all foreigners to obtain permission for any research to be carried out in Turkey prior to entering the country. ARIT fellowship applicants are personally responsible for obtaining their own research permission. Forms should be obtained from the Cultural Office, Turkish Embassy, 1606 23rd Street NW, Washington, DC 20008. Since replies for permission may take as long as six months, applicants are urged to apply well in advance of the time they expect to carry out the research. ARIT reserves the right to withhold payment of fellowship stipends if appropriate research permission has not been obtained.

47. American Water Foundation

P.O. Box 15577
Denver, CO 80215
(303) 236-6960

Research Fellowships

Program Description The American Water Foundation (AWF) sponsors research in conformance with the aims of the American Water Foundation which are summarized in its statement of purpose: The foundation's activities are designed to benefit agricultural and water resources interests. American methods, systems, and equipment in agricultural production are of interest. Particular emphasis is placed on irrigation and drainage, but all aspects of water resources development are addressed.

Eligibility/Limitations The AWF is seeking applicants who are students in a degree program such as civil engineering, agricultural engineering, agriculture, geology, law, economics, and political science.

Fiscal Information Fellowships are awarded in the range of $200 to $1,000.

Application Information Application forms are available upon request from the foundation.

Deadline(s) Proposal deadline is May 31.

48. Ameritech Foundation

30 South Wacker Drive, 34th Floor
Chicago, IL 60606
(312) 750-5223

Grants

Program Description The Ameritech Foundation serves as the philanthropic organization for Ameritech—the parent company of the Bell companies serving Illinois, Indiana, Michigan, Ohio, and Wisconsin and several other communications-related companies—contributing to the attainment of corporate goals by designing and executing programs which match Ameritech's interests to community and social needs. The foundation concentrates on providing grants to recognized institutions which address three issues: research and programs designed to determine ways that communications can contribute to the long-term betterment of society and quality of life; programs and activities that stimulate and improve the economic vitality of the Great Lakes area, including grants to major educational and cultural organizations; and research and development aimed at reshaping policy into forms more relevant to the current and future nature of the communications industry.

Sample Grants In support of the commission's 1934 Communications Act legislative history project, $5,000 to the Golden Jubilee Commission on Telecommunications, Washington, DC (1986). In support of the center's Telecommunications Policy Research Conference, $3,000 to Center for Media Law, Inc., New York (1986). In support of EEOC research on age and equal pay, $5,000 to Education Fund for Individual Rights, New York (1986). In support of the institute's Leadership Council and tax reform research, $50,000 to Northeast-Midwest Institute, Washington, DC (1986). For second payment of a three-year $170,000 pledge to the university's Corporate Council Center for the School of Law's study program on regulation, $57,000 to Northwestern University, Evanston, IL (1986).

Eligibility/Limitations Applicant organizations must be tax-exempt under Section 501(c)(3) of the Internal Revenue Code. The foundation limits its contributions to significant organizations that are regional or national in orientation or impact. The foundation also recognizes its obligation to Chicago as Ameritech's headquarter city and may elect to contribute to selected local organizations. The foundation does not make direct contributions to individuals, to individual community organizations, or to local chapters of national organizations.

Fiscal Information The foundation awarded 82 grants totaling $1.6 million in 1986.

Application Information Organizations which qualify under the foundation's guidelines should provide a brief letter of inquiry before a formal proposal is submitted. It should include: a description of the organization, its history and purpose; an overview of the proposed project for which funding is requested; a summary of the program's budget; an indication of the level of support requested; a list of sources and amounts of other funding obtained, pledged, or requested for this purpose; the population and geographic area served; and documentation of 501(c)(3) public charity status. If the initial review is favorable, a formal proposal will be requested. Preliminary inquiries by telephone or personal visits are discouraged.

Deadline(s) There is no deadline for submitting proposals.

49. Amoco Foundation Inc.

200 East Randolph Drive
Chicago, IL 60601
(312) 856-6306

Grants

Program Description Since Amoco Foundation was organized in 1952, it has maintained a commitment to improve the social and economic development in areas where Amoco Corporation operates. The foundation also emphasizes and promotes excellence in education. Since 1980, Amoco has made a major commitment to urban neighborhood organizations working in areas of housing, jobs, energy, and education to help residents stabilize and improve their communities. With operations in more than 40 countries, Amoco strives to be an ambassador of goodwill in foreign lands. In support of this policy, the Amoco Foundation makes grants overseas to hospitals, schools, museums, and other institutions in areas where the company has operations. Local and national groups that are dedicated to improving conditions for the citizens in the host country also receive foundation support.

Eligibility/Limitations Amoco Foundation makes its domestic contributions only to organizations exempt from federal income tax under Section 501(c)(3) of the Internal Revenue Code, and that are not private foundations as defined in Section 509(a) of the code. It does not normally make grants to organizations that already receive operating support through the United Way, to primary and secondary schools, or to religious, fraternal, social, or athletic organizations. Endowment grants are not provided for any purpose.

Fiscal Information The foundation made grants in 1987 totaling nearly $10 million.

Application Information All requests for grants or other information about the foundation should be directed to the address listed above. Requests for funding must be submitted in writing and should include: a brief description of the organization; a specific purpose for requesting the grant and the benefits it is expected to make possible; the amount of the grant requested and plans to evaluate its effectiveness; budget information including an annual report and a copy of the latest IRS Form 990 report; and a copy of letter(s) from the Internal Revenue Service declaring that the organization is exempt from federal income taxes under Section 501(c)(3) and is not a private foundation under Section 509(a) of the Internal Revenue Code.

Deadline(s) Application deadlines are not announced.

50. The Annenberg/CPB Project
901 E Street, NW
Washington, DC 20004
(202) 879-9600

Materials Development Projects

Program Description The Annenberg/CPB Project was created in 1981 to enhance the quality and availability of higher education through the use of telecommunication and information technologies. With funding provided by The Annenberg Foundation to the Corporation for Public Broadcasting (CPB), the project seeks to develop new course materials, tools and delivery systems that increase opportunities for those who wish to obtain a college-level education, especially to the baccalaureate level. To achieve that end, the project provides funds to develop innovative, academically rigorous course materials. When the project speaks about "materials development projects," it means college-level courses that can be taken for credit by students who find it difficult to participate in regularly scheduled, campus-based courses. The range of possible subject areas mirrors the undergraduate curriculum, and all good ideas are encouraged, although the project has determined that it might make a special contribution by developing introductory courses that are particularly difficult to teach well. Three broad areas have emerged as fields particularly worth tackling. They are the sciences, including such fields as biology, astronomy, and the history of science and technology; cultural and cross cultural studies, including both the American experience and that of other regions of the world; and business, including management and public administration, designed to enlarge the understanding of the liberal arts student.

Sample Grants Support for the Media and Society Seminars of the Columbia University Graduate School of Journalism which has produced a 13-program political science television-based course designed to inform students about current public policy issues concerning individual rights and liberties (1984).

Eligibility/Limitations Any group or institution, profit or nonprofit, is eligible to apply. In unusual circumstances, an individual may initiate a proposal but prior discussion with the project staff is recommended. All projects are expected, either in the short or long run, to have the potential to improve the education of nontraditional learners who, because of constraints on time, resources, or available options, are unable to work toward an undergraduate degree by attending regularly scheduled campus-based classes.

Fiscal Information The project has funding of $10 million a year.

Application Information All applicants must submit a preliminary application, a brief document that describes the proposed concept and provides basic information about need, innovation, and key personnel. Preliminary applications may be submitted either for projects that are ready to move swiftly to completion or for those that need development funds. The preliminary applications are screened by the project's staff and discussed with the Annenberg/CPB Council. Based on that evaluation, the most promising projects are then asked to submit a full proposal. Preliminary application guidelines are available upon request.

Deadline(s) Preliminary applications will be accepted at any time. Action on them is keyed to the meetings of the Annenberg/CPB Project Council in April, July, and December. For submission dates for each council meeting, contact the project's staff.

Additional Information In addition to material development projects, Annenberg/CPB will fund demonstration projects that explore new and better applications of technology to meet the needs of higher education. Proposals may be in either category or may combine them.

51. The Arca Foundation
1425 21st Street, NW
Washington, DC 20036
(202) 822-9193

Grants

Program Description Nancy Susan Reynolds established the Arca Foundation in 1952, stating that philanthropy should not "take the easy way out" by avoiding risk or controversy. She stressed the need to reach toward long-term goals instead of expecting immediate results. In the 1980s, the foundation applied these principles to the field of foreign policy, reserving a small portion of its grant total to domestic concerns. Motivated by reports of gross violations of human rights in countries supported by U.S. aid and by revelations of covert action against established governments, the foundation has sought to promote broad public debate of foreign policy issues in the United States, investigate analysis of the U.S. role abroad, and greater understanding of movements for social justice in Third World countries. In 1989 grants focused heavily on U.S. policies towards the Central American region.

Sample Grants In support of this organization for its efforts to monitor abuses in country, publish objective, factual reports of their findings, and disseminate this information throughout the U.S. and elsewhere to build public awareness regarding human rights problems in South Africa, $20,000 to Lawyers Committee for Human Rights, New York (1987). In support of their work uncovering abuses in ongoing U.S. government surveillance, infiltration and disruption of dissident citizen groups, $10,000 to the Center for Investigative Reporting, Inc., San Francisco, CA (1987).

Eligibility/Limitations The foundation provides support only to nonprofit, tax-exempt organizations as defined under section 501(c)(3) of the United States Internal Revenue Code. Proof of tax-exempt status must accompany all formal grant applications. Although the foundation's concerns are international in scope, grantmaking is limited to U.S.-based organizations whose main locus of activity is in the United States. The foundation does not make grants to individuals. Nor does it provide support for capital projects, endowments, scholarship funds, academic research, direct social services, or counseling programs.

Fiscal Information The foundation's grant total is approximately $1 million. Most awards range from $5,000 to $20,000.

Application Information Although The Arca Foundation welcomes all inquiries, grant application information should be made by letter whenever possible. Applicants are requested to submit a brief two- or three-page summary of the project with budget figures and proof of tax-exempt status. All such letters will be answered, and if the project coincides with the foundation's interests, the directory may request that a complete grant proposal be prepared.

Deadline(s) The deadline for submitting proposals, once requested by the foundation, is March 15 for the spring board meeting and September 15 for the fall board meeting.

52. ARCO Foundation

Public Affairs
515 South Flower Street
Los Angeles, CA 90071
(213) 486-3342

Direct Grants

Program Description The ARCO Foundation awards most of its grants in geographic areas where ARCO has major operations and large numbers of employees. The foundation's target priorities are education, community programs, humanities and the arts, public information programs, and environmental programs.

Sample Grants For policy analysis on hazardous waste and water quality, $5,000 to the Environmental Law Institute, Washington, DC (1987). For an environmental liability law program, $15,000 to the University of Houston Law Foundation, Houston, TX (1987).

Eligibility/Limitations Eligible organizations must be nonprofit, tax-exempt public charities as defined in Sections 501(c)(3) and 509(a) of the Internal Revenue Code. The foundation considers funding of the following: recognized national policy study organizations; organizations that inform the public about the importance of individual responsibility to the private and nonprofit voluntary sector; organizations with a proven record of balanced analysis and judgment on natural resources and land-use issues; programs that promote environmental education; programs to preserve ecologically unique land; programs for wildlife conservation; balance policy studies on environmental issues.

Fiscal Information The foundation awarded direct grants totaling over $14 million in 1988.

Application Information Qualified applicants should submit a concise proposal, not more than two double-spaced typewritten pages. The proposal should contain the following information: a brief description of the organization, including its purpose and an explanation of how it meets the ARCO Foundation's stated guidelines and priorities; a statement of need for the proposed project; the amount of time needed to complete the project; the total cost of the project, other sources of funding, and the amount requested from the ARCO Foundation; and a statement describing community support for or involvement in the project and organization. In addition, the following support data should be submitted: a current budget and the most recent audited financial statement, an annual report, and a copy of the IRS letter of designation as a publicly supported, tax-exempt organization; a copy of the organization's most recent Form 990-A submitted to the IRS; and a list of the organization's board of directors, including their outside affiliations.

Deadline(s) Applications may be submitted at any time. Proposals are accumulated by category and judged with similar requests on a periodic basis.

Additional Information Local and regional organizations must initiate their requests through regional ARCO public affairs offices. Contact the foundation office for a list of regional public affairs offices.

53. The Asia Foundation

465 California Street
San Francisco, CA 94104
(415) 982-4640

Grants

Program Description The Asia Foundation is committed to assisting Asians in the growth and development of their own societies and to the strengthening of Asian-American understanding, cooperation, and friendship. The foundation seeks to encourage the growth of more open and just societies in Asia concerned with individual rights and opportunities and with broader popular participation in local and national affairs; and to strengthen Asian indigenous public and private institutions which contribute to stable national development, equitable economic growth, constructive social change and cooperative international relationships. The foundation attempts to serve each Asian country in the manner best suited to that nation's needs. It concentrates its activities in the following broad fields: education and human resource development; law and judicial administration; public administration and civil service training; international relations studies programs; communications, publications and library development; private community development programs; and business administration, management and private entrepreneurship. The foundation's activities in the U.S. support and supplement its programs in Asia.

Sample Grants For a conference on Malaysia's legal history and development, $4,158 to the University of Malaya, Faculty of Law (1987). For a conference on judicial administration for magistrates from Sabah and Sarawak, $4,992 to the Judicial Department (1987). For two midcareer officers to undertake graduate studies at The Fletcher School of Law and Diplomacy, $47,100 to the Ministry of Foreign Affairs (1987).

Eligibility/Limitations Grants are available to persons nominated by Asian or Pacific institutions in fields of interest to the foundation.

Fiscal Information Over $22 million in grants was awarded in 1987.

Application Information For additional information and eligibility guidelines, contact the foundation.

54. AT&T Foundation

Secretary
550 Madison Avenue, Room 2700
New York, NY 10022
(212) 605-6680

Grants

Program Description AT&T Foundation is the principal source of philanthropic activity by AT&T and its subsidiaries. The foundation's scope is national, emphasizing support for higher education, health care, social action and the arts. Grants in the social action category support projects with national application and national institutions addressing socioeconomic problems. Projects of special interest are those that advance one or more of the following objectives: foster the progress of equal opportunity throughout our society for minorities and women, the physically and mentally disabled, and young people and the elderly; improve the quality of life in America by undertaking initiatives in community development, job training and employment, and the conservation of energy and the environment; and enhance the effectiveness of the not-for-profit and public sectors. Institutions engaged in the study of international trade, tax and industrial competitiveness within and without the field of telecommunications may apply for project support.

Sample Grants To support the American Bar Association Fund for Public Education, $5,000 (1987). To support the American Law Institute, PA, $100,000 (1987). To support the Center for Law and Social Policy, Washington, DC, $10,000 (1987).

Eligibility/Limitations The foundation seeks to fund institutions, organizations and projects whose aim is to advance the full participation of women and minorities in our society. The foundation does not award grants to individuals, buy advertisements or donate equipment. Except in rare instances it does not fund conferences or contribute to the creation of new organizations. Other excluded organizations and purposes are: organizations not classified as tax exempt under Section 501(c)(3) of the Internal Revenue Code; organizations that discriminate by race, color, creed, gender or national origin, organizations whose chief purpose is to influence legislation; political organizations or campaigns; or local chapters of national organizations.

Fiscal Information In 1988 the foundation awarded over $30 million in support.

Application Information If you wish to determine foundation interest in receiving a proposal, please write to the Contributions Coordinator at the above address. Letters of inquiry should contain no more than three pages with the following information: a description of the institution or organization; a statement relating its purpose to the general interests and specific priorities of the foundation; a summary of the purpose for which the grant is sought and evidence of need for the activity; an overall operating budget for the current fiscal year showing anticipated sources of revenue and expenses; and (if project support is sought) a detailed budget of the project.

Deadline(s) No deadlines are announced.

Additional Information AT&T helps meet the needs of local communities through corporate contributions budgets that are prepared and administered by local AT&T managers.

55. Mary Reynolds Babcock Foundation
102 Reynolda Village
Winston-Salem, NC 27106-5123
(919) 748-9222

Grants

Program Description The Mary Reynolds Babcock Foundation provides grants and program-related investments or loans to tax-exempt organizations for programs to support active citizen participation primarily in the following areas: environmental protection, development of public policy, education, well-being of children and adolescents, philanthropy, the arts, grassroots organizing, rural issues, and women's concerns.

Sample Grants To allow Supreme Court Watch to continue its research on potential nominees to the Supreme Court and to begin an evaluation of the American Bar Association's procedures in the nomination process and an initiative to augment the roles of minority and women's bar associations, $15,000 to Nation Institute, New York (1988). To help establish a center to address and resolve the critical issues of toxic water pollution, land abuse, and harm to citizens caused by surface coal mining in Southern Appalachia, $25,000 to the Environmental Law Institute, Washington, DC (1988). To support research to assess current barriers to blacks in higher education and to explore effective legal strategies to remove those barriers, $25,000 to the Higher Education Research Project, NAACP Legal Defense and Education Fund, New York (1988). To support five judicial seminars in the Southeast, $20,000 to the Women Judges' Fund for Justice (1989). To support a citizen effectiveness training project about reproductive choice and the legislative process, $23,000 to the Citizens Leadership Development Fund, Durham, NC (1989).

Eligibility/Limitations Tax-exempt organizations are eligible to apply. The foundation does not make grants to individuals or for construction or restoration projects, international programs, film or video production, research programs, or activities of tax-supported educational institutions outside North Carolina. The majority (75 percent) of grants are made to organizations working in North Carolina and the Southeast, but the foundation also makes grants on a national basis.

Fiscal Information During 1989 the foundation board awarded over $3 million in grants. The foundation makes interim grants between board meetings for projects needing emergency support. Interim grants do not exceed $7,000.

Application Information Applicants are encouraged to approach the foundation well ahead of the announced deadlines to explore the possibility of foundation interest in proposed programs. This may be done by telephone, by letter, or in person. Additional information and application guidelines are available from the foundation.

Deadline(s) The foundation's board of directors meets in May and November to consider grant applications. All application materials should be postmarked by the application deadlines, March 1 and September 1, preceding each meeting.

Additional Information The foundation will consider exceptions to their general guidelines.

56. BankAmerica Foundation
Dept. 3246
P.O. Box 37000
San Francisco, CA 94137
(415) 953-3175

Grants Program

Program Description BankAmerica Foundation funds private, nonprofit, tax-exempt organizations which provide a range of services primarily to communities in California, but also in metropolitan areas across the United States and in foreign countries where BankAmerica Corporation operates. The foundation focuses its activities on realizing the vision the corporation set for itself—to achieve leadership in serving people. The major funding areas are: health, human services, community and economic development, education, and culture and the arts. The foundation provides support to a limited number of institutions and organizations whose primary purpose is public policy research and the dissemination of information on issues that are important to society in general and to financial institutions in particular. These fall into the general areas of issues research and communication, environment and ecology, justice and the law, and consumer and ethnic issues.

Eligibility/Limitations Applicant organizations must be tax exempt under 501(c)(3) of the Internal Revenue Code. The foundation does not support memorial campaigns, fund-raising events, individuals, religious organizations for sectarian purposes, political, labor, fraternal, social or other organizations where funding would be used for purposes primarily benefiting the organization membership, or travel expenses. As a general rule, the foundation does not provide support for endowment drives. Public policy grants may support conferences, seminars, publications and research. Grants in support of public policy research are made selectively and are reviewed annually. The foundation recognizes the need to conduct capital campaigns in the areas listed above.

Fiscal Information The foundation awarded over $5.5 million in contributions in 1989.

Application Information Organizations interested in a grant should carefully review the description of funding policies available from the foundation. An organization that qualifies under those policies should send a one- or two-page letter with the following information: name and address of organization; name and telephone number of person to be contacted; organization's mission (brief statement); population and geographic area served by organization (brief description); purpose for which grant is requested (brief description); total cost of accomplishing that purpose; specific amount requested from foundation; and list of sources and amounts of other funding obtained, pledged, or requested for this purpose.

Deadline(s) Decisions regarding funding requests are reviewed quarterly. Capital campaign requests are considered on an annual basis; applications must be submitted prior to July 1.

57. Benton Foundation

1776 K Street, NW, Suite 605
Washington, DC 20006
(202) 429-7350

Grants

Program Description The Benton Foundation is a private grant-making foundation committed to increasing public understanding and use of communications in our democracy. The foundation is concerned with the communications policy issues raised by new technologies and encourages public participation in the policy debate. The foundation also supports innovative uses of the media that broaden public understanding of complex issues. Finally, the foundation offers educational and training opportunities to nonprofit groups that seek greater access to the new tools of communications.

Sample Grants For continued support for the Project on Privacy and Technology, which addresses significant privacy issues posed by the application of new communications and information technologies by business and government, $50,000 to the American Civil Liberties Union Foundation, Washington, DC (1986). In support of the Fifth Annual Benton National Moot Court Competition in Information Law and Privacy, a competition involving 42 law schools who debated the issue of liability in electronic publishing, $12,500 to The John Marshall Law School, Chicago, IL (1986). For the Project on Information Technology and Civil Liberties, which represents an expansion of work supported earlier that examined privacy concerns arising as a result of information technologies and whose broadened scope addresses more general civil liberties implications of the use of computer and communications technologies by the government, $50,000 to American Civil Liberties Foundation, Washington, DC (1987). For the second and third year of a three-year commitment to Citizens Communications Center for legal research and litigation in the communications field, $20,000 to Georgetown University Law Center, Washington, DC (1988). For continued public education and media work on the Right to Know, protecting public access to government information, $45,000 to People for the American Way, Washington, DC (1988).

Eligibility/Limitations Priority is given to projects of national or regional significance. Grants are usually made to educational, charitable, or civic nonprofit groups. The foundation does not ordinarily support books, periodicals, or newsletters. Contributions to capital fund drives or for general operating support are not likely to be considered.

Fiscal Information Grants and projects supported in 1988 totaled more than $400,000. Grants range in size from $500 to $50,000. In addition, the foundation contributes board and staff assistance to projects to which it is committed.

Application Information Grant applicants are asked to submit in letter form a brief description of their project, including a statement of goals, the personnel to be involved, budget, and funds requested. If further information is required, it will be requested by program staff.

Deadline(s) Funding decisions are made by the board of directors, which normally meets in March, June, and November.

Additional Information Although the foundation encourages film and television productions, a relatively small grants budget limits such support. However, two such grants are awarded annually to works that are judged to contribute to international peace and understanding.

58. The William Bingham Foundation

1250 Leader Building
Cleveland, OH 44114
(216) 781-3275

Grants

Program Description The foundation currently contributes to a wide range of organizations in the areas of education, the arts, health, and welfare, reflecting the diverse interests of the trustees. Programs relating to environmental preservation and conflict resolution, including nuclear arms control, have been of significant interest to the foundation, with emphasis on programs with practical application in these areas.

Sample Grants For the first-year payment of a three-year, $450,000 grant for support of this environmental law organization's Fund for Environmental Conflict Negotiation, $150,000 to the Natural Resources Defense Council, New York (1987). For processing by the Schlesinger Library of papers from the estate of Alice Paul, leading suffragist and author of the proposed Women's Rights Amendment, $25,000 to Radcliffe College, Cambridge, MA (1987). To publish a microfilm edition of the papers of Susan B. Anthony and Elizabeth Cady Stanton, 19th-century leaders of the movement for women's political equality in the United States, $30,000 to the University of Massachusetts, Amherst, MA (1987).

Eligibility/Limitations Grants are made primarily to tax-exempt organizations in the eastern United States. Grants are not made to individuals.

Fiscal Information Grants paid in 1988 totaled over $1.7 million.

Application Information To apply for a grant, submit to the executive director a letter not to exceed two pages, outlining the nature of the project, budget requirements, and the contribution requested. If the project coincides with the foundation's interests, a trustee or the executive director may request a meeting with the applicant and request preparation of a complete grant proposal. Complete proposals should be submitted only at the request of the foundation.

Deadline(s) The query letter may be submitted at any time throughout the year. When the foundation requests a complete grant proposal, the proposal will be due two months before the next semiannual meeting of the board of trustees, usually held in May and October.

59. Boehm Foundation

500 Fifth Avenue
New York, NY 10110-0296
(212) 354-9292

Program Description The Boehm Foundation supports programs which assist the development of human democratic rights both at home and abroad. Since its inception in the early 1960s the primary emphasis of the foundation has been social justice and support for democracy. The foundation continues to voice its concern in the field of race relations as well as its support of other underrepresented groups of citizens seeking to exercise their constitutional rights. Specific areas of interest have always included issues of peace, human rights, education and government accountability. Since 1983 the foundation has increased support for programs promoting peace, disarmament and antinuclear activities. The national debate over U.S. foreign policy in Central America has prompted an additional focal point for financial aid.

Sample Grants For general support of legal and educational work on behalf of public employees who expose misconduct and illegalities of government agencies, $5,000 to the Government Accountability Project (1987). For a project providing legal representation and education to community organizations in Harlem, $4,000 to the National Conference of Black Lawyers (1988). For education among Israeli youth about civil liberties principles, $6,500 to American-Israeli Civil Liberties Coalition, Inc. (1987). For their Peace Law and Education Project, $10,000 to Meiklejohn Civil Liberties Institute (1987). For the National Lawyers' Guild summer internship program, $5,000 to Capp Street Foundation (1988). For the Dean's discretionary fund, $12,000 to CUNY Law School at Queens College (1988). For institutional support to the Lawyers' Committee on Nuclear Policy (1988).

Eligibility/Limitations The foundation does not make grants to individuals. The foundation supports well-established, recognized organizations, as well as newer, experimental, and "grass roots" approaches to the problems of an ever more complex world.

Fiscal Information Grants awarded in 1988 totaled over $568,737.

Application Information No formal grant application forms are available. Proposals should be presented in a letter briefly outlining the objectives and significance of the project, the plans for carrying the project to completion and the qualifications of the organization and personnel concerned. A preliminary budget and letter proving tax-exempt status should be included.

Deadline(s) The foundation board meets once a month.

60. Booth Ferris Foundation
30 Broad Street
New York, NY 10004
(212) 269-3850

Contribution Program

Program Description The foundation's primary interests are in the field of private education, especially theological education, smaller colleges, and independent secondary schools. A limited number of grants is made in the areas of social service and culture in New York City.

Eligibility/Limitations Grants are made to charitable organizations that are exempt from federal taxes under Section 501(c)(3) of the Internal Revenue Code and that are not classified as private foundations. Grants are not made to organizations whose primary work is conducted outside the United States, and grants are not made to individuals, to federated campaigns, or to work with specific diseases or disabilities. Proposals from educational institutions for scholarships and fellowships and for unrestricted endowment are discouraged, as are proposals for individual research at such institutions. Proposals from social service and cultural institutions outside the metropolitan New York area will not be considered.

Fiscal Information Expenditures during 1987 included over $4.8 million for payments of 88 grants.

Application Information One copy of the proposal is sufficient and should be accompanied by an annual report. Financial data, including the organization's current budget and its latest audited financial statement, should be submitted as well.

Deadline(s) The trustees meet six times a year at approximately equal intervals; therefore, applications may be submitted at any time.

61. Borg-Warner Foundation
Corporate Contributions
200 South Michigan Avenue
Chicago, IL 60604
(312) 322-8657

Contributions

Program Description The mission of the Borg-Warner Foundation is to strengthen the individual's capacity to participate in and contribute to society and to serve as one mechanism through which the corporation carries out its citizenship responsibilities. To carry out this mission the foundation seeks to promote opportunities that encourage and enable individuals to expand their personal horizons, community systems to function effectively, and partnerships among individuals and institutions. Foundation contributions are viewed as an investment in overall community well-being. Through donations, the foundation strives to: respond to a wide spectrum of quality of life issues; serve as a catalyst for innovation; take risks in supporting valuable ideas; and build on community strengths.

Sample Grants Grant in the amount of $3,000 in support of a public interest law internship, Chicago, IL (1986). Grant in the amount of $10,000 to Northwestern University School of Law, Chicago, IL (1986). Grant in the amount of $5,000 for the Law and Economics Program, University of Chicago, Chicago, IL

(1986). Grant in the amount of $5,000 to the Mexican American Legal Defense and Education Fund, Chicago, IL (1987).

Eligibility/Limitations In general contributions are confined to tax-exempt organizations in the Chicago area. The foundation will consider providing seed money, capital support, endowment funds, challenge grants, support for general operations, and special project funding. Grants are not given to foreign-based institutions; testimonial dinners, fund-raising events, or advertising; medical or academic research; or to individuals.

Fiscal Information Contributions in 1988 totaled over $1.7 million.

Application Information There is no grant application form. The foundation requests that you submit a cover letter summarizing why financial aid is requested; the amount of money sought; and the name, daytime phone number and relationship to the organization of an individual who may be contacted regarding the request. Applicants must submit a funding proposal—preferably no more than 10 pages long—including the following information about the applicant organization: purpose and history; objectives for the coming year and the activities necessary to carry them out; who is served; the membership of each of the governing boards; projected income and expenses for the current fiscal year, with an audited financial statement from the previous year; size and source of corporate and foundation grants; proof of tax-exempt status; documentation of the needs to be met or problems to be solved; and a statement of the agency's qualifications for getting the job done. If the applicant is seeking support for a specific project, include a specific budget and program description for this project in addition to the above information.

Deadline(s) Requests are accepted throughout the year.

62. The Robert Bosch Foundation
CDS International, Inc.
330 Seventh Avenue, 19th Floor
New York, NY 10001
(212) 760-1400

Fellowship Program

Program Description To strengthen the ties of friendship and understanding between the United States and Germany, the Robert Bosch Foundation annually sponsors an intensive work/study fellowship program in Germany. The program aims to provide young American professionals and executives with a comprehensive overview of the political, economic, and cultural environment of Europe, especially Germany. The twofold goal of the program is to contribute to the professional competence and expertise of the participants and broaden their cultural horizons, while advancing American/German-European relations.

Eligibility/Limitations Applicants for the fellowship must be U.S. citizens who have a graduate or professional degree or equivalent professional experience in business administration, economics, public affairs, political science, law, journalism or mass communications. Prerequisites include an outstanding academic background, public commitment, and character traits indicative of leadership qualities. Some professional experience is desirable. Knowledge of German is strongly recommended, though not required for application.

Fiscal Information Fellows will receive DM 3,000 per month to cover expenses incurred for food and lodgings during the nine-month fellowship program. Married participants whose spouses accompany them may be entitled to receive a monthly supplement. In addition, the foundation will provide, for participants only, all program-related travel, including round-trip air transportation between U.S. residence and Germany; health and accident insurance for the duration of the stay; and accommodations for the fellowship recipient during the intensive language course at the outset of the program, as well as in Brussels, Paris, and at the two-program evaluation seminars. The foundation will also cover the cost of German language instruction between the time the fellows are selected and when they depart for Germany.

Application Information Applicants must submit the following documents: application form (available from the foundation), completed and duly signed; resume; official transcript of graduate studies (or of undergraduate studies, if applicant has no graduate level transcript); a supporting statement in English and German (prepared by a translator, if necessary) describing the applicant's expectations and personal objectives relevant to the proposed stay in Germany, with preference indicated as to the employment experience desired; and two letters of reference.

Deadline(s) Applications, complete with all requisite documentation, must be submitted by October 15. The selection panel will announce its final choices by January. The program will run from September through the following May.

63. The Boston Foundation Inc.

60 State Street, Sixth Floor
Boston, MA 02109
(617) 723-7415

Grants

Program Description The Boston Foundation will consider any proposal for a program that seeks to meet in a significant way health, human service, educational, housing, environmental, or cultural needs in the Greater Boston community. The foundation favors: programs that will serve a broad sector of the community and that will assist those who are not being adequately served by existing community resources; demonstration projects that propose practical approaches to specific community problems; programs that help coordinate community services; programs that will provide leverage for generating additional funds and community support; and building, renovation, and energy conservation projects that will improve the delivery of basic services.

Sample Grants For technical assistance costs, $10,000 to Christians for Urban Justice (1987). For the John & Ethel Goldberg Fund V, $7,050 to the National Judicial College (1987). For the Social Law Library Endowment Fund, $50,000 (1987).

Eligibility/Limitations Grants are made only to tax-exempt organizations as defined by 501(c)(3) of the Internal Revenue Code. In general, grants are not made from undesignated funds for general operating expenses; medical, scientific, or academic research; scholarships, fellowships, or loans; the writing, publication, or distribution of books or articles; conferences or symposiums; travel; the production or distribution of films, radio, or television programs; audio and/or video equipment; or capital campaigns of institutions that have nationwide support. In addition, grants are not made from undesignated funds to individuals, organizations outside the Boston geographic area, or to national or international organizations.

Fiscal Information Grants paid in 1988 totaled more than $12 million.

Application Information A formal written proposal should include: a cover letter, signed by the organization's president and executive director, outlining a brief summary of the request and the amount requested; a report on the expenditure of any previous grant; a copy of the most recent 501(c)(3) IRS ruling; a description of the organization's background, history, purpose, current programs, and the people it serves; a list of board members, officers, and staff; financial statements from the last three years of operation, including the organization's most recent audit and the current operating budget; project description and an estimate of the number of people to be served; specific plans for evaluating the project; project budget; the amount requested; the amount raised or expected from other sources; an explanation of how the project is to be funded; a contact person; and a telephone number.

Deadline(s) The foundation considers grant proposals four times a year, generally in March, June, September, and December. A minimum of 10 weeks before scheduled meetings is required to process proposals. A longer advance period may be necessary in the case of a proposal that requires an unusual amount of preliminary investigation.

64. The Boston Globe Foundation

135 Morrissey Boulevard
Boston, MA 02107
(617) 929-2895

Grants

Program Description The Boston Globe Foundation makes grants to nonprofit organizations from funds made available by Affiliated Publications, Inc. The foundation has seven areas of giving: community services, culture and the arts, education, science and the environment, hospitals and health care, summer camps, and media business.

Sample Grants Seed money for Boston Conference combating racism and corruption in the national judicial system, $1,500 to the Institute for Justice for All, Philadelphia, PA (1986). Annual payment toward multiple-year $100,000 pledge, $20,000 to Harvard University, Center on Press, Politics and Public Policy, Cambridge (1986). To provide support for multiracial study/ action/reflection programming which addresses issues of faith and social justice beginning with the point of view of women's experience, $3,000 to Women's Theological Center, Back Bay, MA (1986). To fund the expense of research and publication of study on integration of handicapped/disabled children under Chapter 766 in Massachusetts public schools, $20,000 to Massachusetts Advocacy Center, Boston (1986).

Eligibility/Limitations The foundation approves grants for operating expenses, special projects, and capital drives to agencies located within the Greater Boston area. Gifts are made to regional or national groups, but the main purpose of the foundation is to service and assist communities in the Boston area.

Fiscal Information The foundation completed its seventh year of operation in 1988 with total contributions in excess of $6.7 million.

Application Information Application guidelines and required application forms are available from the foundation and will be supplied upon request. Foundation staff reviews all proposals, investigates agencies, evaluates the budgetary requirements, and then makes recommendations to the board of directors of the foundation.

Deadline(s) Requests for grants may be submitted at any time. Allow three to four months for processing of a proposal.

65. The Lynde and Harry Bradley Foundation, Inc.

777 East Wisconsin Avenue, Suite 2285
Milwaukee, WI 53202
(414) 291-9915

Grants

Program Description To carry out the foundation's general purposes, the board of directors authorizes grants for support of programs in the following areas of interest: Milwaukee area community affairs, including the application of public policy research findings to the tasks of local and state government; independent colleges and universities of Wisconsin; public affairs, including national public policy research, international and strategic policy research; and education, including higher education and gifted children.

Sample Grants To support the Standing Committee on Law and National Security, $25,000 to the American Bar Association Fund for Justice and Education, Washington, DC (1988). To support study of the judicial selection process, $16,000 to the American Enterprise Institute for Public Policy Research, Washington, DC (1988). To support a research project on the future of federalism, $75,000 to Brookings Institution, Washington, DC (1988). To support a study on nuclear nonproliferation, $4,800 to Columbia University Law School, New York, NY (1988). Continued support for research on the case Nollan v. California Coastal Commission, $50,000 to Pacific Legal Foundation, Sacramento, CA (1988). Continued support for the Center for Applied Jurisprudence, $75,000 to Pacific Research Institute for Public Policy, San Francisco, CA (1988).

Eligibility/Limitations The foundation will award grants only to organizations and institutions exempt from federal taxation under section 501(c)(3) of the Internal Revenue Code.

Fiscal Information Grants paid in fiscal year 1988 totaled over $23 million.

Application Information Two steps are required in the application process. First, the applicant should prepare a brief letter of inquiry, describing the applicant's organization and intended project. If the foundation determines the project to be within its policy guidelines, the applicant will receive a brochure describing the foundation's program and general guidelines and a basic checklist indicating information the proposal should contain. The second step is the actual submission of the proposal.

Deadline(s) Proposals should be submitted by December 15, March 15, July 15, or September 15.

66. The Brookings Institution
1775 Massachusetts Avenue, NW
Washington, DC 20036
(202) 797-6000

Research Fellowships in Economic Studies

Program Description The Brookings Institution awards a limited number of resident fellowships for policy-oriented predoctoral research in economics. The fellowships are designed for doctoral candidates whose dissertation topics are directly related to public policy issues and thus to major interests of the institution. Current Brookings research in economics includes the general fields of economic growth, international economics, human resources, industrial organization, regulation, public finance, monetary economics, and economic stabilization. Essential criteria for the award are relevance of the topic to the Brookings research program and evidence that the research will be facilitated by access to the institution's resources or to federal government agencies.

Eligibility/Limitations Only candidates nominated by graduate departments can be considered for these fellowships; applications from individuals not so nominated cannot be accepted. Candidates must have completed the preliminary examinations for the doctorate no later than February 15.

Fiscal Information The fellowships carry a stipend of $10,000, payable on a 12-month basis, for 11 months of research in residence at Brookings and one month of vacation. The institution will provide supplementary assistance for typing and other essential research requirements in an amount not to exceed $500, plus access to computer facilities. Fellows will be expected to pursue their research at Brookings beginning between July 1 and September 1. Fellows are protected by the institution's health insurance policies during the period of their appointment.

Application Information Candidates are nominated by letters addressed to the Economics Studies Program at the institute's address. One or two candidates may be nominated by any department from among the present or recent graduate students of the department.

Deadline(s) Nominations must be received no later than December 16.

67. The Brookings Institution
1775 Massachusetts Avenue, NW
Washington, DC 20036
(202) 797-6000

Research Fellowships in Foreign Policy Studies

Program Description The Brookings Institution awards a limited number of resident fellowships for policy-oriented predoctoral research in U.S. foreign policy and international relations. The fellowships are designed for doctoral candidates whose dissertation topics are directly related to public policy issues and thus to major interests of the institution. Current Brookings topics place special emphasis on security policy and international economic issues and focus primarily on the regions of East Asia, the Soviet Union and Eastern Europe, and the Middle East. Research in each area examines both the substance of key issues and the processes by which they are resolved in and among governments. Candidates interested in other topics will be considered when it can be shown that their stay at Brookings would be mutually advantageous.

Eligibility/Limitations Only candidates nominated by graduate departments can be considered for these fellowships; applications from individuals not so nominated cannot be accepted. Candidates must have completed the preliminary examinations for the doctorate no later than February 15.

Fiscal Information The fellowships carry a stipend of $10,000, payable on a 12-month basis, for 11 months of research in residence at Brookings and one month of vacation. The institution will provide supplementary assistance for typing and other essential research requirements in an amount not to exceed $500, plus access to computer facilities. Fellows will be expected to pursue their research at Brookings beginning between July 1 and September 1. Fellows are protected by the institution's health insurance policies during the period of their appointment.

Application Information Candidates are nominated by letters addressed to Research Fellowships in Foreign Policy Studies at the institute's address. One or two candidates may be nominated by any department from among the present or recent graduate students of the department.

Deadline(s) Nominations must be received no later than December 16.

68. The Brookings Institution
1775 Massachusetts Avenue, NW
Washington, DC 20036
(202) 797-6000

Research Fellowships in Governmental Studies

Program Description The Brookings Institution awards a limited number of resident fellowships for policy-oriented predoctoral research in governmental studies. The fellowships are designed for doctoral candidates whose dissertation topics are directly related to public policy issues and thus to major interests of the institution. Current research in governmental studies includes studies of American political institutions and politics, economic and social policy, and governmental regulation.

Eligibility/Limitations Only candidates nominated by graduate departments can be considered for these fellowships; applications from individuals not so nominated cannot be accepted. Candidates must have completed the preliminary examinations for the doctorate no later than February 15.

Fiscal Information The fellowships carry a stipend of $10,000, payable on a 12-month basis, for 11 months of research in residence at Brookings and one month of vacation. The institution will provide supplementary assistance for typing and other essential research requirements in an amount not to exceed $500, plus access to computer facilities. Fellows will be expected to pursue their research at Brookings beginning between July 1 and September 1. Fellows are protected by the institution's health insurance policies during the period of their appointment.

Application Information Candidates are nominated by letters addressed to Research Fellowships in Governmental Studies at the institute's address. One or two candidates may be nominated by any department from among the present or recent graduate students of the department.

Deadline(s) Nominations must be received no later than December 16.

69. John Carter Brown Library
Brown University
Box 1894
Providence, RI 02912
(401) 863-2725

John Carter Brown Library Fellowships

Program Description The John Carter Brown Library is an outstanding collection of primary materials relating to virtually all aspects of the discovery, exploration, and development of the New World. Collections range from the late fifteenth century to about 1830, when direct European involvement in American affairs came to an end. Numerous legal works reflect the response of European legal systems to the growth of overseas empires and in particular deal with the development of international law. Regular library fellowships are available for research in the collections of the library for periods of one to four months.

Eligibility/Limitations Fellowships are open to Americans and foreign nationals who are engaged in predoctoral, postdoctoral, or independent research. Fellows are expected to be in regular residence at the library and to participate in the intellectual life of Brown University. Therefore, preference may be given to applicants able to take up the fellowship during the course of the academic year.

Fiscal Information Fellowships range from one to four months with a monthly stipend of $800. (Foreign nationals are advised that the monthly stipend may not be sufficient to cover all of a fellow's travel and living expenses.)

Application Information Application forms are available on request.

Deadline(s) Applications should be postmarked no later than January 15.

Additional Information For qualified scholars who wish to use the collections of the library for periods of less than two months, the library has funds available for small, travel reimbursement grants. The amount of these grants will vary with the distance traveled and will not exceed $600 in any one case.

70. John Carter Brown Library

Brown University
Box 1894
Providence, RI 02912
(401) 863-2725

National Endowment for the Humanities Fellowships

Program Description The John Carter Brown Library is an outstanding collection of primary materials relating to virtually all aspects of the discovery, exploration, and development of the New World. Collections range from the late fifteenth century to about 1830, when direct European involvement in American affairs came to an end. Numerous legal works reflect the response of European legal systems to the growth of overseas empires and in particular deal with the development of international law. Long-term fellowships funded by the National Endowment for the Humanities are available in support of research appropriate to the holdings of the John Carter Brown Library.

Eligibility/Limitations Applicants must hold a doctorate and be American citizens or have been a resident in the United States for the three years immediately preceding the term of the fellowship.

Fiscal Information Fellowships consist of either two six-month awards, carrying a stipend of $13,750 each, or a single twelve-month award with a stipend of $27,500. Fellows are expected to be in regular residence at the library and to participate in the intellectual life of Brown University. Therefore, preference may be given to applicants able to take up the fellowship during the course of the academic year.

Application Information Application forms may be obtained from the director of the library.

Deadline(s) Applications should be postmarked no later than January 15.

Additional Information For qualified scholars who wish to use the collections of the library for periods of less than two months, the library has funds available for small, travel re-

imbursement grants. The amount of these grants will vary with the distance traveled and will not exceed $600 in any one case.

71. Mary Ingraham Bunting Institute of Radcliffe College

34 Concord Avenue
Cambridge, MA 02138
(617) 495-8212

Affiliation Program

Program Description The Mary Ingraham Bunting Institute of Radcliffe College is a major postdoctoral research and fellowship center for women scholars, scientists, creative writers and artists. Approximately 40 fellows from across the United States and around the world are in residence at the institute each year, working on projects that promise to make significant contributions to their respective fields and to their own careers. Affiliates come with funding from another fellowship and are provided with private office or studio space, along with access to Harvard/Radcliffe resources.

Eligibility/Limitations Women scholars, creative writers, and visual and performing artists are eligible. Scholars must have held the Ph.D. or appropriate terminal degree at least two years prior to appointment. Nonacademic applicants, such as artists, writers, social workers, lawyers, journalists, etc., need to have professional experience equivalent to a doctorate and some postdoctoral work. Affiliates are required to present a public lecture or reading in the institute colloquium series or an exhibition in the institute gallery.

Fiscal Information Appointment is without stipend, but includes office or studio space and other resources available to all fellows.

Application Information Application forms and additional information are available from the institute.

Deadline(s) The postmarked deadline for applications is February 15.

72. Mary Ingraham Bunting Institute of Radcliffe College

34 Concord Avenue
Cambridge, MA 02138
(617) 495-8212

Berkshire Summer Fellowship

Program Description The Mary Ingraham Bunting Institute of Radcliffe College is a major postdoctoral research and fellowship center for women scholars, scientists, creative writers and artists. Approximately 40 fellows from across the United States and around the world are in residence at the institute each year, working on projects that promise to make significant contributions to their respective fields and to their own careers. This fellowship is designed to support women historians at the postdoctoral level.

Eligibility/Limitations Women historians at the postdoctoral level are eligible to apply. Women doing historical study who do not hold a Ph.D. in history are ineligible. Preference is given to applicants who do not live in the Boston area and do not normally have access to Harvard/Radcliffe libraries.

Fiscal Information The fellowship carries a stipend of $3,000.

Application Information Additional information and application forms are available from the institute.

Deadline(s) The postmarked deadline is February 15.

73. Mary Ingraham Bunting Institute of Radcliffe College

34 Concord Avenue
Cambridge, MA 02138
(617) 495-8212

The Bunting Fellowship Program

Program Description The Mary Ingraham Bunting Institute of Radcliffe College is a major postdoctoral research and fellowship center for women scholars, scientists, creative writers and artists. Approximately 40 fellows from across the United States and around the world are in residence at the institute each year, working on projects that promise to make significant contributions to their respective fields and to their own careers. These fellowships are designed to support women who wish to pursue independent study in academic and professional fields, in creative writing, in the visual and performing arts, and in music and thereby advance their careers.

Eligibility/Limitations Women scholars, professionals, creative writers, poets, visual and performing artists, and musicians at various levels of career development are eligible to apply. Scholars must have held the Ph.D. or appropriate terminal degree at least two years prior to appointment. Nonacademic applicants, such as artists, writers, social workers, lawyers, journalists, etc., need to have professional experience equivalent to a doctorate and some postdoctoral work. Fellows are required to present a public lecture or reading in the institute colloquium series or an exhibition in the institute gallery.

Fiscal Information Award of the fellowship carries a stipend of $20,500 for a one-year appointment, office or studio space, and access to libraries and other resources of Radcliffe College and Harvard University. Residence in the Boston area is required during the fellowship appointment.

Application Information For information and application forms contact the Fellowship Program of The Bunting Institute.

Deadline(s) Applications and recommendations must be postmarked by October 2.

74. Mary Ingraham Bunting Institute of Radcliffe College

34 Concord Avenue
Cambridge, MA 02138
(617) 495-8212

The Carnegie International Distinguished Visitor Program

Program Description The Mary Ingraham Bunting Institute of Radcliffe College is a major postdoctoral research and fellowship center for women scholars, scientists, creative writers and artists. Approximately 40 fellows from across the U.S. and around the world are in residence at the institute each year, working on projects that promise to make significant contributions to their respective fields and to their own careers. This program is designed to support women from developing countries, preferably sub-Saharan Africa or the Caribbean, working on issues concerning women and development, such as maternal and child health, education, the family, employment, or science and technology.

Eligibility/Limitations Midcareer or senior women researchers or practitioners from developing countries are eligible. Projects in the humanities and creative arts are ineligible.

Fiscal Information Award of the fellowship carries a stipend of $9,500 for a six-month appointment. A shorter term is negotiable, but a minimum of four months is required. There are additional funds for travel, housing, and research. Private office space and access to Harvard/Radcliffe resources are provided.

Application Information For information and application forms contact the institute.

Deadline(s) Applications and recommendations must be postmarked by February 15.

75. Mary Ingraham Bunting Institute of Radcliffe College

34 Concord Avenue
Cambridge, MA 02138
(617) 495-8212

The Peace Fellowship

Program Description The Mary Ingraham Bunting Institute of Radcliffe College is a major postdoctoral research and fellowship center for women scholars, scientists, creative writers and artists. Approximately 40 fellows from across the United States and around the world are in residence at the institute each year, working on projects that promise to make significant contributions to their respective fields and to their own careers. The Peace Fellowship is designed to support women actively involved in finding peaceful solutions to conflict or potential conflict among groups or nations. Involvement with peace issues may be of an activist or scholarly nature. The range of past projects includes the effect of public policy on nuclear disarmament, U.S./Soviet military relations, the relocation of refugees in Guatemala, the role of nonviolent action in Sri Lanka, and the efficacy of divestment in South Africa.

Fiscal Information The fellowship carries a stipend of $20,500 for the year. Private office space is provided, as well as access to Harvard/Radcliffe resources.

Application Information For information and application contact the Fellowship Program of the institute.

Deadline(s) Application postmark deadline is February 15.

76. Florence V. Burden Foundation

630 Fifth Avenue, Suite 2900
New York, NY 10111
(212) 489-1063

Grants

Program Description The foundation has two major fields of interest—currently, the elderly and crime and justice. In both fields, the foundation seeks projects which are at the cutting edge of social innovation and will demonstrate new ways to solve basic enduring problems.

Sample Grants To support a conference on public safety, law enforcement and civil liberties, $40,000 to the American Civil Liberties Union Foundation, New York (1987). To support collection of best practices from successful family mediation programs as an effective alternative to the traditional handling of status offenders in juvenile courts and to disseminate this information to courts, social service agencies, juvenile justice planners and other interested organizations, $29,400 to The Institute of Judicial Administration, New York (1987).

Eligibility/Limitations Although many grants are made in the greater New York area, the foundation's basic interest is in issues of broad national importance; so the foundation welcomes inquiries from all parts of the United States.

Fiscal Information Grants in 1987 totaled over $750,000. Grants range in size from less than $5,000 to $50,000.

Application Information Before an application for a grant is made, a preliminary letter of intent is required to determine whether the foundation's current interests and funds permit consideration of a given proposal. This letter should briefly describe the capabilities of the sponsoring organization and explain why funds are needed, what will be accomplished as a result, and indicate the amount requested. This information is usually sufficient for the foundation to determine whether the request will be considered further. Other materials may be subsequently requested and meetings arranged as appropriate.

Deadline(s) A letter of intent should be submitted by April 1, August 1, or December 1. Meetings of the board of directors to consider grant applications are normally held in February, June, and October. Grant applications must be submitted no later than January 1 for the February meeting, May 1 for the June meeting, and September 1 for the October meeting.

77. Bureau of Justice Statistics

Department of Justice
Washington, DC 20531
(202) 724-7770

Criminal Justice Statistics Development

CFDA Program Number 15.550

Program Description The objectives of this program are to provide financial and technical assistance to state governments regarding the collection, analysis, utilization, and dissemination of justice statistics. The program seeks to improve the administration of justice by encouraging the development of state-level capabilities for collecting, analyzing, and disseminating statistical information pertaining to crime and criminal justice, and for providing statistical information to the federal government for national compilations.

Eligibility/Limitations Eligible beneficiaries are state agencies whose responsibilities include statistical activities consistent with the specific programs.

Fiscal Information Financial assistance for projects range from $30,000 to $150,000, with an average grant of $50,000.

Application Information Application forms are available through inquiry to the Grants Contracts Management Division, OJP, Department of Justice, Washington, DC 20531.

Deadline(s) Contact the headquarters office for application deadlines.

78. Business and Professional Women's Foundation

2021 Massachusetts Avenue, NW
Washington, DC 20036
(202) 293-1200

Sally Butler Memorial Fund for Latina Research

Program Description This fund supports research on a range of issues of importance to women, although economic and employment issues and issues of concern to Latinas are a priority for funding. This programs goals include assisting women scholars of Latin American descent or citizenship at crucial points in their careers; facilitating understanding among women of the Americas; and supporting research which promotes equity for Latinas.

Eligibility/Limitations Applicants must be Latin American women by descent or citizenship, including women in the Caribbean, North, South, and Central American regions. Applicants must be postdoctoral scholars or doctoral candidates whose proposal for research has been approved by academic authorities in an accredited graduate school. Predoctoral candidates must have completed all course work and passed their qualifying exams. Individuals able to demonstrate that the proposed research will be conducted under standards of scholarship recognized at the doctoral level may also apply.

Fiscal Information Awards range from $500 to $3,000. The average fellowship award is $2,000. Fellowship support is for direct research costs and applicants may request any level of funding between $500 and $3,000. Grants are made directly to the award recipient; institutional overhead is not a permissible cost.

Application Information Applications are available between September 1 and December 15. To receive an application form applicants must send a one-page letter including a concise statement about the proposed research subject and the applicant's academic level. Candidates should indicate Latina background in the initial letter. Applications will be sent only after eligibility is ascertained.

Deadline(s) Applications must be postmarked on or before January 1. Letters of reference, mailed directly by the recommender to the foundation, also must have a January 1 postmark. Only completed applications with the required supporting materials will be considered.

Additional Information Due to limited monies, the BPW Foundation's Board of Trustees has decided to defer awarding research grants. The foundation will not accept 1991 applications.

79. Business and Professional Women's Foundation

2021 Massachusetts Avenue, NW
Washington, DC 20036
(202) 293-1200

Educational Programs

Program Description The Business and Professional Women's (BPW) Foundation offers the following scholarships: the BPW Career Advancement Scholarship, the Clairol Scholarship, and the New York Life Foundation Scholarship for women in the health professions.

Eligibility/Limitations To be eligible for the scholarships, applicants must: demonstrate critical financial need; be 25 or older (30 or older for the Clairol Scholarship); be U.S. citizens; be officially accepted into a program of study at an accredited U.S. institution; be graduating within 24 months of the time they apply for a scholarship; be receiving a degree or certificate at the conclusion of their studies; be acquiring marketable skills that will increase their economic security; and be entering the work force after they receive their degree or certificate. BPW scholarships do not cover study at the doctoral level, except for medical and law students. New York Life Foundation scholarships do not cover any study at the doctoral level.

Fiscal Information Tuition, fees, and related expenses are covered by these funds.

Application Information The application procedure is a two-step process. Applicants must first request a preapplication screening form. This form is available between September 1 and November 31. To receive the preapplication screening form, send a request with a self-addressed, business-sized stamped envelope to the Scholarship Department of the foundation between September 1 and November 31. The preapplication screening form must then be completed and returned to BPW Foundation for review. If the application meets all eligibility requirements, an application form will be mailed. Application forms are mailed between October 1 and December 15.

Deadline(s) All application materials must be postmarked by February 28.

80. Business and Professional Women's Foundation

2021 Massachusetts Avenue, NW
Washington, DC 20036
(202) 293-1200

Lena Lake Forrest Fellowships/BPWF Research Grants

Program Description These awards fund women and men engaged in contemporary and historical research in the United States on economic issues of importance to today's working women. Research topics of primary interest to the BPW Foundation include: occupational segregation; comparable worth; technological change in women's work; job satisfaction; analyses of women's cooperative efforts to improve the quality of their work lives; dependent care; work and the seasons of a woman's life; and the relationship of the "gender gap" to women's economic status. Goals for this program include: (1) to support research which working women can use in their efforts to achieve economic equality and to balance the demands of their dual roles in the workplace and at home; (2) to support research which can be used to aid the formation of effective policies toward women as permanent members of the work force; and (3) to foster the development of feminist scholars, especially by funding those in the early stages of career development.

Eligibility/Limitations Applicants must be citizens of the United States. Applicants must be postdoctoral scholars or doctoral candidates whose proposal for research has been approved by academic authorities in an accredited graduate school. Predoctoral candidates must have completed all course work and passed their qualifying exams. Individuals able to demonstrate that the proposed research will be conducted under standards of scholarship recognized at the doctoral level may also apply.

Fiscal Information Awards range from $500 to $3,000. The average fellowship award is $1,500. Fellowship support is for direct research costs and applicants may request any level of funding between $500 and $3,000. Grants are made directly to the award recipient; institutional overhead is not a permissible cost.

Application Information Applications are available between September 1 and December 15. Applicants are required to write a one-page letter requesting an application form and including a concise statement about the proposed research subject and the applicant's academic level. Applications will be sent only after eligibility is ascertained.

Deadline(s) Applications must be postmarked on or before January 1. Letters of reference, mailed directly by the recommender to the foundation, also must have a January 1 postmark. Only completed applications with the required supporting materials will be considered.

Additional Information Due to limited monies, the BPW Foundation's Board of Trustees has decided to defer awarding research grants. The foundation will not accept 1991 applications.

81. The Bydale Foundation
299 Park Avenue, 17th Floor
New York, NY 10171
(212) 207-1968

Grants

Program Description The foundation supports projects concerned with cultural programs, economics, environmental quality, international understanding, law and civil rights, and public policy research.

Eligibility/Limitations Grants are not made to individuals. The foundation will provide funds for research, publications, seminars, special projects, and matching funds.

Fiscal Information Grants totaled over $500,000 in 1988.

Application Information The foundation does not publish application guidelines. Send a preliminary letter or full proposal.

Deadline(s) The foundation prefers that proposals be submitted in July or August. The deadline for receipt of proposals is October 1.

82. Canadian Embassy
Academic Relations
501 Pennsylvania Avenue, NW
Washington, DC 20001
(202) 682-1740

Canadian Studies Conference Grant Program

Program Description The Canadian Studies Conference Grant Program has as its purpose the support of major conferences addressing important and timely Canadian or Canada/U.S. issues. It is intended to secure a greater understanding of the background, complexity and ramifications of these issues. The grants are designed to assist an institution to hold a conference and to publish the resultant papers and proceedings in a scholarly fashion.

Eligibility/Limitations This grant is intended for four-year U.S. colleges and universities, research and policy-planning institutes or other established research institutions which undertake a major conference on a Canadian or Canada/U.S. issue.

Fiscal Information Funding will be in the range of $5,000 to $15,000 (U.S. currency). Grants are provided to help defray only direct costs related to conference activities initiated by the institution. These costs may include travel, honoraria, secretarial services, computer time and possible publishing fees. No provision is made for released-time stipends nor for overhead costs to the institution.

Application Information Application forms and additional information are available from the Academic Relations Office, Canadian Embassy.

Deadline(s) Applications must be postmarked by June 15.

Additional Information Authored papers will remain the exclusive property of the writers. However, the Embassy requires two copies of the papers and/or proceedings once published.

83. Canadian Embassy
Academic Relations
501 Pennsylvania Avenue, NW
Washington, DC 20001
(202) 682-1740

Canadian Studies Faculty Enrichment Program

Program Description The Canadian Studies Faculty Enrichment Program is designed to provide faculty members with an opportunity to develop new courses that will be offered as part of their regular teaching load. Courses in social sciences, business, environment, humanities, law, and fine arts with a unique relevance to Canada are eligible for consideration.

Eligibility/Limitations This program is intended for full-time faculty members at accredited four-year U.S. colleges and universities. The applicants must have held a full-time teaching position for at least two years at their present institution. The candidates should be able to demonstrate that they are already teaching, or will be authorized to teach in the very near future, courses with a substantial Canadian content (50 percent or more). This award is not available two years in a row to the same recipient. All applicants must personally apply for a grant and carry out their own research. When the award provides the sole source of financial support, the period of the award must be used exclusively for the proposed project. Applicants are expected to conduct research in Canada for a period of time during the award period.

Fiscal Information Faculty may request funding in monthly increments of $1,500 (U.S. currency) for a period of up to three months. Grants are intended to help defray direct costs related to a project, including travel, equipment, books, materials, and per diem. No provision is made for released-time stipends nor for overhead costs to the institution.

Application Information Application forms and guidelines are available on request from the nearest Canadian Consular post or the Academic Relations Office, Canadian Embassy.

Deadline(s) All applications should be postmarked no later than October 31 and sent directly to the Academic Relations Office, Canadian Embassy.

84. Canadian Embassy
Academic Relations
501 Pennsylvania Avenue, NW
Washington, DC 20001
(202) 682-1740

Canadian Studies Faculty Research Grant Program

Program Description The Canadian Studies Faculty Research Grant Program is designed to promote research in social sciences, humanities, law, and fine arts with a unique relevance to Canada. The purpose of the grant is to assist scholars in writing an article-length manuscript of publishable quality and reporting their findings in scholarly publications with a view to contributing to the development of Canadian Studies in the United States.

Eligibility/Limitations This program is intended for full-time faculty members at accredited four-year colleges and universities, as well as scholars at American research and policy-planning institutes who undertake significant Canadian or Canadian-U.S. research projects and who did not receive this award last year. Applicants must personally apply for grants and carry out their own research. Contractual or commissioned research does not qualify for support, and grants are not given for work undertaken as part of the applicants' formal program of studies leading to a degree.

Fiscal Information Faculty members and scholars may request funding from $1,000 to $6,000 (U.S. currency). Research grants are intended to defray only direct costs related to a project, including travel, books, materials, secretarial services, computer time, and possible publishing costs. No provision is made for released-time stipends nor for overhead costs to the institution.

Application Information Application forms and guidelines are available on request.

Deadline(s) All applications should be postmarked no later than September 30 and sent directly to the Academic Relations Office, Canadian Embassy.

85. Canadian Embassy
Academic Relations
501 Pennsylvania Avenue, NW
Washington, DC 20001
(202) 682-1740

Canadian Studies Graduate Student Fellowship Program

Program Description The Canadian Studies Graduate Student Fellowship Program is designed to promote research in social sciences, business, environment, humanities, law, and fine arts with a view to contributing to the development of Canadian Studies in the United States. The purpose of the program is to assist graduate students in offering them an opportunity to conduct part of their doctoral research in Canada.

Eligibility/Limitations This program is intended for full-time doctoral students at accredited four-year U.S. colleges and universities whose dissertations are related in substantial part to the study of Canada. Candidates must be citizens or permanent residents of the United States and should have completed all doctoral requirements except their dissertation when they apply for a grant. Applicants must personally apply for grants and carry out their own research. Funds are to be provided only for work undertaken as part of the applicant's formal doctoral program of studies and are to be given only to help defray direct costs resulting from a period of time spend in Canada while doing research.

Fiscal Information A total amount of $750 (U.S. currency) may be awarded monthly to candidates for a designated period of up to eight months.

Application Information Application forms and guidelines are available on request.

Deadline(s) All applications should be postmarked no later than October 31 and sent directly to the Academic Relations Office, Canadian Embassy.

Additional Information All rights to the dissertation remain, of course, the exclusive property of the candidates; the Embassy requires a copy of the dissertation when completed.

86. Canadian Embassy
Academic Relations
501 Pennsylvania Avenue, NW
Washington, DC 20001
(202) 682-1740

Canadian Studies Institutional Research Grant Program

Program Description The Canadian Studies Institutional Research Grant Program encourages major multidisciplinary research projects undertaken by a group of scholars at the same institution or with scholars at other institutions on topics related to Canada or Canada-U.S. relations. The purpose of the grant is to assist researchers to complete their studies and publish the results in scholarly journals or in book form, with a view to contributing to the development of Canadian Studies in the United States. Research projects in the social sciences, business, environment, humanities, law and fine arts are eligible for consideration.

Eligibility/Limitations This program is intended for a group of full-time faculty members at accredited four-year U.S. colleges and universities, as well as scholars at research and policy-planning institutions and other established research institutions who undertake major Canadian or Canadian-U.S. research projects or professional academic activities (seminars, conferences, etc.), and who did not receive this award last year.

Fiscal Information The principal investigator may request, on behalf of the group, funding for up to $15,000 (U.S. currency). Grants are to be given only to help defray direct costs related to a research project or professional activities initiated by the research team or the institution. Contractual or commissioned research does not qualify for support. No provision is made for released-time stipends nor for overhead costs to the institution.

Application Information Application forms and guidelines are available on request.

Deadline(s) All applications should be postmarked no later than September 30 and sent directly to the Academic Relations Office, Canadian Embassy.

Additional Information The Government of Canada, through the Canadian Embassy, Washington, DC, at its discretion, may provide a matching grant to support Canadian Studies Programs and projects funded by a major private foundation or funding institution. Four-year, fully accredited, U.S. colleges, universities, and research institutes are eligible. There is no specific deadline. For further information, write or call the Academic Relations Officer, Canadian Embassy.

87. Canadian Embassy
Academic Relations
501 Pennsylvania Avenue, NW
Washington, DC 20001
(202) 682-1740

Canadian Studies Outreach Grant Program

Program Description This grant program is designed to assist institutions of higher education to provide instructional and curriculum support to teachers and schools involved in learning about Canada. Among the activities included for grant consideration are workshops and seminars and the development of curriculum guides and teaching aids and publication and dissemination of these and other educational media, as well as of newsletters and program delivery assistance.

Eligibility/Limitations This grant is intended for four-year U.S. colleges and universities which undertake major Canadian or Canada-U.S. professional academic activities and are desirous of providing outreach services to schools, educators and boards of education. Long-term outreach proposals spanning several years are encouraged. Support will normally be given only to those institutions with demonstrated competency in Canadian Studies and with experience in outreach projects.

Fiscal Information Institutions may request funding in the range of $5,000 to $15,000 (U.S. currency) per year. Grants are provided to help defray only direct costs related to outreach activities initiated by the institution. These costs include travel, honoraria, materials, printing, program delivery assistance, computer time and possible publishing fees. No provision is made for released-time stipends nor for overhead costs to the institution.

Application Information Application forms and additional information are available from the Academic Relations Office, Canadian Embassy.

Deadline(s) Applications must be postmarked by June 15.

88. Canadian Embassy
Academic Relations
501 Pennsylvania Avenue, NW
Washington, DC 20001
(202) 682-1740

Canadian Studies Program Development Grant

Program Description This grant program is designed to encourage scholarly inquiry and multidisciplinary professional academic activities which will contribute to the development and/or expansion of a Canadian Studies Program at the applying institution. Among the activities included for grant consideration are professional travel, symposia, lecture and film series, publication of associated proceedings, visiting lectureships, scholarly liaison between U.S. and Canadian academics as well as newsletters and program delivery assistance.

Eligibility/Limitations This grant is intended for four-year U.S. colleges and universities which undertake major Canadian or Canada-U.S. professional academic activities to further the development of a Canadian Studies Program at their institution. Long-term program development proposals spanning several years are encouraged.

Fiscal Information Institutions may request funding in the range of $3,000 to $25,000 (U.S. currency) per year. Grants are provided to help defray only direct costs related to professional activities initiated by the institution. These costs include travel, honoraria, materials, printing, secretarial services, computer time and possible publishing fees. No provision is made for released-time stipends nor for overhead costs to the institution.

Application Information Application forms and additional information are available from the Academic Relations Office, Canadian Embassy.

Deadline(s) Applications must be postmarked by June 15.

89. Canadian Embassy

Academic Relations
501 Pennsylvania Avenue, NW
Washington, DC 20001
(202) 682-1740

Canadian Studies Senior Fellowship Award

Program Description The Canadian Studies Senior Fellowship Award is designed to provide senior scholars with an opportunity to complete and publish a major study which will significantly benefit the development of Canadian Studies in the United States. A limited number of fellowships are awarded only to academics having a lengthy track record in teaching, researching, and publishing on Canada. Preference in such instances is to fund a project once a publisher has expressed interest.

Eligibility/Limitations This program is intended for full-time tenured faculty members at accredited four-year U.S. colleges and universities who are fully involved in Canadian Studies. These "Canadianists" should be in the process of completing their research for a book or major monograph. The study must be on a subject of widespread interest to the Canadian Studies community in the United States, as well as in Canada. This award is not available two years in a row to the same recipient.

Fiscal Information A monthly stipend not to exceed $3,000 (U.S. currency) may be awarded for a period of up to six months. Funds are given only to defray direct costs related to a research project initiated by the applicants who must apply on their own behalf. Whenever the award represents the sole source of financial support, the period of the award must be used exclusively and on a full-time basis for the proposed project. The expectation is that persons receiving additional funding from other sources will still devote a significant amount of time to the project.

Application Information Application forms and guidelines are available on request.

Deadline(s) All applications should be postmarked no later than October 31 and sent directly to the Academic Relations Office, Canadian Embassy.

Additional Information All rights to a manuscript will remain, of course, the exclusive property of the grantees. The Embassy requires a copy of the book once published.

90. Carnegie Corporation of New York

437 Madison Avenue
New York, NY 10022
(212) 371-3200

Grants

Program Description Although its purposes are broadly stated, the corporation has a policy of selecting a few areas at a time in which to concentrate its grants. Currently the corporation is concentrating on four program areas. (1) The goal of the Education Science, Technology and the Economy program is the education of all Americans, especially youth, for a scientifically and technologically based society. (2) Toward Healthy Child Development: The Prevention of Damage to Children program seeks to explore ways to prevent four serious kinds of harm to children and young adolescents: school failure, school-age pregnancy, childhood injury, and substance abuse. (3) The priorities of the Strengthening Human Resources in Developing Countries are based on a view of development as a process of expanding indigenous human capacity to identify and solve social and economic problems and on the conviction that scientific research provides knowledge and technologies that can help societies achieve development that is sustainable—economically, environmentally, and socially. (4) The program in Avoiding Nuclear War has four main emphases. The first involves support of efforts to develop new ideas and analyses pertinent to decreasing the chances of nuclear war and to relate this work closely to the policymaking, policy-advising community. The program supports interdisciplinary research and analysis of selected problems with particular bearing on the avoidance of nuclear war, which, because of their complexity or technical difficulty, require attention by the most competent experts, independent of, as well as in, government. The second involves support of serious educational efforts to build a broad nonpartisan interest in the results of this work. The third involves exploration of what the behavioral sciences have to offer in near-term, applied advice about negotiations, decision making, and conflict resolution and long-term understanding of human conflict and its resolution. The fourth is directed at the possibilities for fundamental, long-term change in the relationship between the United States and the Soviet Union.

Sample Grants To the Puerto Rican Legal Defense and Education Fund, for education and advocacy activities, $450,000 (1988). To the NAACP Legal Defense and Educational Fund, for activities including a nationwide survey of racial attitudes, $275,000 (1988). To the American Civil Liberties Union Foundation, for training programs for community leaders who are in the process of bringing suit against alleged violators of the Voting Rights Act, $200,000 (1988). To People for the American Way, for extension of voter outreach and education on constitutional issues, $100,000 (1988). To the Lawyers Committee for Human Rights for monitoring and analysis of Soviet legal reform, $250,000 (2 yrs.) (1989). To the Mexican American Legal Defense and Educational Fund, for education, litigation and advocacy, $750,000 (3 yrs.) (1990). To the Aspen Institute for Humanistic Studies, $33,000 for meetings on U.S. relations with southern Africa for American lawyers (1990).

Eligibility/Limitations The corporation makes grants primarily to academic institutions and national and regional organizations.

Fiscal Information The corporation commits between $35 and $40 million each year to grants, primarily for the people of the United States.

Application Information Program policy statement and guidelines are available on request. There is no formal procedure for submitting a proposal. All that is necessary for preliminary consideration is a statement describing the project's aims, methods, personnel, and the amount of financial support required.

Deadline(s) None. The board reviews quarterly.

91. The Carthage Foundation

P. O. Box 268
Pittsburgh, PA 15230
(412) 392-2900

Grants

Program Description The Carthage Foundation confines most of its grant awards to programs that will address public policy questions concerned with national and international issues.

Sample Grants To the National Defense Institute, $10,000 (1988). To the National Center for Public Policy Research, $35,000 (1988). To the Washington Legal Foundation, $100,000 (1987).

Eligibility/Limitations The foundation does not make grants to individuals.

Fiscal Information Grants awarded in 1988 totaled more than $1 million.

Application Information Initial inquiries to the foundation should be in letter form, signed by the organization's president or authorized representative and having the approval of the organization's board of directors. The letter should include a concise description of and budget for the specific purpose for which funds are requested. Additional information must include the organization's current annual budget, latest audited financial statement and annual report. A copy of the current determination letter from the Internal Revenue Service evidencing tax-exempt status under section 501(c)(3) of the IRS Code is required. Additional information may be requested if need for further evaluation.

Deadline(s) The foundation normally considers grants at meetings held in the first and fourth quarters of each year. However, requests may be submitted at any time and will be acted upon as expeditiously as possible.

92. Mary Flagler Cary Charitable Trust

350 Fifth Avenue, Room 6622
New York, NY 10118
(212) 563-6860

Conservation of Natural Resources Grants

Program Description The trust's purpose in conservation is to preserve coastal barrier islands and beaches in their natural state, to discourage public subsidy of private development in critical coastal areas, and to further an ecosystem approach to the management of natural resources in the coastal zone. The trust offers grants for land acquisition, legal protection, and ecosystem management. Legal protection grants offer support for public interest law groups which monitor federal and state agencies and, when necessary, litigate to prevent illegal or inappropriate public subsidy of private development on barrier islands and in coastal wetlands.

Sample Grants To provide the public with information on the Coastal Zone Management Act, the EPA and NOAA coastal programs and the Coastal Barrier Resources System, $15,000 to Coast Alliance, Inc., Washington, DC (1987). To support a publication of a legal and economic analysis of wetland protection, $15,000 to The Environmental Law Institute, Inc. (1988).

Eligibility/Limitations Grants are generally awarded to groups in the eastern coastal states who are tax exempt under Internal Revenue Code section 501(c)(3) and are not a private foundation under section 509(a).

Fiscal Information The trust makes grants both for general operating support and for program support toward a specific objective or project. In 1988 over $1 million in grants was awarded for conservation projects.

Application Information The trust does not use a grant application form. Instead, as a first step, a letter should be sent to the trust containing a concise statement of the program or project, the amount of funding requested and how it fits within the overall budget of the applicant, a brief description of the nature and activities of the applicant, its legal name, and a current list of the applicant's officers and directors or trustees. If, after studying a written grant request, the trustees decide that there is a possibility of support, additional information will be requested.

Deadline(s) The trustees met at least once every month and a response is made to every applicant. Meetings between applicants and trustees are discouraged until it has first been determined that grant action by the trust is possible.

93. Center for Defense Information

1500 Massachusetts Avenue, NW
Washington, DC 20005
(202) 862-0700

Internships

Program Description The center offers an intern program to undergraduate students, graduate students, and recent graduates who have strong interests in U.S. military issues and related public policy issues. Interns perform a variety of professional support functions, but serve mainly as research and outreach assistants. They work closely with the center staff, usually with considerable responsibility. Intern projects have included such diverse research subjects as U.S. military nuclear wastes, United States arms transfer policy, and Soviet-American naval comparisons, as well as media activities.

Eligibility/Limitations There is no preferred academic background. Fields of study might encompass the social and policy sciences, physical sciences, and preprofessional curricula. Although prior course work in U.S. military issues and related public policy areas is not required, high academic achievements are important. Writing skills are essential.

Fiscal Information Interns generally receive a modest monthly stipend of $600. Interns are expected to work on a full-time basis for periods of four months.

Application Information All internship correspondence should be addressed to the intern program coordinator. Program guidelines are available on request.

Deadline(s) The deadline for receipt of materials for the spring term is November 1, for the summer term April 1, and for the fall term July 1. Candidates are advised to apply early.

94. Center for International Affairs

Harvard University
1737 Cambridge Street, Room 416
Cambridge, MA 02138
(617) 495-2137

John M. Olin Fellowships in National Security

Program Description These fellowships are designed to promote research by younger scholars in the broad area of security affairs. Of particular interest is research into the causes and conduct of war, military strategy and history, defense policy and institutions, and the ways in which the United States and other societies can provide for their security in a dangerous world.

Eligibility/Limitations Eligible applicants include postdoctoral scholars and doctoral candidates at the dissertation stage of their graduate program.

Fiscal Information Postdoctoral fellowships carry a stipend of approximately $22,000 per academic year and the dissertation fellowships carry a stipend of $1,100 per month. Both fellowships will provide some funds to help defray the cost of health insurance, if necessary.

Application Information Applications consist of: a current curriculum vitae, including a bibliography; a 1,500-word description of the proposed research project to be undertaken if accepted as a fellow; one or two samples of writing pertinent to the application, if possible; and the names of two or three persons qualified to evaluate confidentially the applicant's project and scholarly qualifications.

Deadline(s) Applications should be transmitted to the center as early as possible, but in no case later than March 15.

95. Center for International Security and Arms Control

Stanford University
320 Galvez Street
Stanford, CA 94305-6165
(415) 723-9626

Fellowships

Program Description The Stanford Center seeks to contribute to the training of a new generation of scholars and practitioners thoroughly competent to deal with the complex technologies and hard political realities which characterize the fields of arms control and international security. Each year the center invites applications from advanced predoctoral students and postdoctoral scholars for an academic year of specialized study in the fields of international security relations and arms control. The competition is open to all scholars from relevant disciplines, including (although not limited to) political science, history, international relations, law, medicine, psychology and sociology.

Eligibility/Limitations Those eligible to apply include graduate students who have made substantial progress toward the completion of their dissertations, as well as more advanced scholars (Ph.D. or equivalent degree) from U.S. and foreign universities who wish to add a specialization in arms control and international security through an academic year of concentrated study. The center is especially interested in receiving applications from scholars interested in U.S.-Soviet security relations, regional security issues, and problems of peace and international cooperation, particularly in the Asian-Pacific area. The center encourages women and minority applicants.

Fiscal Information The value of fellowship awards is determined by the level of the student's graduate education, work experience, and number of dependents. Stipends for advanced graduate students and postdoctoral scholars range from $12,000 to approximately $24,000 for the academic year. Some funds are available to fellows for such research-related expenses as travel, photocopying and manuscript typing. Successful applicants will be provided office space. It should be noted that there are no provisions for summer support.

Application Information Application guidelines and additional information are available from the director of fellowship programs at the center.

Deadline(s) The deadline for receipt of completed applications is March 5.

96. Center for International Security and Arms Control

Stanford University
320 Galvez Street
Stanford, CA 94305
(415) 723-9626

International Security and Arms Control Fellowships

Program Description The Stanford Center for International Security and Arms Control seeks to contribute to the training of a new generation of scholars and practitioners thoroughly competent to deal with the complex technologies and hard political realities which characterize the fields of arms control and international security. The center is especially interested in receiving applications from scholars working on U.S.-Soviet security relations, regional security issues, problems of peace and international cooperation, particularly in the Asian-Pacific area, and other innovative research topics.

Eligibility/Limitations Eligible applicants include Ph.D. candidates who have made substantial progress toward completion of their dissertations, as well as more advanced scholars (Ph.D. or equivalent degree) from the United States and abroad who plan an academic year of concentrated research and writing.

Fiscal Information The value of fellowship awards is determined by the level of the applicant's graduate education and background. Stipends range from $12,000 (for graduate students) to approximately $24,000 for the nine-month academic year. Some funds are also available for research-related expenses. It should be noted that there are no provisions for summer support.

Application Information For further information on the application procedure and/or application forms, contact the director of fellowship programs at the center.

Deadline(s) The deadline for completed applications is March 5.

Additional Information The center also offers one or two fellowships each year for civilian and/or military officers attached to the U.S. government, members of military or diplomatic services from other countries, and journalists interested in arms control and international security issues.

97. Center for Italian Renaissance Studies

Harvard University, Department of Comparative
  Literature
401 Boylston Hall
Cambridge, MA 02138
(617) 495-2543

Villa I Tatti Fellowships

Program Description The Harvard Center for Italian Renaissance Studies at Villa I Tatti will award stipendiary fellowships for independent study on any aspect of the Italian Renaissance.

Eligibility/Limitations I Tatti offers fellowships for scholars of any nationality, normally postdoctoral and in the earlier stages of their careers. Fellows must be free to devote full time to study. It is in keeping with the purposes of I Tatti that fellows not be absent for protracted periods during the academic year, although they certainly are expected to come and go in the course of carrying out necessary work and making visits elsewhere.

Fiscal Information Stipends will be given in accord with the individual needs of the approved applicants and the availability of funds. The maximum grant will be no more than $22,000; most are considerably less. Each fellow is offered a place to study, use of the Biblioteca Berenson and Fototeca, lunches during weekdays, participation in the activities of the Center, and an opportunity to meet scholars from the United States and other countries working in related fields.

Application Information Applicants should send their curriculum vitae and a description of their project to the Director at Via di Vincigliata, 50135 Florence, Italy, and duplicates to Professor Walter Kaiser at the above address.

Deadline(s) Applications must be received by November 1.

Additional Information I Tatti offers a limited number of nonstipendiary fellowships for scholars working in Florence on Renaissance subjects with support from other sources. Nonstipendiary fellows should have the same qualifications and will have the same privileges as those whose stipends are derived from I Tatti funds. Scholars interested in these fellowships should apply by November 1.

98. Center for Medieval and Renaissance Studies

University of California, Los Angeles
405 Hilgard Avenue
Los Angeles, CA 90024-1485
(213) 825-1970 and 825-1880

Postdoctoral and Visiting Scholars

Program Description The center extends campus privileges to scholars in Medieval and Renaissance fields who obtain a postdoctoral or visiting fellowship to pursue research at UCLA.

Eligibility/Limitations Postdoctoral applicants should hold the Ph.D.

Fiscal Information These positions carry no stipend, but provide library privileges, parking facilities, personal contacts, and professional orientation.

Application Information Application information is available on request from the director of the center.

Additional Information The center, in cooperation with individual departments, hosts visiting professors in the fields of Medieval and Renaissance Studies.

99. Center for Medieval and Renaissance Studies
University of California, Los Angeles
405 Hilgard Avenue
Los Angeles, CA 90024-1485
(213) 825-1970 and 825-1880

Research Assistantships

Program Description The center offers a number of research assistantships on a competitive basis to graduate students from the United States and abroad who are studying for the Ph.D. in some phase of Medieval, Renaissance, or Byzantine Studies.

Eligibility/Limitations Research assistants must be admitted to the Graduate Division of UCLA and to the department in which he or she chooses to study for the doctorate.

Fiscal Information The assistantship carries a stipend that ranges from approximately $916 to $1,055 per month.

Application Information Procedures for application are available by request from the director of the center.

Deadline(s) Applications must be received by March 15.

100. Center for the Humanities
Weslyan College
The Center for the Humanities
Middletown, CT 06457

Andrew W. Mellon Postdoctoral Fellowships in the Humanities

Program Description The purpose of these fellowships is to promote interdisciplinary interests among younger humanists, to direct their attention to problems of pedagogy on the undergraduate level, and to associate them with a distinguished teaching and research faculty in their immediate postgraduate years.

Eligibility/Limitations Scholars who have received their Ph.D. within the last three years in any field of humanistic inquiry are eligible to apply.

Fiscal Information The stipend is $27,500 plus $500 for support of research and instruction.

Application Information There is no official application form. Applicants should submit: a full statement of current research interests; a statement of teaching interest, with specific descriptions of two interdisciplinary courses for undergraduates; a full curriculum vitae; a dossier from the graduate school from which the doctorate was received, or not less than three letters of recommendation; copies of published work, extracts from the dissertation; or drafts of work in progress (not to exceed 50 pages).

Deadline(s) Postmark deadline for applications is November 1.

101. Center for the Study of Human Rights
Columbia University
1108 International Affairs Building
New York, NY 10027
(212) 854-2479

Health Care and Human Rights Fellowship

Program Description The Center for the Study of Human Rights supports a general research program to the study of health care and human rights with a particular emphasis on AIDS. The subject will be examined in the light of international human rights standards from national, comparative and transnational perspectives. The program seeks to promote research within and between different disciplines, including law, political science, medicine, social work, sociology, and other sciences.

Eligibility/Limitations The center invites applications from postdoctoral scholars interested in working in this field. Scholars will be expected to engage in research and related activities on aspects of the year's theme, e.g.: (1) historical and empirical studies of domestic health care policies and provisions from the perspective of evolving human rights concepts and practices; (2) theoretical and legal analyses of the right to health care on the premises and strategies of different health care policies; the promotion of the health care rights of disadvantaged groups; health care claims across national borders; (3) the application of human rights standards to the particular problem of AIDS.

Fiscal Information Scholars will participate fully in the center's programs and have full use of university facilities, access to faculty and other scholars, and the aid, support and services of the center, including assistance with publication. Scholars must be self-supporting, but the center will attempt to assist scholars in obtaining funding.

Application Information Applicants should submit a detailed research proposal and biographical information to the center. Funding or proposed funding sources should be described.

Deadline(s) Applications should be submitted as soon as possible and at least by February 1.

102. Center for the Study of Human Rights
Columbia University
1108 International Affairs Building
New York, NY 10027
(212) 854-2479

Human Rights Fellowships

Program Description The Center for the Study of Human Rights offers a dissertation fellowship in support of work which reflects familiarity with human rights theory, specifically addresses rights, preferably in a cross-national perspective, and promises to advance human rights scholarship.

Eligibility/Limitations All students registered in the Columbia University Graduate School of Arts and Sciences are eligible if their dissertation topics have been approved by their departments.

Fiscal Information The fellowship carries a stipend of $12,500 for the academic year.

Application Information Applications must include: three copies of the approved dissertation outline; three copies of the candidate's biography; and a confidential recommendation by the chair of the candidate's department.

Deadline(s) Complete applications must be received by March 1.

103. Center for Women in Government
University at Albany
1400 Washington Avenue, Draper Hall, Room 302
Albany, NY 12222
(518) 442-3900

Fellowship on Women and Public Policy

Program Description This program is designed to encourage graduate students to pursue careers in public policy while increasing the capacity of New York State government to address issues of concern to women. The fellowship combines academic work and placement in the New York State Legislature or in a state agency. All placements are in Albany.

Eligibility/Limitations Fellowships are open to matriculated students in graduate programs at all accredited colleges and universities in New York State. Applicants must have completed 12 credits of graduate work. Candidates must have demonstrated interest in research, employment or volunteer activities designed to improve the status of women.

Fiscal Information The fellowship carries a $9,250 stipend and 12 graduate credits from the Graduate School of Public Affairs.

Application Information Applications are available from the center.

Deadline(s) Applications and all supporting materials must be submitted by May 27.

104. Chevron U.S.A. Inc.
P.O. Box 7753
San Francisco, CA 94120-7753
(415) 894-4193

Grants

Program Description Chevron contributes to a broad variety of educational, environmental, health, human service, civic, cultural and international activities. The company gives priority to programs that encourage local environmental conservation and education, and creative math and science programs for grade levels K-12.

Eligibility/Limitations Eligible applicants must be private, tax-exempt organizations with certified 501(c)(3) status under the Internal Revenue Code. Generally excluded from consideration are grants to individuals; religious, veteran, labor, fraternal, athletic, or political organizations—except for specific projects that benefit the community; capital funds for buildings and equipment (exceptions may be made to renovate existing facilities for selected institutions that have broad community support in areas where Chevron has significant business operations); endowment funds; conferences and seminars; operating expenses for organizations receiving support through the United Way; school-related bands and sports organizations and events; sports activities; national health, medical and human service organizations specializing in research; travel funds; films, videotapes, or audio productions; fund-raising events or benefits; tickets for benefits; courtesy advertising; or product requests.

Fiscal Information Total contributions in 1988 exceeded $25.8 million.

Application Information Requests should be in concise letter form, preferably not more than two pages, plus attachments, and should include: brief description of activity or project; description of need and how the projects meets identified needs; timetable for project implementation; expected results; method of evaluating project effectiveness and communicating results to donors and similar organizations; project budget; and plans for continued funding. Contact the Manager, Corporate Contributions at the address listed above for additional information.

Deadline(s) Proposals are accepted and reviewed on a continuing basis. However, processing time is usually three months.

105. The Edna McConnell Clark Foundation
250 Park Avenue
New York, NY 10017
(212) 986-7050

Program for Justice

Program Description This program seeks to develop a more humane, just and effective system of criminal sanctions for adults and juveniles by supporting litigation and other means of ensuring constitutional conditions in adult and juvenile correctional institutions and jail; efforts to reduce unnecessary incarceration of adults and juveniles by developing community-based sanctions and encouraging their use; and clusters of projects in selected states that seek to reduce prison populations and increase community-based sanctions.

Sample Grants For a study of Georgia's graduated sanction program, $84,000 to the RAND Corporation, Santa Monica, CA (1988). For support of its National Institute for Sentencing Alternatives to organize a major national meeting on juvenile justice reform, $85,000 to Brandeis University, Waltham, MA (1988). For a study of the problems caused by overcrowding in California Youth Authority institutions and a plan for solving

them, $77,275 to Commonweal, Bolinas, CA (1988). For a media awards program on coverage of criminal justice issues, $5,160 to the Board of Trustees of the University of Alabama, Inc. (1989). To support two monographs exploring juvenile justice issues, $40,000 to Alternative Media Information Center, Inc., New York (1989).

Eligibility/Limitations The foundation primarily supports organizations with a 501(c)(3) tax exemption. The foundation does not consider requests for capital purposes, endowments, deficit operations, scholarships, or grants to individuals.

Fiscal Information Grants in 1989, in the Program for Justice, totaled over $4.3 million.

Application Information To apply, grant seekers should write a brief letter describing the program for which they are seeking funds. The letter should include the purpose of the grant, a description of the proposed activity, the identification of key participants, and an estimated budget and timeframe. It should be sent to the foundation in an envelope clearly marked "Proposal Letter." It will be reviewed by the program director, usually within one week to a month. If the proposed work fits the program's goals, the program director will ask for more information and a formal proposal.

Deadline(s) Proposals are acted upon by the trustees of the foundation at one of their five regular meetings each year.

106. Robert Sterling Clark Foundation, Inc.
112 East 64th Street
New York, NY 10021
(212) 308-0411

Grants

Program Description The Robert Sterling Clark Foundation was incorporated in 1952 and since then has provided financial assistance to a wide variety of charitable organizations. Over the years, program guidelines have evolved and changed. At present, the foundation is concentrating its resources in the following three fields: improving the performance of public institutions; ensuring access to family planning services; and strengthening the management of cultural institutions. Foundation interest in public institutions is based on the belief that foundations can play an extremely useful and important role both in working with government in pursuit of common objectives and in supporting organizations that criticize government where it appears to be responding inappropriately. The foundation will consider support of initiatives designed to: (1) monitor human services delivery programs to ensure that funds are not wasted and that recipients of service receive that to which they are entitled; (2) ensure that public institutions preserve and protect our environment in accordance with federal and state mandates; (3) encourage the kinds of linkages and relationships between the public and private sectors that will promote the development of New York's economic base; and (4) improve the effectiveness and accountability of New York City and New York State agencies.

Sample Grants For continued support of the Children's Rights Project's activities in New York State, $60,000 to the American Civil Liberties Union Foundation, New York (1987). For economic and environmental analyses of city and state waste disposal policy initiatives, $50,000 to Environmental Defense Fund, New York (1988). For litigation and public education, $70,000 to the American Civil Liberties Union Foundation Reproductive Freedom Project, New York (1988).

Eligibility/Limitations The foundation has elected to focus on the activities of government agencies in New York City and State.

Fiscal Information In 1988, the foundation appropriated grants totaling over $1.4 million. Grants ranged in size from $2,000 to $60,000 for periods of one to three years in length.

Application Information The foundation is interested in learning as much as possible about applicants. Consequently, the foundation requires that the following information accompany all proposals: one-page proposal summary; organization budget for the past year, current year, and projected year; most recent audited financial statement; IRS letter explaining tax status; names and occupations of board of directors; major sources of current financial support; resumes of key staff; and examples of past accomplishments. The main body of the application should not exceed 10 pages. If the applicant is requesting support for a particular project, the proposal should include the following information: description of project; project budget; expected results; detailed workplan; plans for evaluation; plans for future support; other contributors; and names of other organizations where the proposal has been submitted.

Deadline(s) The board of directors considers proposals throughout the year.

107. The Cleveland Foundation
1400 Hanna Building
Cleveland, OH 44115
(216) 861-3810

Program Description The foundation awards grants in five "program areas": health, social services, civic affairs, education, and cultural affairs. The foundation supports innovative programs that address problems to be solved, or opportunities to be seized, in the Greater Cleveland area. The foundation seeks new and more effective ways of doing things—for ideas that require no small amount of foresight and, perhaps, some risk taking.

Eligibility/Limitations Grants support both private and public services. They are made primarily to tax-exempt private agencies (which the Internal Revenue Service classifies as 501(c)(3) organizations, public charities under the law) and sometimes to governmental agencies in which case the limits of eligibility are more strictly defined. The Foundation does not make grants to individuals. Only programs in the Greater Cleveland area are considered for support.

Fiscal Information In 1988 The Cleveland Foundation awarded grants totaling $22.2 million. Grants ranged from $200 to $500,000. Most grants are for one-year awards. Multiyear grants are sometimes considered, although a first-time grant for a project never extends beyond three years.

Application Information Application information is detailed in a brochure, "Guidelines for Grant Seekers," available from the foundation.

Deadline(s) Deadlines for receipt of full proposals are December 15, March 31, June 15, and August 31.

108. College of William and Mary
Marshall-Wythe School of Law
Williamsburg, VA 23185

Commonwealth Center Fellow in American Legal History/Culture at the Institute for Bill of Rights Law

Program Description The Commonwealth Center for the Study of American Culture is devoted to the interdisciplinary study of American culture over the period extending from approximately 1815 to the present. The mission of the center is to encourage scholarship in such diverse fields as ethnohistory, gender studies, anthropology, the study of science, technology and medicine, as well as the more conventional disciplines of economic, social and political history. The Institute for Bill of Rights Law of the Marshall-Wythe School of Law at the College of William and Mary, in conjunction with the Commonwealth Center for the Study of American Culture, invites applications and nominations for the position of senior fellow. Funded by the center but resident in the institute, the senior fellow will hold a concurrent appointment as Visiting Professor of Law.

Eligibility/Limitations Candidates need not posses a law degree, but must have a record of distinguished scholarship in the area of American legal history or culture relevant to 19th- and 20th-century American studies.

Fiscal Information The stipend is competitive and commensurate with experience.

Application Information Additional information and application guidelines are available upon request.

Deadline(s) Review of applications begins on November 15 and continues until the position is filled.

Additional Information The Commonwealth Center also offers postdoctoral and senior fellowships for interdisciplinary research on topics of interest to the center. Contact the Director, Commonwealth Center for the Study of American Culture, College of William and Mary, Williamsburg, VA, 23185, for additional information.

109. Columbia Foundation
1090 Sansome Street
San Francisco, CA 94111
(415) 986-5179

Program Description The Columbia Foundation is currently focusing its grant program on projects that address critical issues and offer promise of significant positive impact in the following areas: preservation of the natural environment; enhancement of urban community life and culture; international and cross-cultural understanding; reversal of the arms race worldwide; and protection of basic human rights.

Sample Grants For start-up funding to establish a statewide public foundation to accept contributions made as a condition of environmental dispute settlements and to redirect the funds and grants to conservation projects, $30,000 over three years to California Fund for the Environment, Los Altos (1988). For the Task Force on Implementation of the Immigration Reform Act, which will work together with a coalition of immigrant-serving agencies to develop and support a public education program to inform newcomers about qualifications procedures for legalizations and to develop immigrant services, $25,000 to Northern California Grantmakers, San Francisco (1988).

Eligibility/Limitations The foundation focuses its program primarily on projects that seek common ground between the San Francisco community and the shared global concerns facing an interdependent world. Applications from San Francisco Bay Area organizations are given priority consideration. The foundation will consider grants only to organizations certified by the IRS as "public charities."

Fiscal Information Total grants awarded in the year ending May 31, 1988, were $935,491. Grants ranged in size from $1,000 to $250,000. The foundation generally does not provide support for operating budgets of established agencies, recurring expenses for direct services or ongoing administrative costs, individual fellowships or scholarships to agencies that are wholly supported by federated campaigns or heavily subsidized by government funds.

Application Information Preliminary inquiry by letter to the executive director at the address listed above is preferred. This preliminary letter of inquiry should include a brief summary of the proposed project or activity, the financial support needed, and a brief profile of the organization, its purpose, activities and personnel. A full proposal will be requested if the application is to be considered further by the foundation. Foundation profile and grants list are available on request.

Deadline(s) Grant applications are accepted on an ongoing basis. Application review can take two to three months.

110. Committee on International Security
Harvard MacArthur Scholarships, Center for
   International Affairs, Box 3
1737 Cambridge Street
Cambridge, MA 02138
(617) 495-2137

Harvard MacArthur Scholarships in International Security

Program Description These graduate awards are designed for students who have completed the training phase of their doctoral studies and who are now ready to go deeper into the field of international security, preparing themselves to become scholars and practitioners.

Eligibility/Limitations Applications are invited from any Harvard doctoral candidate working in international security. Applicants must be in the dissertation-writing stage of their work, having completed all graduate course requirements and general examinations by the beginning of the academic year for which they seek support.

Fiscal Information Approximately 10 scholarships of $12,500 each will be awarded.

Application Information The following materials are required for a complete application: a cover letter indicating the applicant's desire to be considered for an award; a curriculum vitae; a one-page summary of the planned dissertation project; a statement demonstrating how the applicant's research relates to international security and how support from the committee will promote that research; a statement showing a general description of the applicant's financial situation and needs; copies of all graduate transcripts; three letters of recommendation. All application materials should be sent to the address listed above.

Deadline(s) The deadline for receipt of all materials is March 1.

111. Committee on Scholarly Communication with the People's Republic of China
National Academy of Sciences
2101 Constitution Avenue, NW
Washington, DC 20418
(202) 334-2718

American Scholars to China Program

Program Description This program is open to candidates in the humanities only (not in the social or natural sciences and engineering) from outside the China studies field, in support of research, collaborative projects and seminars in China.

Eligibility/Limitations Applicants must have received the doctoral degree or its equivalent at the time of application. Applicants must be U.S. citizens or permanent residents at the time of application. Preference to scholars whose visits will initiate or continue long-term research and collaboration.

Fiscal Information Grants include travel to and from China, living allowance, research and educational materials and in-China travel allowances. There is no stipend or financial support for dependents.

Application Information Additional information and application forms are available upon request.

Deadline(s) The deadline for mailing all application materials is October 14.

112. Committee on Scholarly Communication with the People's Republic of China
National Academy of Sciences
2101 Constitution Avenue, NW
Washington, DC 20418
(202) 334-2718

China Conference Travel Grants

Program Description China Conference Travel Grants provide partial travel support to American humanists and social scientists presenting papers at research conferences in the PRC. Eligible conferences must be concerned with the humanities or social sciences, and preference will be given to supporting travel to conferences concerned with some aspect of China area studies.

Eligibility/Limitations Eligible scholars must be specialists in some aspect of the study of China; hold the Ph.D. degree; be U.S. citizens or permanent residents; and after the conference, disseminate a report describing the results of the conference to their colleagues in the United States. Applicants must explain how they will do this in the application itself. Preference is given to scholars who have not previously attended academic conferences in the PRC.

Fiscal Information The amount of support offered will be slightly less than the cost of round-trip airfare, and no additional allowance can be made for personal expenses or maintenance.

Application Information Application forms and additional information are available on request.

Deadline(s) Applications will be evaluated on a rolling basis but must be received no later than three months before the conference.

113. Committee on Scholarly Communication with the People's Republic of China
National Academy of Sciences
2101 Constitution Avenue, NW
Washington, DC 20418
(202) 334-2718

Fellowships for Graduate Program in China

Program Description The Committee on Scholarly Communication with the People's Republic of China (CSCPRC) was founded in 1966 under the joint sponsorship of the American Council of Learned Societies (ACLS), the National Academy of Sciences (NAS), and the Social Science Research Council (SSRC). The CSCPRC supports the exchange of scholars between the PRC and the United States. The Graduate Program provides support for American graduate students in the social sciences and humanities to carry out long-term (ten to twelve months) study or research in substantive fields at Chinese universities.

Sample Grants Support for a history project, "Pettifoggers and the Late Imperial Chinese Legal Culture" (1988-89). Support for a political science project, "Lawmaking and the Economy in China: Bureaucratic Process in a Changing Sector" (1988-89). Support for a political science project, "Norm Building, Organizational Legitimacy, and Policy Implementation: The Case of Water Pollution Prevention in the PRC" (1990-91). Support for an environmental policy project, "Environmental Policy Implementation in South China's New Economic Development" (1990-91).

Eligibility/Limitations The program offers support for individuals with the M.A. for course work and/or dissertation research in the social sciences and humanities. Application is open to U.S. citizens and permanent residents regardless of national origin, race, sex, or religious affiliation. Applicants must have received a bachelor's degree and must have completed three years, or the equivalent, of modern standard Chinese.

Fiscal Information Full fellowships for graduate students include travel to China, tuition and room fees, monthly stipend, and travel and educational material allowances. No allowance is made for support of any kind for dependents.

Application Information Address requests for information and application forms to CSCPRC.

Deadline(s) Applications must be postmarked by October 14.

114. Committee on Scholarly Communication with the People's Republic of China
National Academy of Sciences
2101 Constitution Avenue, NW
Washington, DC 20418
(202) 334-2718

Program for Research in China

Program Description The Committee on Scholarly Communication with the People's Republic of China (CSCPRC) was founded in 1966 under the joint sponsorship of the American Council of Learned Societies (ACLS), the National Academy of Sciences (NAS), and the Social Science Research Council (SSRC). The CSCPRC supports the exchange of scholars between the PRC and the United States. Open to candidates in the social sciences and humanities (not the natural sciences and engineering), the research program supports in-depth research on China, the Chinese portion of a comparative study, or exploratory research on an aspect of contemporary China. It will support limited research in Hong Kong or elsewhere in East Asia to supplement research within the PRC.

Sample Grants Support for a literature project: "Chinese New-Era Literature About the Legal System" (1989-90). Support for a history project, "Bandits, Brotherhoods and Qing Law in Guangdong, 1770-1839" (1990-91).

Eligibility/Limitations Applicants must have the Ph.D. or its equivalent. There is no minimum language requirement, but the necessity of Chinese language skills for a particular research plan is considered in reviewing the feasibility of proposals. Application is open to U.S. citizens and permanent residents regardless of national origin, race, sex, or religious affiliation.

Fiscal Information Grants for research scholars include travel to and from China, monthly stipend and living allowance, research and educational materials and in-China travel allowance. There is no financial support for dependents.

Application Information Address requests for information and application forms to CSCPRC.

Deadline(s) Applications must be postmarked by October 14.

115. Compton Foundation
10 Hanover Square
New York, NY 10005
(212) 510-5040

Program Description The foundation's directors determine funding priorities. The areas of interest given precedence may change from time to time when, in the opinion of the directors, adjustments are appropriate in response to social change, unanticipated needs of the community, or emerging opportunities. At present, the foundation's priorities include: global human survival, education, social welfare and social justice, religion, and culture and the arts.

Eligibility/Limitations The Compton Foundation makes grants only to organizations and institutions that qualify under requirements of the federal Tax Reform Act of 1969. Grants are not awarded to individuals.

Fiscal Information Grants authorized and paid in 1986 totaled more than $2.5 million.

Application Information The Compton Foundation has no application forms. Inquiries may be made by writing a concise letter clearly stating the objectives of the proposal, the means by which they are to be accomplished, the qualifications of the personnel involved, and a budget. Evidence of the organization's status under provisions of the Internal Revenue Code should be included. Prospective applicants are encouraged to determine that the proposal is relevant to the foundation's interests before applying. An annual report, delineating the foundation's interests and grant-making policies and significant grants made, is available on request from the foundation.

Deadline(s) None.

116. The Conservation and Research Foundation
Connecticut College, Foundation Call Box
New London, CT 06320
(203) 873-8514

Environmental Grants

Program Description The purposes of the foundation are to promote the conservation and enlightened use of our renewable natural resources, to encourage related research in the biological sciences, and to deepen understanding of the intricate relationships between man and the environment that supports him. These purposes are implemented by direct grants to organizations to aid their conservation programs; initiating studies, supporting activities and publishing information that might have a catalytic impact upon the preservation of environmental quality;

and supporting biological research in neglected areas, especially those having environmental implications.

Eligibility/Limitations Only those research investigations that might, for one reason or another, be ineligible to receive funding from conventional granting agencies will be considered.

Fiscal Information Grants rarely exceed $5,000. Indirect costs are usually not allowed. From January 1988 through August 1989 the foundation awarded 17 grants totaling $47,600.

Application Information Initial inquiry regarding the possibility of support should be in the form of an exploratory letter addressed to the foundation outlining the nature of the proposal, the amount of funding required, and reasons why the project might fit into the program of the foundation.

Deadline(s) No deadlines are announced.

117. Consulate General of Japan
Public Information and Cultural Affairs Section
250 East First Street, Suite 1507
Los Angeles, CA 90012
(213) 624-8305

Monbusho Scholarships

Program Description Monbusho offers scholarships to foreign students who wish to study at a Japanese university as a research student. Fields of study include the humanities and social sciences (including law, politics, commerce, and history) and the natural sciences.

Eligibility/Limitations Applicants must be nationals of the United States; under 35 years of age; university or college graduates; willing to study the Japanese language; and in good health.

Fiscal Information A monthly living allowance, transportation to and from Japan, an arrival allowance, a field of study allowance, and school fees are included in the scholarship.

Application Information Application forms and additional information are available upon request. Applicants should write the Japanese consulate nearest their place of residence or where they attend college.

Deadline(s) The deadline for receipt of completed application forms and related materials is July 29.

118. Corporation for Public Broadcasting
Radio Program Fund
901 E Street, NW
Washington, DC 20004-2006
(202) 879-9600

National Radio Program Production

Program Description The Corporation for Public Broadcasting (CPB) has available a fund to support national radio program production. Through this program fund, the CPB supports public radio system projects of high quality, diversity, excellence and innovation obtained from diverse sources, with strict adherence to objectivity and balance in programming of a controversial nature. Priorities are for projects that yield quality programming that is illuminating and inspiring, as well as appealing; that take programmatic risk; and that advance public radio's mission of serving an increasing number of Americans. Projects meeting the first priority will reflect programming that recognizes and incorporates the diversity and complexity of life, culture and society; or will present the unknown or underrepresented corners of life; or will present artistic and cultural work of the highest quality; or may provide programming alternatives to that which is available from other media. Projects meeting the risk priority will take creative risk in content and approach and will take business risk through the uncertain process of becoming established in the public radio marketplace. Projects meeting the third priority may hold the prospect of emerging as major new services or series or will be original and compelling projects of national significance but more limited in scope.

Eligibility/Limitations Any individual, association, foundation, institution, partnership, corporation or other business entity may submit a proposal. CPB invites submission of both production and laboratory-type proposals.

Fiscal Information No floor or ceiling exists on the amount of funds available for an individual project. CPB will evaluate all proposals from a "cost-for-product" perspective. Although not the major or only consideration in making final choices, awards to otherwise equal proposals may be determined by budget factors.

Application Information Additional information and application forms are available from the Vice President, Telecommunications, at the corporation's address.

Deadline(s) September 11.

119. Corporation for Public Broadcasting
Television Program Fund
901 E Street NW
Washington, DC 20004-2006
(202) 879-9600

Television Program Fund

Program Description The program fund of the Corporation for Public Broadcasting (CPB) announces an open solicitation process through which independent producers and public television stations may submit proposals for the development and production of programs for public television. Proposals may be submitted in three areas: news and public affairs; cultural and children's; and drama and arts.

Sample Grants Support for a documentary exploring the case of Leonard Poltier, a Native American whose trial for the murder of two FBI agents in 1975 remains a source of controversy to this day, to Apparatus/Lym Productions, New York (1989). Support for a dramatic biography of Clarence Darrow, a lawyer during the American Industrial Revolution, to Heus/Stept Productions, Los Angeles, CA (1989).

Eligibility/Limitations Independent producers and public television stations are eligible to submit program proposals. Submissions from women and minorities are encouraged, as are coproductions between independent producers and public television stations. The open solicitation requires projects to conform to traditional broadcast lengths, e.g., 28 minutes, 58 minutes, etc. Proposed programs must be visual, of more than local or regional interest, and must adhere to accepted technical, ethical, and artistic or journalistic standards. The credentials of the production team and whether or not a subject has received, or is likely to receive, adequate coverage elsewhere are also factors in the selection process.

Fiscal Information There are no restrictions on the amount of funds that may be requested, although the program fund reviews all budgets submitted and encourages producers to obtain other sources of funding. Major projects inevitably require several funding sources because the total cost places too great a demand on program fund resources.

Application Information Guidelines and submission requirements are available from the CPB.

Deadline(s) Proposals are preselected by staff for review by an advisory panel three times each year. The closing dates for submissions are January 19 and September 14. Proposals not received at CPB by close of business (5:30 p.m.) on the closing date will be held for consideration in the next funding round. There will be no exceptions. Packages received after the closing date but postmarked on or before said date are not acceptable.

120. Council for European Studies
Columbia University
Box 44 Schermerhorn
New York, NY 10027

Predissertation Fellowships on Topics Related to the European Communities

Program Description The basic purpose of these fellowships is to enable graduate students in the social science disciplines to pursue short-term, exploratory research in the European Communities to explore proposed dissertations on European Communities-related issues. Eligible disciplines are history, political science, economics, and sociology. All topics related to the Treaties of Paris and Rome and the Single European Act are eligible.

Sample Grants Support for a project in political science, "Administrative Legality and Local Politics in France and Britain, 1950-1975" (1988). Support for a project in law and political science, "Judicial Review and the Decline of Parliamentary Opposition: The Changing Nature of British Constitutional Discourse" (1989).

Eligibility/Limitations Students whose dissertation prospectuses have received formal approval from their departments are ineligible, as are graduate students who are in Europe at the time of competition. Applicants must be enrolled in a doctoral program at an American university and have completed the equivalent of at least two years of full-time graduate study prior to the beginning date of their proposed research. Fellowships are restricted to citizens of the United States.

Fiscal Information Fellowships provide $3,000 for expenses connected with the predissertation research phase.

Application Information Potential applicants should contact the council in writing at the address above and request additional information and application guidelines.

Deadline(s) The deadline for application is February 1. Applications must be requested by January 15.

Additional Information The council's Committee on Workshops invites proposals for the organization of workshops on the European Communities. The council will provide a maximum of $2,500 per workshop as seed money, and maintenance or travel for workshop participants. Contact the council for additional information.

121. Council for International Exchange of Scholars
3400 International Drive, NW, Suite M-500
Washington, DC 20008-3097
(202) 686-7866

Fulbright Scholar Program—Distinguished Lecturing

Program Description This program supports a small number of scholars who are prominent in their fields.

Eligibility/Limitations Prospective applicants should have U.S. citizenship at the time of application. In some programs, language proficiency may be required. Persons who have lived abroad for the full 10-year period immediately preceding the time of application are ineligible. In general, preference is given to persons who have not already had lecturing or research grants. A previous grantee may, however, apply for a second award if three years have elapsed between the end of the first grant period and the beginning of the second. In accordance with a new ruling by the Board of Foreign Scholarships, scholars who have already held two (or more) Fulbright scholar awards are no longer prohibited from making application. Such applicants should bear in mind, however, that preference will be given to those who have not participated in the program and who do not have substantial recent experience abroad.

Fiscal Information Grant benefits include: round-trip travel for the grantee and for a principal dependent of a grantee whose appointment is for a full academic year; a maintenance allowance, paid either in local currency, in dollars, or in local currency with a dollar supplement (allowance amounts vary by grant category, the country and duration of the grant, and family status); incidental allowances for baggage, for books and services essential to the assignment, and for travel within the host country; housing (or housing allowance) in certain countries; and tuition allowance in certain countries (where available, tuition reimbursement is provided for tuition costs of accompanying dependents enrolled in elementary or secondary schools of the host country).

Application Information Only one application may be filed in an annual competition, but applicants may name up to three alternate countries. To obtain an application form and more detailed information, write or call CIES.

Deadline(s) Deadlines vary from country to country. Contact CIES for additional information.

122. Council for International Exchange of Scholars
3400 International Drive, NW, Suite M-500
Washington, DC 20008-3097
(202) 686-7866

Fulbright Scholar Program—Faculty Grants for Lecturing

Program Description The Fulbright Scholar Program serves two primary purposes. It enables Americans to learn firsthand about other countries and cultures, and it promotes academic and professional development. Some 700 awards are offered in support of university lectureships; many of these also offer some opportunity for research. Areas for lecturing include but are not limited to comparative law, comparative legal systems, American legal practices rights of minorities, right to life, free speech, judicial theory and theorists, tax law, environmental law, etc.

Eligibility/Limitations Prospective applicants should have U.S. citizenship at the time of application. For lecturing, usually a doctoral degree at the time of application and postdoctoral college or university teaching experience at the level and in the field of the lectureship is required. In some programs, language proficiency may be required. Persons who have lived abroad for the full 10-year period immediately preceding the time of application are ineligible. In general, preference is given to persons who have not already had lecturing or research grants. A previous grantee may, however, apply for a second award if three years have elapsed between the end of the first grant period and the beginning of the second. In accordance with a new ruling by the Board of Foreign Scholarships, scholars who have already held two (or more) Fulbright scholar awards are no longer prohibited from making application. Such applicants should bear in mind, however, that preference will be given to those who have not participated in the program and who do not have substantial recent experience abroad.

Fiscal Information Grant benefits include: round-trip travel for the grantee and for a principal dependent of a grantee whose appointment is for a full academic year; a maintenance allowance, paid either in local currency, in dollars, or in local currency with a dollar supplement (allowance amounts vary by grant category, the country and duration of the grant, and family status); incidental allowances for baggage, for books and services essential to the assignment, and for travel within the host country; housing (or housing allowance) in certain countries; and tuition allowance in certain countries (where available, tuition reimbursement is provided for tuition costs of accompanying dependents enrolled in elementary or secondary schools of the host country).

Application Information Only one application may be filed in an annual competition, but applicants may name up to three alternate countries. To obtain an application form and more detailed information, write or call CIES.

Deadline(s) Application deadline for faculty lectureship awards vary from country to country. Contact CIES for specific deadlines. A brochure is produced in November announcing awards for which there are insufficient numbers of candidates. For those unfilled awards, applications will continue to be accepted. Applications will also be accepted for some lecturing awards after the announced deadline. Interested persons may inquire at any time during the year.

123. Council for International Exchange of Scholars
3400 International Drive, NW, Suite M-500
Washington, DC 20008-3097
(202) 686-7866

Fulbright Scholar Program—Faculty Grants for Lecturing/Research

Program Description The Fulbright Scholar Program serves two primary purposes. It enables Americans to learn firsthand about other countries and cultures, and it promotes academic and professional development. Some awards are designed to combine both lecturing and research. Areas for lecturing/research include, but are not limited to, development of Western law, comparative law, public policy, advocacy, environmental law, informal justice, law and economics, international trade, tax law, and human rights.

Eligibility/Limitations Prospective applicants should have U.S. citizenship at the time of application. For lecturing, usually a doctoral degree at the time of application and postdoctoral college or university teaching experience at the level and in the field of the lectureship is required. In some programs, language proficiency may be required. Persons who have lived abroad for the full 10-year period immediately preceding the time of application are ineligible. In general, preference is given to persons who have not already had lecturing or research grants. A previous grantee may, however, apply for a second award if three years have elapsed between the end of the first grant period and the beginning of the second. In accordance with a new ruling by the Board of Foreign Scholarships, scholars who have already held two (or more) Fulbright scholar awards are no longer prohibited from making application. Such applicants should bear in mind, however, that preference will be given to those who have not participated in the program and who do not have substantial recent experience abroad.

Fiscal Information Grant benefits include: round-trip travel for the grantee and for a principal dependent of a grantee whose appointment is for a full academic year; a maintenance allowance, paid either in local currency, in dollars, or in local currency with a dollar supplement (allowance amounts vary by grant category, the country and duration of the grant, and family status); incidental allowances for baggage, for books and services essential to the assignment, and for travel within the host country; housing (or housing allowance) in certain countries; and tuition allowance in certain countries (where available, tuition reimbursement is provided for tuition costs of accompanying dependents enrolled in elementary or secondary schools of the host country).

Application Information Only one application may be filed in an annual competition, but applicants may name up to three alternate countries. To obtain an application form and more detailed information, write or call CIES.

Deadline(s) Application deadline for research and lecturing awards vary from country to country. A brochure is produced in November announcing awards for which there are insufficient numbers of candidates. For those unfilled awards, applications will continue to be accepted. Applications will also be accepted for some lecturing awards after the announced deadline. Interested persons may inquire at any time during the year.

124. Council for International Exchange of Scholars
3400 International Drive, NW, Suite M-500
Washington, DC 20008-3097
(202) 686-7866

Fulbright Scholar Program—Faculty Grants for Research

Program Description The Fulbright Scholar Program serves two primary purposes. It enables Americans to learn firsthand about other countries and cultures, and it promotes academic and professional development. Some 300 grants are offered in support of research in most disciplines.

Eligibility/Limitations Prospective applicants should have U.S. citizenship at the time of application. A doctorate at the time of application, or comparable professional qualifications is required. In some programs, language proficiency may be required. Persons who have lived abroad for the full 10-year period immediately preceding the time of application are ineligible. In general, preference is given to persons who have not already had lecturing or research grants. A previous grantee may, however, apply for a second award if three years have elapsed between the end of the first grant period and the beginning of the second. In accordance with a new ruling by the Board of Foreign Scholarships, scholars who have already held two (or more) Fulbright scholar awards are no longer prohibited from making application. Such applicants should bear in mind, however, that preference will be given to those who have not participated in the program and who do not have substantial recent experience abroad.

Fiscal Information Grant benefits include: round-trip travel for the grantee and for a principal dependent of a grantee whose appointment is for a full academic year; a maintenance allowance, paid either in local currency, in dollars, or in local currency with a dollar supplement (allowance amounts vary by grant category, the country and duration of the grant, and family status); incidental allowances for baggage, for books and services essential to the assignment, and for travel within the host country; housing (or housing allowance) in certain countries; and tuition allowance in certain countries (where available, tuition reimbursement is provided for tuition costs of accompanying dependents enrolled in elementary or secondary schools of the host country).

Application Information Only one application may be filed in an annual competition, but applicants may name up to three alternate countries. To obtain an application form and more detailed information, write or call CIES.

Deadline(s) Application deadline for faculty research awards vary from country to country. Contact CIES for specific deadlines. Applications for research normally are not accepted after the deadline. Interested persons may inquire at any time during the year.

125. Council for International Exchange of Scholars
3400 International Drive, NW, Suite M-500
Washington, DC 20008-3097
(202) 686-7866

Fulbright Scholar Program—Junior Lecturing and Junior Research

Program Description The Fulbright Scholar Program serves two primary purposes. It enables Americans to learn firsthand about other countries and cultures, and it promotes academic and professional development. These awards are designed primarily for younger scholars who are recent Ph.D., recipients or advanced Ph.D. candidates.

Eligibility/Limitations Prospective applicants should have U.S. citizenship at the time of application. In some programs, language proficiency may be required. Persons who have lived abroad for the full 10-year period immediately preceding the time of application are ineligible. In general, preference is given to persons who have not already had lecturing or research grants. A previous grantee may, however, apply for a second award if three years have elapsed between the end of the first grant period and the beginning of the second. In accordance with a new ruling by the Board of Foreign Scholarships, scholars who have already held two (or more) Fulbright scholar awards are no longer prohibited from making application. Such applicants should bear in mind, however, that preference will be given to those who have not participated in the program and who do not have substantial recent experience abroad.

Fiscal Information Grant benefits include: round-trip travel for the grantee and for a principal dependent of a grantee whose appointment is for a full academic year; a maintenance allowance, paid either in local currency, in dollars, or in local currency with a dollar supplement (allowance amounts vary by grant category, the country and duration of the grant, and family status); incidental allowances for baggage, for books and services essential to the assignment, and for travel within the

host country; housing (or housing allowance) in certain countries; and tuition allowance in certain countries (where available, tuition reimbursement is provided for tuition costs of accompanying dependents enrolled in elementary or secondary schools of the host country).

Application Information Only one application may be filed in an annual competition, but applicants may name up to three alternate countries. To obtain an application form and more detailed information, write or call CIES.

Deadline(s) Application deadline for research and lecturing awards varies from country to country. Contact CIES for deadlines. A brochure is produced in November announcing awards for which there are insufficient numbers of candidates. For those unfilled awards, applications will continue to be accepted. Applications will also be accepted for some lecturing awards after the announced deadline. Interested persons may inquire at any time during the year.

126. Council for International Exchange of Scholars
3400 International Drive, NW, Suite M-500
Washington, DC 20008-3097
(202) 686-7866

Fulbright Scholar Program—Professional

Program Description The Fulbright Scholar Program serves two primary purposes. It enables Americans to learn firsthand about other countries and cultures, and it promotes academic and professional development. These awards are designed primarily for professionals.

Eligibility/Limitations Prospective applicants should have U.S. citizenship at the time of application. In some programs, language proficiency may be required. Persons who have lived abroad for the full 10-year period immediately preceding the time of application are ineligible. In general, preference is given to persons who have not already had lecturing or research grants. A previous grantee may, however, apply for a second award if three years have elapsed between the end of the first grant period and the beginning of the second. In accordance with a new ruling by the Board of Foreign Scholarships, scholars who have already held two (or more) Fulbright scholar awards are no longer prohibited from making application. Such applicants should bear in mind, however, that preference will be given to those who have not participated in the program and who do not have substantial recent experience abroad.

Fiscal Information Grant benefits include: round-trip travel for the grantee and for a principal dependent of a grantee whose appointment is for a full academic year; a maintenance allowance, paid either in local currency, in dollars, or in local currency with a dollar supplement (allowance amounts vary by grant category, the country and duration of the grant, and family status); incidental allowances for baggage, for books and services essential to the assignment, and for travel within the host country; housing (or housing allowance) in certain countries; and tuition allowance in certain countries (where available, tuition reimbursement is provided for tuition costs of accompanying dependents enrolled in elementary or secondary schools of the host country).

Application Information Only one application may be filed in an annual competition, but applicants may name up to three alternate countries. To obtain an application form and more detailed information, write or call CIES.

Deadline(s) Application deadline for research and lecturing awards varies from country to country. Contact CIES for deadlines. A brochure is produced in November announcing awards for which there are insufficient numbers of candidates. For those unfilled awards, applications will continue to be accepted. Applications will also be accepted for some lecturing awards after the announced deadline. Interested persons may inquire at any time during the year.

127. Council for International Exchange of Scholars
3400 International Drive, NW, Suite M-500
Washington, DC 20008-3097
(202) 686-7866

Fulbright Scholar Program—Travel Only

Program Description These awards provide round-trip transportation to the country where the scholar will conduct research.

Eligibility/Limitations Prospective applicants should have U.S. citizenship at the time of application.

Fiscal Information The cost of round-trip transportation to the country where the scholar will conduct research will be provided.

Application Information Only one application may be filed in an annual competition, but applicants may name up to three alternate countries. To obtain an application form and more detailed information, write or call CIES.

Deadline(s) Deadlines vary from country to country. Contact CIES for additional information.

128. Council for International Exchange of Scholars
3400 International Drive, NW, Suite M-500
Washington, DC 20008-3097
(202) 686-7866

Fulbright Scholar-in-Residence Program

Program Description This program supports American colleges and universities hosting a visiting scholar in the humanities or social sciences, or in scientific or professional specializations with a strong international focus. Of particular interest for the current program are proposals to bring foreign specialists in the fields of communications, education, U.S. constitutional law and related subjects, as well as foreign scholars in U.S. studies (history, literature, and politics).

Eligibility/Limitations American colleges and universities are eligible to apply.

Fiscal Information Grants support visiting scholars for all or part of the academic year. The program provides roundtrip travel for the grantee, and for awards for the full academic year, one accompanying dependent; a maintenance allowance; and incidental allowances. The host institution is expected to share in the support of the visiting scholar.

Application Information Detailed program guidelines, proposal forms and further information is available on request.

Deadline(s) The deadline for receipt of proposals is November 1.

129. Council for International Exchange of Scholars
3400 International Drive, NW, Suite M-500
Washington, DC 20008-3097
(202) 686-4025

Indo-American Fellowship Program—Advanced Research in India

Program Description This program is sponsored by the Indo-U.S. Subcommission on Education and Culture and is funded by the United States Information Agency, the National Science Foundation, the Smithsonian Institution, and the Government of India. The objective of the program is to draw into educational exchange Americans who are not India area specialists and who have had limited or no prior experience in the country. The program seeks to open new channels of communication between academic and professional groups in the two countries and to encourage a wider range of research activity than now exists. Awards are offered in all academic fields and in professional areas such as architecture, business, law, museum work, and creative arts.

Eligibility/Limitations Applicants must be U.S. citizens at the postdoctoral or equivalent professional level.

Fiscal Information Both long-term awards (six to ten months) and short-term awards (two to three months) are available. Each award carries a basic stipend of $1,500 per month, of which $350 per month is payable in dollars and the rest in rupees; an allowance of from $325 to $500 in rupees for research expenses/books; and international travel for all grantees and an allowance of 2,000 rupees for study/travel in India. For long-term grantees only: a $400 excess baggage allowance; international travel for dependents; a monthly allowance of $100 per dependent up to a maximum of $250 per month. Upon request, and subject to approval, a supplementary research allowance of up to 34,000 rupees may be available to long-term fellows.

Application Information Application forms should be requested from CIES.

Deadline(s) Application deadline is June 15.

Additional Information Other fellowships or grants may be received concurrently with these awards, provided benefits are not duplicated. No deduction will be made for sabbatical salary, but other funding must be reported and will be taken into consideration in determining the amount of the grant.

130. Council for International Exchange of Scholars
3400 International Drive, NW, Suite M-500
Washington, DC 20008-3097
(202) 686-6240 or (202) 686-6242

NATO Advanced Research Fellowships and Institutional Grants

Program Description A limited number of advanced research fellowships and related disciplines will be offered to candidates from NATO member countries. Awards are to promote research leading to publication on political, security, and economic issues directly affecting the health of the alliance. Candidates are invited to submit applications for research within the following subject areas: (1) internal and external problems arising for Western security; (2) public perceptions of the alliance and the Soviet threat; (3) in the context of Article 2 of the Washington Treaty, analysis of the alliance's role in contributing to peaceful international relations; (4) European contributions to NATO; and (5) NATO strategy and emerging technologies.

Eligibility/Limitations Research applicants must have the Ph.D. or equivalent professional status at the time of application, and be American citizens. Fellowships are intended for scholars of established reputation. Institutional proposals from departments of political science or economics, international affairs institutes, centers for security studies, or research teams are welcome.

Fiscal Information Grants are intended to provide supplemental support for travel and other research expenses. Duration of the grant is flexible to the needs of the scholar.

Application Information Special application forms are required for these awards; contact CIES in September for applications.

Deadline(s) Deadline for application is January 1.

131. Council for International Exchange of Scholars
3400 International Drive, NW, Suite M-500
Washington, DC 20008-3097
(202) 686-7878

NATO Advanced Research Fellowships and Institutional Grants: Fellowships in Studies of Democratic Institutions

Program Description A limited number of advanced research fellowships in the social sciences and related disciplines will be offered to candidates from NATO and Warsaw Treaty Organization countries. Awards are to promote research leading to publication on democratic institutions and their functioning. Candidates are invited to submit applications for research within the following subject areas: study of the executive, legislative, and judicial branches of government; the role of media and nongovernmental organizations in democratic institutions; and the political, economic, and social dimensions of the democratic system.

Eligibility/Limitations Applicants must have the Ph.D. or equivalent status at the time of application, and be U.S. citizens. Fellowships are intended for scholars of established reputation.

Fiscal Information A fixed-sum grant of approximately 180,000 Belgian francs or the equivalent in the currency of any other member country is available for individual fellowship awards. International travel for grantee is also provided, plus transport required for research within western Europe (subject to NATO approval).

Application Information Special application forms are required for these awards. Write or telephone for supplemental materials and NATO application forms.

Deadline(s) The deadline for application is January 1. Special NATO application forms are available after September 15.

132. Council for International Exchange of Scholars
3400 International Drive, NW, Suite M-500
Washington, DC 20008-3097
(202) 686-4025

Pacific Islands Research Program

Program Description Up to two awards for three to six months to conduct research on the society and culture of the Pacific island nations, not including Australia and New Zealand, are available. Projects should lead to increased U.S. knowledge and understanding of these countries and the southwest Pacific region.

Eligibility/Limitations Preference is for applications in anthropology, economics, history, political science, and sociology.

Fiscal Information The award includes approximately $2,500 per month, plus initial allowance of $8,860 to $10,445 to cover such items as international travel, excess baggage, settling in, books, and services, based on number of dependents and countries where research will be conducted.

Application Information Additional information and application guidelines are available from CIES.

Deadline(s) The application deadline is June 15.

133. Council for International Exchange of Scholars
3400 International Drive, NW, Suite M-500
Washington, DC 20008-3097
(202) 686-4028

Regional Awards: African Regional Research Program

Program Description About 10 awards in all academic fields for research in one to four sub-Saharan African countries over periods of three to nine months. African specialists are encouraged to apply, but applications are also welcome from scholars who may have had no previous experience in Africa.

Eligibility/Limitations Both Africanists and non-Africanists are expected to include evidence in their proposals of host-country support for their research. This can be done by enclosing a letter of invitation or one expressing interest in the research from an African colleague or university. Applicants for non-English-speaking countries should have sufficient language ability to conduct the proposed research.

Fiscal Information The grant carries an award of approximately $2,350 to $3,400 per month (U.S. currency), plus initial allowance of $3,395 to $10,740 to cover such items as international travel and excess baggage, depending on country and number of dependents. Separate allowance will be provided for purchase of educational materials to be left in host country. Tuition reimbursement for accompanying K-12 children of $12,000 for grants of nine months and over, or $8,000 for grants of four to eight months. Deductions may be made if the host institution provides a local salary, international travel, or housing.

Application Information Because grantees are responsible for obtaining their own research clearances and visas, scholars should request information on procedures from colleagues in Africa and/or the U.S. Information Agency at an early date. Applicants are also encouraged to discuss their proposals with

CIES Africa area staff well in advance of the application deadline.

Deadline(s) The application deadline is August 1.

Additional Information Two to three awards for three to nine months are offered for research on any aspect of the Southern Africa Development Coordination Council.

134. Council for International Exchange of Scholars
3400 International Drive, NW, Suite M-500
Washington, DC 20008-3097
(202) 686-6236

Regional Awards: American Republics Research Program

Program Description This program offers up to 25 research awards, each for six months, in any discipline for one or more countries of the Caribbean, Mexico, or South America. Non-academic professionals in business, journalism, law, and government are also encouraged to apply. Research topics may be contemporary or historical, regional or comparative. Applications are encouraged from scholars whose projects involve collaboration with colleagues in the host country and who are willing to give occasional lectures.

Eligibility/Limitations Candidates must have Ph.D. or equivalent professional status. Applicants for non-English-speaking countries should have sufficient language ability to conduct the proposed research.

Fiscal Information The grant carries an award of approximately $2,000 to $2,500 per month (U.S. or local currency), depending on country and number of dependents. In addition, international travel for grantee, and in some countries, tuition reimbursement for accompanying K-12 children up to $8,000 is awarded.

Application Information Additional information and application guidelines are available from CIES.

Deadline(s) The application deadline is June 15.

135. Council for International Exchange of Scholars
3400 International Drive, NW, Suite M-500
Washington, DC 20008-3097
(202) 686-6238

Regional Awards: Central American Republics Research and Lecturing Program

Program Description CIES offers an expanded program of Fulbright awards for research and lecturing in Belize, Costa Rica, El Salvador, Guatemala, Honduras, Nicaragua, and Panama. Up to 20 awards are offered for three to six months of research in any field in one or several countries of the area (fields may be restricted in some countries). The research topic may be contemporary or historical, regional or comparative.

Eligibility/Limitations Candidates must have the Ph.D. or other terminal degree. Applicants for Spanish-speaking countries should have sufficient language ability to conduct the proposed research.

Fiscal Information Awards carry stipends of from $2,500 to $2,900 per month (U.S. currency), plus an initial allowance of $3,000 to $3,200 to cover such items as international travel, excess baggage, settling in, books and services. Tuition reimbursement for accompanying K-12 children is offered up to $8,000.

Application Information Additional information and application guidelines are available from CIES.

Deadline(s) The application deadline is June 15.

136. Council for International Exchange of Scholars

3400 International Drive, NW, Suite M-500
Washington, DC 20008-3097
(202) 686-4019

Regional Awards: Middle East, North Africa, South Asia Regional Research Program

Program Description Projects may be comparative or regional in scope and must involve work in more than one country of the Middle East, North Africa, or South Asia. Proposals may treat contemporary or historical topics. Applications are encouraged from scholars whose projects involve collaboration with host country colleagues and who will give occasional lectures or seminars.

Eligibility/Limitations College and university faculty, independent scholars, and established practitioners in professional fields are eligible to apply. Appropriate language proficiency is required.

Fiscal Information Monthly stipends and initial allowances for travel and settling-in expenses vary with the cost of living in and travel costs to each location. Consult CIES program staff for specific information on award amounts. Tuition reimbursement for accompanying K-12 children up to $12,000 for grants of nine months or up to $8,000 for grants of four to eight months is available.

Application Information Additional information and application guidelines are available from CIES.

Deadline(s) The deadline for application is August 1.

137. Council for International Exchange of Scholars

3400 International Drive, NW, Suite M-500
Washington, DC 20008-3097
(202) 686-4020

Regional Awards: Southeast Asian Regional Research Program

Program Description Up to seven awards for three to nine months to conduct research on Southeast Asian society and culture are available. Fields include humanities, social sciences, communications, education, law, and business. Countries of study include Brunei, Indonesia, Malaysia, Philippines, Singapore, and Thailand.

Eligibility/Limitations Proposals with intercountry travel and collaborative research will be considered. Applicants should have level of language facility appropriate to their project.

Fiscal Information Benefits vary, depending on country. Contact CIES for specific information.

Application Information Applications and additional information are available from CIES.

Deadline(s) Application deadline is August 1.

138. Council for International Exchange of Scholars

3400 International Drive, NW, Suite M-500
Washington, DC 20008-3097
(202) 686-4020

Regional Awards: Western European Regional Research Program

Program Description Approximately eight to ten awards for research on European politics, society, and culture are available. Applications are accepted in any discipline within the social sciences and humanities. Proposals are welcomed in a wide range of subject areas, including anthropology, history, literature, sociology, business, political science, law, economics, and public policy. Projects should be regional or comparative in scope, historical or contemporary in focus, and must involve significant time in each of two or more of the following countries: Austria, Belgium, Cyprus, Denmark, Finland, France, Germany, Greece, Iceland, Ireland, Italy, Luxembourg, Malta, the Netherlands, Norway, Portugal, Spain, Sweden, Switzerland, Turkey, and the United Kingdom. Research in Eastern Europe is not funded under this program.

Eligibility/Limitations Where appropriate, applicants should submit documentation demonstrating access to archives, individuals to be interviewed, or European colleagues. Language competency or arrangements for translation must be demonstrated if required for completion of the project.

Fiscal Information Grants are for a minimum of three months and a maximum of nine months, with a preference for projects of six months or less. Benefits include $2,000 per month stipend, prorated for periods involving parts of a month, plus a travel/incidental allowance of $3,000 to cover such items as international travel, excess baggage, settling in, books and services, etc.

Application Information Applications and additional information are available from CIES.

Deadline(s) Application deadline is August 1.

139. Council for International Exchange of Scholars

3400 International Drive, NW, Suite M-500
Washington, DC 20008-3097
(202) 686-7866

Spain Research Fellowships

Program Description Approximately 20 postdoctoral fellowships of three to ten months' duration will be awarded for research under the Agreement of Friendship, Defense, and Cooperation between the United States and Spain. Fields of preference are anthropology, archeology, arts, communications, economics, education, geography, history, law, linguistics, literature, logic, philosophy, political science, psychology and sociology.

Eligibility/Limitations Competence in oral and written Spanish is required, according to the needs of the proposed research project. The doctorate is required at the time of application.

Fiscal Information Fellowships carry an award of approximately $1,200 to $1,800 per month, the total to be based on the number of accompanying dependents; $1,000 for books and settling-in expenses; round-trip travel for grantee, and, if the grant period is seven or more months, for one accompanying dependent.

Application Information Special application forms are available from CIES.

Deadline(s) Application deadline is January 1.

140. Council on Foreign Relations

58 East 68th Street
New York, NY 10021
(212) 734-0400

International Affairs Fellowships

Program Description The fellowships, for individuals from the government, business, professional, and academic communities, seek to bridge the gap between analysis and action in foreign policy by supporting a variety of policy studies and active experiences in policy-making. Academic and other professionals from the private sector spend their fellowship tenures in public service, whereas opportunities for the systematic assessment of key issues in foreign policy, in a research environment, are given to government officials on leave. Because the focus of the program is the provision of a contrasting career experience for the young and exemplary foreign policy professional, a change of residence is generally required. The competition is multidisciplinary; past recipients having included scholars and practitioners representing the fields of political science, economics, history, anthropology, sociology, psychology, philosophy, law, journalism, business, and government.

Sample Grants Fellowship support for a study of "Law and the Challenge of International Terrorism" (1987-88). Fellowship support for a study of "Law and Foreign Policy in the Reagan Administration" (1987-88). Fellowship support for a study of "Law and the United States Policy toward the United Nations," (1988-89).

Eligibility/Limitations The program is open to all men and women holding American citizenship between the ages of 27 and 35 (inclusive) in the calendar year of their application. The program does not fund predoctoral or postdoctoral scholarly research, work toward a degree, nor the completion of projects on which substantial progress has been made prior to the fellowship period. For the academic applicant, although the Ph.D. or its equivalent is not a firm requirement, given the caliber of candidates, those who have not yet completed their doctorate and first professional "tour of duty" do not typically fare well. Similarly, successful candidates from government or business communities generally hold advanced degrees and possess a solid record of work experience in the international field.

Fiscal Information The stipend is determined according to individual budget statements in consultation with the program administration. Within the fixed maximum, the program generally will attempt to meet the major portion of a fellow's current income. If necessary, modest supplementary funding may be sought from outside sources to close the gap, at least partially, between the stipend ceiling and the fellow's earnings. The program does not provide support for research assistance or computer time, and fellows are responsible for arranging their own housing, insurance, benefits, and travel. The duration of the fellowship is one year. Short-term projects are not eligible for consideration. No extensions are granted.

Application Information Interested individuals who feel that their backgrounds and goals mesh with those of the program are encouraged to forward a brief outline of their proposal, the ways in which they intend to carry it out, and a curriculum vitae to the Director, International Affairs Fellowship Program at the council's address. After internal council review, an invitation to apply, application forms, and supplementary information on procedures will be sent to those satisfying the preliminary requirements.

Deadline(s) The deadline for nominations is September 15; applications are due by October 31.

141. Council on Legal Education Opportunity

1800 M Street, NW, Suite 290, North Lobby
Washington, DC 20036
(202) 785-4840

CLEO Program

Program Description The CLEO Program is designed to remedy the effects of the historic exclusion of the economically disenfranchised person from participation in the legal profession. Specifically, it is designed to serve those economically and educationally disadvantaged persons who, but for CLEO, would have little opportunity to attend an accredited law school due to financial and admission credential limitations.

Eligibility/Limitations The prototype of the CLEO participant is an individual who is usually a first generation college graduate. He or she may fall within a broad spectrum of ethnic backgrounds including Black, Chicano, Puerto Rican, Appalachian, Asian American, American Indian, Caucasian, Spanish American, Cuban, Dominican, etc. Although no age limitations are associated with participation in CLEO, the typical student is usually between 22 and 30. Participants must be either a U.S. citizen or a permanent resident of the trust territory of the Pacific Islands; or, the individual will have demonstrated intentions of becoming a permanent resident of the United States and will reside in this country for other than a temporary purpose.

Fiscal Information CLEO participants who have successfully completed the six-week Regional Summer Institute program and demonstrate a probability of success in law school are certified as CLEO fellows. As such they are eligible to receive law school placement assistance and the annual CLEO stipend award for their three years of legal study. The CLEO stipend is to be used for education-related expenses only.

Application Information The financial assistance that CLEO offers is contingent upon successful completion of a CLEO summer institute. However, application to the CLEO Regional Summer Institutes is not an application to law school. The student must apply independently to the law schools of his or her choice. Contact the CLEO for additional information.

Deadline(s) The deadline for receipt of all documents required for CLEO application is March 1.

142. Council on Library Resources

1785 Massachusetts Avenue, NW, Suite 313
Washington, DC 20036
(202) 483-7474

Cooperative Research Grants

Program Description Under the Cooperative Research Program, the Council on Library Resources (CLR) makes a limited number of grants each year to support research projects proposed jointly by librarians and members of faculties in library science or, when appropriate, other pertinent disciplines. The purpose is threefold: to stimulate productive communication between teaching faculty and librarians; to encourage librarians to develop more fully their research skills; and to increase the quantity and improve the quality of research and analytical studies related to library operations.

Sample Grants Support for research on the impact of automation on a law school library budget.

Eligibility/Limitations Librarians, members of faculties in library science, and members of faculties in other pertinent disciplines are eligible to apply.

Fiscal Information Grants are limited to a maximum of $3,000 and are intended to fund such incremental research costs as the organization of data, the hiring of interviewers or other assistants, and charges for computer time. Grants may not be used for the salaries of principals, purchase of equipment, or indirect costs.

Application Information Applications must be submitted jointly by the investigators and should include evidence of institutional support for the work. Each proposal should be submitted in the form of a letter to the Council on Library Resources and should include the following information: a brief abstract (no more than 50 words) of the proposal; a description of proposed work, including objectives, brief discussion of previous work on the topic, methodology, and plans for evaluation; curriculum vitae of each of the principal investigators; the anticipated duration of the project; an assessment of the potential utility of research results; a detailed budget; and plans for disseminating the results. Applicants should provide the original and four copies of the application.

Deadline(s) Grants are awarded twice each year, in the spring and fall. The spring deadline is April 1, and the fall deadline is November 1.

143. William Nelson Cromwell Foundation

Mr. Henry N. Ess, III, Sullivan & Cromwell
250 Park Avenue
New York, NY 10177
(212) 558-4000

Grants

Program Description The foundation supports research on American legal history.

Application Information Sends letters of inquiry to Mr. Ess at the address listed above.

Deadline(s) No deadlines are announced.

144. The Charles E. Culpeper Foundation, Inc.

Ten Stamford Forum, Suite 800
Stamford, CT 06901
(203) 975-1240

Grants

Program Description The foundation was established under the last will and testament of Charles E. Culpeper, one of the early pioneers in the bottling and marketing of Coca-Cola. The foundation engages in a program of general giving. The fields of health, education and the arts comprise approximately 65 percent of the foundation's annual grant program. Other areas in which the foundation is interested are science and technology, youth, and administration of justice.

Sample Grants In support of a graduate program for judges, $55,000 to the University of Virginia Law School (1985). In support of a study to reduce civil litigation costs, $50,000 to the Center for Public Resources (1985).

Eligibility/Limitations The foundation does not make grants to attend conferences or seminars or to engage in travel and approves only a limited number of requests for endowment purposes or building programs. It does not make grants to individuals or to organizations which merely distribute funds to beneficiaries of the latter's choosing. It encourages applications from regions where access to local private funding may not be available However, it makes grants to assist projects located only in the United States.

Fiscal Information Grants totaling more than $5.1 million were awarded in 1987.

Application Information The foundation does not use a standard form of application. Therefore, applicants should write a letter containing the following information: a succinct description of the project; its purpose; a detailed budget; and a copy of the applicant's tax-exempt letter. If the foundation's preliminary review determines an interest in the project, further information will be requested.

Deadline(s) The foundation's board meets quarterly to consider and take final action on grant requests presented to it by the grants committee. The foundation advises every applicant in writing as to the disposition of any proposal.

145. Cummins Engine Foundation

Mail Code 60814, Box 3005
Columbus, IN 47202-3005
(812) 377-3114

Program Description The foundation gives special consideration for funding to programs in three major categories: youth and education; equity and justice; and quality of life. In the area of youth and education, the foundation seeks ways to help young people grow up to be full participants in a complex world. In equity and justice, the foundation's focus is on those who face discrimination, are dispossessed, or are poorly served by society. The foundation also encourages opportunities for leadership development among women and minorities. A limited number of grants is made annually to promote economic development and human rights abroad. In quality of life, the foundation looks for programs that refresh the spirit and enhance the general environment in communities where Cummins and its subsidiaries have manufacturing plants. The foundation also seeks new and unusual ways to support the arts and artists.

Sample Grants General support for the principal monitor and defender of civil rights law and enforcement, $15,000 to NAACP Legal Defense and Education Fund, New York, NY (1987). General support for the leading civil rights organization working on equity issues for women and girls, $2,500 to NOW Legal Defense and Education Fund, New York, NY (1987).

Eligibility/Limitations Cummins does not support political causes or candidates, or sectarian religious activities. Grants are not made to individuals. The foundation makes virtually all its local grants in communities where Cummins and its subsidiaries have manufacturing plants.

Fiscal Information Grant awards range from $500 to $30,000. Total grants and donations in 1988 exceeded $3 million and included $342,460 to projects in the equity and justice program area.

Application Information A preliminary proposal should include a brief description of the problem being addressed, specifically what the program hopes to achieve, operating plan and cost, description of key leadership and how one will be able to tell whether or not the program worked. Upon receipt of the proposal, the foundation staff will respond regarding the possibility of funding.

Deadline(s) Inquiries and proposals may be submitted in writing at any time during the year, though to be on the agenda for a specific meeting, proposals should be received no later than the first of the previous month. The foundation directors meet in February, July, September, and December to consider new programs and approve grants. The staff has authority to make small grants from its discretionary budget between meetings.

146. Charles and Margaret Hall Cushwa Center

University of Notre Dame
Room 614, Memorial Library
Notre Dame, IN 46556
(219) 239-5441

Hibernian Research Award

Program Description This award is designed to promote scholarly study of the Irish in the United States.

Eligibility/Limitations Applicants must be postdoctoral scholars from any academic discipline who are engaged in a research project related to the study of the Irish people in the United States.

Fiscal Information The award carries a stipend of $2,000.

Application Information Application forms are available from the center on request.

Deadline(s) Applications must be postmarked no later than December 31.

147. Charles and Margaret Hall Cushwa Center

University of Notre Dame
Room 614, Memorial Library
Notre Dame, IN 46556
(219) 239-5441

Research Grant Program

Program Description This program is designed to foster research in the archives and library of the University of Notre Dame. The library collection is particularly rich in the following areas: Catholic newspapers, history of midwestern Catholicism, Catholic literature, and history of Catholicism in the United States. The archives have manuscripts of historical personages, records of 20th-century Catholic organizations, reports of European missionary societies, and much more material related to the American Catholic community.

Eligibility/Limitations Applicants must be postdoctoral scholars of any academic discipline who are engaged in projects which require substantial use of the collection of the library and/or archives. The research project must be related to the study of the American Catholic community and must indicate as specifically as possible how the use of the Notre Dame Library and Archives is pertinent to the study.

Fiscal Information Grants range from $1,000 to $2,000.

Application Information Application forms and procedures are available from the center on request.

Deadline(s) Applications must be postmarked no later than November 30.

148. The Danforth Foundation

231 South Bemiston Avenue, Suite 580
St. Louis, MO 63105-1903
(314) 862-6200

Grants

Program Description The Danforth Foundation is a national, educational philanthropic organization, dedicated to enhancing the humane dimensions of life. Activities of the foundation traditionally have emphasized the theme of improving the quality of teaching and learning. Currently, the foundation serves the following areas: higher education through sponsorship of programs administered by the staff; precollegiate education through grant-making and program activities; and urban education in metropolitan St. Louis through grant-making and program activities. Programs administered by the foundation include the Danforth Seminars for Federal Judges and Educators program, which offers workshops for federal judges and educational leaders to examine issues related to education and the courts.

Fiscal Information Grants totaled over $11.5 million in 1988.

Application Information Persons considering the preparation of a grant proposal within the areas funded by the foundation are asked to mail a brief summary of the proposed activity. Staff members study each inquiry and reply promptly with specific information concerning the eligibility of the proposal.

Deadline(s) Applications are accepted at any time.

149. Shelby Cullom Davis Center for Historical Studies

Princeton University
129 Dickinson Hall
Princeton, NJ 08544-1017
(609) 452-4997

Visiting Fellowships

Program Description The center offers visiting fellowships for highly recommended younger scholars, as well as for senior scholars with established reputations, for the seminars organized by the center. Every year a new theme is selected; in 1991-92, the subject of the seminar will be imperialism, colonialism and the colonial aftermath. The center hopes that the topic will attract fellows and speakers from disciplines other than cultural history, such as politics, law, religion, and medicine.

Eligibility/Limitations Candidates must have finished their dissertations and must have a full-time position to which they can return. Fellows are expected to live in Princeton to take active part in the intellectual interchange with other members of the seminar.

Fiscal Information Fellowships may run either for one semester, September to January or February to June; or for the full academic year from September to June. The center is normally only able to offer support for one semester, but it hopes that most fellows will find outside support for a second semester. In calculating support for each fellow, deductions are made for outside grants and sabbatical leave funds that a fellow may bring with him/her. The center will pay each visiting fellow invited for the year, with no outside support, the equivalent of his/her after-tax annual salary paid at his/her home university, up to a maximum of $55,000. Each fellow invited for one semester, with no outside support, will be paid up to a maximum of $27,500. Those with outside support that amounts to less than their normal salary will receive sufficient additional funds from the center (up to a maximum of $55,000 for the year or $27,500 for one semester) to bring their after-tax salaries up to normal. Those with full support from outside will be made visiting fellows without salary, transportation, or research expenses. Support to visiting fellows from abroad, whose base salary scale is below the normal American level, will be adjusted upward to take this into account, but the amount will not exceed the maximum stated above. The center will pay transportation costs for each visiting fellow without outside travel funds, and his or her family, with the following limitations. It will pay for the most economical means of transportation for fellow, spouse, and children. Travel funds for spouse and children are intended only for persons accompanying a visiting fellow for a substantial period of time. The center will allow each visiting fellow, without outside research funds, research expenses of up to $750 per semester, or $1,500 per year, payable on presentation of a statement of expenses.

Application Information Inquiries and requests for fellowship application forms should be addressed to the secretary of the center.

Deadline(s) The deadline for receipt of applications and letters of recommendation is December 1.

150. Dayton Hudson Foundation

777 Nicollet Mall
Minneapolis, MN 55402-2055
(612) 370-6555

Grants

Program Description Dayton Hudson's policies emphasize a strong commitment to serve communities where the corporation has operating facilities. The corporation's giving, therefore, is principally local (in 47 states). Dayton Hudson has established the following priority funding categories and has assigned guidelines to each: social action (40 percent); arts (40 percent); and miscellaneous (20 percent) support for the efforts of community-based institutions, organizations and programs that are dedicated to meeting other critical community needs. In the social action category, funds are contributed to programs and projects that result in: (a) the economic and social progress of individuals; and/or (b) the development of community and neighborhood strategies that respond effectively to critical community social and economic concerns.

Eligibility/Limitations Dayton Hudson strives to be a contributions leader in its Twin cities headquarters area (Minneapolis-St. Paul) and in the communities where the corporation has operating company headquarters: Hayward, CA; Detroit, MI; Oklahoma City, OK; Phoenix, AZ; and Woburn, MA. On a more limited basis, grants are made in other communities where there is a major Dayton Hudson presence. Dayton Hudson, its operating companies, and the foundation consider requests from organizations which have been given 501(c)(3) tax-exempt status by the IRS. Dayton Hudson rarely funds organizations during their first year of operation. Grants are not made to individuals. Grants are rarely made to educational institutions or research groups.

Fiscal Information Grant funds distributed in 1988 totaled more than $17 million. Grants are made for general operations, special projects and occasionally capital purposes. Grants are not normally made for endowments.

Application Information The foundation encourages informal inquiries in advance of formal proposals. Requests from organizations in Minnesota should be sent directly to the foundation. Requests from organizations located outside Minnesota should be sent to the giving officer of the Dayton Hudson facility in the local community; a list of companies and locations is available from the foundation at the address listed above. Informal inquiries in advance of a formal application are encouraged. Dayton Hudson does not use an application form. To apply, send a letter and include the following: a description of the proposed program or project, the need, the people to be served, and the time period to be covered by the grant; an explanation of the results to be accomplished and how those results will be evaluated; a description of your organization, its mission, objectives, names and qualifications of those who would manage the project or program, and a list of officers and directors. Also enclose a copy of your IRS tax-exempt certification, a financial statement for the most recent fiscal year, organization and program budgets for last year and the current year showing anticipated expenses and income sources; and provide a representative list of donors who contributed to your organization in the last 12 months.

Deadline(s) Applications are accepted at any time.

151. Deer Creek Foundation
818 Olive Street, Suite 949
St. Louis, MO 63101
(314) 241-3228

Grants

Program Description The Deer Creek Foundation is a private philanthropy interested primarily in the advancement and preservation of the governance of society by rule of the majority, with protection of basic rights as provided by the Constitution and the Bill of Rights, and in education in its relation to this concept.

Eligibility/Limitations Grants are most often made to organizations and institutions.

Fiscal Information Foundation guidelines normally preclude support for endowment, construction, equipment, or general operating expenses.

Application Information No specific application form is required. Applicants should submit a letter stating briefly the objectives of the project and program design, the qualifications of the organization and individuals concerned, the mechanism for evaluating the results, a budget, and the latest annual report or audited financial statement, if available. This letter should be accompanied by a copy of the applicant's tax-exempt status determination letter from the Internal Revenue Service.

Deadline(s) No deadlines are announced.

152. The Gladys Krieble Delmas Foundation
40 West 57th Street, 27th Floor
New York, NY 10019

Grants for Venetian Research

Program Description The foundation announces its program of predoctoral and postdoctoral grants for research in Venice, Italy. The following areas of study will be considered: the history of Venice and the former Venetian empire in its various aspects— art, architecture, archaeology, theatre, music, literature, natural science, political science, economics, and the law. Also included are studies related to the contemporary Venetian environment such as ecology, oceanography, and urban planning and rehabilitation.

Eligibility/Limitations Applicants must be citizens of the United States, have some experience in advanced research, and, if graduate students, have fulfilled all doctoral requirements except for completion of the dissertation.

Fiscal Information Applications will be entertained for grants from $500 up to a maximum of $10,000. Funds will also be available eventually for aid in the publication of such studies resulting from research made possible by those grants as are deemed worthy by the trustees and advisory board.

Application Information There are no formal application forms. For guidelines for application contact the foundation.

Deadline(s) Applications for grants should be received by December 15.

153. Department of Education
Center for International Education, Office of Assistant
    Secretary for Postsecondary Education, ROB-3, Mail
    Stop 3308
7th & D Streets, SW
Washington, DC 20202
(202) 708-9291

Fulbright-Hays Training Grants—Doctoral Dissertation Research Abroad

CFDA Program Number 84.022

Program Description This program is designed to provide opportunities for graduate students to engage in full-time dissertation research abroad in modern foreign language and area studies. The program is designed to develop research knowledge and capability in world areas not widely included in American curricula. Awards will neither be available for projects focusing primarily on Western Europe nor in countries where the United States has no diplomatic representation.

Eligibility/Limitations Institutions of higher education may apply on behalf of doctoral students. Candidates for Doctoral Dissertation Research Fellowships must: (a) be a citizen or national of the United States; (b) be a permanent resident of the United States; (c) provide evidence from the Immigration and Naturalization Service that he or she is in the United States for other than a temporary purpose with the intention of becoming a citizen or permanent resident; or (d) be a resident of the Trust Territory of the Pacific Islands; (e) be a graduate student in good standing at an institution of higher education who, when the fellowship period begins, has been admitted to candidacy in a doctoral degree program in modern foreign languages and area studies at that institution; (f) plan a teaching career in the United States upon graduation; and (g) possess adequate skills in the language(s) necessary to carry out the dissertation research project.

Fiscal Information In fiscal year 1988, grant awards ranged from $1,100 to $57,790, with an average award of $17,378. Awards are made for at least six but not more than 12 months.

Application Information Candidates for dissertation research fellowships apply directly to the institutions at which they are enrolled in a Ph.D. program, not to the Department of Education. Students should send requests for application forms to the office of the graduate dean or his representatives at the graduate schools at which they are enrolled.

Deadline(s) Generally, applications must be received by the last week in October or the first week in November of the year preceding the year of study.

154. Department of Education
Center for International Education, Office of Assistant
    Secretary for Postsecondary Education, ROB-3, Mail
    Stop 3308
7th & D Streets, SW
Washington, DC 20202
(202) 708-8763

Fulbright-Hays Training Grants—Faculty Research Abroad

CFDA Program Number 84.019

Program Description These grants are designed to help universities and colleges strengthen their programs of international studies through selected opportunities for research and study abroad in foreign languages and area studies; to enable key faculty members to keep current in their specialties; to facilitate the updating of curricula; and to help improve teaching methods and materials. Awards will not be available for projects focusing primarily on Western Europe or in countries where the United States has no diplomatic relations.

Eligibility/Limitations Institutions of higher education may apply on behalf of faculty. Candidates for Faculty Research Abroad awards must: (a) be a citizen or national of the United States; (b) be a permanent resident of the United States; (c) provide evidence from the Immigration and Naturalization Service that he or she is in the United States for other than a temporary purpose with the intention of becoming a citizen or permanent resident or (d) be a resident of the Trust Territory of the Pacific Islands; (e) be employed by an institution of higher education; (f) have been engaged in teaching relevant to his foreign language or area of specialization for the two years immediately preceding the date of the award; (g) propose research relevant to his modern foreign language or area specialization which cannot be conducted in the United States, or for which a foreign country or region provides superior research facilities and will contribute to the development or improvement of the study of modern foreign languages or area studies in those fields needed for a full understanding of the area, regions, or countries in which the modern foreign languages are commonly used; (h) not be preparing for dissertation research for a Ph.D.; and (i) possess adequate skills in the language or languages necessary to successfully carry out the project.

Fiscal Information Financial provisions include a stipend in lieu of salary; cost of air fare for award recipient only; baggage allowance; project allowance to purchase expendable materials, services, and supplies. The amount of project assistance in 1988 ranged from $1,860 to $65,020, with an average award of $21,407, for projects that last from three to twelve months.

Application Information Faculty members may address requests for general information to the Advanced Training and Research Branch, Department of Education, but should obtain application forms from the appropriate office at their employing institutions. Applications should be submitted directly to the institution, not to the branch.

Deadline(s) Generally, applications must be received by the last week in October or the first week in November of the year preceding the year of study. Exact deadline is announced in the Federal Register.

155. Department of Education

Center for International Education, Office of Assistant
  Secretary for Postsecondary Education, ROB-3, Mail
  Stop 3308
7th & D Streets, NW
Washington, DC 20202
(202) 732-3294

Fulbright-Hays Training Grants—Group Projects Abroad

CFDA Program Number 84.021

Program Description This program provides grants to educational institutions to conduct overseas group projects in research, training and curriculum development.

Eligibility/Limitations Higher education institutions, private nonprofit educational organizations, state departments of education and consortia of these eligible parties may apply. Individuals participating in group projects must be: (1) citizens or nationals of the United States; and (2) faculty members in foreign language or area studies, experienced educators responsible for conducting, planning, or supervising programs in foreign language or area studies at the elementary, secondary, or junior college levels, or graduate or upper-division students who plan teaching careers in foreign language, area studies, or world affairs.

Fiscal Information Grant funds may be used for international travel; maintenance allowances; purchase of artifacts, books, other teaching materials; rent for instructional facilities in the country of study; project-related travel in the overseas area; and clerical and professional services in the country of study. Awards in 1988 ranged from $28,000 to $202,000, with an average award of $56,000, for projects ranging from six weeks to twelve months.

Application Information Specific guidelines for preparation of proposals as published in the Federal Register are available upon request from the Office of International Programs. The standard application forms as furnished by the federal agency and required by OMB Circular No. A-102 must be used for this program.

Deadline(s) Generally, applications must be received by the first week in November of the year preceding the year of overseas activity.

156. Department of Education

Center for International Education, Office of Assistant
  Secretary for Postsecondary Education, ROB-3, Mail
  Stop 3308
7th & D Streets, SW
Washington, DC 20202
(202) 732-3292

Summer Seminars Abroad (Fulbright Exchange)

CFDA Program Number 84.018

Program Description This program is designed to increase mutual understanding between the people of the United States and those in other countries by offering qualified American teachers and other educational personnel the opportunity to participate in short-term training seminars abroad.

Eligibility/Limitations Teachers at different levels in varying subject fields, social studies supervisors, and curriculum directors are eligible to apply for seminars abroad. Applicants must have at least a bachelor's degree and be citizens of the United States at the time of application; they must have at least three years successful full-time teaching, administering or supervising experience; and they must be employed currently in the subject field.

Fiscal Information Grants to study abroad provide round-trip transportation to some countries. No dependents are to accompany grantees participating in seminars.

Application Information Applications should be submitted on forms available on request from the International Studies Branch, Center for International Education. Program regulations and guidelines are detailed in "Opportunities Abroad for Educators" available from the International Education Program.

Deadline(s) Applications must be received by December 30 of the year preceding the grant during an academic year to attend a seminar overseas.

157. Department of Education

Division of Higher Education Incentive Programs, Office
  of Postsecondary Education
7th & D Streets, SW
Washington, DC 20202
(202) 732-4395

Law School Clinical Experience Program

CFDA Program Number 84.097

Program Description The objectives of this program are to establish and expand programs in law schools to provide clinical experience to students in the practice of law; expand programs of clinical experience including, but not limited to, any of the following: (1) development of new areas of clinical experience; (2) increase in the number of participating students; and (3) development and implementation of new teaching techniques. Preference shall be given to those programs providing legal experience in the preparation and trial of actual cases, including administrative cases and the settlement of controversies outside the courtroom.

Eligibility/Limitations Individually accredited law schools and a combination or consortium of accredited law schools may apply.

Fiscal Information Grants are limited to not more than 90 percent of the total cost of establishing or expanding a clinical law program. No law school may receive more than $100,000 in any fiscal year under this grant. Costs are limited to expenditures for planning, preparation of related teaching materials, and administration; faculty training, payment for the director and other faculty or attorneys directly involved in supervision; travel and per diem for faculty and students; and other related activities in connection with the program.

Application Information Instructions and forms detailing application procedures are mailed to all accredited law schools. This program is subject to the provisions of OMB Circular No. A-110.

Deadline(s) Contact the program for deadlines.

158. Department of Education
Division of Higher Education Incentive Programs, Office of Postsecondary Education
7th & D Streets, SW
Washington, DC 20202
(202) 732-4393

Legal Training for the Disadvantaged
CFDA Program Number 84.136

Program Description The objectives of this program are to provide educationally and economically disadvantaged students, many with marginal or less than traditional admissions credentials, an opportunity to attend an ABA-accredited law school by operating (with the cooperation of accredited law schools) seven six-week summer institutes, and providing fellowships to students during their enrollment in law school.

Eligibility/Limitations Applicants must be either U.S. citizens or permanent residents of the Trust Territory of the Pacific Islands or intend to become permanent residents of the United States and reside in this country for other than temporary purposes. Any person from a low-income or economically disadvantaged background who will have graduated from college by the beginning of the summer may apply.

Fiscal Information The grant carries stipends ranging from $1,500 to $1,700.

Application Information Apply directly to the Council on Legal Education Opportunity, 1800 M Street, NW, Suite 290, North Lobby, Washington, DC, 20006.

Deadline(s) The deadlines are established by the Council on Legal Education Opportunity.

159. Department of Education
Fund for the Improvement of Postsecondary Education, Office of the Assistant Secretary for Postsecondary Education
7th & D Streets, ROB-3, Room 3100
Washington, DC 20202
(202) 732-5750

Fund for the Improvement of Postsecondary Education (FIPSE)
CFDA Program Number 84.116

Program Description The fund proves assistance for innovative programs that improve the access to and the quality of postsecondary education. Priority is given to activities which relate to: (1) improvement of undergraduate liberal arts education, and (2) broad dissemination and impact. Consideration, but low priority, is given to requests for student aid and equipment.

Eligibility/Limitations The full range of providers of postsecondary education services including, but not limited to, two- and four-year colleges and universities, community organizations, libraries, museums, consortia, student groups, and local government agencies may apply.

Fiscal Information Grant awards range from $5,000 to $150,000 with an average award of $65,000.

Application Information The fund recommends that potential applicants contact the program prior to application. Application forms are furnished by the fund.

Deadline(s) Contact the fund for deadlines.

160. Department of Education
Library Development Staff, Library Programs, Office of Educational Research and Development
555 New Jersey Avenue, NW, Room 402M
Washington, DC 20208
(202) 357-6315

College Library Technology and Cooperation Grants
CFDA Program Number 84.197

Program Description The purpose of this program is to encourage resource-sharing projects among the libraries of institutions of higher education through the use of technology and networking and to improve the library and information services provided to them by public and nonprofit private organizations, as well as to conduct research or demonstration projects to meet special needs in using technology to enhance library and information sciences.

Eligibility/Limitations Eligible applicants include institutions of higher education, combinations of institutions of higher education, and public and nonprofit private organizations, which provide library information services to institutions of higher education on a formal, cooperative basis.

Fiscal Information The range of awards is $15,000 to $125,000. The average size of an award is: networking grant, $30,000; combination grant, $125,000; services to institutions grant, $25,000; research and demonstration grant, $100,000.

Application Information The standard application forms as furnished by the federal agency and required by OMB Circular No. A-102 must be used for this program. This program is eligible for coverage under E.O. 12372, "Intergovernmental Review of Federal Programs." An applicant should consult the office or official designated as the single point of contact in his or her state for more information on the process the state requires to be followed in applying for assistance, if the state has selected the program for review.

Deadline(s) Applications are submitted annually. Check the headquarters office for application deadlines.

161. Department of Education
Library Development Staff, Library Programs, Office of Educational Research and Development
555 New Jersey Avenue, NW, Room 402L
Washington, DC 20208
(202) 357-6320

Library Research and Demonstration
CFDA Program Number 84.039

Program Description The objectives of the program are to award grants and contracts for research and/or demonstration projects in areas of specialized services intended to improve library and information sciences practices. Research and demonstration projects relating to the improvement of libraries include the promotion of economical and efficient information delivery, cooperation efforts related to librarianship, and developmental projects; the improvement of training in librarianship; and for the dissemination of information derived from such projects with special emphasis on services to selected clientele.

Eligibility/Limitations Applications for grants and contracts may be submitted by an institution of higher education or a public or private agency, institution or organization.

Fiscal Information The estimated range of awards is $50,000 to $100,000. Projects may run from one to five years.

Application Information The standard application forms as furnished by the federal agency and required by OMB Circular No. A-102 must be used for this program. This program is eligible for coverage under E.O. 12372, "Intergovernmental Review of Federal Programs." An applicant should consult the office or official designated as the single point of contact in his or her state for more information on the process the state requires to be followed in applying for assistance, if the state has selected the program for review.

Deadline(s) No specific deadlines have been established. Applications are submitted annually. Check headquarters office for deadline dates.

162. Department of Education

Library Development Staff, Library Programs, Office of
Educational Research and Development
555 New Jersey Avenue, NW
Washington, DC 20208
(202) 357-6322

Strengthening Research Library Resources

CFDA Program Number 84.091

Program Description The objectives of this program are to
promote research and education of high quality throughout the
United States by providing financial assistance: (1) to help
major research libraries maintain and strengthen their collections, and (2) to assist major research libraries in making their
holdings available to individual researchers and scholars outside
their primary clientele and to other libraries whose users have
need for research materials. Grants may be used for the acquisition of books and other library materials, indexing and abstract-
ing, equipment and supplies, additional staff, and communication with other institutions. Applicants are encouraged to design
projects to adapt, convert or create library records for unique
research materials which complement a national data base; to
augment unique collections of special materials; or to preserve
and promote the sharing of library resources.

Eligibility/Limitations Public or private nonprofit institutions
with major research libraries, including the library resources of
an institution of higher education, independent research libraries, and state or other public libraries may apply.

Fiscal Information Grants range in size from $42,410 to
$506,839, with an average award of $147,282.

Application Information The standard application forms as furnished by the federal agency and required by OMB Circular No.
A-102 must be used for this program. This program is eligible
for coverage under E.O. 12372, "Intergovernmental Review of
Federal Programs." An applicant should consult the office or
official designated as the single point of contact in his or her
state for more information on the process the state requires to
be followed in applying for assistance, if the state has selected
the program for review.

Deadline(s) Applications are submitted annually. Check headquarters office for deadline dates.

163. Department of Education

School Improvement Programs, Office of Elementary
and Secondary Education
400 Maryland Avenue, SW
Washington, DC 20202
(202) 732-4357

Law-Related Education Program

CFDA Program Number 84.123

Program Description The objectives of this program are to
support programs at the elementary and secondary school levels
by developing and implementing model projects designed to
institutionalize law-related education (LRE); to provide assistance from established LRE programs to other state and local
agencies; and to support projects to develop, test, demonstrate,
and disseminate new approaches or techniques.

Eligibility/Limitations State educational agencies, local educational agencies, public or private nonprofit agencies, organizations, and institutions may apply.

Fiscal Information Grants range from $20,000 to $400,000.

Application Information The standard application forms as furnished by the federal agency and required by OMB Circular No.
A-102 must be used for this program. This program is eligible
for coverage under E.O. 12372, "Intergovernmental Review of
Federal Programs." An applicant should consult the office or
official designated as the single point of contact in his or her
state for more information on the process the state requires to
be followed in applying for assistance, if the state has selected
the program for review.

Deadline(s) Deadlines are announced in the Federal Register.

164. The Dirksen Congressional Center

Broadway & Fourth Street
Pekin, IL 61554
(309) 347-7113

Congressional Research Grants Program

Program Description The Dirksen Congressional Center is an
independent research and educational organization devoted to
the study of Congress, especially congressional leadership. The
center's first interest is to fund the study of the leadership in the
Congress, both House and Senate. The research for which assistance is sought must be original, culminating in new knowledge
or new interpretation or both. The grants program was developed to support work intended for publication in some form or
for application in a teaching or policy-making setting.

Eligibility/Limitations The competition is open to anyone with a
serious interest in studying Congress. The center seeks applications specifically from political scientists, historians, biographers,
scholars of public administration or American studies, or journalists. Graduate students may also apply.

Fiscal Information An award can cover any aspect of a qualified
research project. Stipends will be awarded to individuals on a
competitive basis. Awards range from a few hundred to $3,500.
Salary compensation will be limited to $1,500 per month.
Grants will not be awarded for purchase of equipment or for
subsidizing publication costs.

Application Information There are no standard application
forms. Applicants are responsible for showing the relationship
between their work and the grant program guidelines. An applicant must submit one copy of the following: (1) a cover sheet
listing name, address, and telephone numbers for work and
home, social security number, institutional affiliation when appropriate, project title, project abstract (not to exceed 100
words), and total amount requested; (2) a description of the
project, typed and double-spaced, explaining the project's goals,
methods, and intended results and demonstrating clearly its
importance to understanding Congress or congressional leadership; (3) a vita including a list of publications; and (4) a budget
indicating how funds will be spent and the extent of matching
funds available.

Deadline(s) Applications must be postmarked March 31.

165. Geraldine R. Dodge Foundation, Inc.

95 Madison Avenue, P.O. Box 1239
Morristown, NJ 07962-1239
(201) 540-8442

Grants

Program Description For the effective focus of the foundation's
energies, the trustees have found it necessary to exclude major
fields from consideration. Among these are higher education,
health and religion. The foundation's focus is on four areas:
animal welfare and local projects; secondary education; the arts;
and public issues. The foundation's focus in the area of animal
welfare is directed toward projects with national implications.
Humane activities at local levels fall outside the foundation's
programs. Projects within the state of New Jersey in the public
interest and in the arts are considered. The foundation's focus
on secondary education includes projects in New Jersey and at
NALIS schools in the Northeast and Middle Atlantic states and
programs with a national audience.

Sample Grants For first-year support of the "Successful Communities" growth management program in New Jersey, with a
major focus on Clinton Township, and including technical assistance in the development of model ordinances, $50,000 to the
Conservation Foundation, Washington, DC (1988). To assist the
development of a pilot workshop for New Jersey leaders and
citizens to enable communities to work effectively with the
federal Right-to-Know law, $50,000 to Environmental Law In-
stitute, Washington, DC (1988). In support of a two-year cam-

paign to mobilize public support for legislation to attack the fouling of the New Jersey coast by pollutants and floatables, $10,000 to the American Littoral Society, Sandy Hook, NJ (1988).

Eligibility/Limitations The foundation does not support scholarship funds or make direct awards to individuals nor does it administer programs which it supports. Also, it does not typically consider requests for grants to conduit organizations, which pass on funds to other organizations. The foundation does not ordinarily consider proposals for capital purposes, endowment funds, or deficit operations.

Fiscal Information Grants in 1988 totaled over $8.9 million.

Application Information A grant request should be initiated by a letter describing the proposed project, its expected impact, the qualifications of staff, a detailed expense budget and certified audit of the financial statements, the time frames, and other funding sources, as well as copies of the applicant organization's tax-exempt rulings stating that it is described in Section 501(c)(3) of the Internal Revenue Code and is not a private foundation.

Deadline(s) Proposals should be postmarked no later than the following deadlines, to allow adequate time for review: January 1 for animal welfare and local projects; April 1 for secondary education; July 1 for the arts; and October 1 for public issues.

166. The William H. Donner Foundation, Inc.

500 Fifth Avenue, Suite 1230
New York, NY 10110
(212) 719-9290

Program Grants

Program Description The foundation supports projects in U.S.-Canadian relations. In addition, the foundation is making exploratory grants in various other areas that are of potential interest to the trustees. These include, but are not limited to, public affairs, education, mental health and wildlife conservation. After a short period of exploratory grantmaking, the foundation's trustees intend to adopt new program areas.

Sample Grants In support of a pilot project to use two technical protocols of the Cartagena Convention for the Protection and Development of the Marine Environment for the Wider Caribbean Region as points of departure in encouraging wider participation by Gulf and Southern state governments in the Cartagena Convention, $24,900 to the Council for Ocean Law (1987). In support of the annual Berkeley Seminars on Federalism to focus serious attention on North American federalism and intergovernmental relations, $70,000 to the Institute for International Studies, Canadian Studies Program, University of California, Berkeley (1987). In support of a lecture series on aspects of international economic policy and decision-making process, $25,000 to the University of Rochester, New York (1988).

Eligibility/Limitations The geographic scope of the foundation's program is national. Applicants must be charitable, tax-exempt organizations under Section 501(c)(3) of the Internal Revenue Code. The proposed projects must fall within an existing or exploratory area of interest to the trustees.

Fiscal Information In 1989 the foundation awarded more than $5 million. The foundation does not fund construction or renovation of buildings, endowment funds, capital campaigns, annual charitable drives, grants to individuals, or provide general operating support, fund operating deficits, or make loans to individuals or organizations.

Application Information Applicants should determine first if their project falls into one of the foundation's program fields and within the program criteria. Next, the applicant should send the foundation a letter outlining briefly the proposed project. The letter should include a comprehensive summary of the proposed project, a brief statement of the project's objectives, and an explanation of how applicants propose to meet those objectives. In addition, the letter should name and describe the interests and qualifications of the key personnel involved in the

project and sponsoring organization. It must also include an estimate of the level of support to be requested from the foundation and a listing of other funding sources, if any, and their anticipated levels of support. The foundation will respond to all such inquiries, usually within two weeks.

Deadline(s) Applications will be accepted at any time and will be acted on as expeditiously as possible. To be considered for a particular meeting of the trustees, proposals must be received at the foundation according to the following schedule: August 1 for October board meeting; December 1 for February board meeting; and April 1 for June board meeting.

167. Earhart Foundation

2929 Plymouth Road, Plymouth Building, Suite 204
Ann Arbor, MI 48105
(313) 761-8592

Fellowship Research Grants

Program Description The foundation funds research in such disciplines from the social sciences and humanities as economics, philosophy, international affairs and political science.

Eligibility/Limitations Established scholars are eligible to apply. Such persons must be associated or affiliated with educational or research institutions and the effort supported should lead to the advancement of knowledge through teaching, lecturing and publication.

Fiscal Information There were 55 research grants in 1987. The maximum was $20,000 and the minimum $300, with an average of $8,183.

Application Information The applications evaluated must include a personal history statement; a full description of the proposed research; an abstract of approximately one page (single-spaced); a list of referees; and a statement about applications pending elsewhere.

Deadline(s) Proposals should be submitted not less than 120 days before commencement of the projected work period.

Additional Information The foundation supports two additional programs. H.B. Earhart Fellowships are awarded to move talented individuals through graduate study. Awards are made to graduate students nominated by faculty sponsors. Grants are occasionally made, upon application, to "publicly supported" educational and research organizations qualified for private foundation support. Written inquiries are preferable before formal submission of grant proposals.

168. The Educational Foundation of America

23161 Ventura Boulevard, Suite 201
Woodland Hills, CA 91364
(818) 999-0921

Grants

Program Description The Educational Foundation of America grants are awarded in areas of interest including, but not limited to, population issues, education, the environment, medical research, and native American enhancement.

Sample Grants In support of scholarships to help qualified minority students attend school, $25,000 to Whittier College School of Law, Los Angeles, CA (1985). In support of an affiliate development program, $100,000 to National Abortion Rights Action League Foundation (1989).

Eligibility/Limitations In general, the foundation makes grants only for specific projects and does not provide funds for endowment or building programs, for grants to individuals, or for annual fund-raising campaigns. Though not exclusive, projects focusing on the United States are preferred.

Fiscal Information Grants vary from $5,000 to $150,000.

Application Information Applicants are requested to send an informal letter of inquiry, two pages maximum, signed by an authorized official of the organization. The letter should briefly identify the organization, including date of founding, location, region of focus, name and very brief description of the foun-der(s), and affiliation with other organizations. Furthermore, it should describe the purpose of the project, its intended results and duration, and the amount of funds requested. Accompany-ing these must be a copy of a letter of determination from the IRS indicating permanent 501(c)(3) status certifying that the organization is tax exempt and is not a private foundation under Code 509(a). An officer of the organization must attest that this status remains in effect. Financial statements showing all sources of the organization's support and expenses for the immediate preceding four years must also be attached. The foundation staff will review the letter of inquiry and notify the writer whether or not to submit a full proposal.

Deadline(s) Although there are specific deadlines for accumula-tion of materials before any particular board meeting, proposals and inquiries are welcomed by the foundation at any time during the year.

169. Environmental Law Institute
Director of Communications
1616 P Street, NW
Washington, DC 20036
(202) 328-5150

Scholarships

Program Description The institute provides scholarships to indi-viduals who require financial assistance to attend American Law Institute-ABA/Environmental Law Institute conferences or courses.

Eligibility/Limitations Law students and professionals working with environmental matters in nonprofit organizations or gov-ernment agencies are eligible to apply for assistance.

Deadline(s) Applications are due two months before the con-ference date. Conferences are scheduled yearly in mid-October and mid-February.

Additional Information The institute awards summer internships to law students interested in environmental law. Contact the institute for application information.

170. Ernst & Young Foundation
227 Park Avenue
New York, NY 10172
(212) 407-1500

Tax Research Grant Program

Program Description The program was established for two major purposes: to promote a fair and equitable tax system and to improve accounting education. The program seeks to promote objective tax research in departments and schools of accounting. To encourage a broad range of tax research, proposals may be submitted on any aspect of federal, state or local taxation. These include policy, planning, history, education, compliance and comparative systems. The research may be either theoretical or applied. The foundation encourages interdisciplinary research that involves accounting faculty and faculty members from other disciplines, such as economics, finance, behavioral sci-ences, and law.

Sample Grants To study the effects of various tax law provisions that are purported to penalize the elderly, $24,100 to faculty from Texas A&M University (1989). To estimate the effective-ness of tax policy in stimulating new savings, $15,200 to faculty from the University of North Carolina at Chapel Hill and the State University of New York at Albany (1989).

Eligibility/Limitations The principal researcher must be an ac-counting faculty member who holds a full-time teaching ap-pointment and who possesses terminal degree qualifications as prescribed by the American Assembly of Collegiate Schools of Business. Coresearchers must also be full-time faculty members and hold appropriate academic credentials.

Fiscal Information The size of individual grants is limited to $50,000.

Application Information Interested researchers must submit each proposal in triplicate, spelling out its objectives, methodology and relevance. Include an itemized budget and an estimated completion date for each phase of the project. The budget should be as detailed as possible. The grant will not pay over-head charges at a percentage rate, but will reimburse researchers for incurred expenses. Proposals should be mailed to: Program Director, The Tax Research Grant Program, Ernst & Young, 1950 Roland Clarke Place, Reston, VA, 22091-1490.

Deadline(s) Proposals should be sent by October 31.

171. Exxon Corporation
225 East John W. Carpenter Freeway
Irving, TX 75062
(214) 444-1000

Grants

Program Description Exxon Corporation awards grants in the following program areas: environment, public information and policy research; education; health, welfare and community ser-vices; arts, museums and historical associations; and public broadcasting programming.

Sample Grants For an international dispute resolution program focusing on tropical forest management in Latin America and pollution control in European countries, $50,000 to the Con-servation Foundation, Washington, DC (1988). Toward a pro-gram for placing law students in summer internships with public interest law firms, $15,000 to the Civil Rights Law Program, Columbia University, New York, NY (1988). In support of a membership group that promotes public awareness of the Con-stitution and publishes *Constitution* magazine, $25,000 (of a special grant, $75,000 over three years) to the Foundation for the United States Constitution, New York, NY (1988). For seminars to help prevent, mitigate and resolve Third World conflicts, $5,000 to the International Peace Academy, New York, NY (1988).

Eligibility/Limitations Educational institutions or organizations that are located in the United States, its territories or posses-sions, and that are qualified as eligible charitable donees by the Internal Revenue Service are eligible for grants. The foundation does not make grants to individuals. Grants are not ordinarily made to: (1) support the adoption of established educational or administrative methods or materials; (2) provide funds for cap-ital purposes (equipment, buildings, or endowment); (3) support institutional scholarship funds; or (4) fund those standard course or curriculum development activities normally covered by in-stitutional budgets. (This does not include special course or curriculum development efforts that would involve unusual ex-penditures for the institution.) The foundation is less likely to respond to requests for operating funds for an existing college or university program.

Fiscal Information In 1988 Exxon made contributions of $15.5 million.

Application Information An institution or organization wishing to submit a project for consideration should send the foundation a proposal outline. Guidelines for the proposal outline are avail-able from the foundation.

Deadline(s) There are no specific closing dates for submission of the proposal outline; each will be reviewed as it is received.

Additional Information The corporation has moved to head-quarters from New York City. The company and foundation will phase out grants made to local organizations in New York and become involved with local organizations in the Dallas area.

172. Exxon Education Foundation

P.O. Box 101
Florham Park, NJ 07932-1198
(201) 765-3002

Grants

Program Description The mission of the Exxon Education Foundation is to support improvements in the quality of education. Proposals for funding may be submitted under the foundation's Curriculum & Teaching program (higher education portion) and its Management in Higher Education program. Curriculum & Teaching grants support efforts that will lead to improvement in instructional methodology and content, as well as the evaluation and dissemination of such efforts. The foundation is especially interested in projects that cross traditional lines between disciplines, professions, and institutions, and in projects that promote interaction between humanists and social scientists and representatives of scientific, technical, and professional fields. Priority is given to projects involving reexamination of basic educational purposes, programs, and requirements and to efforts to introduce consideration of values issues into professional and graduate training. Preference is given also to projects that reflect a concern for the international dimension of education and the need for heightened awareness of global issues. Under the Management of Higher Education program, the foundation is interested in projects that will foster improved allocation and use of resources among and within educational institutions and systems, improved understanding of the economic forces affecting educational services and institutions, and improved institutional response to economic change.

Sample Grants To develop an international environmental dispute resolution program focusing on tropical forestry issues in Asia and Latin America, $50,000 to the Conservation Foundation, Washington, DC (1989). In support of dispute resolution program, $10,000 to the Center for Public Resources, New York, NY (1989). In support of Center for Law, $20,000 to Columbia University, New York, NY (1989). In support of a communications program on federal legislative issues, $10,000 to the General Federation of Women's Clubs, Washington, DC (1989).

Eligibility/Limitations Educational institutions or organizations that are located in the United States, its territories or possessions, and that are qualified as eligible charitable donees by the Internal Revenue Service are eligible for grants. The foundation makes no grants to individuals. Grants are not ordinarily made to: (1) support the adoption of established educational or administrative methods or materials; (2) provide funds for capital purposes (equipment, buildings, or endowment); (3) support institutional scholarship funds; or (4) fund those standard course or curriculum development activities normally covered by institutional budgets. (This does not include special course or curriculum development efforts that would involve unusual expenditures for the institution.) The foundation is less likely to respond to requests for operating funds for an existing college or university program.

Fiscal Information In 1989 Exxon organizations made contributions of $21.8 million.

Application Information An institution or organization wishing to submit a project for consideration should send the foundation a proposal outline. Guidelines for the proposal outline are available from the foundation.

Deadline(s) There are no specific closing dates for submission of the proposal outline; each will be reviewed as it is received.

173. The FERIS Foundation of America

34 South Oak Ridge Road
Mount Kisco, NY 10549
(914) 666-5720

The Albert Gallatin Fellowship in International Affairs

Program Description The FERIS Foundation of America was established in 1972 to promote study and research in international affairs and to foster cultural understanding between the United States and other countries. The foundation finances fellowships at the Graduate Institute of International Studies in Geneva, Switzerland, a leading center for the study of international law and politics, international economics, international institutions and international development.

Sample Grants To support a doctoral dissertation on "The World Health Organization and the Transnational AIDS Network" (1989). To support a doctoral dissertation on "Procedural Issues in International Arbitration" (1989). To support a doctoral dissertation on "The Principle of Non-Appropriation of Outer Space and Celestial Bodies" (1987).

Eligibility/Limitations American candidates for the Ph.D. who are actively engaged in dissertation research for the doctorate.

Fiscal Information The fellowship provides a stipend in Swiss francs, 1,700 a month for living and other expenses for the academic year, October to July; round-trip travel from New York to Geneva; an allowance for travel outside of Geneva, if required by fellow's research, to be determined in consultation with the fellow's supervisor; an allowance for purchase or transport of books related to research.

Application Information Applications forms which contain further information on the fellowship and its requirements may be obtained from the foundation.

Deadline(s) The closing date for receipt of application is March 13.

174. Firestone Trust Fund

205 North Michigan Avenue, Suite 3800
Chicago, IL 60601-5965
(312) 819-8548

Firestone Community Investment Program

Program Description There are four major categories in which contributions are considered: education, health and welfare, culture and the arts, and civic and community. In the civic and community category, contributions are made to ensure the availability of an adequate level of community services, sufficient housing and a healthy and pleasant environment for employees and their neighbors. Consideration is also given to examining new solutions to community and environmental problems. Assistance is given for community and neighborhood improvements; environment and energy conservation; justice and law; housing and urban revitalization; civil rights and equal opportunity; voter registration and education; and job training.

Eligibility/Limitations Contributions are limited to 501(c)(3) tax-exempt organizations.

Fiscal Information Grants paid in 1988 were over $6 million.

Application Information Applications for grants from the fund must be submitted in writing and should include specific details on purpose, goals and costs of the request. Evidence of the organization's 501(c)(3) tax-exempt status should be included.

Deadline(s) Major funding proposals normally are reviewed biannually (February and August).

175. The Fluor Foundation

Community Affairs Coordinator
3333 Michelson Drive
Irvine, CA 92730
(714) 975-6797

Grants

Program Description The Fluor Foundation was established to handle philanthropic matters for the Fluor Corporation. Contributions are given in the areas of education, health and welfare, cultural activities, and civic programs.

Eligibility/Limitations The foundation does not support the endeavors of individuals, medical research, or guilds, auxiliaries, and support groups. It is the policy of the foundation to consider contribution requests from nonprofit, 501(c)(3) organizations as determined by the IRS. These organizations must be located in the communities where Fluor has permanent offices. Contribution requests from national organizations will only be considered when local organizations do not exist.

Fiscal Information Contributions in 1987 totaled over $500,000.

Application Information The proper procedure for financial consideration is to submit a letter of introduction explaining the purpose and goals, the amount requested, and how the grant will be used. If the request falls within foundation guidelines, a Contribution Request Application will be forwarded.

Deadline(s) No deadlines are announced.

176. Folger Shakespeare Library
Fellowship Committee
201 East Capitol Street, SE
Washington, DC 20003
(202) 544-4600

NEH Senior Fellowships and Folger Senior Fellowships

Program Description A limited number of NEH Senior Resident Fellowships and Folger Senior Fellowships are available to senior scholars who are pursuing research projects appropriate to the collections of the Folger. The Folger Library houses one of the world's finest collections of Renaissance books and manuscripts. Its principal collections are in the following areas: Shakespeareana; English, American, and European literature and drama (1500-1800); English, American, and continental history (1500-1715); political, economic, and legal history (1500-1715); history of philosophy, art, music, religion, science and medicine, and exploration (1500-1715). Applications are welcome in all areas covered by the Folger collection for work on projects which draw significantly on Folger holdings.

Eligibility/Limitations Senior scholars who have made substantial contributions in their fields of research and who are pursuing research projects appropriate to the collections of the Folger are eligible to apply.

Fiscal Information Fellowships are for a period of six to nine months and carry stipends of $15,000 to $27,500.

Application Information Applicants should submit six copies of both a 500-word description of the research project and a curriculum vitae including a list of publications. Applicants should also have three letters of reference sent directly to the fellowship committee.

Deadline(s) The deadline for application is November 1.

Additional Information Short-term postdoctoral fellowships with stipends of up to $1,500 per month for a term of one to three months are available. A completed application will consist of three copies of the applicant's curriculum vita and three copies of a 500-word description of the research project plus three letters of recommendation submitted directly to the fellowship committee. The deadline for application is March 1.

177. The Ford Foundation
320 East 43rd Street
New York, NY 10017
(212) 573-5000

Education and Culture

Program Description The Ford Foundation's domestic and international work is coordinated within six areas of general concern: urban poverty, rural poverty and resources, human rights and governance, education and culture, international affairs, and population. The foundation's Education and Culture Program aims to build social capacity and realize individual potential by broadening access, assuring equity, and enriching teaching and scholarship in selected fields. Programs are supported to increase the presence of minority faculty and students in higher education, to deepen the engagement of faculty in teaching and scholarship, and to improve the quality of education in the social sciences, international studies, Afro-American studies, and women's studies.

Sample Grants For projects promoting access and equity, $40,000 to NOW Legal Defense and Education Fund, New York, NY (1988). For administration and policy research, $40,000 to NOW Legal Defense and Education Fund, New York, NY (1988).

Eligibility/Limitations Activities supported by foundation grants must be charitable, educational, or scientific as defined under the appropriate provisions of the U.S. Internal Revenue Code and Treasury Regulations. Most of the foundation's grant funds are given to organizations. Although the foundation also makes grants to individuals, such grants are few in number relative to demand; limited to research, training, and other activities related to the foundation's program interests; and subject to certain limitations and procedural requirements of the U.S. Internal Revenue Code. In the main, foundation grants to individuals are awarded either through publicly announced competitions or on the basis of nominations from universities and other nonprofit institutions.

Fiscal Information Grants paid in 1989 total over $46.8 million.

Application Information Before any detailed formal application is made, a brief letter of inquiry is advisable to determine whether the foundation's present interests and funds permit consideration of the proposal. There is no application form. Proposals should be set forth in the following manner: objectives; the proposed program for pursuing objectives; qualifications of persons engaged in the work; a detailed budget; present means of support and status of applications to other funding sources; and legal and tax status.

Deadline(s) Applications are considered throughout the year.

178. The Ford Foundation
320 East 43rd Street
New York, NY 10017
(212) 573-5000

Governance and Public Policy

Program Description The Ford Foundation's domestic and international work is coordinated within six areas of general concern: urban poverty, rural poverty and resources, human rights and governance, education and culture, international affairs, and population. The foundation's Governance and Public Policy Program seeks to enhance pluralism and increase disadvantaged groups' participation in the governing process; to improve the responsiveness of government institutions; and to encourage independent research on major public policy issues. In the United States the program is organized into three areas: efforts to improve the processes of governance and to strengthen philanthropy and the nonprofit sector; analysis of policies affecting disadvantaged minorities, a leadership development program for minorities, and a graduate fellowship program for minorities in public policy and international affairs; and research and analysis focused on U.S. economic and social policy, and public policies and community and public policies and community programs responding to the AIDS pandemic.

Sample Grants For dispute resolution, $1,320,000 to the National Institute for Dispute Resolution, Washington, DC (1988). For public policy analysis, $260,000 to the Center for Immigration Studies, Washington, DC (1988). For training, technical assistance and the publication of materials to help motivate large law firms to make an increased commitment to pro bono activities, $155,000 to the American Bar Association (1989).

Eligibility/Limitations Activities supported by foundation grants must be charitable, educational, or scientific as defined under the appropriate provisions of the U.S. Internal Revenue Code and Treasury Regulations. Most of the foundation's grant funds are given to organizations. Although the foundation also makes grants to individuals, such grants are few in number relative to demand; limited to research, training, and other activities related to the foundation's program interests; and subject to certain limitations and procedural requirements of the U.S. Internal Revenue Code. In the main, foundation grants to individuals are awarded either through publicly announced competitions or on the basis of nominations from universities and other nonprofit institutions.

Fiscal Information Grants paid in 1989 totaled over $37.5 million.

Application Information Before any detailed formal application is made, a brief letter of inquiry is advisable to determine whether the foundation's present interests and funds permit consideration of the proposal. There is no application form. Proposals should set forth objectives, the proposed program for pursuing objectives, qualifications of persons engaged in the work, a detailed budget, present means of support and status of applications to other funding sources, and legal and tax status.

Deadline(s) Applications are considered throughout the year.

179. The Ford Foundation

320 East 43rd Street
New York, NY 10017
(212) 573-5000

Human Rights and Social Justice

Program Description The Ford Foundation's domestic and international work is coordinated within six areas of general concern: urban poverty, rural poverty and resources, human rights and governance, education and culture, international affairs, and population. The foundation's Human Rights and Governance Program supports a broad range of research, education, litigation, and advocacy activities aimed at encouraging adherence to international human rights standards; clarifying the rights and responsibilities of refugees and migrants; enhancing the status of blacks, Hispanics, and Native Americans and promoting better intergroup relations; advancing the legal rights and economic well-being of women, particularly low-income and minority women; and providing low-income groups with access to legal services and examining legal issues that affect the disadvantaged.

Sample Grants In support of international human rights law, $175,000 to the Minnesota Lawyers International Human Rights Committee (1988). For support of refugees' and migrants' rights, $75,000 to the American Immigration Law Foundation, Washington, DC (1988). In support of work on social justice/legal services, $50,000 to Women Judges' Fund for Justice, Washington, DC (1989). To support worldwide activities to promote the rule of law and human rights, $400,000 to the International Commission of Jurists, Switzerland (1985). To support a series of seminars to familiarize judges in the United States with the main body of international human rights law and its possible domestic applications, $120,000 to the Aspen Institute of Humanistic Studies, Queenstown, MD (1989).

Eligibility/Limitations Activities supported by foundation grants must be charitable, educational, or scientific as defined under the appropriate provisions of the U.S. Internal Revenue Code and Treasury Regulations. Most of the foundation's grant funds are given to organizations. Although the foundation also makes grants to individuals, such grants are few in number relative to demand; limited to research, training, and other activities related to the foundation's program interests; and subject to certain limitations and procedural requirements of the U.S. Internal Revenue Code. In the main, foundation grants to individuals are awarded either through publicly announced competitions or on the basis of nominations from universities and other nonprofit institutions.

Fiscal Information Grants paid in 1989 totaled over $32.4 million.

Application Information Before any detailed formal application is made, a brief letter of inquiry is advisable to determine whether the foundation's present interests and funds permit consideration of the proposal. There is no application form. Proposals should set forth objectives, the proposed program for pursuing objectives, qualifications of persons engaged in the work, a detailed budget, present means of support and status of applications to other funding sources, and legal and tax status.

Deadline(s) Applications are considered throughout the year.

180. The Ford Foundation

320 East 43rd Street
New York, NY 10017
(212) 573-5000

International Affairs

Program Description The Ford Foundation's domestic and international work is coordinated within six areas of general concern: urban poverty, rural poverty and resources, human rights and governance, education and culture, international affairs, and population. The foundation's International Affairs Program supports a wide range of research, training, and educational activities in seven areas: key policy problems in international economics and development; international refugees and migration; international peace, security, and arms control; international organizations and law; U.S. foreign policy; international relations, primarily of developing countries; and foreign-area studies, primarily of the Soviet Union and Eastern Europe.

Sample Grants In support of international organizations and law, $228,275 to the American Society of International Law, Washington, DC (1988). In support of work on refugee and migration policy, $1,337,500 to the RAND Corporation, Santa Monica, CA (1988). In support of policy analysis and public education concerning ocean law and policy, $150,000 to the Council on Ocean Law, Washington, DC (1989). In support of a planning grant, $42,600 to Harvard Law School, Boston, MA (1989).

Eligibility/Limitations Activities supported by foundation grants must be charitable, educational, or scientific as defined under the appropriate provisions of the U.S. Internal Revenue Code and Treasury Regulations. Most of the foundation's grant funds are given to organizations. Although the foundation also makes grants to individuals, such grants are few in number relative to demand; limited to research, training, and other activities related to the foundation's program interests; and subject to certain limitations and procedural requirements of the U.S. Internal Revenue Code. In the main, foundation grants to individuals are awarded either through publicly announced competitions or on the basis of nominations from universities and other nonprofit institutions.

Fiscal Information Grants paid in 1989 totaled over $24 million.

Application Information Before any detailed formal application is made, a brief letter of inquiry is advisable to determine whether the foundation's present interests and funds permit consideration of the proposal. There is no application form. Proposals should be set forth in the following manner: objectives; the proposed program for pursuing objectives; qualifications of persons engaged in the work; a detailed budget; present means of support and status of applications to other funding sources; and legal and tax status.

Deadline(s) Applications are considered throughout the year.

181. The Ford Foundation

320 East 43rd Street
New York, NY 10017
(212) 573-5000

Rural Poverty and Resources

Program Description The Ford Foundation's domestic and international work is coordinated within six areas of general concern: urban poverty, rural poverty and resources, human rights and governance, education and culture, international affairs, and population. The foundation's Rural Poverty and Resources Program supports efforts that analyze factors limiting agricultural productivity; encourage more efficient and equitable management of natural resources; increase the capacity of individuals and institutions to contribute to the formulation of rural policies; help women and other vulnerable groups increase their income from agricultural and off-farm enterprises; and strengthen community-based and intermediary organizations providing credit, training, and other services to the rural poor.

Sample Grants For policy development, $16,000 to the Public Affairs Committee, New York, NY (1988). For policy development, $250,000 to the National Center for Policy Alternatives, Washington, DC (1988). In support of land and water management program, $500,000 to the American Indian Lawyer Training Program, Oakland, CA (1989).

Eligibility/Limitations Activities supported by foundation grants must be charitable, educational, or scientific as defined under the appropriate provisions of the U.S. Internal Revenue Code and Treasury Regulations. Most of the foundation's grant funds are given to organizations. Although the foundation also makes grants to individuals, such grants are few in number relative to demand; limited to research, training, and other activities related to the foundation's program interests; and subject to certain limitations and procedural requirements of the U.S. Internal Revenue Code. In the main, foundation grants to individuals are awarded either through publicly announced competitions or on the basis of nominations from universities and other nonprofit institutions.

Fiscal Information Grants paid in 1989 totaled over $27.3 million.

Application Information Before any detailed formal application is made, a brief letter of inquiry is advisable to determine whether the foundation's present interests and funds permit consideration of the proposal. There is no application form. Proposals should be set forth in the following manner: objectives; the proposed program for pursuing objectives; qualifications of persons engaged in the work; a detailed budget; present means of support and status of applications to other funding sources; and legal and tax status.

Deadline(s) Applications are considered throughout the year.

182. The Ford Foundation

320 East 43rd Street
New York, NY 10017
(212) 573-5000

Urban Poverty

Program Description The Ford Foundation's domestic and international work is coordinated within six areas of general concern: urban poverty, rural poverty and resources, human rights and governance, education and culture, international affairs, and population. The foundation's Urban Poverty Program aims to improve the lives of the U.S. urban poor through two major lines of work: strengthening community and neighborhood development; improving services for children, youth and families; and cross-disciplinary research on poverty.

Sample Grants For projects in physical, economic or social revitalization, $830,000 to the National Economic Development and Law Center, Berkeley, CA (1988). For projects in physical, economic or social revitalization, $112,000 to the National Housing and Community Development Law Project, Berkeley, CA (1988). For policy research and program evaluation, $200,000 to the Arkansas Institute for Social Justice, Little Rock, AR (1988). For policy research and program evaluation, $100,000 to NAACP Legal Defense and Education Fund, New York, NY (1989).

Eligibility/Limitations Activities supported by foundation grants must be charitable, educational, or scientific as defined under the appropriate provisions of the U.S. Internal Revenue Code and Treasury Regulations. Most of the foundation's grant funds are given to organizations. Although the foundation also makes grants to individuals, such grants are few in number relative to demand; limited to research, training, and other activities related to the foundation's program interests; and subject to certain limitations and procedural requirements of the U.S. Internal Revenue Code. In the main, foundation grants to individuals are awarded either through publicly announced competitions or on the basis of nominations from universities and other nonprofit institutions.

Fiscal Information Grants paid in 1989 totaled over $39.9 million.

Application Information Before any detailed formal application is made, a brief letter of inquiry is advisable to determine whether the foundation's present interests and funds permit consideration of the proposal. There is no application form. Proposals should be set forth in the following manner: objectives; the proposed program for pursuing objectives; qualifications of persons engaged in the work; a detailed budget; present means of support and status of applications to other funding sources; and legal and tax status.

Deadline(s) Applications are considered throughout the year.

183. Ford Motor Company Fund

The American Road, P.O. Box 1899
Dearborn, MI 48121-1899
(313) 845-8711

Grants

Program Description The fund contributes to the betterment and improvement of humankind through grants to organizations operating exclusively for charitable, scientific, literary, or educational purposes, primarily in geographic areas of interest to the fund. A major segment of the fund's activities concern grants in support of cultural organizations, the United Way, urban affairs projects, social welfare, educational institutions and selected national charities and associations. The fund also supports economic education projects.

Sample Grants In support of a visiting scholar program of study of government regulations, $100,000 to the American Enterprise Institute, Washington, DC (1986). In support of the RAND Corporation Institute for Civil Justice, $20,000, Santa Monica, CA (1986).

Eligibility/Limitations Grants are made only to organizations and institutions and never directly to individuals.

Fiscal Information Contributions in 1988 totaled over $17.7 million.

Application Information Proposals are generally submitted in brief narrative form, and, if the project appears to be in the fund's area of interest, further data and detailed exhibits will be requested. For applicants interested in more detailed information, an annual report on the fund's activities is available for a $3.00 charge.

Deadline(s) No deadlines are announced.

184. Foreign Policy Research Institute

3615 Chestnut Street
Philadelphia, PA 19104
(215) 382-0685

Thornton D. Hooper Fellowship in International Affairs

Program Description The Thornton D. Hooper Fellowship Competition seeks to promote original research on issues affecting U.S. interests. It is designed to attract the participation of international relations specialists, political scientists, economists, historians, and members of related disciplines.

Eligibility/Limitations Fellows must have received or be about to receive a doctoral degree or have equivalent experience.

Fiscal Information The applicant who is selected will spend a year in residence at the Foreign Policy Research Institute and will receive a stipend commensurate with his or her experience.

Application Information Applicants should submit copies of three publications (or writings accepted for publication), a curriculum vitae, three letters of recommendation, and a 1,000-word research proposal on some aspect of international affairs.

Deadline(s) Application deadline is December 15.

Additional Information FPRI offers internships to promising undergraduate and graduate students contemplating a career in international affairs.

185. Foreign Policy Research Institute

3615 Chestnut Street
Philadelphia, PA 19104
(215) 382-0685

Senior Fellowship Program

Program Description The institute is an independent, nonprofit organization devoted to the study of the political, economic, social, and military dimensions of contemporary international developments. The institute's major activities include a broad-based research program on critical issues affecting U.S. interests abroad; an internationally renowned publications program; seminars, conferences, and workshops for business, government, and academic leaders; and a fellowship program designed to provide training in foreign policy analysis to promising scholars. The FPRI takes special pride in its fellowship program, which provides training in policy analysis to aspiring scholars and often serves as a springboard to active participation in the policy-making process itself. The training program relates academic skills to the theoretical and operational aspects of U.S. foreign policy and offers exposure to diverse disciplines.

Fiscal Information FPRI offers stipends to its fellows, normally to defray tuition costs and dissertation fees and to enable the fellows to conduct research in cooperation with resident staff.

Application Information Application information is available upon request.

Deadline(s) Contact the institute for deadlines.

186. Foundation for Child Development

345 East 46th Street
New York, NY 10017
(212) 697-3150

Project Grants

Program Description The foundation supports work in three major areas: child-development research, public policy and advocacy, and direction-action initiatives. The research component of the foundation's program emphasizes the integration of action and research. Researchers seeking support from the foundation should make explicit the potential connections between their research and the lives of children and families at risk. In the policy area the foundation seeks to increase understanding between the research community and policymakers. The direct-action programs of the foundation should be social research probes to develop new policy initiatives.

Sample Grants For creation of a Bench Book for Family Court Judges, $25,000 to the Task Force on Permanency Planning for Foster Children, Inc., New York (1988-89). For analysis of policies aimed at improving the coordination of New York State services to children, $25,000 to the State Communities Aid Association, New York (1988-89). In support of technical assistance for state implementation of the Family Support Act, a two-year grant of $150,000 to the Children's Defense Fund, Washington, DC (1988-89). In support of a project aimed at coordination of services for children, $33,960 to the Youth Law Center (1988-89). In support of training, technical assistance, counsel, policy analysis and research, and public education on the Family Support Act, $49,870 to the Center for Law and Social Policy (1988-89).

Eligibility/Limitations The foundation considers applications from nonprofit organizations for support of projects. The foundation does not provide support for projects outside New York that are largely service oriented or for building supplies and renovations.

Fiscal Information Grant disbursements during 1989 totaled over $1.4 million.

Application Information A grant request should be initiated through a letter to the foundation from the applicant organization requesting support for the project. The request should include: a description of the proposed project, the amount requested, and qualifications of the project director; an estimate of the time involved in conducting the project; for projects, both a budget and an overall organization budget, the project budget to identify direct and indirect costs, with an explanation of how the latter are allocated; for general institutional support, the overall budget; a brief description of the applicant organization (except in the case of universities); reference to other funding sources; the project's relationship to the project directory's total endeavor; the project's significance in relation to the foundation's interests; a statement as to whether the applicant organization has received exemption from federal taxation under the Internal Revenue Code, including information on the applicant's classification as either a public charity or a private operating or nonoperating foundation. A copy of the Internal Revenue Service ruling should accompany the proposal.

Deadline(s) No deadlines are announced.

187. The Frost Foundation, Ltd.

650 South Cherry Street, Suite 205
Denver, CO 80222
(303) 388-1687

Program Description Where possible, the foundation utilizes its contributions as "seed money" providing the initial impetus for new programs or the nucleus for attracting matching funds, whether from the private or public sector. It is prepared to review applications from the perspective of long-range development of educational, charitable, and religious facilities and programs, with preference to be given to such facilities and programs within the following states: Louisiana, Colorado, Arkansas, New Mexico, Texas, Arizona, and Oklahoma. The foundation attempts to encourage self-reliance, creativity, and ingenuity on the part of prospective recipients.

Sample Grants To purchase a personal computer system for NARF's attorney staff in Boulder, $10,000 to Native American Rights Fund, Boulder, CO (1987). To develop, through citizen involvement, new strategies for decision-making about groundwater quality problems in the southwestern states, $10,000 to Western Network, Santa Fe, NM (1987).

Eligibility/Limitations The foundation awards funds to organizations determined as 501(c)(3) under the Internal Revenue Code. As a general rule, the foundation does not contribute to operating expenses which are generally beneficial only for the short term.

Fiscal Information Generally, the foundation does not consider gifts of small amounts because it is likely that these could be made from other sources. It concentrates on large and significant needs in the areas where a contribution would have a more permanent, as opposed to temporary, effect. Grants paid in 1988 totaled over $1.2 million.

Application Information Grant applications should include the following information: name of organization, address, telephone number, and the name of project director; brief history of the organization; purposes and objectives of organization; structure of organization and department concerned; IRS determination letter, 501(c)(3); concise description of need or problem to be addressed; brief general description of project or program designed to meet the need or solve the problem; specific project or program objectives in measurable terms; estimates of cost, amount requested from the foundation, and proposed sources of other funding; copy of project budget; procedures used for planning project or program; plans for providing qualified personnel to staff project or program and nature of qualifications (include individual resumes); estimated time for implementation and duration of program; plans for cooperation with other institutions or organizations, if any; proposed plan for evaluation of project; signature and title of chief executive officer indicating organizational approval of request; and a copy of most recent financial statement (audit). Applicants must submit four copies of the grant proposal.

Deadline(s) The foundation's directors meet in mid-February and late September of each year. The deadline for the receipt of proposals to be considered at the February meeting is December 1, and the deadline for the receipt of proposals for consideration at the September meeting is July 1.

188. Lloyd A. Fry Foundation

135 South LaSalle Street, Suite 1910
Chicago, IL 60603
(312) 580-0310

Grants

Program Description The Lloyd A. Fry Foundation makes grants in the following broad fields: education; health; arts and culture; and civic affairs and social service. Priority is given to proposals for the initiation of new programs rather than for the support of ongoing programs of direct service.

Eligibility/Limitations Grants are made only to tax-exempt organizations and are rarely made to organizations outside the Chicago metropolitan area. Grants are not made to individuals.

Fiscal Information Grants totaled over $2.1 million in 1988.

Application Information Inquiries preceding the submission of formal proposals are welcome and will receive a prompt response. Such inquiries should include a brief statement of the proposed project and a project budget. Contact the foundation for additional information and proposal guidelines.

Deadline(s) Proposals may be submitted at any time. The board of directors of the foundation meets four times a year to consider requests for grants. Normally these meetings are held in February, May, August, and November.

189. Fund for Research on Dispute Resolution

1901 L Street, NW, Suite 600
Washington, DC 20036
(202) 785-4637

Research Grants

Program Description The fund supports a broad range of research which connects the study of disputing and dispute handling to social, psychological, economic, political or legal theory. It seeks to promote understanding of the conditions under which individuals, groups and organizations do or do not express grievances and become involved in disputes. The fund supports exploration of the way social, political and legal institutions encourage, inhibit or resolve grievances and disputes. The fund welcomes efforts to understand the effects on individuals, society and policy of disputing and dispute handling. It supports research that examines how different patterns of disputing and dispute handling affect the rights of disputants and others, how they enhance or diminish opportunities for democratic participation and how they speak to the needs of powerless or "at-risk" groups. It encourages researchers to engage in critical examination of disputing and dispute handling and will support studies that are both theoretically grounded and socially useful. Preference will be given to projects that collect new data or develop new analyses of existing data. Longitudinal, comparative and historical research projects are appropriate. A wide range of methodologies and approaches are encouraged.

Sample Grants For a study of two hospital units to explore why some patients initiate claims in response to medical error and malpractice, whereas many others do not, $57,060 to the American Bar Foundation (1988). To examine the effects of "bargaining in the shadow of the law" in the context of divorce negotiations, $65,092 to the Center for Urban Affairs and Policy Research, Northwestern University (1988). To investigate the increase in the nation's business disputes and commercial litigation since 1960, $89,152 to Dispute Processing Research Program, University of Wisconsin (1989).

Eligibility/Limitations The fund will not support research on conflict and conflict resolution among and between nations; projects that merely describe dispute handling techniques; or program evaluation which seeks to determine whether the goals of a particular experiment or program have been attained.

Fiscal Information The fund does not provide funding for any indirect costs. Under its 1990 program, the fund will award grants totaling approximately $800,000.

Application Information The application process includes a competitive two-step process with the submission of brief concept papers for review, followed by invitations to some applicants to submit full proposals. Applicants must submit 15 copies of a brief concept paper that describes the proposed research in no more than six double-spaced typewritten pages. These papers should describe the proposed research indicating what important social problems will be addressed, what hypotheses or questions guide the research, and what methods of study and analysis will be employed; indicate its theoretical justification, demonstrating how the proposed research will address basic questions in social, psychological, economic, political or legal theory; clearly state the relevance of the proposed work to research traditions in the dispute-processing field and indicate the likely contribution to knowledge arising from the proposed research. Applicants must also provide a budget summary which should include the total amount requested, the total project budget and a budget breakdown including the basis for estimates of salaries, wages and fringe benefits.

Deadline(s) Concept papers are due on March 15 and September 15. Applicants will be notified within approximately six weeks whether to submit a full proposal to the fund.

Additional Information The fund announces a special initiation to encourage research on disputing and dispute resolution focusing on minorities, the poor, the underclass, and dependent populations. The fund welcomes concept papers addressing important research issues in these areas and anticipated providing support for several projects addressing these social problems in upcoming grants rounds.

190. Gates Foundation

3200 Cherry Creek South Drive, Suite 630
Denver, CO 80209-3247
(303) 722-1881

Grants

Program Description The purpose of the Gates Foundation is to aid, assist, encourage, help initiate or carry on activities which will promote the health, welfare and broad education of humanity whether by means of research, grants, publications, its own agencies and activities or through cooperation with agencies and institutions already in existence, or by any other means which, from time to time, shall seem appropriate to the foundation.

Sample Grants First of three $15,000 annual grants for general operating support to the Mountain States Legal Foundation, Denver, CO (1987).

Eligibility/Limitations The foundation will grant funds only to properly documented tax-exempt organizations. The foundation generally does not make grants to organizations outside Colorado; support projects involving court actions; grant individual awards or scholarships; or reconsider previously denied proposals.

Fiscal Information Grants awarded in 1988 totaled more than $4 million.

Application Information Many proposers find it useful to call the executive director or program officer of the foundation for the purpose of reviewing the substance of the proposed project prior to filing a full formal request. There is certain basic information that the foundation requires. The foundation will need a preliminary summary, which does not exceed two pages. It should be written in narrative form and should contain no adjectives. The information needed is described below, and should be presented in the order given: name of organization and a brief history; geographic location—state, city, or town; mission, purposes and/or goals; a description of the applying organization, including size (in terms of physical plant), number of people involved, and annual operating income and expense; a clear description of the project for which the funds are being raised; what the project will cost over what period of time; how much money has been raised for the project to date and from what general sources; and a statement as to why the project is important and whom it will affect. In addition to this summary, the foundation may request further information it deems necessary to complete its investigation.

Deadline(s) For each proposal to be thoughtfully studied, it is important for the applying organization to have their final proposal in the hands of the foundation staff at least eight weeks prior to the trustees' meeting. More time could be required if a proposal is either highly specialized and requires outside consultation or is so significant that it requires a full on-site study by the trustees. Proposals should be submitted by January 15 for the April 1 meeting; April 15 for the June 15 meeting; July 15 for the October 1 meeting; and October 15 for the December 15 meeting.

191. General Electric Foundations

3135 Easton Turnpike
Fairfield, CT 06431
(202) 373-3216

Program Description The foundations seek to improve the way we educate our young, care for our health, protect our natural environment, nurture our arts, assist people and communities whose jobs have been lost to competition, and provide for those least able to provide for themselves. The role of the foundations is to stimulate change in all these areas. The foundations see their grants as "risk capital" seeding the ideas of those whose imagination and drive are already at work.

Sample Grants For general support, $25,000 to the American Law Institute (1988).

Eligibility/Limitations The foundations do not award scholarships or fellowships directly to individuals, nor do they support requests from individuals for research or study grants. Assistance is not customarily provided for capital, endowment or other special purpose campaigns.

Fiscal Information Foundations grants totaled over $19.1 million in 1988.

Application Information The foundations do not have formal grant application forms. Requests for funding should be made by letter and should include the following information: brief description of the organization, including its legal name, its primary purpose and history; amount of grant request and how it will be used; clear statement of the purpose of the organization program(s), including the benefits it is expected to provide; the official contact person; budget information; any additional factual information related to the organization or the request that may be useful for evaluation (e.g., list of support from other donors); and documents affirming that the organization is exempt from federal income tax under section 501(c)(3) of the Internal Revenue Code.

Deadline(s) No deadlines are announced.

192. General Foods

Corporate Contributions Committee & The General
  Foods Fund, Inc.
250 North Street
White Plains, NY 10625
(914) 335-7961

Contributions and Grants

Program Description General Foods' Contributions Program consists of cash contributions made directly by General Foods Corporation and its U.S. and foreign subsidiaries and grants made by The General Foods Fund, Inc. Gifts are made at the local and national levels. GF supports programs or projects in the following categories: education in nutrition and the food sciences, general education, socioeconomic development, cultural affairs, and public policy and food industry issues. In the cultural affairs category, GF assists local civic and cultural organizations and programs, including performing arts, museums, libraries, parks and zoos. On a highly selective basis, GF contributes to nationally prominent performing arts companies and cultural organizations and programs.

Sample Grants For general support, $25,000 to the American Law Institute (1988). For general support, $10,000 to the Earl Warren Legal Training Program (1988). For general support, $25,000 to Environmental Law Institute (1988).

Eligibility/Limitations General Foods and subsidiaries intend to support nonprofit, tax-exempt organizations and programs which address needs, issues and concerns of society consistent with GF's contributions policy and program objectives; benefit a broad segment of the community served; which, through responsible sponsorship and competent management, have demonstrated their effectiveness and/or promise for producing desired results in the future; which hold themselves accountable to donors and beneficiaries, regularly report on their financial condition, including sources of funding, their fund-raising practices and costs and administrative expenses; and which if in the United States, qualify as tax-exempt under Section 501(c)(3) of the Internal Revenue Code. GF will not contribute to organizations which discriminate by race, color or national origin; religious organizations or activities for the propagation of a particular faith or creed; individuals; or goodwill advertising. GF prefers not to make donations for capital or endowment funds, memorial purposes, testimonial dinners, conferences or related travel expenses.

Fiscal Information Annual contributions and grants combined totaled $18.5 million in 1988.

Application Information All requests and proposals should be in written form, brief and concise, stating the purpose for which funds are sought and containing a brief description of the sponsoring organization, its history, leadership, services offered, constituencies served, accomplishments, current financial statements, support sources, and evidence of tax-exempt status. Where applicable, primarily in local communities, the extent of actual or potential use of facilities and services by employees of GF and/or subsidiary companies and their families should be furnished. Requests for support in local GF communities should be address to the senior official at the GF or subsidiary unit. Requests for support of organizations and programs of national scope and specifically for education in nutrition and food sciences, general education, and public policy and food industry issues should be addressed to the secretary of the Corporate Contributions Committee, General Foods Corporation, White Plains, NY 10625.

Deadline(s) No deadlines are announced.

193. General Mills Foundation

P.O. Box 1113
Minneapolis, MN 55440
(612) 540-3337

Grants

Program Description The General Mills Foundation originally focused its primary attention on education, but in 1969 widened its range of interest to include the areas of education, social service, health, cultural affairs and civic affairs. Its current giving favors those communities where substantial numbers of General Mills employees live and work, and favors grants that address the current needs of families, children and youth.

Sample Grants Scholarship Program support, $4,000 to Mexican Americans Legal Defense and Educational Fund, Los Angeles, CA (1989). To support legal policy activities, $5,000 to the Lawyers Committee for Civil Rights Under Law, Washington, DC (1989). To support Immigration Law Reform Project, $7,500 to the Legal Aid Society of Minneapolis, MN (1989).

Eligibility/Limitations It is the practice of the foundation to make grants to organizations that have secured their own 501(c)(3) and 509(a) Internal Revenue Service rulings and not to make "pass-through" grants to fiscal agents for expenditure by another agency. The foundation does not make grants to individuals; support travel, either by groups or individuals; basic or applied research; for-profit organizations; or advertising. Generally, the foundation will not make grants to: subsidize publications; support conferences, seminars, workshops, or symposia, endowment campaigns or capital funds; or testimonial dinners or fund-raisers. In distributing its grants, the foundation gives most of its attention to those communities in which its parent company has a major facility and a substantial number of employees.

Fiscal Information Total grant amounts given by General Mills Foundation in 1989 were over $6.8 million.

Application Information Proposals to the foundation do not require a prescribed application form. A brief letter, with adequate documentation, is an acceptable application. Such a letter should include: a description of the purpose for which the grant is sought; specific details on how this purpose will be achieved by the grant; description of the constituency which will benefit from the project; evidence that there is a need for the activity or project; evidence that the persons proposing a project are able to carry it to completion; a planned method for evaluating the proposed program after its completion; a specific budget for the project, as well as the operating budget for the organization's current fiscal year, showing anticipated sources of revenue, as well as expenses; a brief description of the organizations requesting support, with a list of its officers and board members; an audited financial statement and the most recent Form 990 (including Schedule A) Income Tax Return of Organizations Exempt from Income Tax; a major donor list for the most recent and the current fiscal years listing the amount of support from each donor and sources of assured or anticipated support for the project proposed; and evidence that the organization requesting support has been granted tax exemption under Section 501(c)(3) of the Internal Revenue Code and is not a private foundation within the meaning of Section 509(a). The foundation earnestly requests that all initial inquiries from prospective applicants be made by mail, not by telephone or by personal visits to the foundation office.

Deadline(s) The General Mills Foundation trustees meet periodically throughout the year. There is, therefore, no "best" time to submit applications to the foundation.

194. General Motors Foundation, Inc.

General Motors Building, Room 13-145
3044 West Grand Boulevard
Detroit, MI 48202-3091
(313) 556-4260

Grants

Program Description The General Motors Foundation makes contributions to local and national organizations. With regard to local contributions, the foundation places primary emphasis on communities in which a significant number of GM employees work and live. Similarly, contributions are made to national organizations that have a broad appeal and are recognized for their excellence. The categories of primary interest to the foundation are education and community relations. Included in the latter category are support for health and welfare, cultural, and various other activities. To promote the participation of minorities in handling its legal affairs, and increase the number of minority lawyers graduating from law schools, GM has created a $600,000 fund at 514 major law schools to assist in the development of minority lawyers.

Eligibility/Limitations The foundation contributes only to publicly supported organizations exempt from federal income tax under section 501(c)(3) of the Internal Revenue Code. The foundation does not generally support endowments or special interest groups or projects.

Fiscal Information In 1989, combined charitable and educational contributions from General Motors and the General Motors Foundation totaled $42.4 million.

Application Information Contribution requests should include: a statement summarizing the expected use of the proposed grant; a copy of the organization's 501(c)(3) IRS determination letter; historical organizational information; detailed budget information for the previous three years; a detailed budget proposal; a list of major annual contributors for the previous three years; and a brief description of the organization's activities and operations for the current year.

Deadline(s) No deadlines are announced.

195. General Semantics Foundation

14 Charcoal Hill
Westport, CT 06880
(203) 226-1394

Project Grants

Program Description Grants are awarded to support research in general semantics. Projects must be specifically in the field of general semantics, or explicitly related to the field of general semantics.

Eligibility/Limitations Applicants must have knowledge of general semantics and present evidence to that effect.

Fiscal Information Stipends range from $300 to $4,500.

Application Information Inquiries should include documentation of ongoing work in general semantics, usually under university support.

Deadline(s) Applications are accepted at any time.

196. General Service Foundation

P.O. Box 4659
Boulder, CO 80306
(303) 447-9541

Program Description The foundation has selected as its areas of concern international peace, population, and resources. Because the foundation's areas of concern are broad, the board has determined guidelines within each area. All applicants are urged to submit only applications coming within the following guidelines. The foundation is interested in making contributions only in the nonmilitary aspects of international peace, particularly as follows: research and education on U.S. international relations that would contribute to international peace; international working groups concerned with increasing understanding and cooperation; policy and program analysis leading to development of alternatives to war; and research and education on the relationships between economic, environmental, and political development and international peace. In the area of population, the primary interest is in making contributions to organizations, tax-exempt under U.S. laws, for population work overseas, preferably in Latin America. Preferred applications include: programs for the introduction and better distribution of family planning information and services, including abortion and voluntary sterilization; programs which improve maternal and child health, family planning, agricultural and economic development; and programs relating to reproductive health care and reproductive rights. Population interests in the United States include programs for primary adolescent pregnancy prevention, family life education, and contraceptive development; and programs relating to reproductive health care and reproductive rights. In the area of resources, the foundation is interested in improving the use, management, and quality of water in the United States, particularly west of the Mississippi River, and developing food, water, fuel, forage, forests, and/or fertilization on a sustainable basis in developing countries, and particularly tied in with family planning education and services.

Sample Grants To support their Caribbean Development Project to establish mechanisms of consultation between Caribbean organizations and U.S. policymakers and assist the Caribbean organizations to develop the skills to communicate their development experiences into policy analysis, $27,500 to The Development Group for Alternative Policies (1988). To support their Security Program, which is examining resource-related conflict and how efficiency in extraction, trade and use of energy and critical materials can enhance national and world security, $30,000 to Rocky Mountain Institute (1988). Continued support to the Reproductive Freedom Project, which uses litigation, public education and policy development to defend reproductive privacy rights for all women, $56,000 to American Civil Liberties Union Foundation (1988). To support the Development Law and Policy Program, which promotes law and policy change in the fields of population, family planning, health and the status of women by providing information, technical assistance and financial support to developing world policymakers, legislators and lawyers, $33,500 to Columbia University, Center for Population and Family Health (1988). To support work on reproductive rights, $19,000 to the National Women's Law Center (1989). To support graduate program in water resources administration, including water law, $5,000 to the Natural Resource Center, University of New Mexico (1989).

Eligibility/Limitations Contributions are made to organizations that are tax-exempt under U.S. laws. The foundation prefers projects and/or programs which give promise of significant contribution and which are new, innovative, demonstrational, and/or research oriented in nature. In general, contributions are not made to operating budgets, or to annual campaigns of established organizations. The foundation does not ordinarily contribute to capital (physical plant, equipment, endowment) to individuals, or for relief.

Fiscal Information Grants paid in 1989 totaled over $1.1 million.

Application Information Contribution policies, guidelines, and application procedures are available from the foundation upon request. There are no specific application forms. Prospective applicants may wish to discuss their particular proposal if they are uncertain as to whether it comes within approved contribution policy and guidelines. If so, please call the foundation.

Deadline(s) March 1 and September 1.

Additional Information The foundation will make occasional contributions to exceptional proposals in the three areas but not coming strictly within the approved guidelines; and, in addition, to specifically approved projects or programs proposed by directors from time to time.

197. The Wallace Alexander Gerbode Foundation
470 Columbus Avenue, Suite 209
San Francisco, CA 94133
(415) 391-0911

Grants

Program Description The foundation's interests generally fall under the following categories: arts, education, environment, health and urban affairs.

Sample Grants To support Tenants Rights Project $10,000 to the Asian Law Caucus, Oakland, CA (1987). To support a film documentary "The Judge Who Changed America: the Life and Times of Earl Warren," $25,000 to the Catticus Corporation, Emeryville, CA (1987).

Eligibility/Limitations The foundation is primarily interested in programs and projects impacting the residents of Alameda, Contra Costa, Marin, San Francisco, and San Mateo counties in California and the state of Hawaii. However, the foundation will, on occasion, and as a second priority, award grants to efforts that it finds to be exceptionally compelling in other northern California communities. The foundation generally does not support: direct services, deficit budgets, general operating funds; building and equipment funds; general fund-raising campaigns, religious purposes, publications, scholarships and grants to individuals.

Fiscal Information Grants in 1988 totaled over $1.9 million.

Application Information The preferred form of contact is a letter of inquiry with a short description of the project and a proposed budget.

Deadline(s) Applications are accepted on an ongoing basis.

198. German Academic Exchange Service (DAAD)
950 Third Avenue, 19th Floor
New York, NY 10022
(212) 758-3223

Legal Studies and Internships—Grants for Young Lawyers

Program Description The German Academic Exchange Service (DAAD) is a private, self-governing organization of the universities in Germany. It was founded in 1925, reestablished in 1950, and has, according to its statutes, the task of promoting international relations between institutions of higher education, especially in the field of academic and scientific exchange. The purpose of the Grants for Young Lawyers program is to familiarize the applicant with the structure and function of German law during a 10-month program in Germany.

Eligibility/Limitations Applicants must have a JD or LLB and have passed the bar exam. Applicants must have good command of German (equivalent to two years of college-level German). The age limit of applicants is 32 years.

Fiscal Information The stipend includes tuition and fees, a monthly allowance and a travel subsidy.

Application Information Requests for application forms must reach DAAD at least two weeks prior to deadline.

Deadline(s) The deadline for applications is April 1.

Additional Information DAAD also sponsors study visits and research grants for faculty, recent Ph.Ds and Ph.D. candidates, and graduate students/graduating seniors. Contact DAAD for further information about these programs.

199. The German Marshall Fund of the United States
11 Dupont Circle, NW, Suite 750
Washington, DC 20036
(202) 745-3950

Environmental Fellowship Program

Program Description The German Marshall Fund, in cooperation with the Institute for European Environmental Policy (IEEP), is offering up to seven short-term fellowships for American environmentalists interested in gaining firsthand knowledge of selected European environmental policies. Fellows will spend three to eight weeks in two or three European countries, under the guidance of the IEEP staff in Bonn, London, and Paris, who will seek to tailor each program to individual interests, background, and experience. Fellows will examine specific issues of environmental policymaking which must be of direct relevance to their current work. Eligible fields of interest include managing the environment, open space conservation, and environmental policy communication and education.

Eligibility/Limitations The fellowship is open to qualified individuals engaged full-time in environmentally oriented activities of either (1) a public or other nonprofit institution or (2) private industry. Applicants must have had at least three years of professional training and experience in one or more of the eligible fields of interest. They must have a good working knowledge of another language (French, German, Italian or Spanish) in addition to English.

Fiscal Information The fellowship provides a weekly stipend of up to $600; one transatlantic round-trip airfare; and a reasonable sum for travel expenses within Europe. Applicants from industry will be requested to contribute 50 percent of their support.

Application Information Applications must include the following: a letter of no more than four pages in length describing the applicant's specific areas of environmental expertise and professional responsibilities, subject matter to be pursued in Europe, ways in which the applicant would disseminate knowledge acquired to other professionals, and language capability; a resume; three professional recommendations focusing on the applicant's qualifications and the potential impact of a fellowships on his or her work in the United States; a letter from the applicant's employer endorsing the request.

Deadline(s) Application deadline is May 15.

200. The German Marshall Fund of the United States
11 Dupont Circle, NW
Washington, DC 20036
(202) 745-3950

Grantsmaking Program

Program Description Three policies govern the fund's grant-making. (1) All projects must address issues important to both nations in Western Europe and the United States and involve persons or institutions on both sides of the Atlantic. Other industrial and developing countries may sometimes be included if the purpose is to reflect their increasing effect on the United States and Europe. The U.S.-European dimension is always primary. (2) Preference is given to projects focused on policy-relevant cross-national comparisons and transfer of experience, especially those projects involving practitioners or policymakers. (3) A plan for dissemination of observations and/or implementation of new approaches must be included. Proposals limited to analysis or research can be considered only if tied closely to dissemination and/or implementation of policy.

Sample Grants For an international workshop on the use of "critical loads" as a means of controlling transboundary air pollution, $40,000 to the Environmental Law Institute, Washington, DC (1988). For a conference in Germany on tax policy issues, $5,000 to the Manhattan Institute for Policy Research, New York, NY (1988). For conference on the Basic Law of the Federal Republic, $12,000 to the University of Pennsylvania, Philadelphia, PA (1989). For a conference in Budapest on reform of the Hungarian constitution and attendant judicial institutions to the American Association for the International Commission of Jurists, Inc., New York, NY (1990).

Eligibility/Limitations Most grants are given to organizations. In general, the fund makes grants in trustee-approved program areas for workshops or conferences (usually binational), trans-atlantic travel/study programs, policy-oriented analysis, public education and information, and short-term travel by individuals and groups. Grants to individuals are, in the main, awarded through publicly announced competitions on the basis of nominations from independent selection committees or for transatlantic travel to participate at conferences.

Fiscal Information The fund expends about $6.3 million a year for grants and related expenses. In the year ending May 31, 1988, 141 grants were made to institutions, with a median commitment of $13,000. In addition, 246 grants were made to individuals; the majority of these resulted from competitions.

Application Information Individuals and institutions seeking support from the fund should first send a brief letter of inquiry outlining: the purpose and policy importance of the project; its international dimensions and potential for cross-national transfer; plans for dissemination of project findings; other potential funding sources; and qualifications of the applicant (a curriculum vitae for individuals; descriptive brochures or annual reports for institutions). Inquiries should be sent to the fund's principal office in Washington.

Deadline(s) Applications for grants are considered throughout the year. Requests which are eligible for funding in excess of $25,000 must be submitted in final form, i.e., must satisfy the substantive requirements of the program officer, at least six weeks before a scheduled meeting of the fund's board of trustees. These meetings take place in early October, mid-February, and late May.

201. The German Marshall Fund of the United States

11 Dupont Circle, NW
Washington, DC 20036
(202) 745-3950

Research Fellowships

Program Description The German Marshall Fund of the United States offers grants for research that seeks to improve the understanding of significant contemporary economic, political, and social developments involving the United States and Western Europe. Projects may focus on either comparative domestic or international issues. Projects should establish the potential importance of their findings either by comparative analysis of a specific issue in more than one country or by an exploration of

that issue in a single country in ways that can be expected to have relevance for other countries.

Sample Grants A fellowship was awarded in support of research on the influence of German ideas on American jurisprudence in the 19th and 20th centuries (1988). A fellowship was awarded in support of research on activist judicial lawmaking in West Germany (1989).

Eligibility/Limitations The fund seeks to assist U.S. scholars at various stages of their academic careers. Applicants must have completed the Ph.D. by the time of application, and should have previously completed substantial research projects which have received critical review. Usually the earlier research experience will have focused on Europe, but, assuming adequate previous preparation, experts on U.S. topics may apply for work on their subject in Europe. The fund particularly wishes to identify great promise in younger scholars whose research accomplishments are outstanding, but perhaps still limited in number and less well known. A younger applicant for a fellowship will, typically, have earned a doctorate two to seven years prior to submitting an application. He or she will be seeking support either to extend dissertation research in new directions or to launch a new research project after publication of research from the dissertation. Senior scholars may also apply. They will be expected to present distinguished records of past research achievements. The fund will not support preparation for any degree.

Fiscal Information A fellowship is intended to allow the recipient to work on research full time, without teaching, administrative, or other professional responsibilities, during an academic term or up to one year. Short-term projects (three months or less) are not eligible for consideration. Within a fixed maximum ($28,000), the fellowships will help meet, but not exceed, a fellow's current income. Additional funds up to $2,000 are provided to cover necessary travel but there is no support for research assistance, computer time, or other project costs. Fellows will be responsible for arranging their own housing, insurance, benefits, and travel (including visas).

Application Information For application forms and additional information contact the fund.

Deadline(s) Applications must be postmarked no later than November 15.

202. The German Marshall Fund of the United States

11 Dupont Circle, NW
Washington, DC 20036
(202) 745-3950

Short-Term Travel Awards

Program Description A limited number of short-term transatlantic travel grants are offered to encourage the exchange of ideas and experience between scholars and practitioners in fields relevant to the fund's program of interests. Awards are made solely to assist participation (i.e., presentation of a paper or scheduled role as discussant) at conferences. Awards can be made to applicants whose participation in a conference fits within one of the fund's program areas. Currently these are U.S.-European economic issues, U.S.-European relations, employment, environment, energy conservation, immigration, and urban issues.

Sample Grants To participate in an international workshop held in Sweden on critical loads for sulfur and nitrogen, a travel grant was awarded to a member of the Environmental Law Institute, Washington, DC (1988). To participate in an international meeting of the Intergovernmental Panel on Climate Change Response Strategies, a travel grant was awarded to a member of the Environmental Law Institute, Washington, DC (1989).

Eligibility/Limitations Eligible applicants include: (1) officials, professionals, and practitioners in government, business, trade unions, public interest groups, and international organizations in Europe and North America who have been invited to participate in an academic or research conference on the other side of the Atlantic; and (2) scholars from universities or research institutions in Europe or North America who have been invited to participate in a conference organized by a government agency, business corporation, trade union, public interest group, or international organization on the other side of the Atlantic. Conferences must take place in North America or Europe. Applicants are eligible for only one award in a two-year period. Awards will not be made for scholars or academics to participate in scholarly or research conferences.

Fiscal Information A maximum award of $1,000 is intended to defray travel expenses (economy class round-trip airfare, local transportation, lodging, meals) and may not cover the entire cost of the trip.

Application Information There are no application forms for this program. Each application must include: a cover letter from the applicant describing his/her role in the conference, relating it to the fund's fields of interest and identifying the importance of the applicant's participation for transatlantic exchange of experience; the applicant's curriculum vitae; an invitation from the conference organizers, on official letterhead, specifying the participation requested and giving dates and purposes of the conference, and additional background information on the conference organizers; and a letter of endorsement from the applicant's supervisor or academic dean, where applicable. Applications should be plainly marked "Short-Term Travel Award."

Deadline(s) Applications must be received by the fund no less than six weeks (and no more than six months) before the conference dates.

203. William T. Grant Foundation

515 Madison Avenue
New York, NY 10022-5403
(212) 752-0071

Research Grants

Program Description The foundation's primary mission is improving children's mental health. It pursues this goal primarily by support of research. The current focus is the field of problem behaviors in the school-age child. Support from the foundation is channeled through five mechanisms: (1) investigator-initiated research; (2) a faculty scholars program; (3) research on community-based social interventions; (4) consortia; and (5) officers' discretionary grants. Research in any discipline is supported, but it is expected that most scholars will come from pediatrics, child psychiatry, education, epidemiology, and the behavioral sciences.

Sample Grants To support the "Community Watch" program, a project which seeks to end discrimination in housing against children with mental disabilities, $200,000 to Mental Health Law Project (1988-1990). In support of coverage of issues affecting children and youth, including reports and commentary of child psychology and child development, education, child health, and children and the law, $75,000 to National Public Radio (1986-1991).

Eligibility/Limitations Grants are limited, without exception, to established tax-exempt organizations and institutions which are described under Section 501(c)(3) of the Internal Revenue Code. Applicant institutions must submit photocopies of their most recent determination letters from the IRS, which must include the applicant's classification under Section 509(a) of the Code, "Private Foundation Status." As a rule, the foundation does not support or make contributions to: building funds; fund-raising drives; or the operating budgets of ongoing service agencies or educational institutions.

Fiscal Information Grants paid in 1988 totaled over $7.6 million. The foundation received 879 applications and funded 98.

Application Information The foundation does not have formal grant application forms. The initial request should be in the form of a letter, briefly describing the project or program, and indicating its financial needs. Alternatively, full research applications may be submitted, but it is preferable to determine if the project falls within the foundation's mission area first. The

application or letter should identify all other agencies to which application has been made for support of the project. If it is determined that the project falls within the current program interests and priorities of the foundation, a full proposal will be requested for further consideration.

Deadline(s) Proposals are reviewed and evaluated by the staff and selected for recommendation to the board of trustees. The board meets four times per year. Applications may be received at any time, although there is no guarantee that the foundation will be able to complete its review in time for the next board meeting.

204. The Daniel and Florence Guggenheim Foundation

950 Third Avenue
New York, NY 10022
(212) 755-3199

Grants

Program Description The foundation's resources are devoted to the promotion, through charitable and benevolent activities, of the well-being of humankind throughout the world. The foundation emphasizes support of projects in the field of criminal justice. Accordingly, requests for grants should only be presented if there is criminal justice content.

Eligibility/Limitations Grants are not awarded to individuals.

Fiscal Information Grants paid in 1988 totaled $356,451.

Application Information Application information is available upon request from the foundation.

Deadline(s) Requests should be received by January 15.

205. The Harry Frank Guggenheim Foundation

527 Madison Avenue
New York, NY 10022-4301
(212) 644-4907

Career Development Awards

Program Description The foundation sponsors a program of research to advance the understanding of human social problems related to dominance, aggression, and violence. Career Development Awards are designed to recognize an outstanding young scientist or academic leader in studies pertinent to the foundation's interests.

Eligibility/Limitations Consideration for a Career Development Award can be initiated only by nomination. Candidates may be from any country. They must be at least three years beyond receipt of the doctorate and not yet 40 years of age by the date on which funding is scheduled to begin. Candidates should have demonstrated outstanding capability and exceptional promise for significant future achievement. In addition, candidates should be investigators with substantial potential to contribute to the foundation's long-term aim to improve the human social condition through a better understanding of the causes and consequences of dominance, aggression, and violence.

Fiscal Information Awards are paid to the recipient's institution with the understanding that suitable space and general facilities will be provided by the institution and that the total amount of the award will be made available to the investigator. The foundation does not contribute to institutional overhead costs. The awards provide salary and research expenses in an amount averaging $37,500 a year for three years.

Application Information Instructions and forms for nominators are available from the Career Development Awards program officer at the address listed above.

Deadline(s) Nominations and supporting material must be submitted by August 1, for a decision in December, and funding to begin in July, August, or September of the following year.

206. The Harry Frank Guggenheim Foundation

527 Madison Avenue
New York, NY 10022-4301
(212) 644-4907

Dissertation Fellowship

Program Description The foundation sponsors an international program of scientific research and scholarly study with a long-term aim to improve the human social condition through a better understanding of the causes and consequences of dominance, aggression, and violence. Awards are made only for research clearly relevant to human dominance, aggression, and violence. The foundation will consider research proposals from any discipline that will further the foundation's intellectual and practical objectives, including but not limited to anthropology, biology, history, psychology, sociology and political science.

Eligibility/Limitations Dissertation Fellowships are awarded each year to individuals who will complete the writing of the dissertation within the award year. Applicants may be citizens of any country and studying at colleges or universities in any country.

Fiscal Information Fellowships carry a stipend of $10,000.

Application Information Additional information and application guidelines are available from the foundation.

Deadline(s) Applications must be received by February 1.

207. The Harry Frank Guggenheim Foundation

527 Madison Avenue
New York, NY 10022-4301
(212) 644-4907

Grants for Research

Program Description The foundation sponsors an international program of scientific research and scholarly study concerning human relationships to one another. The long-term aim is to improve the human social condition through a better understanding of the causes and consequences of dominance, aggression, and violence. Awards will be made only for projects with well-defined aims clearly germane to the human case (but not necessarily restricted to studies of humans). The foundation will consider projects designed to reveal basic physiological mechanisms, processes, and interrelations, or otherwise advance knowledge from any discipline that will further the foundation's intellectual and practical objectives.

Sample Grants Individual supported research on "Reason and Justice in the Behavior of Dominant Groups" (1988). Faculty support for research on "Exclusion from Justice and Destructive Interpersonal Conflict," Columbia University, NY (1988-89).

Eligibility/Limitations Grants are made to individuals for individual projects, not to institutions for institutional programs. Awards may be made either to an institution on behalf of an individual or directly to an individual.

Fiscal Information The foundation expects to make most awards in the range of $15,000 to $30,000 a year for periods of one or two years. Applications for larger amounts and longer durations must be very strongly justified. Requests will be considered for salaries, employee benefits, research assistantships, computer time, supplies and equipment, field work, essential secretarial and technical help, and other items necessary for the successful completion of the project.

Application Information Additional information and application procedures are available from the foundation.

Deadline(s) The biannual deadlines are August 1 and February 1.

208. John Simon Guggenheim Memorial Foundation

90 Park Avenue
New York, NY 10016
(212) 687-4470

Fellowships to Assist Research and Artistic Creation

Program Description To improve the quality of education and the practice of the arts and professions, to foster research, and to provide for the cause of better international understanding, the John Simon Guggenheim Memorial Foundation offers fellowships to further the development of scholars and artists by assisting them to engage in research in any field of knowledge and creation in any of the arts, under the freest possible conditions and irrespective of race, color, or creed.

Sample Grants Support for a law professor for research on the market paradigm, Yale University (1988). Support for a law professor for research on the history of the United States Supreme Court, 1921-1930, University of California, Berkeley, School of Law, CA (1990).

Eligibility/Limitations Fellowships are awarded through two annual competitions: one open to citizens and permanent residents of the United States and Canada, and the other open to citizens and permanent residents of all other American states, of the Caribbean, of the Philippines, and of the French, Dutch, and British possessions in the Western Hemisphere. Fellows are usually between 30 and 45 years of age, but there are no age limits. The fellowships are awarded to men and women of high intellectual and personal qualifications who have already demonstrated unusual capacity for productive scholarship or unusual creative ability in the arts.

Fiscal Information Appointments are ordinarily made for one year, but in no instance for less than six consecutive months. The amount of each grant will be adjusted to the needs of the fellows, considering their other resources and the purpose and scope of their studies. Members of the teaching profession receiving sabbatical leave on full or part salary are eligible for appointment, as are holders of appointments under the Fulbright program, but Guggenheim Fellowships may not be held concurrently with other fellowships. In 1990 the foundation awarded 143 U.S. and Canadian fellowships for a total of $3,765,000. The average grant was for $26,329. There were 3,218 applicants.

Application Information Application forms will be mailed on request.

Deadline(s) Applications for fellowships must be made in writing on or before October 1 by the applicants themselves in the form prescribed. Fellows of the foundation who seek further assistance must apply before October 15 of each year. It should be noted that the foundation does not grant immediate renewals of its fellowships.

209. The George Gund Foundation

One Erieview Plaza
Cleveland, OH 44114-1773
(216) 241-3114

Program Description Foundation trustees have established specific program areas of foundation activity and allocated available foundation funds to each based on priorities which are under periodic review. Currently, these program areas include education, economic and community revitalization, human services, environmental quality, the arts, and civic affairs. Within each of these broad fields, specific focuses for foundation efforts have been selected. Grants in assistance of environmental quality reflect a continuing interest in educational programs related to the environment, the development of more effective public policy, and advocacy, in particular related to the Great Lakes ecosystem and the general field of environmental security. Grants in civic affairs support education and research related to strengthening the effectiveness of governmental organization and functions.

Sample Grants For a joint study with the Citizens League to establish standards of performance for independent public agencies, $35,000 to Governmental Research Institute, Cleveland, OH (1988). For a county government effectiveness study, $50,000 to Cleveland Tomorrow, Cleveland, OH (1988).

Eligibility/Limitations The foundation makes grants only to qualified educational, community service, and philanthropic organizations, as defined under federal and state laws as permissible grantees of private foundations. Grantees must have satisfied, therefore, Internal Revenue Code requirements as nonprofit, tax-exempt agencies having public charity status or be approved as qualified government-related agencies or religious institutions. The foundation does not generally consider grants for "bricks and mortar," equipment, or endowment purposes. Grants for operating budget support will be considered only if the need is for limited duration. The foundation does not make direct awards to individuals.

Fiscal Information In 1988 the foundation made a total of $10.2 million in grant payments.

Application Information All grant applications and requests for information should be addressed to the fund. Although there are no special forms for application, the application should normally be a letter or formal statement, covering the following: an abstract of the proposal, organizational background information, a project description, a budget, and IRS classification.

Deadline(s) Proposals are accepted according to the following deadlines for consideration at the next regularly scheduled meeting of the trustees: January 15 for March consideration, March 30 for June consideration, June 30 for September consideration, and September 30 for December consideration.

210. Hagley Museum and Library

P.O. Box 3630
Wilmington, DE 19807
(302) 658-2400

Advanced Research Fellowships

Program Description These fellowships support independent study in Hagley's fields of interest at its Center for the History of Business, Technology, and Society.

Eligibility/Limitations Scholars from any humanistic discipline or from related social sciences are encouraged to apply. These fellowships are restricted to individuals pursuing advanced research; awards will not be made to degree candidates or to persons seeking support for work leading to a degree. Applicants must be American citizens or have been resident in the United States for three years immediately preceding the term of the fellowship.

Fiscal Information Funded by the National Endowment for the Humanities and the Andrew W. Mellon Foundation, the fellowship carries a maximum stipend of $27,500 for an academic year, and the minimum residency is six months.

Application Information Application forms and additional information are available from the Hagley.

Deadline(s) Completed applications must be received by November 15.

Additional Information Additional fellowships include dissertation fellowships in support of doctoral work in the topical fields of Hagley's research and collecting interest, fellowships in support of research in the arts and industries, regional fellowships, and a residential dissertation fellowship.

211. Hagley Museum and Library

P.O. Box 3630
Wilmington, DE 19807
(302) 658-2400

Grants-in-Aid

Program Description The Hagley Museum and Library announces the availability of grants-in-aid designed to support short-term (two to eight weeks) research in Hagley's imprint, manuscript, pictorial, and artifact collections.

Eligibility/Limitations Grants are available to degree candidates as well as to advanced scholars working in Hagley's areas of collecting and research interest. There is no restriction on the applicant's field of study.

Fiscal Information The grants-in-aid will not exceed $1,000 per month.

Application Information To apply, send the following information to the Executive Administrator, Center for the History of Business, Technology, and Society, Hagley Museum and Library: current curriculum vitae or resume; a brief (one to three pages) description of the research project to be pursued at Hagley (be certain to include a discussion of specific collections, artifacts, buildings, gardens or archaeological digs to be studied, and a statement of purpose for the study, whether for publication, exhibition, restoration, etc.); a statement of the period in which you expect to use the grant; and the amount of stipend requested.

Deadline(s) Applications for grants-in-aid may be submitted throughout the year and will be processed as received. Awards will be made in February, June, and October.

212. The Hague Academy of International Law

Peace Palace
Carnegieplein 2, 2517 KJ, The Hague, the Netherlands

Summer Sessions in International Law

Program Description Every year the academy offers two summer sessions in areas of international law.

Eligibility/Limitations Applicants must be under 40 years of age.

Fiscal Information The amount of the scholarship is paid to the holders by the treasurer of the academy after their arrival at The Hague. In 1990 the amount of a scholarship was 1,300 florins covering general expenses incurred during the three weeks of one of the summer sessions. Traveling expenses are not refunded.

Application Information The academy does not have special application forms. Applicants must submit materials directly to the Secretariat of the academy, and include a statement of his or her surname, first name, qualities, profession, nationality, place and date of birth with a photograph and a statement of the evidence which the applicant considers to be of value in support of his or her candidacy. Every application must be typewritten and accompanied by a recommendation from a professor of international law. The candidate should, if possible, attach copies of any scientific publications. As documents forwarded by applicants are not returned, university certificates or other diplomas must be submitted in the form of copies duly verified by a competent authority.

Deadline(s) All applications must reach the Secretariat on March 1. The summer session for which the candidate wants to be registered should be clearly stated.

Additional Information The academy offers seven residential scholarships for doctoral candidates whose theses are in an advanced stage of preparation. These scholarships are given for a period of two months (from July 1 onwards) to be spent at the academy. These scholarships are meant for candidates from developing countries who reside in their home country and who do not have access to scientific sources. Applications for these scholarships, duly typed out, must be sent to the Secretariat before March 1. They should be accompanied by a recommendation from the professor under whose direction the thesis is being written. The title of the thesis should be mentioned. The thesis may be concerned with either private international law or public international law. The holders of these scholarships will receive an allowance of 75 florins per day. Financial help toward traveling expenses may be granted to participants, taking into account the distance of their country of normal residence.

213. Harvard University Mellon Faculty Fellowships

Lamont Library 202
Cambridge, MA 02138
(617) 495-2519

Andrew W. Mellon Faculty Fellowships in the Humanities

Program Description The Andrew W. Mellon Foundation has provided Harvard University with a grant for a fellowship program to support experienced but nontenured junior faculty in the humanities. The program's primary purpose is to seek out promising humanists in different parts of the United States and to offer them time to develop current research and an opportunity to demonstrate scholarly potential at a critical point in their careers. Applicable fields of study include: Afro-American studies, American studies, classics, comparative literature, English, fine arts, folklore, history, history of science, languages and literature programs, linguistics, music, philosophy, religion, visual and environmental studies.

Eligibility/Limitations Applicants must have the Ph.D., received prior to June 30 of the year preceding the fellowship deadline, and have completed at the time of appointment at least two years postdoctoral teaching in the humanities at the college or university level—usually as assistant professors. Special consideration will be given to candidates who have not recently had access to the resources of a major research university.

Fiscal Information Fellows will hold one-year appointments with departmental affiliation, full access to libraries and other benefits of membership in the Harvard University community. Annual salary will be $30,000.

Application Information Each applicant should submit the following and ensure that all materials have been received by the deadline: a full curriculum vitae; a statement of current research and teaching interests and a proposal describing how these interests might be pursued at Harvard; and two or more letters of recommendation.

Deadline(s) Deadline for applications is November 1.

214. The Hastings Center

255 Elm Road
Briarcliff Manor, NY 10510
(914) 762-8500

Student Intern Program

Program Description The Hastings Center supports sustained, professional investigation of the social and ethical impact of the biological revolution. A resident staff and fellows—representing the natural and social sciences, law, philosophy, theology, and medicine—engage in research and discussion organized around projects in bioethical issues such as abortion, death and dying, aging, neonatal care, allocation of resources, occupational health, health professional-patient relationships, AIDS, surrogate motherhood, and artificial reproduction, etc. The Student Intern Program is open to any student actively pursuing a degree who is interested in doing serious and independent research on ethical issues in medicine, the life sciences, and the professions.

Eligibility/Limitations Applicants should be pursuing a degree. Interns come from undergraduate, professional, and graduate school. The intern's research project must centrally focus on bioethical issues, and he or she must have an adequate prior preparation in bioethics.

Fiscal Information No stipends are available.

Application Information For information and application forms contact the center. The fundamental element of the application for this program is the proposal for a specific research project to be completed during the internship; it is intended to focus the applicants' preparation for their internships and to serve as a basis for their work at the center.

Deadline(s) For January internships, applications should be postmarked by November 15; the summer deadline is April 15.

215. The Hastings Center

255 Elm Road
Briarcliff Manor, NY 10510
(914) 762-8500

Visiting Scholar Program

Program Description The Hastings Center supports sustained, professional investigation of the social and ethical impact of the biological revolution. A resident staff and fellows—representing the natural and social sciences, law, philosophy, theology, and medicine—engage in research and discussion organized around projects in bioethical issues such as abortion, death and dying, aging, neonatal care, allocation of resources, occupational health, health professional-patient realtionships, AIDS, surrogate motherhood and artificial reproduction, genetic engineering, and animal welfare. Visiting scholars are accepted at the center on the basis of their potential contribution to the center's ongoing work and on the likelihood that their stay will be of significant scholarly benefit to them. Though the center is eager to welcome as many scholars as possible, applicants should understand that space is limited and that the availability of space during the requested period of residence will be a consideration. The program is intended to allow senior scholars the opportunity to do independent research at the center on ethical issues in medicine, the life sciences and professions for brief periods of time (a few weeks to six months) and to participate in the center's meetings and projects while in residence.

Eligibility/Limitations This program is open to academic, medical, and legal professionals with advanced degrees.

Fiscal Information The award carries no stipend.

Application Information For information and application forms contact the center.

Deadline(s) No deadlines are announced.

Additional Information The Corporate Fellowship Program permits individuals from the corporate sector to do short-term (one or two weeks) research on a particular ethical issue that has arisen in the setting of their company.

216. The Hearst Foundations

90 New Montgomery Street, Suite 1212
San Francisco, CA 94105
(415) 543-0400

Grants

Program Description The Hearst Foundation, Inc., was founded in 1945 by publisher and philanthropist William Randolph Hearst. In 1948, the California Charities was established. Soon after Mr. Hearst's death in 1951, the name was changed to the William Randolph Hearst Foundation. Both foundations reflect the philanthropic interests of William Randolph Hearst: human services education, health care, and culture. The foundations have established the following priority areas of interest: programs to aid poverty-level and minority groups; education programs with emphasis on private secondary and higher education; health-delivery systems and medical research; cultural programs with records of public support; programs affiliated with religious institutions. Organizations serving larger geographical areas are generally favored over those of a neighborhood or narrow community nature. Charitable goals of the two foundations are essentially the same. For economy they are administered as one. Grant proposals should be addressed to The Hearst Foundations.

Sample Grants For William Randolph Hearst Endowed Scholarships for students who want to work (full or part time) while in law school, $25,000 to the William Mitchell College of Law, Saint Paul, MN (1988).

Eligibility/Limitations Grants from the foundations must be used exclusively for charitable purposes within the United States and its possessions. Grants are not made to individuals. Grants may not be used for political purposes. The foundations do not purchase tickets, tables or advertising for fund-raising events. Grants will be made only to tax-exempt organizations that are not private foundations. Only one proposal is reviewed from an organization within one year.

Fiscal Information Grants totaled over $5 million in 1988.

Application Information The foundations do not have formal application forms. Proposals need not be elaborate and should include the following: amount requested; brief description of basic needs and objectives of project or program; budget showing project costs and how funds will be used; brief history of organization making request; names and primary affiliations of officers and board members; most recent audited financial report; other actual and potential sources of funding; IRS documentation certifying applicant is tax-exempt under section 501(c)(3) and not a private foundation under section 509(a).

Deadline(s) Board meetings on grant decisions are held in March, June, September, and December. Proposals may be submitted throughout the year.

Additional Information Applicants headquartered *east* of the Mississippi River should mail appeals to: The Hearst Foundations, 888 Seventh Avenue, 27th Floor, New York, NY 10106, telephone (212) 586-5404. Applicants headquartered *west* of the Mississippi River should mail appeals to The Hearst Foundations at the address listed above.

217. The William R. and Flora L. Hewlett Foundation
525 Middlefield Road
Menlo Park, CA 94025-3495
(415) 329-1070

Conflict Resolution Program

Program Description Since 1978 the foundation has been interested in encouraging improvements in the ways our society resolves disputes. In 1984 the foundation established the conflict resolution program to support work across disciplines, and in a wide variety of settings. The foundation emphasizes general support grants, intending to devote resources to the development of the field as a whole. Grants are made in three categories: support for theory development; grants to mediation and other practitioner organizations; and support to organizations that train or educate potential users about conflict resolution techniques or otherwise promote the field as a whole.

Sample Grants For general support of the Program on Negotiation, $300,000 to Harvard University, Cambridge, MA (1988). For general support of the Research Center on Conflict Resolution, $150,000 to Stanford University Law School, Stanford, CA (1988). For general support of the Disputes Processing Research Program, $250,000 to the University of Wisconsin, Madison, Institute of Legal Studies, Madison, WI (1988). For general support of the Standing Committee on Dispute Resolution, $125,000 to American Bar Association, Fund for Justice and Education, Los Angeles, CA (1988). For general support of the Institute for Civil Justice, $250,000 to the RAND Corporation, Santa Monica, CA (1989). For alternative dispute resolution activities, $40,000 to the National Judicial College, University of Nevada, Reno, NV (1989).

Eligibility/Limitations Normally, the foundation will not consider support for grants or loans to individuals; grants for basic research; capital construction funds; grants in the medical or health-related fields; or general fund-raising drives. It will not make grants intended directly or indirectly to support candidates for political office or to influence legislation.

Fiscal Information Grants authorized in 1989 in this program category totaled over $3 million. There is no fixed minimum or maximum with respect to the size of grants; applicants should provide a straightforward statement of their needs and aspirations for support, taking into account other possible sources of funding.

Application Information The most efficient means of initial contact with the foundation is a letter of inquiry, addressed to the president. The letter should contain a brief statement of the applicant's need for funds and enough factual information to enable the staff to determine whether or not the application falls within the foundation's areas of preferred interests or warrants

consideration as a special project. Applicants who receive a favorable response to their initial inquiry will be invited to submit a formal proposal.

Deadline(s) Grants must be approved by the board of directors, which meets quarterly. Meeting dates are available upon request, but applicants should realize that even proposals which are recommended for board approval cannot in every case be reviewed at the first meeting following their receipt. All inquiries and proposals are reported to the board, including both those that lie clearly outside the foundation's declared interests and those declined at the staff level.

Additional Information Letters of application will be briefly acknowledged upon their receipt. But because the foundation prefers to operate with a small staff, a more detailed response will in some cases be delayed. Applicants who have not had a substantive reply after a reasonable period of time should feel free to make a follow-up inquiry.

218. The William R. and Flora L. Hewlett Foundation
525 Middlefield Road
Menlo Park, CA 94025-3495
(415) 329-1070

Education Program

Program Description Grants in the education program are made to promote the underlying strengths of recipient institutions rather than to meet their short-term, specific needs. Most of the grants are made in the following categories: grants to strengthen networks of major research libraries; proposals that promise benefits to university presses; and grants to strengthen comprehensive teaching and research programs of academic institutions in the United States and Mexico that focus on relations between these countries.

Sample Grants For a project with El Colegio de Mexico on U.S.-Mexico drug enforcement collaboration, $25,000 to Harvard Law School, Cambridge, MA (1988). For the U.S.-Mexico Transboundary Resources Institute, $300,000 to the University of New Mexico School of Law, Albuquerque, NM (1989). A challenge grant, $300,000 to the Fletcher School of Law and Diplomacy, Tufts University, Medford, MA (1989).

Eligibility/Limitations The foundation does not encourage requests to fund student aid, construction, equipment purchases including computers, education research, basic scientific research, health research, or health education programs. In general, the foundation discourages requests benefiting individual institutions except when these may explicitly relate to other foundation objectives.

Fiscal Information Grants authorized in 1989 for education totaled over $9.7 million. There is no fixed minimum or maximum with respect to the size of grants; applicants should provide a straightforward statement of their needs and aspirations for support, taking into account other possible sources of funding.

Application Information The most efficient means of initial contact with the foundation is a letter of inquiry, addressed to the president. The letter should contain a brief statement of the applicant's need for funds and enough factual information to enable the staff to determine whether or not the application falls within the foundation's areas of preferred interests or warrants consideration as a special project. Applicants who receive a favorable response to their initial inquiry will be invited to submit a formal proposal.

Deadline(s) Grants must be approved by the board of directors, which meets quarterly. Meeting dates are available upon request, but applicants should realize that even proposals which are recommended for board approval cannot in every case be reviewed at the first meeting following their receipt. All inquiries and proposals are reported to the board, including both those that lie clearly outside the foundation's declared interests and those declined at the staff level.

Additional Information Letters of application will be briefly acknowledged upon their receipt. But because the foundation prefers to operate with a small staff, a more detailed response will in some cases be delayed. Applicants who have not had a substantive reply after a reasonable period of time should feel free to make a follow-up inquiry.

219. The William R. and Flora L. Hewlett Foundation
525 Middlefield Road
Menlo Park, CA 94025-3495
(415) 329-1070

Environment Program

Program Description The goals of the environment program are to improve decision-making on environmental issues and to encourage more intelligent and rewarding uses of the natural environment for education, conservation and development. The program includes four categories of grants: support for organizations that produce policy-oriented studies or that disseminate information on a broad range of environmental issues of concern to U.S. policymakers; grants to organizations that study, document, or demonstrate how environmental decision-making process could be improved; grants to selected university and college environmental studies programs at the graduate and undergraduate levels and to university consortiums focused on specific problem areas; and support for a limited number of organizations that conduct coordinated efforts on a national scale to acquire, preserve, or improve the management of unique, ecologically significant land.

Sample Grants For general support, $300,000 to the Environmental Law Institute, Washington, DC (1989). For general support of the Public Policy Program's work on environmental decision-making, $150,000 to UCLA Department of Humanities and Social Sciences, Los Angeles, CA (1987).

Eligibility/Limitations Normally, the foundation will not consider for support grants or loans to individuals; grants for basic research; capital construction funds; grants in the medical or health-related fields; or general fund-raising drives. It will not make grants intended directly or indirectly to support candidates for political office or to influence legislation.

Fiscal Information Grants authorized in 1989 for the environment totaled over $3 million. There is no fixed minimum or maximum with respect to the size of grants; applicants should provide a straightforward statement of their needs and aspirations for support, taking into account other possible sources of funding.

Application Information The most efficient means of initial contact with the foundation is a letter of inquiry, addressed to the president. The letter should contain a brief statement of the applicant's need for funds and enough factual information to enable the staff to determine whether or not the application falls within the foundation's areas of preferred interests or warrants consideration as a special project. Applicants who receive a favorable response to their initial inquiry will be invited to submit a formal proposal.

Deadline(s) Grants must be approved by the board of directors, which meets quarterly. Meeting dates are available upon request, but applicants should realize that even proposals which are recommended for board approval cannot in every case be reviewed at the first meeting following their receipt. All inquiries and proposals are reported to the board, including both those that lie clearly outside the foundation's declared interests and those declined at the staff level.

Additional Information Letters of application will be briefly acknowledged upon their receipt. But because the foundation prefers to operate with a small staff, a more detailed response will in some cases be delayed. Applicants who have not had a substantive reply after a reasonable period of time should feel free to make a follow-up inquiry.

220. The William R. and Flora L. Hewlett Foundation
525 Middlefield Road
Menlo Park, CA 94025-3495
(415) 329-1070

Population Program

Program Description Within this broad field of interest, the foundation plans to continue support of a range of programs, from research on the key variables affecting fertility behavior to efforts to evaluate and implement fertility-reducing development policies. Specific interests are in the following areas: the training of population experts, primarily at university-based population centers; policy-related research on population issues, particularly the relationship of social and economic factors to fertility; and the support of comprehensive family planning services.

Sample Grants For a program to improve judicial education in the field of reproductive issues, $20,000 to the Women Judges' Fund for Justice, Washington, DC (1988).

Eligibility/Limitations The foundation generally provides organizational, rather than project, support. The foundation does not support biomedical research on reproduction or population education programs directed toward the general public.

Fiscal Information Grants authorized in 1989 for population totaled over $7.4 million. There is no fixed minimum or maximum with respect to the size of grants; applicants should provide a straightforward statement of their needs and aspirations for support, taking into account other possible sources of funding.

Application Information The most efficient means of initial contact with the foundation is a letter of inquiry, addressed to the president. The letter should contain a brief statement of the applicant's need for funds and enough factual information to enable the staff to determine whether or not the application falls within the foundation's areas of preferred interests or warrants consideration as a special project. Applicants who receive a favorable response to their initial inquiry will be invited to submit a formal proposal.

Deadline(s) Grants must be approved by the board of directors, which meets quarterly. Meeting dates are available upon request, but applicants should realize that even proposals which are recommended for board approval cannot in every case be reviewed at the first meeting following their receipt. All inquiries and proposals are reported to the board, including both those that lie clearly outside the foundation's declared interests and those declined at the staff level.

Additional Information Letters of application will be briefly acknowledged upon their receipt. But because the foundation prefers to operate with a small staff, a more detailed response will in some cases be delayed. Applicants who have not had a substantive reply after a reasonable period of time should feel free to make a follow-up inquiry.

221. The William R. and Flora L. Hewlett Foundation
525 Middlefield Road
Menlo Park, CA 94025-3495
(415) 329-1070

Regional Grants

Program Description Through the regional grants program, the foundation responds to requests from organizations based in or near the San Francisco Bay area that serve local residents. There are five categories in this program area: community development, youth employment, homelessness, selected human services, and minority leadership development.

Sample Grants For support of the Bay Area Regional Economic Development Project, $47,000, and for general support of the California Community Economic Development Association, $75,000 to the National Economic Development and Law Center, Berkeley, CA (1988). For the Regional Support Center for Homelessness Policy and Programs, $250,000, and for a feasibility study for a Regional Support Center for Homelessness Programs, $25,000 to the Association of Bay Area Governments, Oakland, CA (1988).

Eligibility/Limitations The foundation will consider different types of grants—general, program, or project support. Limited program funds dictate that only a few of the requests reviewed can be supported.

Fiscal Information Regional grants authorized in 1989 totaled over $4.7 million. There is no fixed minimum or maximum with respect to the size of grants; applicants should provide a straightforward statement of their needs and aspirations for support, taking into account other possible sources of funding.

Application Information The most efficient means of initial contact with the foundation is a letter of inquiry, addressed to the president. The letter should contain a brief statement of the applicant's need for funds and enough factual information to enable the staff to determine whether or not the application falls within the foundation's areas of preferred interests or warrants consideration as a special project. Applicants who receive a favorable response to their initial inquiry will be invited to submit a formal proposal.

Deadline(s) Grants must be approved by the board of directors, which meets quarterly. Meeting dates are available upon request, but applicants should realize that even proposals which are recommended for board approval cannot in every case be reviewed at the first meeting following their receipt. All inquiries and proposals are reported to the board, including both those that lie clearly outside the foundation's declared interests and those declined at the staff level.

Additional Information Letters of application will be briefly acknowledged upon their receipt. But because the foundation prefers to operate with a small staff, a more detailed response will in some cases be delayed. Applicants who have not had a substantive reply after a reasonable period of time should feel free to make a follow-up inquiry.

222. The Hitachi Foundation

1509 22nd Street, NW
Washington, DC 20037
(202) 457-0588

Grants

Program Description The Hitachi Foundation has been established to help develop the human resources, skills, and understanding necessary to enrich the lives of individuals in the increasingly complex and technological world of today and tomorrow. The foundation is committed to supporting programs which enable individuals to lead more productive lives and help them to participate with more awareness as citizens in an increasingly international environment. Grants are made to programs that have practical purpose and far-reaching impact. Finally, the foundation encourages proposals that will bring together diverse institutions and organizations to help resolve human and social concerns, to stimulate learning, and to address the humanistic dimension of technological development. The foundation supports the following program areas: community and economic development, education, technology and human resource development, the arts, and museums.

Sample Grants To support a two-year strategic planning and assessment process at the institution, $74,000 to Tufts University, Fletcher School of Law and Diplomacy, Medford, MA (1987).

Eligibility/Limitations Applicant organizations must be tax exempt. The foundation will not consider requests related to: organizations whose activities or policies include specific political purposes; capital improvement projects/building funds; projects in which the primary purpose is publications, conferences, seminars or research; sectarian or denominational religious activities; endowments, fund-raising campaigns, recruitment or advertising; funds for individuals.

Fiscal Information Grants approved in 1989 totaled $910,030.

Application Information A request for funding is considered in two stages. The preliminary stage should be a letter no more than three pages in length. The preliminary request should include the following: a statement of need for the project, and a description of those whom it will serve; a summary of the proposed project activities, its specific purpose, and how the project is an improvement upon present practice; the amount of the grant being requested, and other sources of funds to be committed to the project; a brief description of the applicant organization, its objectives, activities and scope (this may be appended); verification of tax-exempt status. If the proposed project is of interest to the foundation, a more detailed proposal will be invited for formal consideration.

Deadline(s) The foundation will review preliminary requests two times a year. These review periods begin in February and October. Preliminary requests received by the first of February and October will be reviewed and given a response regarding foundation interest within six weeks. Any preliminary requests received after the beginning of each of the review periods will be considered automatically in the following review period.

223. The Honor Society of Phi Kappa Phi

Louisiana State University
P.O. Box 16000
Baton Rouge, LA 70893
(504) 388-4917

Graduate Fellowships

Program Description Fellowships in support of first year graduate work, normally undertaken within the year following receipt of the baccalaureate degree, are awarded by the Honor Society of Phi Kappa Phi.

Eligibility/Limitations Recipients must be active members of Phi Kappa Phi on the date the awards are made. Applications will be accepted from individuals selected for membership but not yet initiated. Applicants must have initiated plans to enroll as a candidate for an advanced degree in a recognized graduate or professional school, preferably in an American college or university. Students registering in a professional school such as law, medicine, or engineering as well as individuals pursuing academic programs in fine, applied, or performing arts are eligible. In general, preference will be given to candidates with a definite purpose of proceeding to the doctorate or other advanced professional degree. The awards are intended for the support of students undertaking first-year graduate study within 12 months of receipt of the baccalaureate degree. However, persons of any age having delayed graduate study for a year or more may compete through the chapter of initiation or chapter of current membership for consideration.

Fiscal Information Awardees may accept fellowships with the full $6,000 stipend, a reduced stipend adjusted on the basis of other financial support, a $500 monetary award, or an award without stipend. It is expected that a person accepting a Phi Kappa Phi Graduate Fellowship with full or partial stipend will devote full time to graduate study. Awardees desiring to hold other remunerative scholarships, assistantships, or fellowships (except for waiver of tuition and/or fees) must obtain prior approval of the Phi Kappa Phi Fellowship Committee.

Application Information Application forms and further information are available upon request.

Deadline(s) Applications must be filed with the secretary of the local chapter by the established deadline (normally February 1) on special forms available from the office of each chapter secretary.

Additional Information Applicants must obtain application forms from the local chapter secretary and then obtain the chapter's nomination to enter the national competition.

224. Hoover Institution on War, Revolution and Peace

Stanford University
Stanford, CA 94305-6010
(415) 723-0603

National Fellows Program

Program Description The National Fellows Program allows particularly gifted younger scholars to spend one full year on unrestricted, creative research and writing at the Hoover Institution. During this period fellows are free from all other academic responsibilities. Accordingly, the fellowships afford scholars a unique opportunity to advance their professional careers by completing an original and significant research project. Research projects deal with both current and historical policy issues in domestic and foreign affairs. Special emphasis is placed on those proposals that consider important policy issues facing the United States today. A fellow may concentrate research and writing in one or more fields of study such as political science, economics, modern history, international relations, law, and sociology. Fellowships are awarded with the clear expectation that the fellows will take advantage of this opportunity to complete a publishable manuscript while in residence at the Hoover Institution.

Sample Grants Fellowship support for "The Political Economy of Cloning Human Beings: Policy Implications on the Light of Legal and Political Theory," Emory University (1989). Fellowship support for "The Novelty Requirement in Patent Law," Graduate School of Public Policy, University of California, Berkeley (1989).

Eligibility/Limitations Candidate qualifications should include a Ph.D. degree or its equivalent, approximately three or four years' experience beyond the doctorate, clear indications of intellectual competence, and promise as a productive scholar.

Fiscal Information Approximately 14 to 16 National Fellowships are awarded each year, 12 national and peace fellows, and four public affairs fellows.

Application Information Admission to the program is based primarily on nomination and recommendation of leading scholars throughout the United States, as well as on submission of a carefully prepared research proposal.

Deadline(s) Applications should be submitted to the executive secretary prior to January 15 of the year for which the fellowship is desired.

225. Hoover Presidential Library Association, Inc.
P.O. Box 696
West Branch, IA 52358
(319) 643-5327

Hoover Presidential Library Fellowship and Grant Program

Program Description The program seeks to encourage scholarly use of the Herbert Hoover Presidential Library. It specifically promotes the study of Herbert Hoover's private and public careers, national public policy issues of the period when Hoover held office (1921-1933), and topics that are supported by related library holdings. With the recent opening of the Lou Henry Hoover Papers, the scope of the fellowship and grant program has been expanded to include research into the professional, political, and social contributions of Lou Henry Hoover. Proposals that do not meet these criteria will not be considered.

Sample Grants For research on "The Selling of Supreme Court Nominees: Politics and the Senate Confirmation Process," to an assistant professor of political science, $1,000, University of Georgia, Athens, GA (1990).

Eligibility/Limitations Current graduate students and postdoctoral researchers are eligible to apply.

Fiscal Information Fellowships of up to $10,000 per applicant will be awarded as stipends for extended postdoctoral research. Grants of up to $1,000 per applicant will be awarded for travel costs and per diem expenses for graduate and postdoctoral research.

Application Information Application forms are available from the association.

Deadline(s) Deadline for receipt of applications is March 1.

226. Houston Endowment, Inc.
P.O. Box 52338
Houston, TX 77052
(713) 223-4043

Grants

Program Description The purpose of the Houston Endowment, Inc., is the support of any charitable, educational, or religious undertaking. The endowment has concentrated much of its interest in the broad field of education.

Sample Grants In support of the Leland Professional Internship Program for Congressional and Senate offices, $50,000 to Center for Public Policy, Houston, TX (1987-88). For scholarships, $409,000 to South Texas College of Law, Houston, TX (1987-88). For educational programs of the Southwestern Law Enforcement Institute, $10,000 to Southwestern Legal Foundation, Dallas, TX (1987-88). For an endowment fund for faculty research, $4 million to University of Texas Law School Foundation, Austin, TX (1987-88).

Eligibility/Limitations Educational institutions are eligible for support.

Fiscal Information In 1987-88 the endowment paid over $46.8 million in grants.

Application Information Applications should be in the form of a letter briefly describing the purposes of the applicant organization, the objectives of the project, and a budget of required expenditures. Proof of tax exemption should be enclosed, together with a statement from the Internal Revenue Service that the applicant is classified as "not a private foundation" under the provisions of the Tax Reform Act of 1969.

Deadline(s) Requests for grants are reviewed at regular monthly meetings of the trustees.

227. Hudson River Foundation
40 West 20th Street, 9th Floor
New York, NY 10011
(212) 924-8290

Grants Program

Program Description The Hudson River Fund is dedicated to supporting scientific, ecological, and related public policy research on issues and matters of concern to the Hudson River, its tributaries and its drainage basin with emphasis given, but not limited to, mitigating fishery impacts caused by power plants, providing information needed to manage the fishery resources of the Hudson River, understanding the factors relating to abundances and structure of fish populations, and gaining knowledge of the condition of the Hudson River ecosystem. To address some of the goals of the Hudson River Fund, the foundation has chosen the following areas for directed research: biology of resource species; base of Hudson River food webs; source, disposition and role of toxic substances; hydrodynamics and sediment transport; education, public policy and decision-making. In this final category, the foundation's purpose is to encourage scientifically sound policies and to help the public better understand and develop policies related to the river. Studies and programs that encourage public awareness of the river in all its aspects, more effective decision-making, and informed conflict resolution are sought. Studies of public policies and decisions, legal disputes, or other public actions significantly affecting the natural resources of the Hudson River are of particular interest.

Eligibility/Limitations Proposals are welcome from individual researchers; researchers at colleges and universities; nonprofit/nonacademic institutions; profit-making institutions; and government (local, state, and federal) agencies.

Fiscal Information There is no funding limit specified for these grants, but annual budgets rarely exceed $75,000.

Application Information Standardized application forms, which should be used for each application, are available from the foundation.

Deadline(s) Proposals are due in the foundation office by 5:00 p.m. E.S.T. on March 15. Notice of the foundation's decision on applications normally will be sent within three to four months of the submission deadline.

Additional Information Travel grants, grants for the study of emergency situations, summer scholarships for graduate and undergraduate students, and graduate fellowships are also available from the foundation. Contact the foundation for information about these additional programs.

228. The S.S. Huebner Foundation for Insurance Education

The Wharton School, University of Pennsylvania
3641 Locust Walk
Philadelphia, PA 19104
(215) 898-5644

Research Grants

Program Description The foundation supports research in the field of risk and insurance.

Eligibility/Limitations Eligible applicants are full-time faculty at colleges and universities in the United States and Canada, who hold terminal degrees such as the Ph.D., D.B.A., or a law degree or are fellows in an actuarial society.

Fiscal Information Grants carry awards of up to $10,000.

Application Information Further information is available on request.

Deadline(s) The deadline for applications is March 1.

229. Immigration History Research Center

University of Minnesota
826 Berry Street
St. Paul, MN 55114
(612) 373-5581

Grants-in-Aid of Research

Program Description The Immigration History Research Center (IHRC) announces a limited number of grants available to qualified scholars wishing to use the center's collections. The IHRC was founded in 1965 with a dual purpose—to encourage study of the role of immigration and ethnicity in shaping the society and culture of the United States and to collect and preserve the records of 24 American ethnic groups originating from Eastern, Central, and Southern Europe and the Near East. The collections consist of all types of manuscript and printed materials, often in the language of the immigrants, and include personal papers; archives of ethnic fraternal associations, mutual aid societies, and cultural organizations; records of immigrant aid organizations such as the American Council for Nationalities Service and the International Institutes; files of more than 650 newspapers and 2,000 periodicals; and thousands of books, almanacs, and albums. Although the collections are primarily historical, their rich diversity makes them valuable for researchers in disciplines such as sociology, political science, linguistics, literature, and folklore.

Eligibility/Limitations Graduate students, faculty, and independent scholars are eligible to apply. Applicants must provide evidence of competence in languages required for research.

Fiscal Information Grants carry an award of up to $750 to help defray travel costs and living expenses for research requiring a minimum of one week at the center.

Application Information Application procedures are available upon request.

Deadline(s) Deadlines for applications are March 1 and September 1.

230. The Institute for Advanced Study

Olden Lane
Princeton, NJ 08540
(609) 734-8000

Visiting Member Awards

Program Description The Institute for Advanced Study is devoted to the encouragement, support, and patronage of learning—of science, in the old, broad, and undifferentiated sense of the word. The academic work of the institute opened with the appointment of its first professors, eminent in pure mathematics and mathematical physics. Later, appointments were made in the various fields of archaeological and historical study and in economics. These initial appointments, like the faculty appointments to be made later, helped to define, though they did not limit, the fields of study at the institute. Although there is no policy of excluding members whose interests are remote from those of any member of the faculty, the institute tends to support with special emphasis fields in which exists a tradition of fruitful activity. At present the academic work of the institute is carried out in four schools. The School of Historical Studies reflects the interests of the faculty: Greek archaeology, epigraphy, Greek philosophy and philology, Roman history, palaeography, medieval history, the history of art, modern history, the history of modern philosophy, American intellectual history, and the history of mathematics and the sciences. The School of Social Science brings together a small number of scholars using the methods and perspectives of the social sciences to examine historical and contemporary materials with the aim of elucidating the processes of social change. Visitors under this program have been drawn from the disciplines of anthropology, economics, history, political science, psychology, linguistics, and sociology, among others. The members of the School of Mathematics are for the most part pure mathematicians, and the members of the School of Natural Sciences are theoretical physicists, astrophysicists, and astronomers. A principal function of the institute is to provide for members who come to the institute for short periods.

Eligibility/Limitations Applicants usually must hold the doctorate. The major consideration in choosing a visiting member is the expectation, based on past performance, that his or her term at the institute will result in work of significance and high quality. The largest number of visiting members are selected because their proposed research project falls within the special interests of one or more faculty. In its selection of members, the institute maintains and always has maintained a nondiscriminatory policy with respect to sex, race, creed, and country of origin. Throughout its history it has invited both men and women to be members and faculty.

Fiscal Information About half of the institute's members are supported by grants-in-aid from funds available to the schools and supplementary specific purpose funds of the institute; the other half are supported by the members' own institutions, by the United States and foreign governments, and by private foundations.

Application Information Most applications arrive unsolicited. Solicited applications do not guarantee appointment. Application information and forms indicating the necessary supporting information are available from the school administration officer in the respective schools.

Deadline(s) Applications should be made by October 15 of the preceding year for the School of Historical Studies, and by December 1 of the preceding year for the School of Social Science.

Additional Information The institute is independent and maintains most of the facilities necessary for academic life. It also relies on a fortunate symbiosis with Princeton University, from which the institute is organically and administratively separate, but with whom it enjoys close academic and intellectual relations. Thus the institute has several libraries, partially adequate for the fields in which faculty and members work; but it also makes use of the libraries of Princeton University and the Princeton Theological Seminary, to which full access is available, as well as the libraries and museums of other institutions and those of both Philadelphia and New York.

231. Institute for Humane Studies
George Mason University
4400 University Drive
Fairfax, VA 22030
(703) 323-1055

Leonard P. Cassidy Summer Fellowships in Law and Philosophy

Program Description The purpose of these fellowships is to promote research in jurisprudence.

Eligibility/Limitations Eligible applicants include graduate students in accredited law or philosophy programs.

Fiscal Information The fellowships carry an award of $4,000.

Application Information For more information contact the institute.

Deadline(s) The deadline for application is February 15.

232. Institute for Humane Studies
George Mason University
4400 University Drive
Fairfax, VA 22030
(703) 323-1055

Claude R. Lambe Fellowships

Program Description The purpose of these fellowships is to support outstanding students with a demonstrated interest in the classical liberal tradition intent on pursuing an intellectual/scholarly career in the social sciences, law, humanities, or journalism.

Eligibility/Limitations Eligible applicants include graduate students/undergraduates with junior or senior standing in the next academic year at accredited colleges and universities.

Fiscal Information The fellowships carry an award of $10,000.

Application Information For more information contact the institute.

Deadline(s) The deadline for application is January 15.

233. Institute for Humane Studies
George Mason University
4400 University Drive
Fairfax, VA 22030
(703) 323-1055

John M. Olin Fellowships

Program Description The purpose of these fellowships is to support outstanding students with a demonstrated interest in the principles of a free society who are taking advanced degrees at Oxford University, Cambridge University, or the University of London.

Eligibility/Limitations Eligible applicants are graduate students in economics, law, government, history, political science, or philosophy who are U.S. citizens.

Fiscal Information The fellowships carry awards up to $16,500.

Application Information For more information contact the institute.

Deadline(s) Deadline for application is December 15.

234. Institute for Research on Poverty
University of Wisconsin-Madison
1180 Observatory Drive, 3412 Social Science Building
Madison, WI 53706
(608) 262-6358

Small Grants and Sabbatical Grants Program

Program Description Two broad questions define the area of invited empirical research. First, to what degree have private and government efforts in the United States succeeded in preventing or alleviating poverty and related problems? To what extent have changes in the economy or in society (e.g., in family and household structure, in the legal system) influenced the effectiveness of these efforts? Second, what have been the intended and unintended consequences of government intervention against poverty in the United States? These questions can be addressed from a variety of disciplines—anthropology, economics, history, law, philosophy, political science, psychology, public administration, sociology, social work—and can employ either quantitative, qualitative, or ethnographic data. Cross-national perspectives may be included. Use of new data sets and methodologies is encouraged.

Sample Grants For research on "Determinants of Child Support Outcomes" Old Dominion University (1989).

Eligibility/Limitations Researchers who have received salary support from the institute within the last five years are ineligible to apply. Assistance received while a graduate student is not considered salary support. Previous small grant winners are ineligible. Grants are made to individuals only and not to their institutions. Applicants must hold the doctorate or the highest degree appropriate for their discipline.

Fiscal Information Small grants will cover the equivalent of up to two months of salary (usually for a summer) and will be paid as a personal services contract. No overhead or fringe benefits will be paid. The grant will cover round-trip travel expenses to and from Madison, but not living expenses for those who are in residence in Madison. Sabbatical grants cover the equivalent of up to 4.5 months of salary.

Application Information Contact the institute for additional information and application guidelines.

Deadline(s) Applications sent by mail must include six copies and be postmarked by February 16.

235. Institute for the Study of World Politics
Fellowship Competition
1755 Massachusetts Avenue, NW, Suite 500
Washington, DC 20036

Fellowships

Program Description Fellowships promote scholarly examination of political, economic, and social issues that affect the security, well-being, and dignity of the peoples of the world. The range of topics of interest to the institute is necessarily quite broad. The following general categories indicate its concerns: Limitation of strategic nuclear arms, control of the proliferation of nuclear weapons, and restriction of the growing traffic in conventional weapons. Development of means for the prudent and equitable distribution and management of technology, raw materials, energy, food, and other resources, and development of more stable balances between these factors, population growth and migration, and the capacities of the natural environment. Improvement of levels of health, nutrition, education, economic security, and social welfare within the developing countries, and establishment of more stable, mutually beneficial relationships between North and South. Definition and recognition of fundamental human rights and development of more effective international mechanisms for the protection of such rights.

Eligibility/Limitations Institute fellowships are awarded to (1) doctoral candidates conducting dissertation research—but not to graduate students at earlier stages of work, and (2) postdoctoral scholars undertaking special research projects.

Fiscal Information Fellowships vary in amount according to the recipients' needs and resources. They are awarded for periods of three to nine months, may include funds for travel or other field-research costs if these are essential to the study, and may be combined with support from other sources.

Application Information Application forms and additional information are available from the institute.

Deadline(s) Applications must be postmarked no later than February 16.

236. Institute of Current World Affairs—The Crane-Rogers Foundation

Wheelock House, 4 West Wheelock Street
Hanover, NH 03755
(603) 643-5548

Fellowship Program

Program Description The purpose of the institute is to identify an area or issue of the world outside the United States in need of in-depth understanding and then to select a young person of outstanding promise and character to study and write about that area or issue for a minimum fellowship period of two years.

Eligibility/Limitations The institute provides fellowships to individuals of varied academic and professional backgrounds. Fellows are expected to have finished their formal education.

Fiscal Information Fellowships provide full support for periods ranging from two to four years. Fellowships are not awarded to support work toward academic degrees nor to underwrite specific studies or programs of research as such. In 1989 $187,767 was spent on fellowships and grants.

Application Information The institute has no application forms for fellowships. Instead, candidates are invited to write to the executive director, enclosing a resume or curriculum vitae and explaining briefly the personal background and professional experience that would qualify them for fellowships of their own devising or for study of the fellowship areas supported.

Deadline(s) Applications may be submitted at any time.

Additional Information From time to time, the institute offers a series of fellowships focused on continuing themes or specific issues. One such series, known as Forest & Man Fellowships, offers people with graduate degrees in forestry or forest-related specialities an opportunity to broaden their understanding of the relationship of forest-resource problems to humans, including policymakers, environmentalists, peasants, scientists and forest-product industrialists.

237. Institute of International Education

809 United Nations Plaza
New York, NY 10017-3580
(212) 984-5330

Fulbright Fixed Sum Grants

Program Description The Institute of International Education is under contract to the U.S. Information Agency to organize publicly, receive and process applications, and, through its National Screening Committee, make recommendations to the Board of Foreign Scholarships for graduate study grants under the Fulbright Program. Under agreements with foreign governments, universities and private donors, the institute performs the same functions with regard to grants sponsored by them. Fulbright Fixed Sum Grants provide a fixed sum payment in U.S. dollars for predoctoral study or research abroad.

Eligibility/Limitations Applicants must be U.S. citizens and have received the majority of their high school and undergraduate college education at educational institutions in the United States. Applicants must hold a B.A. degree or the equivalent before the beginning date of the grant. Applicants may not hold a doctoral degree at the time of application, but may hold a J.D. at the time of application. Applicants must have sufficient proficiency in the written and spoken language of the host country to communicate with the people and to carry out the proposed study. Such proficiency is especially important to students wishing to undertake projects in the social sciences and humanities. Although the majority of these grants are reserved for graduate students who, in most cases, will be engaged in research for the doctoral dissertation, it is the policy of the Board of Foreign Scholarships that awards also be available to

other graduate students, graduating seniors, and candidates who wish to further their careers in the creative and performing arts.

Fiscal Information Most grants will be awarded for programs of study or research that will require an academic year. Grant amounts vary from country to country. In certain countries, grantees who, upon arrival, can submit proof that they have been admitted to doctoral candidacy and have completed all requirements except the writing of their dissertations may receive higher stipends.

Application Information Application forms and additional information are available from IIE. Before filling out an application, a prospective candidate should confirm that there will be awards in the country in which he or she is interested. Applicants who are enrolled in U.S. colleges and universities should contact their Fulbright Program Advisers for the latest information. Others should write to IIE.

Deadline(s) Requests for applications received after October 15 will not be honored. Receipt deadline is October 31.

238. Institute of International Education

809 United Nations Plaza
New York, NY 10017-3580
(212) 984-5330

Fulbright Full Grants

Program Description The Institute of International Education is under contract to the U.S. Information Agency to organize publicly, receive and process applications, and, through its National Screening Committee, make recommendations to the Board of Foreign Scholarships for graduate study grants under the Fulbright Program. Under agreements with foreign governments, universities and private donors, the institute performs the same functions with regard to grants sponsored by them.

Eligibility/Limitations Applicants must be U.S. citizens and have received the majority of their high school and undergraduate college education at educational institutions in the United States. Applicants must hold a B.A. degree or the equivalent before the beginning date of the grant. Applicants may not hold a doctoral degree, but may hold a J.D. at the time of application. Applicants must have sufficient proficiency in the written and spoken language of the host country to communicate with the people and to carry out the proposed study. Such proficiency is especially important to students wishing to undertake projects in the social sciences and humanities.

Fiscal Information Most grants will be awarded for programs of study or research that will require an academic year. Full grants provide round-trip transportation, language or orientation courses (where appropriate), tuition, books, maintenance for one academic year in only one country, and limited health and accident insurance. Most of these benefits are payable in local currency. The maintenance allowance is based on living costs in the host country and is sufficient to meet the normal expenses of a single person.

Application Information Application forms and additional information are available from IIE. Before filling out an application, a prospective candidate should confirm that there will be awards in the country in which he or she is interested. Applicants who are enrolled in U.S. colleges and universities should contact their Fulbright Program Advisers for the latest information. Others should write to IIE.

Deadline(s) Requests for applications received after October 15 will not be honored. Receipt of application is October 31.

239. Institute of International Education

809 United Nations Plaza
New York, NY 10017-3580
(212) 984-5330

Fulbright Travel Only Grants

Program Description The Institute of International Education is under contract to the U.S. Information Agency to organize publicly, receive and process applications, and, through its National Screening Committee, make recommendations to the Board of Foreign Scholarships for graduate study grants under the Fulbright Program. Under agreements with foreign governments, universities and private donors, the institute performs the same functions with regard to grants sponsored by them. In general, Fulbright Travel Grants are tied to specific maintenance and tuition scholarships and may not used to supplement awards other than these.

Eligibility/Limitations In general, applicants must be candidates for Fulbright maintenance and tuition scholarships. Travel Only Grants are available only to Belgium, Finland, France, Germany, Italy, Korea, or New Zealand.

Fiscal Information Travel Grants provide round-trip transportation to the country where the student will pursue studies for an academic year, health and accident insurance, and the cost of an orientation course abroad, if applicable.

Application Information Application forms and additional information are available from IIE. Before filling out an application, a prospective candidate should confirm that there will be awards in the country in which he or she is interested. Applicants who are enrolled in U.S. colleges and universities should contact their Fulbright Program Advisers for the latest information. Others should write to IIE.

Deadline(s) Requests for applications received after October 15 will not be honored. Receipt of application is October 31.

240. Institute of International Education
International Human Rights Internship Program
1400 K Street NW, Suite 650
Washington, DC 20005
(202) 898-0600

International Human Rights Internships Program

Program Description The goals of this program are to provide individuals with practical training in international human rights implementation; to support the efforts of international human rights organizations; and to strengthen the international network of individuals trained in human rights work. The program arranges one-year fellowship placements with organizations in the United States, Europe, Africa, Asia and Latin America. A very small number of short-term placements of two to three months may be considered on a case-by-case basis for individuals and organizations in Africa, Asia, and Latin America.

Eligibility/Limitations Qualified individuals of all nationalities are eligible to apply.

Fiscal Information A fellowship grant covers international travel, a basic living stipend and health insurance for a fellow. It does not provide support for spouses or families. Grants vary depending on the location of the fellowship, ranging normally from $5,000 to $15,000 for a one-year fellowship.

Application Information For information and an application form write to the program director at IIE.

Deadline(s) Annual application deadline for organizations is July 31. Annual application deadline for individuals is August 31.

241. Institute of World Affairs
375 Twin Lakes Road
Salisbury, CT 06068
(203) 824-5135

Summer Seminars

Program Description Each year the Institute of World Affairs brings together students, scholars, and professionals from the United States and other countries to explore topics of contemporary significance and to strengthen international contacts.

Eligibility/Limitations There will be no more than 25 participants, roughly one-third from the United States and the rest from other countries. Admission is without regard to race, color, creed, or sex. The seminar is not designed for those who wish to

engage in extensive research. Young professionals, graduate students, and exceptional students from all parts of the world are encouraged to apply.

Fiscal Information Some scholarship help is available.

Application Information For further information, application blanks and copies of brochures, call or write the institute.

Deadline(s) Contact the institute for deadlines.

242. Inter-American Bar Foundation
1819 H Street, NW, Suite 310
Washington, DC 20006
(202) 293-1455

Program Description The Inter-American Bar Foundation offers facilitative services for lawyers with five years of experience who want to study law overseas. The foundation will place lawyers with law offices in foreign countries.

Application Information Individuals interested in legal exchanges should contact the foundation.

243. Inter-American Foundation
IAF Fellowship Program
P.O. Box 9486
Arlington, VA 22209-0486
(703) 841-3800

Doctoral Program for Field Research

Program Description The Inter-American Foundation awards fellowships for doctoral dissertation field research on grassroots development topics in Latin America and the Caribbean. More than half of the fellowships will be awarded in disciplines other than anthropology and sociology.

Sample Grants Support for research on "The Experience of Violence: Order, Disorder, and Social Discrimination in Brazil" (1989). Support for research on "Livestock Contractual Arrangements in the Mexican Tropics: Dynamics and Consequences for the Poor" (1989).

Eligibility/Limitations Fellowships are open to candidates from the social sciences, physical sciences, technical fields, and the professions. Applicants from Latin America, the Caribbean or the United States must be enrolled in U.S. universities, must have completed all other degree requirements, must write and speak the local language, and must establish a formal affiliation with an appropriate Latin American or Caribbean institution.

Fiscal Information Fellowship are granted for a maximum of 18 months.

Application Information Application forms may be obtained by writing to the foundation.

Deadline(s) Applications are due by December 5.

244. Inter-American Foundation
IAF Fellowship Program
P.O. Box 9486
Arlington, VA 22209-0486
(703) 841-3800

Master's Program for Field Research

Program Description The Inter-American Foundation awards fellowships to master's-level students to conduct up to six months of field research in Latin America and the Caribbean on grassroots development topics. Other eligible graduate students include, for example, those studying law or medicine, as well as those conducting predissertation field research.

Sample Grants Support for research on "The Participation of Small-Scale Farmers in the Management of Irrigation Water: The Case of Mendoza, Argentina" (1989).

Eligibility/Limitations Applicants from Latin America, the Caribbean or the United States must be enrolled in U.S. universities, must write and speak the local language, and must establish a formal affiliation with an appropriate local institution.

Fiscal Information Fellowships are granted for a maximum of six months.

Application Information Application forms, help in contacting campus screening committees, and further information about selection procedures can be obtained by writing the foundation.

Deadline(s) The application deadline is March 1 each year for foundation support beginning after May 1 and before the following April 30.

245. International Foundation of Employee Benefit Plans

18700 West Bluemound Road, P.O. Box 69
Brookfield, WI 53008-0069
(414) 786-6700

Graduate Grants for Research on Employee Benefits

Program Description The foundation wishes to encourage research on employee benefits topics. Awards are offered to graduate students for original research on health care benefits, retirement and income security, and other aspects of employee benefits systems.

Eligibility/Limitations Applicants must be citizens of the United States and pursuing a graduate degree from an accredited college or university. Graduate students must have received approval of the thesis topic from their thesis advisor. The following academic disciplines are appropriate backgrounds for grant applicants: business and finance; labor and industrial relations; economics; law; and social/health sciences.

Fiscal Information Grants do not exceed $5,000 for a 12-month period and may be held concurrently with other grants and forms of support.

Application Information Applicants must submit a proposal not to exceed 20 typed, single-spaced pages. In addition to describing the intended topic of study and its potential significance for employee benefits, proposals should include the methodology to be used, the estimated cost of doing the study and the expected timetable for completion. Applicants also are required to provide two letters of recommendation, one of which should be from the thesis or dissertation adviser.

Deadline(s) There is no deadline for submission. Applications will be reviewed within 60 days of receipt.

246. International Foundation of Employee Benefit Plans

18700 West Bluemound Road, P.O. Box 69
Brookfield, WI 53008
(414) 786-6700

Postdoctoral Grants for Research on Employee Benefits

Program Description Awards support original research on employee benefit topics, including health benefits, retirement and income security, and other aspects of the employee benefits system.

Sample Grants Support for research on "Parental Leave: Judicial and Legislative Trends: Current Practices in the Workplace" (1989). Support for research on "Private Employers' Potential Legal Liability for Cost Containment Provisions" (1989).

Eligibility/Limitations Applicants must be citizens of the United States, hold a terminal degree from an accredited institution and be employed by a nonprofit educational or research institution. Applicants from all disciplines are eligible; however, backgrounds in business and finance, labor/industrial relations, economics, law or the social/health sciences are likely to be most appropriate.

Fiscal Information Grants do not normally exceed $10,000 for a 12-month period.

Application Information Applicants must submit a proposal not to exceed 20 typed, single-spaced pages. In addition to describing the intended topic of study and its potential significance for employee benefits, proposals should include the methodology to be used, the estimated cost of doing the study, and the expected timetable for completion.

Deadline(s) There is no deadline for submission. Applications will be reviewed within 60 days of receipt.

247. International Research & Exchanges Board

126 Alexander Street
Princeton, NJ 08540-7102
(609) 683-9500

Developmental Fellowships: Disciplinary Fellowships

Program Description The International Research & Exchanges Board (IREX) offers fellowships to faculty, postdoctoral researchers, and Ph.D. candidates for Soviet or East European language and area studies. This program prepares fellows to undertake field research in the USSR and Eastern Europe and to establish working relationships with Soviet and East European colleagues and institutions. By enabling scholars in a variety of disciplines to use Soviet and East European sources and materials, IREX seeks to stimulate research on these countries. Disciplinary fellowships are open to applicants outside of Soviet and East European studies in fields such as archaeology, anthropology, business, economics, geography and demography, law, musicology, political science, psychology, and sociology, to gain the language and area background necessary to conduct research in the USSR and Eastern Europe.

Eligibility/Limitations Applicants must be U.S. citizens planning doctoral dissertations or postdoctoral research requiring field access to the USSR or Eastern Europe. Fellows are required to apply to an appropriate IREX program following their tenure as Developmental Fellows.

Fiscal Information Applicants may apply for academic tuition, language training or tutoring, stipend, and research allowance.

Application Information Contact IREX by mail or phone indicating the: program for which an application is contemplated; academic affiliation or job title; highest degree and date received; age; citizenship; proposed time abroad; field of specialization; and the proposed project.

Deadline(s) The deadline for application is February 15.

248. International Research & Exchanges Board

126 Alexander Street
Princeton, NJ 08540-7102
(609) 683-9500

Developmental Fellowships: Fellowships in the Study of Soviet Nationalities

Program Description The International Research & Exchanges Board (IREX) offers fellowships to faculty, postdoctoral researchers, and Ph.D. candidates for Soviet language and area studies. This program prepares fellows to undertake field research in the USSR and is open to applicants with a strong background in Soviet-area studies who propose to undertake language and related studies in the non-Russian republics of the USSR.

Eligibility/Limitations Applicants must be U.S. citizens planning doctoral dissertations or postdoctoral research requiring materials available through exchange participation. Applicants must be faculty members, postdoctoral researchers, or Ph.D. candidates.

Fiscal Information Applicants may apply for academic tuition, language training or tutoring, stipend, and research allowance.

Application Information Contact IREX by mail or phone indicating the program for which an application is contemplated; academic affiliation or job title; highest degree and date received; age; citizenship; proposed time abroad; field of specialization; and the proposed project.

Deadline(s) The application deadline is February 15.

249. International Research & Exchanges Board

126 Alexander Street
Princeton, NJ 08540-7102
(609) 683-9500

Developmental Fellowships: Fellowships to Develop Dual-Area Competence

Program Description The International Research & Exchanges Board (IREX) offers fellowships to faculty, postdoctoral researchers, and Ph.D. candidates for Soviet or East European language and area studies. Fellowships to Develop Dual-Area Competence are open to applicants with expertise in a specific world region who propose to develop competence in a second world region for the purpose of comparative research. One of these regions must be the USSR or East Europe. Projects may include comparative study of two East European countries.

Eligibility/Limitations Applicants must be U.S. citizens planning doctoral dissertations or postdoctoral research requiring materials available through exchange participation. Applicants must be faculty members, postdoctoral researchers, or Ph.D. candidates.

Fiscal Information Applicants may apply for academic tuition, language training or tutoring, stipend, and research allowance.

Application Information Contact IREX by mail or phone indicating the program for which an application is contemplated; academic affiliation or job title; highest degree and date received; age; citizenship; proposed time abroad; field of specialization; and the proposed project.

Deadline(s) The application deadline is February 15.

250. International Research & Exchanges Board

126 Alexander Street
Princeton, NJ 08540-7102
(609) 683-9500

Grants for Collaborative Activities and New Exchanges

Program Description To encourage the development of individual and institutional collaboration and exchanges involving humanists and social scientists, the International Research & Exchanges Board (IREX) makes grants in support of specific collaborative projects and new exchanges. Such undertakings as bilateral and multinational symposia, collaborative and parallel research, joint publications (but not publication costs), exchanges of data, comparative surveys, jointly designed software, and the like, as well as brief visits necessary in the planning of such projects, will be considered for funding.

Sample Grants Support for research on "Perceptions of Justice in East and West" (1989).

Eligibility/Limitations Applicants must present evidence that they will be received by the appropriate institutions in one of these countries and that appropriate scholars are prepared to consider the proposed project or exchange. In the case of university-sponsored exchanges between students and faculty, IREX will support the initial planning of such programs, but will not finance the resulting exchanges.

Fiscal Information Applicants may request economy (APEX, when applicable) round-trip airfare and ground expenses as needed. Recipients may be funded in full or in part, depending on funding levels and numbers of applicants.

Application Information Application materials are available by calling IREX or by writing.

Deadline(s) The application deadlines are October 1, February 1, and June 1.

251. International Research & Exchanges Board

126 Alexander Street
Princeton, NJ 08540-7102
(609) 683-9500

Grants for Independent Short-Term Research

Program Description This program is designed for U.S. scholars in the humanities and social sciences to pursue their individual research. Preference generally will be given to proposals for short-term follow-up research by scholars with prior field experience.

Sample Grants Support for interviews and research concerning the Soviet arbitrazh system of deciding economic disputes between state enterprises and cooperatives, (1989). Support for research in the USSR on the role of the Soviet lawyer in the Soviet justice system (1989).

Eligibility/Limitations Awards are for special short-term travel, normally one- or two-week stays by U.S. citizens who have the Ph.D. or an equivalent professional degree and need support for humanities or social sciences projects. In order to encourage wider participation in East-West scholarly contacts, grants may be awarded to U.S. scholars outside the field of Soviet and East European Studies. Grant recipients are responsible for their own visa, travel, and academic arrangements.

Fiscal Information Recipients may receive full or partial provision for round-trip airfare and stipend support of up to two weeks, depending upon the level of funding and the number of applications.

Application Information Application materials are available by calling IREX at the number listed above.

Deadline(s) Application deadlines are October 1, February 1, and June 1.

252. International Research & Exchanges Board

126 Alexander Street
Princeton, NJ 08540-7102
(609) 683-9500

Individual Advanced Research Exchanges: U.S.S.R.

Program Description This program supports short-term and long-term advanced research exchanges with the U.S.S.R. Short-term exchanges last from two to five months; preference is given to faculty-level applicants. Long-term exchanges last from one semester to one academic year; applications are encouraged from all academic levels from senior graduate students to full professors.

Sample Grants Support for research on "Specific Features of Conflicting Laws in the U.S." (1988).

Eligibility/Limitations Applicants should be U.S. citizens and, normally, have full-time affiliation with a North American college or university and be faculty members or advanced doctoral candidates who will have completed all requirements for the Ph.D. (or equivalent professional degree) except the thesis by the time of participation. Many scholars not academically employed, and candidates for the M.A. degree may also be qualified if they are proposing professional-level, independent research projects. Inquiries about eligibility are welcome.

Fiscal Information The program supports periods of stay abroad between two and ten months. The academy prefers that scholars not plan exchange participation during the summer months. The Academy of Sciences provides housing, medical coverage, and a per diem ruble allowance. The academy has agreed to assist in providing suitable accommodations for accompanying family members. IREX provides domestic and international transportation for participants; for graduate students, a small monthly maintenance allowance in addition to host country stipend; and for salaried participants, a partial stipend-in-lieu-of-salary less the value of housing and other benefits received from the host country. Stipends are adjusted to take into account such other resources as fellowships, sabbatical salaries, etc.

Application Information Graduate students should obtain forms from the office of the graduate dean at the school where they are enrolled. Faculty-level applicants should obtain forms from their employing institutions. In both cases, applicants submit them directly to those institutions and not to the Department of Education.

Deadline(s) Application deadline is October 15.

253. International Research & Exchanges Board
126 Alexander Street
Princeton, NJ 08540-7102
(609) 683-9500

Individual Research Exchanges: Eastern Europe

Program Description The International Research & Exchanges Board (IREX) conducts research exchange programs open to applicants in all disciplines with Bulgaria, Czechoslovakia, Germany, Hungary, Poland, Romania, and Yugoslavia.

Sample Grants Support for research on "The Search for Industrial Community: the Theory and Practice of German Labor Law, 1918-1945" (1988). Support for research on "An Analysis of Property Rights Structures in East-West Industrial Cooperation" (1988).

Eligibility/Limitations Applicants should be U.S. citizens, have command of the language of the host country sufficient for research, and, normally, have full-time affiliation with a North American college or university and be faculty members or advanced doctoral candidates who will have completed all requirements for the Ph.D. (or equivalent professional degree) except the thesis by the time of participation. Many scholars not academically employed and candidates for the M.A. degree may also be qualified if they are proposing professional-level independent research projects. Inquiries about eligibility are welcome.

Fiscal Information IREX provides domestic and international transportation; a monthly allowance for graduate students and one-half salary prorated for the grant period for salaried participants; a contribution for family airfare for married grantees with family accompanying for four or more months—graduate students in this category also receive a family maintenance allowance; and allowances for passport, visa fees, and excess baggage expenses. Stipends are adjusted to take into account such other resources as fellowships, sabbatical salaries, etc. Host countries provide a stipend in local currency and book and microfilm allowances. With the exception of Yugoslavia, where only a nominal housing allowance is provided and IREX also pays a housing allowance, host countries pay for housing for the participant and accompanying dependents. Medical and dental care is provided for participants and accompanying dependents except in Germany and Yugoslavia, where medical and dental care is provided for participants only. Details of host support vary from country to country and may vary from year to year. Current information is included in application materials.

Application Information Contact IREX for application guidelines and additional information.

Deadline(s) The application deadline is October 15.

254. International Research & Exchanges Board
126 Alexander Street
Princeton, NJ 08540-7102
(609) 683-9500

Individual Research Exchanges: Mongolian People's Republic

Program Description In May 1988 IREX established a formal exchange of scholars between the United States and the Mongolian People's Republic. The agreement provides for the exchange annually of up to 10 scholars on each side for a total of 20 months and is scheduled to begin in 1990.

Eligibility/Limitations Applicants should be advanced graduate students and specialists holding the Ph.D. or equivalent degree.

Initially preference will be given to established scholars who have demonstrated interest in Inner Asia.

Fiscal Information Exchanges are for from two to ten months. IREX provides domestic and international transportation; for graduate students, a small monthly maintenance allowance in addition to host country stipend; and for salaried participants, a small stipend-in-lieu-of-salary less the value of host country provisions. The host country provides housing, medical care, and a monthly tugrik allowance. All stipends are adjusted to take into account such other resources as fellowships, sabbatical salaries, etc.

Application Information Contact IREX for application guidelines and additional information.

Deadline(s) The application deadline is October 15.

255. International Research & Exchanges Board
126 Alexander Street
Princeton, NJ 08540-7102
(609) 683-9500

Travel Grants for Senior Scholars

Program Description This grant program is designed to support U.S. scholars in the humanities and social sciences who have received formal invitations from an appropriate institution in the Soviet Union, East Europe, or the Mongolian People's Republic. Invitations should be from institutions such as an academy of sciences, a related institution or a university. The grants are intended for the purposes of consultation and/or lecturing and familiarization by a U.S. scholar at the invitation of the host country. Attendance or participation at international conferences is ineligible, unless such conferences have an East-West issue as their main concern.

Sample Grants Support for travel to deliver a series of lectures at the Adam Mickiewicz University of Poznan on legal aspects of government control of transborder communications in the United States. Support for travel to lecture at the University of Lodz in Poland on modern philosophic and jurisprudential underpinnings of a decentralized legal system and economy (1989).

Eligibility/Limitations Applicants should be U.S. citizens and must have received a formal invitation from an appropriate institution in one of the above named countries.

Fiscal Information Applicants may request round-trip APEX airfare only. Grant recipients are responsible for all their visa and travel arrangements.

Application Information Application materials are available by calling IREX at the number listed above or by writing.

Deadline(s) The application deadlines are October 1 and April 1.

256. The International Society for General Semantics
P.O. Box 2469
San Francisco, CA 94126
(415) 543-1747

The Sanford I. Berman Research Scholarships in General Semantics

Program Description The society seeks research proposals which will demonstrate how evaluations and reevaluations of the symbolic environment affect human behavior. Subject areas may range widely from personal and family relationships to teaching, journalism, business, the professions, and other pursuits in human affairs.

Eligibility/Limitations The awards are for graduate research—masters, doctoral or postdoctoral—in how language affects differing views of the world, thought, behavior, communication, or other areas investigated under the heading general semantics.

Fiscal Information Grants are $3,000. Although the awards do not offer complete support, the scholarship committee hopes that this funding will encourage the initiation and completion of research related to general semantics.

Application Information Guidelines which should be followed in submitting a research proposal are available from the society.

Deadline(s) Proposals for grants must be received no later than May 30.

257. The James Irvine Foundation
One Market Plaza, Spear Tower, Suite 1715
San Francisco, CA 94105
(415) 777-2244

Grants

Program Description The James Irvine Foundation was established in 1937 to promote the general welfare of the people of California. Although its historic roots are in Orange County, the foundation is dedicated to enhancing the social, economic, and physical quality of life throughout California, and enriching the state's intellectual and cultural climate. Within these broad purposes, the foundation supports higher education, the cultural arts, medicine and health care, community services and youth programs.

Sample Grants For research and design in the developmental phase of a pilot project in Los Angeles, $30,000 to N.A.A.C.P. Legal Defense & Educational Fund, Legal Defense Fund, New York, NY (1986). To purchase a classroom facility, $25,000 to San Joaquin College of Law, Fresno, CA (1986).

Eligibility/Limitations Grants are limited to charitable uses in the State of California and for the benefit of charities which do not receive a substantial part of their support from taxation nor exist primarily to benefit tax-supported entities. The foundation considers requests for institutional and program development, policy studies and capital projects. Grants generally are not made for basic research, for films or publishing activities, or for festivals or conferences. Exceptions to these policies may occur from time to time solely upon the initiative of the foundation.

Fiscal Information Grant authorizations in 1988 totaled more than $19 million.

Application Information Grant seekers should submit one copy of the proposal with a cover letter signed by an appropriate officer of the organization. The cover letter should briefly summarize the proposed project; identify the applicant, the problem or need to be addressed, the proposed objectives, and strategy to accomplish the objectives; and the amount of support requested from the foundation and the total estimated project costs. The proposal narrative should include the following components: applicant background, problem statement, and proposed project. In addition, the proposal should include: complete financial statements for the last two fiscal years; current year's budget to include year-to-date financial information; copies of original federal and state tax-exemption letters and IRS notification of foundation status under Section 509(a) of the Tax Reform Act of 1969; list of officers and directors/trustees, including names, addresses, occupations/affiliations, board responsibilities, and length of term; a current annual report and/or program brochure, if available; and board endorsement, signed by an officer of the board of directors/trustees, indicating that the proposal is made with board approval.

Deadline(s) The distribution committees meet semiannually, generally in May and November, to consider applications. These meetings are followed by a meeting of the board of directors at which final action is taken.

Additional Information For the purpose of processing inquiries and applications only, the foundation has divided California into northern and southern sections. Applicants from the northern section, which is the area north of San Luis Obispo, Kern and San Bernardino counties, should address their applications to the San Francisco office at the address listed above. Applications from the southern section, which is the area south of and including San Luis Obispo, Kern and San Bernardino counties, should be directed to: The James Irvine Foundation, 450 New-port Center Drive, Suite 545, Newport Beach, CA, 92660, telephone (714) 644-1362.

258. Ittleson Foundation
645 Madison Avenue, 16th Floor
New York, NY 10022
(212) 838-5010

Grants

Program Description The foundation at this time is generally interested in providing seed money for the start-up of innovative programs that will improve the social welfare of the citizens of the United States. The current interests of the Ittleson Foundation are most accurately described as being in the fields of mental health, the environment, the elderly, and crime and justice.

Sample Grants In support of a project on values history process, which records a person's wishes regarding medical treatment, $25,000 (first payment of a two-year $40,000 grant) to The Institute of Public Law at the University of New Mexico, Albuquerque, NM (1988).

Eligibility/Limitations Preference is given to pilot projects, test and demonstration projects, and applied research which ideally should inform public policy, if successful.

Fiscal Information The foundation does not generally support capital building projects, endowments, grants to individuals, scholarships or internships (except as part of a program), or continuing support to existing programs. Nor does the foundation support programs of direct service to individuals with only a local focus or constituency. The foundation does not make international grants.

Application Information There are no application forms. The best way to apply for a grant is to write a brief letter to the executive director describing the work for which the funds are being sought, along with a budget. If the activity falls within the current scope of interests of the foundation and if there is any possibility that the foundation would be willing to have the request placed on an agenda for formal consideration at one of its meetings, the applicant will be asked to supply additional information as may be required.

Deadline(s) There are no application deadlines. Grant requests are reviewed on a continuing basis.

259. The Japan Foundation
142 West 57th Street, 6th Floor
New York, NY 10019
(212) 949-6360

Dissertation Fellowships

Program Description These fellowships are intended to provide doctoral candidates in the social sciences and the humanities with an opportunity to conduct dissertation research in Japan. The foundation would like to encourage applications from well-qualified candidates particularly in fields that are currently understaffed with Japanese specialists, such as political science, law, economics, business, and journalism.

Eligibility/Limitations Applicants must have completed all requirements except the dissertation when they begin the fellowship. Applicants are expected to be proficient enough in the Japanese language to pursue their research in Japan. Candidates should be American citizens or permanent residents of the United States. American citizens residing abroad are also eligible to apply.

Fiscal Information Dissertation fellowships carry monthly stipends of 180,000 yen for periods ranging from four to fourteen months. In addition to monthly stipends, grantees will receive allowances for housing, key money, dependents, luggage, settling-in, research, research travel, and documents. Fellowships include traveler's insurance and business-class air transportation to and from Toyko by the most direct route available. Travel expenses for dependent family members will not be provided.

Fellowships are tenable only in Japan. Fellows are expected to devote full time to the pursuit of the goals described in their applications and may not accept employment in Japan during the term of their awards, with or without remuneration. Grantees may not hold another major grant concurrently with the dissertation fellowship.

Application Information Program announcements and application forms can be obtained from the New York office of the foundation or from the Los Angeles office, 244 South San Pedro Street, Suite 508, Los Angeles, CA 90012, telephone (213) 617-1159. Applications should be sent directly to the New York office.

Deadline(s) Completed applications should be postmarked no later than November 15.

Additional Information Applicants residing in the United States who are not citizens or permanent residents of the United States should contact directly The Japan Foundation headquarters in Tokyo, Park Building, 3-6 Kioi-cho, Chiyoda-ku, Tokyo 102, Japan. Americans with permanent residency status abroad should apply through the foundation's overseas office or Japanese diplomatic mission in the country where they reside.

260. The Japan Foundation
142 West 57th Street, 6th Floor
New York, NY 10019
(212) 949-6360

Institutional Project Support Programs

Program Description The Japan Foundation offers five types of institutional project support programs: visiting professorships, staff expansion grants, research grants, conference/intensive course grants, and study-in-Japan grants. The basic purpose of these programs is to assist in the study and understanding of Japanese culture and society in the United States.

Eligibility/Limitations Any educational, cultural, or public affairs organization classified as a nonprofit institution for federal income tax purposes is eligible to apply. Before making application, institutions should confirm whether they are legally able to receive foreign grants. Projects being considered for the foundation's support must be in the fields of the humanities and social sciences.

Fiscal Information Support will be given on a cost-sharing basis. The foundation does not provide overhead costs, except for the visiting professorship grant program. The number and size of the grants specified in each program are approximate and subject to change. Please note that the foundation cannot consider requests in the following areas: building construction, land or rental costs, support for endowed chairs, contributions to capital funds, museum acquisitions, costs of permanent equipment, and salaries for existing positions.

Application Information Program announcements and application forms can be obtained from the New York office of the foundation or from the Los Angeles office, 244 South San Pedro Street, Suite 508, Los Angeles, CA 90012, telephone (213) 617-1159. Applications should be sent directly to the New York office. Institutions submitting more than one project application are requested to submit their requests on separate forms.

Deadline(s) Completed applications should be postmarked no later than November 15.

Additional Information The foundation's library support program is designed to promote research on and understanding of Japan in the United States through donations of books and other materials substantially related to Japan. The library of any American research or educational institution is eligible to apply for this program. Contact the foundation for further information.

261. The Japan Foundation
142 West 57th Street, 6th Floor
New York, NY 10019
(212) 949-6360

Professional Fellowships

Program Description Professional fellowships are intended for scholars in the social sciences and humanities, journalists, writers, artists and other professionals who wish to conduct research in Japan. The proposal must be related wholly or in substantial part to Japan.

Eligibility/Limitations Candidates for these fellowships should be American citizens or permanent residents of the United States. American citizens residing abroad are also eligible to apply. Proficiency in Japanese language is desirable, but it is not required except in those cases where it is necessary to successfully complete the research project. For those seeking academic degrees and applying in this category, applications will not be accepted unless the dissertation has been successfully defended prior to the date applications are due. Scholars should have an academic position in a research institution as well as substantial experience in research, teaching and writing in their respective fields of study. Applications from researchers in the social sciences, especially economics, including faculty members from professional schools are particularly welcome.

Fiscal Information Professional fellowships carry monthly stipends of 240,000 or 300,000 yen; the amount is determined in accordance with the grantee's professional career. In addition to monthly stipends, grantees of long-term fellowships of four to twelve months in length will receive the following allowances: housing, key money, dependents, luggage, settling-in, research, research travel, and documents. Grantees of short-term fellowships of two to four months in length will receive allowances for: housing, luggage, research, research travel, and documents. Fellowships include traveler's insurance and business-class air transportation to and from Toyko by the most direct route available. Travel expenses for dependent family members will not be provided. Fellowships are tenable only in Japan. Fellows are expected to devote full time to the pursuit of the goals described in their applications and may not accept employment in Japan during the term of the award, with or without remuneration. Grantees may not hold another major grant concurrently with the professional fellowship.

Application Information Program announcements and application forms can be obtained from the New York office of the foundation or from the Los Angeles office, 244 South San Pedro Street, Suite 508, Los Angeles, CA 90012, telephone (213) 617-1159. Applications should be sent directly to the New York office.

Deadline(s) Completed applications should be postmarked no later than November 15.

Additional Information Applicants residing in the United States who are not citizens or permanent residents of the United States should contact directly The Japan Foundation headquarters in Tokyo, Park Building, 3-6 Kioi-cho, Chiyoda-ku, Tokyo 102, Japan. Americans with permanent residency status abroad, however, should apply through the foundation's overseas office or Japanese diplomatic mission in the country where they reside.

262. Japan-United States Friendship Commission
1200 Pennsylvania Avenue, NW, Room 3416
Washington, DC 20004
(202) 275-7712

Grants Programs

Program Description The commission is an independent federal agency dedicated to promoting mutual understanding and cooperation between the United States and Japan. It administers grant programs in the following areas: Japanese studies in the United States; American studies in Japan; policy-oriented research; the arts; and public affairs/education.

Sample Grants For the participation of the executive administrator in the People-to-People Law Delegation to Japan, $3,500 to the Passaic River Coalition (1988). For a comparative study of nuclear regulation and perceptions of nuclear risks in Japan and the United States, $4,750 to Washington State University (1988).

Eligibility/Limitations Nonprofit institutions are eligible to apply.

Fiscal Information The commission awarded over $2.2 million in grants in 1988. The commission welcomes matching grants from other appropriate sources. These and other forms of cooperation will be taken as evidence of broad interest and support for any given proposal.

Application Information Additional information and application guidelines are available from the commission.

Deadline(s) Deadlines for submission of proposals are March 1 and August 1.

263. The J.M. Foundation
60 East 42nd Street, Room 1651
New York, NY 10165
(212) 687-7735

Project Grants

Program Description The J.M. Foundation grants program encompasses several related fields including: rehabilitation of people with disabilities; prevention and wellness; expansion of effective extramural care; health-related policy research; alcohol abuse and other drug dependencies; and selected projects in biomedical research and medical education. The foundation also has a strong interest in educational activities which strengthen America's pluralistic system of free markets, individualism, entrepreneurship, voluntarism, and private enterprise.

Sample Grants To publish and distribute the association's manual on the rights of people with disabilities, $15,000 to the Association of the Bar of the City of New York Fund, New York, NY (1989). To enhance communications and produce educational materials for members at law schools across the United States, $10,000 to the Federalist Society for Law and Public Policy Studies, Washington, DC (1989). For the Civil Liberties Research Project, $15,000 to the Washington Legal Foundation, Washington, DC (1989).

Eligibility/Limitations Any organizations that are tax-exempt under Section 501(c)(3) of the Internal Revenue Code are invited to submit a proposal to the foundation. To maximize the impact of modest resources, the foundation generally declines participation in the following proposal categories: capital campaigns such as renovations and building funds, arts, annual appeals, grants to individuals such as financial aid, and international projects outside the United States.

Fiscal Information Grants paid during 1989 totaled over $2.2 million.

Application Information The J.M. Foundation does not have a printed application form, nor does it have a rigid format for requests. The foundation recommends that an initial letter of inquiry be forwarded to the executive director containing the following information: a brief summary of the proposed project; vita of author researcher or project officer, if applicable; a summary of the need for support including background, objective, time period, key staff, project budget, and evaluation plan; an annual report and organization brochure; the most recent audited financial statements; membership of the governing board; a copy of the IRS exemption letter; a list, including amounts, of organization supporters, current funders of the proposed project, if any, and grant makers with whom proposals are pending for the project; and the expected outcome or results. Proposals determined to be consistent with the interests and capacity of the foundation are examined further and processed for presentation to the directors at one of their four meetings each year.

Deadline(s) The directors meet in January, May, and October.

264. The Lyndon Baines Johnson Foundation
2313 Red River
Austin, TX 78705
(512) 478-7879

Grants-in-Aid of Research

Program Description These funds are dispersed for the sole purpose of helping to defray living, travel, and related expenses incurred while conducting research at the Johnson Library.

Eligibility/Limitations Scholars who wish to conduct research at the Johnson Library are eligible to apply. In accepting a grant, an applicant must agree to the following conditions: that the product of the research which is made possible through these funds will not be used for any political purpose; that the funds are for the purpose of helping to defray expenses while conducting research at the Johnson Library; that the grant is for the year awarded only; that the LBJ Foundation will be provided with a copy of any publication, article, or book resulting from research made possible by the grant.

Fiscal Information Grants generally range from $300 to $1,400. Grant requests should be calculated on the basis of $50 a day per diem plus actual travel costs. Airfare should be calculated on the most economical fare.

Application Information Prior to submitting a proposal, it is strongly recommended that applicants write to the chief archivist to obtain information about materials available in the library on the proposed research topic. Applications should be addressed to the executive director of the foundation.

Deadline(s) Applications must be received by August 31.

265. The Robert Wood Johnson Foundation
College Road, P.O. Box 2316
Princeton, NJ 08543
(609) 452-8701

Grants

Program Description The Robert Wood Johnson Foundation is a private philanthropy interested in improving health in the United States. The foundation is currently supporting or examining programs that improve health-care services; assist the segments of our population most vulnerable to illness; address specific diseases of regional or national concern; or encourage innovations on broad national health issues. The foundation funds projects of several kinds: (1) Projects that reflect the applicant's own interests. For such projects there are no formal application forms or deadlines. (2) Projects, also investigator-initiated, that are developed in response to a foundation call for proposals. The call for proposals describes the program area for which proposals are requested and specifies any necessary application steps or guidelines. (3) Projects that are part of foundation national programs. For these, the foundation sets the program's goals, common elements that all projects should contain, eligibility criteria, timetables and application procedures.

Sample Grants For their endowment fund, $50,000 to the Supreme Court Historical Society, Washington, DC (1989). For research on physician behavior and medical malpractice, $199,997 to the RAND Corporation, Santa Monica, CA (1989). For technical assistance for the Medical Malpractice Program, $74,179 to the University of Virginia Law School foundation, Charlottesville, VA (1989).

Eligibility/Limitations Ordinarily, preference will be given to organizations that have qualified for exemption under Section 501(c)(3) of the Internal Revenue Code, and that are not "private foundations" as defined under Section 509(a). Public instrumentalities performing similar functions are also eligible. Foundation guidelines preclude support for: ongoing general operating expenses or existing deficits; endowment or capital costs, including construction, renovation or equipment; basic biomedical research; conferences, symposia, publications or media projects unless they are related to the foundation's program objectives or an outgrowth of one of its grant programs; research on unapproved drug therapies or devices; international programs and institutions; and direct support to individuals.

Fiscal Information During 1989 the foundation made grants totaling over $98.6 million.

Application Information There are no formal grant application forms. Applicants wishing to apply for funds not in response to a call for proposals or national program announcement are advised to submit a preliminary letter of inquiry rather than a fully developed proposal. Such a letter should be no more than four pages long, should be written on the applicants letterhead and should contain the following information about the proposed project: a brief description of the problem to be addressed; a statement of the project's principal objectives; a description of the proposed intervention; the expected outcome; the qualifications of the institution and the project's principal personnel; a timetable; plans for evaluation; plans for sustaining the project after grant funds expire; and the name of a primary contact person for follow-up.

Deadline(s) Applicant-initiated proposals are accepted throughout the year. The board of trustees meets five times a year to conduct business, review proposals, and appropriate funds.

Additional Information The foundation awards health policy fellowships to faculty of health professional schools to improve their capabilities to study health policy and assume leadership roles in health activities. Contact the foundation for additional information.

266. The Fletcher Jones Foundation
One Wilshire Building, Suite 1210
624 South Grand Avenue
Los Angeles, CA 90017
(213) 689-9292

Grants

Program Description The trustees of the foundation give consideration to charitable, scientific, literary and education areas, plus a minor portion to general-purpose grants. However, from time to time, the trustees may give special emphasis to any of the above-listed areas. At present, special emphasis is being given to private colleges and universities, particularly those in California.

Sample Grants To assist renovation and expansion of the Law Center, $250,000 to the University of Southern California (1986). For general operating support, $10,000 to the Institute for Civil Justice (1986). For general operating support, $5,000 to the Pacific Legal Foundation (1986).

Eligibility/Limitations Grants are made to qualified, nonprofit organizations. Grants are not made to individuals, to carry on propaganda, to influence legislation, or to organizations engaged in such activities. The foundation generally does not favor requests for projects which should be financed by governmental agencies, nor does it normally make grants to operating funds, secondary schools, deficit financing, or contingencies. As a general rule, it does not make grants for conferences, seminars, workshops, travel exhibits, or surveys.

Fiscal Information Grants paid in 1987 totaled over $3.3 million.

Application Information An organization which believes it meets the foundation's criteria for a grant may wish to test the foundation's interest before preparing a formal grant application by submitting a short "Test Letter," highlighting the proposal and stating the amount of grant to be requested. Each such letter will be acknowledged. Two replies are possible: (1) without commitment, the foundation will be pleased to receive and give consideration to an application for the grant as outlined, or (2) the proposal does not appear feasible for foundation support. For applications deemed appropriate, no special application format is required. To facilitate trustee consideration, however, it is suggested that all applications be submitted on one typewritten page. A short cover letter should summarize the essential information. There is no limitation on the number of supporting documents. The following information assists the trustees in making a proper judgment: a fact sheet summarizing significant

statistics and background about the applicant organization, its objectives, its current programs and services, and its chief sources of support; a description of the project and why it is needed; goals to be accomplished and how; applicant's qualifications to carry out the project; detailed financial information relative to the project; the amount requested from the foundation; and how and when the project will be evaluated. Support documents forwarded should include: the most recent financial report, including balance sheet and profit-and-loss statement; IRS Classification Letter showing that the organization is a Section 501(c)(3) nonprofit public charity and not a private foundation; most recent Form 990 filed with the IRS; state Franchise and Income Tax Exemption Letter; list of organization's officers and directors, including their business or professional affiliations; applicant's most recent annual program report and name, address and telephone number of the organization's attorney.

Deadline(s) The foundation accepts applications for grants throughout the year.

267. W. Alton Jones Foundation
433 Park Street
Charlottesville, VA 22901
(804) 295-2134

Secure Society Program

Program Description The goal of the Secure Society Program is to prevent nuclear war. The foundation's grant-making program is designed to address the imperfections in our present "system" of international security and to encourage the development of feasible alternatives.

Sample Grants To support a program of dinner seminars for members of Congress on the key aspects of U.S.-Soviet relations, $20,000 to the Peace Through Law Education Fund, Washington, DC (1987).

Eligibility/Limitations The foundation does not support scholarship funds or make direct awards to individuals.

Fiscal Information Grants payable in 1988 totaled over $4 million. Grant awards range from $4,000 to over $300,000. The foundation ordinarily will not consider proposals for capital purposes, endowment funds, or deficit operations.

Application Information A preliminary inquiry prior to the submission of a detailed proposal is advisable. A grant request should be initiated by a letter describing the proposed project, its expected impact, the qualifications of the staff, a detailed expense budget, the time frames, and other funding sources, as well as copies of the applicant organization's tax-exempt rulings stating that it is described in Section 501(c)(3) of the Internal Revenue Code and is not a private foundation.

Deadline(s) The commitment of grant funds is the responsibility of the board of trustees. The board meets in March, June, September, and December. Proposals should be submitted to the foundation's executive director prior to January 15, April 15, July 15, and October 15 to allow adequate time for review before the quarterly meetings.

268. W. Alton Jones Foundation
433 Park Street
Charlottesville, VA 22901
(804) 295-2134

Sustainable Society Program

Program Description The Sustainable Society Program seeks to keep the earth suitable for long-term habitation by preserving the natural resource base. The program supports proposals for projects which address the conservation of biological diversity worldwide. The goal of this program is to preserve the diversity of the earth's plants, animals, natural communities, and ecosystems and to preserve the ecosystem services required to maintain a livable biosphere.

Sample Grants For litigation, legal counseling, policy analysis, and scientific research to protect the public's health and the region's natural resources, $100,000 (second year of a two-year $200,000 grant) to the Conservation Law Foundation of New England, Boston, MA (1988). In support of litigation, policy analysis, and legal counseling to local environmental organizations throughout the Southeast, $200,000 (fourth year of a four-year $499,700 grant) to Southern Environmental Law Center, Charlottesville, VA (1988).

Eligibility/Limitations The foundation does not support scholarship funds or make direct awards to individuals. The foundation has in the past supported projects which educate the public and the government; monitor the government; foster conservation through land purchases, easements, parks and preserves; include basic and applied research; initiate policy development, litigation, and mediation; and train resource specialists or develop indigenous organizations, especially in the tropics and other species-rich areas.

Fiscal Information Grants payable in 1988 totaled over $4 million. Grant awards range from $4,000 to over $300,000. The foundation ordinarily will not consider proposals for capital purposes, endowment funds, or deficit operations.

Application Information A preliminary inquiry prior to the submission of a detailed proposal is advisable. A grant request should be initiated by a letter describing the proposed project, its expected impact, the qualifications of the staff, a detailed expense budget, the time frames, and other funding sources, as well as copies of the applicant organization's tax-exempt rulings stating that it is described in Section 501(c)(3) of the Internal Revenue Code and is not a private foundation.

Deadline(s) The commitment of grant funds is the responsibility of the board of trustees. The board meets in March, June, September, and December. Proposals should be submitted to the foundation's executive director prior to January 15, April 15, July 15, and October 15 to allow adequate time for review before the quarterly meetings.

269. The Joyce Foundation
135 South LaSalle Street, Suite 4010
Chicago, IL 60603-4886
(312) 782-2464

Program Grants

Program Description The Joyce Foundation awards grants primarily in the fields of conservation, culture, economic development, government, and health. Conservation—the wise use of natural resources and the custodial care of these resources for future generations—is a basic concern of the foundation. The foundation funds projects that have a particularly strong relevance in the Midwest: soil conservation, groundwater protection, reducing atmospheric pollutants, and protecting and enhancing the basic qualities of the Great Lakes. Increasing interest is given to examining the field of biotechnology. The foundation is committed to strengthening the economic vitality of the Midwest and expanding the opportunities for low-income individuals to fully participate in the economy. The foundation supports projects that work directly with low-income individuals to use the economic system to their own advantage. The foundation seeks to encourage greater citizen participation in the electoral process and efforts to strengthen public participation in state and local budget making processes.

Sample Grants For a center for state environmental programs, $50,000 to Environmental Law Institute, Washington, DC (1987). For efforts on new immigration law, $10,000 to Travelers & Immigrants Aid of Chicago, Chicago, IL (1987).

Eligibility/Limitations Applications should be made only by organizations prepared to demonstrate their tax-exempt status by copy of Internal Revenue Service ruling or determination letters. All organizations must be prepared to supply complete financial information and permit the results of a grant to be audited.

Fiscal Information Grants approved in 1989 totaled over $12.9 million. Joyce Foundation funding is unlikely to exceed three consecutive years. Applicants requesting grants for projects or programs of extended duration are urged to provide plans for financial support from others that would permit phasing out the foundation's assistance. When appropriate, grantees are encouraged to challenge constituents to match foundation money. Estimates of dollar amounts to be distributed among fields of interest can be obtained by writing the foundation after January 30 of that year.

Application Information Guidelines are available upon request. It is suggested that these guidelines be reviewed carefully before sending a request to the foundation. Applicants are encouraged first to submit a brief statement of their programs and projects. If an initial staff review is favorable, complete information is requested.

Deadline(s) Grant proposals are reviewed at meetings of the board of directors in the spring, summer, and late fall. Proposal deadlines are January 15 in economic development and education; May 15 in conservation and health; and August 15 in culture and government.

Additional Information Applicants in the field of higher education should contact the foundation at least two months prior to the appropriate proposal deadline and request a higher education questionnaire. Applicants in other program areas should use the general format for proposals provided in the guidelines. The foundation also makes a number of small grants between regularly scheduled meetings of the board. This support is given for special projects and in response to immediate funding needs.

270. Judicial Conference of the United States
Committee on the Bicentennial of the Constitution
231 West Lafayette Boulevard, Room 240
Detroit, MI 48226
(313) 226-6890

Summer Stipends

Program Description The United States Judicial Conference's Committee on the Bicentennial of the Constitution announces a summer stipend program to support research on the history and evolution of the federal courts. Any topic in the field of federal judicial history is eligible for consideration, but the committee encourages proposals that focus on federal courts other than the Supreme Courts. Topics that explore the interaction between the state and the federal judiciaries are also welcome, but projects that deal exclusively with state courts or federal administrative law are not eligible.

Eligibility/Limitations Scholars in such fields as history, political science, and law may apply; there is no disciplinary restriction. Academic affiliation is not required, but applicants should hold a terminal degree in their discipline. Preference will be given to applicants with a clear intention to publish.

Fiscal Information The awards consist of an $8,000 honorarium and a $2,000 travel and expense grant. The committee assumes that grantees will undertake no other major professional activity (e.g., summer school teaching) during the period covered by the award.

Application Information Applicants should submit the following: a description of the overall research project, including a summary of the work completed so far (no longer than five pages); a statement of research goals to be achieved during the summer of the grant (no longer than two pages); an enumeration of the research sites to be visited, with a tentative budget; a curriculum vitae; and two letters of recommendation. Applications should be sent to Judge Frank X. Altimari, U.S. Court of Appeals for the Second Circuit, Uniondale Avenue at Hempstead Turnpike, Uniondale, NY 11553.

Deadline(s) Applications must be received by December 15.

271. The J.M. Kaplan Fund, Inc.
330 Madison Avenue
New York, NY 10017
(212) 661-8485

Grants

Program Description In recent years, as fund assets and grant expenditures have broadened, so has the reach of fund programs. The fund has become increasingly involved in national efforts towards environmental protection, the humane planning and development of cities, and civil liberties and human rights. Nonetheless, the fund continues to favor the local endeavor and those national organizations whose headquarters are in New York City. The program has emerged over time in three broad parts: In the area of land use, the fund is concerned with conservation and enhancement of natural resources; with public gardens, farmlands, and open space; with architecture, historic preservation, and strong neighborhoods; and with rational planning by government including avoidance of nuclear explosion. In the areas of civil liberties and human needs, the fund assists efforts for a more just society, to end prejudice and ensure First Amendment rights and other legal protections; for basic public services; and for worldwide human rights. In the arts, the fund makes grants for books, pictures, and music, with an emphasis on work in New York.

Sample Grants To prepare and publish a series of Preservation Law Updates summarizing important court decisions of concern to preservationists, and distributing them across the country, $25,000 to National Center for Preservation Law, Inc. (1987). For general support, including their Amicus Journal, U.S.-Soviet nuclear test ban verification project, programs for land and water conservation, and a feasibility study for an Urban Environmental Law Center, $265,000 to the Natural Resources Defense Council, Inc. (1987). For general support for their efforts to protect the welfare and civil liberties of all children in America, through research and public education to implement existing laws, $50,000 to the Children's Defense Fund (1987).

Eligibility/Limitations The fund generally does not contribute to the following: operating budgets of educational, medical, and cultural institutions; building programs; charitable organizations that solicit contributions from the general public; organizations whose main activities take place outside the New York area; films or video; scholarships, fellowships, research, conferences, prizes, study or travel; or the personal sponsorship of books, dances, plays, musical compositions, or other works of art. The fund contributes only to tax-exempt, publicly supported organizations and is prohibited from making grants to individuals.

Fiscal Information In 1988 the fund awarded grants totaling over $6.1 million.

Application Information A clear, concise letter describing the organization and the program for which it seeks support serves as application—and should be accompanied by budgets, sources of income, lists of board and staff members, IRS determination letter, and Form 990. Further material may be requested if there is trustee interest in the proposal. Initial inquiries by brief letter or telephone are preferred, after which we will send our application checklist for the complete materials if project is appropriate.

Deadline(s) Requests are considered between March 1 and October 15, and grant decisions are made on a rolling schedule.

272. The Helen Kellogg Institute for International Studies
University of Notre Dame
Notre Dame, IN 46556
(219) 239-6580

Kellogg Institute Residential Fellowships

Program Description The institute aims to advance understanding of Third World development, particularly in Latin America, through research, education and outreach. The institute's research reflects commitments to democracy, development, and social justice, and focuses on five major themes: (1) alternative policies of economic development and their social consequences; (2) responses of those excluded from effective participation in political and economic life; (3) the social roles of religion and the Catholic Church; (4) the processes and possibilities of democratization; and (5) public policies for social justice.

Eligibility/Limitations The institute seeks fellows of high scholarly accomplishment and promise, both at senior and junior levels, whose work and presence will contribute creatively to its major research themes. It welcomes applications from candidates from any country who hold a Ph.D. or equivalent degree in any discipline of the social sciences or history. Candidates will be evaluated individually, but joint projects will be considered.

Fiscal Information Stipends to fellows vary with seniority. Fellows from abroad may receive one direct round-trip economy airfare.

Application Information For application forms and more information contact the institute.

Deadline(s) The deadline for receipt of applications is November 15.

273. W. K. Kellogg Foundation
400 North Avenue
Battle Creek, MI 49017-3398
(616) 968-1611

Grants

Program Description The foundation concentrates its grantmaking in the following programming areas: adult continuing education; community-based, problem-focused health services; a wholesome food supply; and broadening leadership capacity of individuals. The foundation is conducting limited grantmaking in the following five areas to determine if these themes may become major parts of programming: rural America, water resources, management of information systems, philanthropy and volunteerism, and science education.

Sample Grants To help policy officials and citizens make more informed decisions regarding groundwater quality protection by providing educational programming through extension education, $399,934 to Pennsylvania State University, University Park (1989). To provide public policy education through a continuing forum to address Arizona's natural resources, $128,600 to the University of Arizona, Tucson (1989).

Eligibility/Limitations The foundation's geographic scope of programming is the United States, Latin America, the Caribbean, and southern African countries. To be eligible for support, organizations and institutions must qualify under the regulations of the Internal Revenue Service. Grantees must have the financial potential to sustain the project on a continuing basis after foundation funding is ended.

Fiscal Information During the 1989 fiscal year, program payments totaled over $106 million. The foundation does not make loans and does not provide grants for: operational phases of established programs; capital facilities, equipment, conferences, publications, films, or television or radio programs, unless they are an integral phase of a project already funded; endowments or developmental campaigns; basic research; planning and studies; religious purposes; or individuals—except for fellowships in specific areas of foundation programming.

Application Information The foundation does not have grant application forms. To be considered for foundation aid, an institution or organization should write a one- or two-page preproposal letter briefly describing the basic problem and the plan for its solution. The plan should include project objectives, operational procedures, time schedule, and personnel and financial resources available and needed. Proposal letters are carefully evaluated by the foundation. If the proposal is within the foundation's guidelines and interests and if foundation priorities and resources permit consideration of the requested aid, conferences and staff investigation may follow. The organization may be asked to develop a more detailed proposal which includes a plan for evaluation of the project's effect. Proposal letters should be addressed to the chief programming officer of the foundation.

Deadline(s) No deadlines are announced.

274. W. K. Kellogg Foundation
400 North Avenue
Battle Creek, MI 49017-3398
(616) 969-2005

Kellogg National Fellowship Program

Program Description This program offers outstanding American professionals an opportunity to broaden their social and intellectual sensitivity, awareness, and leadership potential. A basic aim of the program is to assist future leaders in developing skills and competencies which transcend traditional disciplinary and professional methods of addressing problems.

Eligibility/Limitations The three-year program is designed for individuals who are in the early years of their professional careers. Fellows may be drawn from business, education, human service agencies, and private practice. Awards will not be made for basic research or to assist in obtaining a degree. Applicants must be U.S. citizens and in the early years of professional activity.

Fiscal Information A total of up to $35,000 each will be awarded during the three-year period. If a fellow is employed by an eligible grantee, the fellow's employer will be reimbursed 12.5 percent of the fellow's annual salary. If the fellow is not employed by an eligible grantee, no salary reimbursement will be awarded; the fellow, however, may be eligible to receive a stipend of up to $300 per month for a maximum of 36 months.

Application Information Contact the foundation for additional information and an application form.

Deadline(s) Completed applications, institutional endorsements and reference forms must be postmarked by December 15.

275. The Joseph P. Kennedy, Jr. Foundation
1350 New York Avenue, NW, Suite 500
Washington, DC 20005
(202) 393-1250

Grants

Program Description The foundation has two objectives: seeking the prevention of mental retardation by identifying its causes; and improving the means by which society deals with its mentally retarded citizens. The guiding strategy of the foundation has been to use its funds and influence in areas where a multiplier effect is possible. This is accomplished by supporting research, by developing innovative models of service through provision of seed money, and by enhancing public awareness and influencing public policy.

Eligibility/Limitations The foundation solicits grantees and also accepts applications from others.

Fiscal Information Grants are not made for construction or capital outlay, and are generally confined to projects and/or research conducted in the United States. The foundation generally does not fund equipment or award indirect costs.

Application Information Applicants should send a two-page preliminary letter of intent. This letter must describe the project and the project's goals, including a proposed budget and outline of how the project might be funded after foundation funds are no longer available, and describing the qualifications of the personnel. After initial screening, proposals deemed worthy of further consideration receive extensive review and applicants are asked to submit an expanded grant application in a format supplied by the foundation.

Deadline(s) Letters of intent must be submitted by October 1 for funding during the next year. The date for completion of full proposals is November 15.

Additional Information To encourage an understanding of how public policy is developed, the foundation sponsors Public Poli-

cy fellowships in Mental Retardation for future national leaders in the field of mental retardation. The program provides outstanding professionals a year-long fellowship during which they experience firsthand the legislative and administrative processes, and learn about the substance and economics of public policy decisions. One or two fellows are selected annually based on their education, professional background, and potential for future leadership in the field of mental retardation.

276. Josiah W. and Bessie H. Kline Foundation, Inc.
42 Kline Village
Harrisburg, PA 17104
(717) 232-0266

Grants

Program Description The objectives of foundation giving are to aid blind or incapacitated persons; to make grants to Pennsylvania colleges and universities, and to hospitals; to make grants for scientific or medical research; and to make grants to finance projects for the improvement of law or to promote a sounder economy in the United States.

Eligibility/Limitations The foundation does not make grants to individuals.

Fiscal Information The foundation does not make grants for general operating support.

Application Information To be considered, submit a letter of request with the following information: a description of the need and purpose, the qualifications of the requesting organization and the location as to where and how the support will be used; a budget for the project and any support that will be received from other sources; the amount of request from the foundation and the dates of the need; a copy of the letter from the IRS showing that the organization is exempt from federal income tax under section 501(c)(3) of the Internal Revenue Code and that the organization is not a private foundation under section 509(a).

Deadline(s) Requests for grants may be submitted at any time. All requests are acted upon by the foundation at meetings which are generally held every March and November.

277. KPMG Peat Marwick Foundation
Three Chestnut Ridge Road
Montvale, NJ 07645-0435
(201) 307-7151

Research Opportunities in International Business Information

Program Description The Research Opportunities in International Business Information program was created to stimulate research on international business information and to provide financial and administrative support to academicians who are prepared to perform such research. Research topics that could contribute to meeting the information technology needs of transnational business include: the use of information systems to overcome nontariff trade barriers (for example, licensing and other obligations where compliance depends on supplying information); structural responses to national differences in tax laws; and the effect of disparate tax rules on global economic growth, for example, the unique conditions in which transnational business operates, the capabilities and problems represented by information technology, and the information needs of transnational business interact to establish the boundaries of the need research.

Sample Grants To determine the effect, if any, of the tax laws of the host country and/or investor country on the international movement of capital, $36,250 to researchers at Texas Tech University (1989).

Eligibility/Limitations To be eligible to apply, an individual must be a Ph.D. candidate or a college or university faculty member.

Fiscal Information Grants of up to $40,000 will be paid according to the plan submitted. If a project requires funds in excess of this amount, the proposal should request funds within the $40,000 limit for a segment of the project that has a defined output. Proposals for follow-up segments can be submitted during subsequent submission periods.

Application Information Additional information and application guidelines are available on request.

Deadline(s) The submission deadline for proposals is October 31.

Additional Information The foundation supports a Research Fellowship Program for accounting faculty and a Doctoral Scholarship Program for students in the second year of a doctoral program in accounting and in auditing via the Research Opportunities in Auditing Program. Contact the foundation for additional information.

278. KPMG Peat Marwick Foundation

Three Chestnut Ridge Road
Montvale, NJ 07645-0435
(201) 307-7151

Tax Research Opportunities

Program Description The foundation encourages researchers to submit research proposals in areas of tax research, including but not limited to, tax policy, revenue modeling, and microcomputer use.

Sample Grants To investigate the potential for using alternatives to penalties as a means of motivating taxpayer compliance, $36,000 to researchers at the University of Colorado, Boulder, CO (1989).

Eligibility/Limitations To be eligible to apply, an individual must be a university faculty member.

Fiscal Information Grants are limited to a maximum of $40,000. If a project requires funds in excess of this amount, the proposal should request funds within the $40,000 limit for a segment of the project that has a defined output. Proposals for follow-up segments can be submitted during subsequent submission periods.

Application Information Additional information and application guidelines are available on request.

Deadline(s) The submission deadline for proposals is October 31.

Additional Information In addition to direct research funds, the program offers administrative support, assistance in gaining access to empirical data and to specialized knowledge and skills available within KPMG Peat Marwick, and help in publishing manuscripts.

279. Kraft Foundation

Kraft Court
Glenview, IL 60025
(312) 998-2419

Corporate Giving

Program Description Kraft is committed to the long-term objective of contributing 2 percent of domestic pretax income to benefit nonprofit organizations whose work improves the well-being of society and, therefore, the environment in which the company operates. A spectrum of activities is supported through four major program categories: arts and culture, civic affairs, education, and health and welfare. Priority is given to those proposals which are most responsive to the focus areas of company concern: nutrition and physical fitness; strengthening educational institutions; economic development; and community development. Additionally, programs addressing the needs of minorities, women, and persons with disabilities are of particular interest and constitute a special focus.

Eligibility/Limitations Generally, the foundation will not consider requests for funding from individuals; organizations with a limited constituency; organizations which restrict their services to members of one religious group; political organizations or those whose primary purpose is to influence legislation or political viewpoint or to promote a particular candidate; travel, tuition and registration fees; membership dues; or goodwill advertisements of any kind.

Application Information Initial contact should be made by mail. An application form is not required; however, a concise statement of the following information is required: general program information including a brief statement of the history, purpose, and achievements of the organization; a proposal including an indication of how the applicant and/or its project meet one or more of the objectives of the focus areas, innovatively responds to an important need, is supported by the targeted constituency it intends to serve and is cost effective; total organization and/or project budgets for both the current and previous fiscal year, if applicable; an audited financial statement for the previous year, or a Letter of Auditability; an IRS letter certifying the applicant as 501(c)(3) or equivalent organization; list of officers and board members; list of other donors; list of accrediting agencies; and statement of fund-raising expenses as a percentage of overall organization, administrative and program costs.

Deadline(s) Proposals are reviewed on a continuous basis.

280. The Kresge Foundation

3215 West Big Beaver Road, P.O. Box 3151
Troy, MI 48007-3151
(313) 643-9630

Grants

Program Description Grants are awarded *only* toward projects involving the construction or renovation of facilities, the purchase of major capital equipment or an integrated system at a cost of at least $75,000, and the purchase of real estate.

Sample Grants For construction of National Center for Continuing Judicial Education, $450,000 to the University of Nevada, Reno, NV (1989). For renovation and expansion of the Legal Research Center, $650,000 to the University of San Diego, CA (1989). For renovation and expansion of the law library, $1,000,000 to New York University, New York, NY (1988).

Eligibility/Limitations Eligible applicants include tax-exempt charitable organizations operating in the following fields: higher education (awarding baccalaureate and/or graduate degrees); health care and long-term care; social services; science and environment; arts and humanities; and public affairs.

Fiscal Information In 1989, the foundation awarded over $57.5 million in grants. Grants are awarded on a challenge basis. No matching formula is involved. The challenge is to raise whatever balance is needed to assure full project funding. The purpose is to encourage additional gift support. The foundation does not grant initial funds or total project support. Grants are for a portion of the costs remaining at the time of grant approval.

Application Information An application must include the scope of the project, specifically defined, including estimates based on advanced architectural plans or actual costs; a detailed plan outlining the anticipated fund-raising progress from the date of submission to the expected date of the announcement of the Kresge grant (a specific dollar amount should be requested); any long-term financing (five years or more), regulatory approvals, or purchase agreements required for completion of the project must be formally committed or imminent prior to applying.

Deadline(s) Applications may be submitted at any time throughout the year, but only once in any 12-month period.

281. Legal Services Corporation

Office of Field Services
400 Virginia Avenue, SW
Washington, DC 20024-2751
(202) 863-1837

Funding for Law School Civil Clinical Programs

Program Description The Legal Services Corporation (LSC) announces that grant funds are available for advancing the provision of civil legal assistance through the Law School Civil Clinical Programs.

Eligibility/Limitations Proposals for grants will be solicited from all law schools that are currently accredited by the American Bar Association, or accredited for purposes of bar admission by the state bar association of the state in which the law school is located. Proposals may be submitted by either a singe law school or a consortium of law schools.

Fiscal Information Each grant will be for up to 12 months and in an amount of up to $75,000 per grant.

Application Information For further information contact the associate director, Office of Field Services.

Deadline(s) Grant proposals must be received by the Office of Field Services on or before April 20.

282. The Max and Anna Levinson Foundation

P.O. Box 125
Costilla, NM 87524
(505) 586-1681

Grants

Program Description The foundation is a small national foundation, concerned with the development of a more humane and rewarding democratic society, in which people have a greater ability and opportunity to determine directions for the future. Projects of national and international impact are supported in the fields of world peace and arms control, civil liberties and human rights, environment and energy, and the Jewish community. Whatever the specific area of interest, the foundation encourages projects which are concerned with promoting social change and social justice, either by developing and testing alternatives or by responsibly modifying existing systems, institutions, conditions and attitudes that block promising innovation.

Sample Grants For their Child Support and Beyond Project, on policies and changes in child support laws, $5,000 to Center for Law and Social Policy (1988). For their program providing educational work and camps with high school students on environmental and social justice issues, $5,000 to Creating Our Future (1988). For support for a field organizer to increase income sharing programs at law schools across the country, which will allow more students to pursue public-interest law work, $10,000 to the National Association for Public Interest Law (1988). For the Women's Economic Justice Center, which develops public policy alternatives on women's and family issues, $10,000 to the National Center for Policy Alternatives (1988).

Eligibility/Limitations The foundation does not consider grants for building programs, scholarships, loans or grants to individuals for travel, study or similar purposes, traditional charitable programs, expansion of existing services, or projects of primarily local significance.

Fiscal Information Grants range in size from $3,000 to $15,000.

Application Information To submit a proposal, write to the foundation (two to six pages) explaining: the "problem" or "opportunity" you are seeking to deal with and the specific changes are you seeking to bring about; the activities you wish to carry out for which you are seeking funding; the chances of success; and the criteria to be used to evaluate the extent to which you have achieved your goals. Send a budget, including expenditures and income by current and anticipated sources. Also include relevant information about your organization and key individuals and your federal tax status.

Deadline(s) Contact the foundation for deadlines.

283. Library Company of Philadelphia

1314 Locust Street
Philadelphia, PA 19107
(215) 546-3181

Summer Research Fellowships in American History and Culture

Program Description The Historical Society of Pennsylvania and The Library Company of Philadelphia offer summer fellowships for research in their collections. These two libraries have comprehensive collections capable of supporting research in a variety of fields and disciplines relating to the history of North America, principally in the 18th and 19th centuries.

Eligibility/Limitations While the program is designed for scholars possessing the Ph.D. or a significant record of professional experience and scholarly publication, several fellowships are reserved for doctoral candidates doing dissertation research.

Fiscal Information The fellowships, which are tenable for one or two months from June to September, carry stipends of $1,100 per month. Fellows will be assisted in finding reasonably priced accommodations.

Application Information To apply, send a vita, the names of three references, and a description of the proposed project to the curator of the library.

Deadline(s) Candidates must apply by February 1.

284. Lilly Endowment, Inc.

2801 North Meridian Street, P.O. Box 88068
Indianapolis, IN 46208
(317) 924-5471

Program Description The endowment accepts proposals in three program areas—religion, education, and community development. Within these broad parameters, the endowment is particularly interested in initiatives that will benefit school-aged youth or that will develop leadership in religious, educational, and community organizations.

Sample Grants For the National Research and Operations Nerve Center, $150,000 to the Pacific Legal Foundation, Sacramento, CA (1989). For general support, $80,000 to Landmark Legal Foundation, Kansas City, MO (1988). For general support, $50,000 to the New England Legal Foundation, Boston, MA (1988).

Eligibility/Limitations Organizations which have been determined tax-exempt under Section 501(c)(3) of the Internal Revenue Code are eligible to apply. Grants are not made to individuals. The endowment gives priority to efforts that improve the quality of life in Indianapolis and Indiana, however, the endowment's work in religion is national in scope.

Fiscal Information Grants paid in 1989 totaled over $76.5 million. The endowment does not fund: loans or cash grants to individuals; health-care and biological science projects; mass-media projects; projects that exceed three years in length; endowments or endowed chairs; libraries; building campaigns, arts and culture, neighborhood and social service projects and general operating funds outside of Indiana.

Application Information The endowment does not use application forms. Applicants should approach the endowment with a preliminary letter of no more than two pages. The letter should introduce the applicant organization, describe the proposed project, and detail how much support will be requested. In cases that warrant further consideration, the endowment will request additional information.

Deadline(s) The full board considers large grants in February, April, June, September, and November. Grants of less than $100,000 are generally considered by the board's executive committee, which meets in March, May, July, October, and December.

285. The Charles A. Lindbergh Fund, Inc.

Grants & Awards Office
P.O. Box O
Summit, NJ 07901
(201) 522-1392

The Lindbergh Grants Program

Program Description This program offers grants to individuals working for a balance between technological progress and the preservation of our natural and human environment to achieve a better quality of life for all. The board of directors of the fund is interested in increasing representation in the following areas: aeronautics/astronautics/aviation, agriculture, the arts and humanities, biomedical research, conservation of natural resources, health and population sciences, intercultural communication, oceanography, water resource management, waste disposal management, and wildlife preservation.

Eligibility/Limitations The Lindbergh Grants Program is international in scope. Citizens of all countries are eligible. The fund welcomes candidates who are affiliated with an academic or nonprofit institution. Grants are awarded to individuals, not to affiliated institutions for institutional programs.

Fiscal Information Grants of up to $10,580 will be awarded annually.

Application Information Copies of the Lindbergh Grants Announcement and application guidelines can be obtained by writing the fund. Enclose a self-addressed, stamped envelope with your request.

Deadline(s) Complete applications should be received by the fund before October 17.

286. The Henry Luce Foundation, Inc.

111 West 50th Street
New York, NY 10020
(212) 489-7700

Program Grants

Program Description The foundation makes grants in the areas of public affairs, Asian affairs, theology and higher education.

Sample Grants To support a study of the separation of powers and the performance of contemporary American political institutions, $225,000 to American Enterprise Institute for Public Policy Research (1989). To support an international roundtable on the First Amendment, $22,000 to the Williamsburg Charter Foundation (1989).

Eligibility/Limitations Qualified nonprofit organizations are eligible to apply.

Fiscal Information In 1989 foundation grant awards exceeded $22.2 million.

Application Information The foundation publishes no formal guidelines, nor does it use special application forms. The staff of the foundation is always happy to answer telephone requests for additional information about specific application procedures.

Deadline(s) Requests for general program grants can be submitted at any time, although the foundation's awards in this category are normally made late in the year.

287. J. Roderick MacArthur Foundation

9333 North Milwaukee Avenue
Niles, IL 60648
(708) 966-0143

Grants

Program Description The primary aims of the J. Roderick MacArthur Foundation in fulfilling its charitable, scientific, literary, and educational purposes are to aid those who are inequitably or unjustly treated by established institutions. The foundation seeks to foster discussion about and needed changes in these institutions by protecting and encouraging freedom of expression, human rights, civil liberties, and social justice and by

eliminating political, economic, social, religious, and cultural oppression. The foundation supports efforts and projects, including litigation, throughout the world to eliminate censorship and protect freedom of expression, including the freedom to hold and express opinions in all media of communications, both within and between nations; foster human rights, including political, social, economic, and cultural rights; protect and foster civil liberties in the United States (including all Constitutional rights) and to encourage their eventual observance in the rest of the world; and foster social justice and the elimination of political, economic, social, religious, and cultural oppression.

Sample Grants To support the publication and distribution in Arab countries of a four-volume text on human rights, law and practice in Arabic, $20,000 to DePaul University (1989). To support their Democracy, Human Rights, and U.S. Political Aid in Latin America Project, which will investigate the impact on human rights of the U.S. government's "Administration of Justice Program," which among other things, gives aid to Third World police forces, $20,000 to the Washington Office on Latin America (1989). To support the research, writing, publishing and distribution of a handbook for students, conveying information on public policy issues concerning the CIA, especially those critical First Amendment issues concerning academic freedom and freedom of speech raised by CIA presence on U.S. college campuses, $20,000 to the Bill of Rights Foundation (1989). To support a law school research project, "The Witherspoon Jurors That Never Were," about the possible development of a broad constitutional challenge against the death penalty and the jury selection process in capital cases, $20,000 to The University of Chicago, Chicago, IL (1988).

Eligibility/Limitations Only nonprofit, tax-exempt organizations as defined under Section 501(c)(3) of the Internal Revenue Code are eligible for funding. Capital projects, endowments, loan requests, ordinary social services of an ongoing nature, programs that are the routine responsibilities of government, and religious/church-based activities ordinarily will not be considered. The foundation will not consider the purchase of blocks of tickets, support for benefits, solicitations from regular development campaigns, and annual contribution drives. Also generally excluded are requests for conference expenses, projects to build statues, memorials, or the like, and organizations already supported by tax revenues.

Fiscal Information Grant awards are usually not more than $20,000. Grants awarded in 1989 totaled over $2.2 million.

Application Information Rather than submit a formal application with supporting materials, potential grantees may wish first to send a preliminary letter of inquiry to determine foundation interest in their request. This letter should describe succinctly the background, programs, personnel, and purposes of the organization and should briefly, but thoroughly, outline the proposal and its cost. When submitting a formal application, provide specific and detailed information. Include the legal name, address, and telephone number of the organization, and the name of a representative who can be contacted by telephone. Submit the organization's most recent budget, audited financial statements (if available), annual reports, and past and current funding information (grantors and the amounts contributed by each). Also include the most recent copies of IRS tax-exempt determination letters indicating status under Sections 501(c)(3) and 509(a) of the Internal Revenue Code, along with a brief history of the organization and its general goals and purposes. Submit a specific statement detailing the objectives of the proposed grant, an itemized budget broken down to show specific costs related to the proposed project, and the names and backgrounds of any individuals involved in carrying it out. Point out any unique facts of the request and what differentiates it from other projects of the same nature. Specify the expected duration of the project and any details regarding other potential funding sources. Include a synopsis of the plans to evaluate the results of the project and any past evaluations done by the organization on similar programs or efforts.

Deadline(s) The foundation has no established deadlines. Proposals are reviewed by the board approximately five to six times per year.

288. The John D. and Catherine T. MacArthur Foundation
140 South Dearborn Street
Chicago, IL 60603
(312) 726-8000

Grants Programs

Program Description The John D. and Catherine T. MacArthur Foundation is a private, independent, grant-making foundation created in 1978 for charitable and public service purposes. It has developed a limited number of innovative programs in areas within which it can act as a catalyst for useful change. There are currently specific areas of sustained foundation emphasis: health, devoted primarily to research on mental health and on the biology of parasitic disease; peace and international cooperation, which seeks to expand and strengthen the field of international security studies and to increase public understanding of complex security issues; world environment and resources, which supports conservation efforts, public education, and policy studies relating to key environmental issues in the tropics; general grants, a locus for foundation interests in justice, mass communications and institutional support; special grants, supporting cultural and community activities in the Chicago and Palm Beach, Florida areas; education programs, which focus on the development of literacy, numeracy, and critical and creative thinking skills; and world population programs, which are exploring new concepts and approaches to the problems posed by the tremendous growth of the world's populations.

Sample Grants For publication and distribution of the ABA Criminal Justice Mental Health Standards, $102,397 to the American Bar Association, Chicago, IL (1988). In support of the activities of the Research Program on Mental Health and the Law, $890,000 over two years to the University of Virginia, Charlottesville, VA (1988). In support of the 1988 U.S.-Soviet Lawyers Dialogue on legal and policy issues on nuclear arms control, $25,000 to Lawyers Alliance for Nuclear Arms Control, Boston, MA (1988). In support of a project on efficient identification and application of dispute resolution procedures, $127,525 to the Institute of Judicial Administration, New York, NY (1988). In support of the Development Law and Policy Program, $330,000 (over three years) to Columbia University, New York, NY (1988).

Eligibility/Limitations The foundation does not solicit and will not consider proposals which seek any of the following: support of programs or activities which are among the routine or accepted responsibilities of government; support for political activities or political campaigns, attempts to influence legislation, or the development or dissemination of propaganda; contributions to capital campaigns, plant construction, equipment purchases, endowment funds, debt retirement, or completed projects; general support of other foundations or institutions, or of regular development campaigns, annual fund-raising drives, institutional benefits or honorary functions, or similar appeals; grants for publications or conferences; grants to religious programs of any denomination; or awards to individuals. Increasingly, grants are made in support of foundation-generated initiatives rather than in response to grant requests.

Fiscal Information Grants approved in 1988 totaled over $111.9 million.

Application Information More detailed information on programs is available from the foundation.

Deadline(s) No deadlines are announced.

289. The John and Mary R. Markle Foundation
75 Rockefeller Plaza
New York, NY 10019-6908
(212) 489-6655

Grants

Program Description The foundation restricts its activities to the field of mass communications, directing its efforts toward the improvement of all media, including media services facilitated by new technology, and the use of computers in transmitting information. The foundation's current program focuses on the following areas: communications technology and political participation, communications technology and the elderly, electronic publishing, new applications of computer software, and communications policy.

Sample Grants To study and test the feasibility of using nonjudicial processes to resolve libel claims against media organizations, $67,000 to the University of Iowa, Iowa Libel Research Project, Iowa City, IA (1989). To continue for one year, support of the Citizens Communications Center, $10,000 to Georgetown University Law Center, Institute for Public Representation, Washington, DC (1989).

Eligibility/Limitations Organizations with 501(c)(3) status are eligible to apply.

Fiscal Information During the fiscal year July 1, 1988 through June 30, 1989, the foundation made grants totaling over $2.7 million.

Application Information The foundation requires no specific form for submitting a proposal. It recommends an initial inquiry by mail to permit an early judgment about the possibility of support. This letter should include a brief outline of the project indicating its purpose, procedures, chief personnel, and the amount requested.

Deadline(s) Grants are approved at meetings of the board of directors in November, March, and June.

290. McDonnell Douglas Foundation
P.O. Box 516
St. Louis, MO 63166-0516
(314) 232-8464

Grants

Program Description The principal interests of the foundation are to improve the quality of human life and to fulfill fundamental human needs by providing financial support to organizations and programs which reasonably may be expected to maximize human understanding, productivity and achievement (principally by gifts to a select group of colleges and universities); alleviate human suffering related to poverty, disability, and disease; enhance the quality of life through cultural activities; develop character and leadership and improve justice and government; and promote international understanding and world peace.

Eligibility/Limitations The foundation prefers to support local organizations and programs in geographic areas where the greatest concentration of McDonnell Douglas Corporation employees are located. Requests from tax-supported institutions will not be considered unless there is joint government/private enterprise.

Fiscal Information Grants awarded in 1988 totaled over $7.8 million.

Application Information The foundation does not have a printed grant application form. Proposals for funding should be as concise as possible and include the following: name, address, phone number, and contact person; statement of the problem or need addressed by the program or organization; identification of the geographic area and number of people served by the program or organization; a statement of the specific purpose for which funds are requested; a specific dollar request; an annual organizational budget and a detailed budget for any capital campaign or program to which the request relates; identification of sources of support; explanation of the novelty of the program or organization; a copy of the IRS 501(c)(3) determination letter designating the organization as a nonprofit, tax-exempt public charity; and identification of the organization's board of directors and key staff members.

Deadline(s) Applications are accepted throughout the year. The foundation board meets every other month to review proposals.

291. James S. McDonnell Foundation

1034 South Brentwood Boulevard, Suite 1610
St. Louis, MO 63117
(314) 721-1532

Grants

Program Description The foundation currently concentrates its efforts in three major areas: research to improve the quality of life, research and innovation in education, and efforts to improve global understanding.

Sample Grants In support of developing new approaches to international conflict resolution, $157,000 to the Kettering Foundation, Dayton, OH (1987).

Eligibility/Limitations Foundation programs are implemented primarily by awarding grants to universities, colleges, schools, and other qualifying nonprofit organizations. Grants are not made to individuals. Generally, foundation programs do not provide support for endowments, capital drives, general funds, or construction and renovation projects.

Fiscal Information The foundation paid $11.9 million in grants in 1988.

Application Information There are no application forms. Before submitting a full proposal, it is advisable to send a preliminary letter of inquiry to the foundation. If the initial review is favorable, the foundation will request a full proposal.

Deadline(s) Applications for support may be submitted at any time.

292. The Andrew W. Mellon Foundation

140 East 62nd Street
New York, NY 10021
(212) 838-8400

Grants

Program Description The purpose of the foundation is to "aid and promote such religious, charitable, scientific, literary, and educational purposes as may be in the furtherance of the public welfare or to tend to promote the well-doing or well-being of mankind." Within this broad charter the foundation currently makes grants on a selective basis to institutions of higher education; in cultural affairs and the performing arts; in medical, public health, and population education and research; and in certain areas of conservation, natural resources, the environment, and public affairs.

Sample Grants For use by Harvard Law School in conducting an American Indian Law symposium, $10,235 to Harvard University, Cambridge, MA (1989). Toward costs of a project on the law on ocean-boundary disputes, $50,000 to the American Society of International Law, Washington, DC (1988). To provide public-interest law scholarships for black students, $150,000 to Earl Warren Legal Training Program, New York, NY (1988). For use by its Center for Oceans Law and Policy for the Law of the Sea Convention Commentary Project, $500,000 to the University of Virginia, Charlottesville, VA (1987). Toward costs of preparing and publishing a manual on natural resources law, $250,000 to the Environmental Law Institute, New York, NY (1987).

Eligibility/Limitations The foundation does not award fellowships or other grants to individuals or make grants to primarily local nonprofit organizations.

Fiscal Information Grants totaled approximately $46 million in fiscal 1989.

Application Information No special application forms are required. Ordinarily a simple letter setting forth the need, the nature, and the amount of the request and the justification for it, together with evidence of suitable classification by the Internal Revenue Service and any supplementary exhibits an applicant may wish to submit, will suffice to assure consideration.

Deadline(s) Applications are considered throughout the year.

293. Richard King Mellon Foundation

525 William Penn Place, 39th Floor
Pittsburgh, PA 15219
(412) 392-2800

Grants

Program Description The major focus of the foundation is on the quality of life in Pittsburgh and western Pennsylvania. The main fields of interest are conservation, education, social services, and medicine and health care. The trustees of the foundation also maintain an interest in the conservation of natural areas in the United States.

Sample Grants To underwrite a project analyzing factors affecting wetlands regulation and developing a policy for their protection, $150,000 to the Environmental Defense Fund, Washington, DC (1989). Two-year support for educational activities regarding the Constitution, $30,000 to the Jefferson Foundation, Inc, Washington, DC (1988).

Eligibility/Limitations The foundation's grant programs emphasize institutions in western Pennsylvania. Proposals will not be given consideration unless they are accompanied by a copy of the applicant's classification ruling under current IRS regulations. The foundation will not consider requests on behalf of individuals and typically does not consider requests for grants to conduit organizations.

Fiscal Information Grants approved in 1989 totaled over $42.4 million.

Application Information There are no special forms for applying for a grant. Applications should take the form of a letter or formal statement from the senior administrative officer of the organization and include: a two-page executive summary providing an overview of the sponsoring organization, the proposed project, and the problem it seeks to address; a background of the organization; detailed information on the proposed project including the project budget and timetable; a current operating budget; an audited financial statement; a copy of the latest IRS determination letter indicating tax-exempt status under Section 501(c)(3) and 509(a).

Deadline(s) The board of trustees meets twice a year, usually in June and November. Proposals should be submitted prior to April 1 and October 1, respectively, to allow adequate time for review before the meetings.

294. The John Merck Fund

11 Beacon Street, Suite 600
Boston, MA 02108
(617) 723-2932

Grants

Program Description The fund supports research projects on developmental disabilities in children, the environment, disarmament/arms control, population policy, and human rights. In the area of the environment, the fund makes grants to projects throughout the world that seek to address environmental threats relating to climate change; projects that seek to protect the natural resources of rural New England; projects to preserve and nurture productive farmland, to encourage forest preservation and to improve forest management; and to protect and encourage responsible use of air, water, land, and scenic resources. In the area of disarmament, the fund targets projects that promote alternative defense. In the area of population policy, the fund limits its grants to programs and projects which, directly or indirectly, contribute to policy research and implementation that will affect population control programs over the long term. In the area of human rights, the fund supports selective efforts by U.S.-based organizations to investigate, document and expose systematic abuses of human rights in target countries; to encourage similar efforts by emerging overseas groups; and to expand opportunities for training law school students and graduates from the United States and the Third World who are interested in careers involving human rights advocacy.

Sample Grants To conduct a seminar for state and federal judges throughout the country on the impact of new reproductive technologies on the law, $15,000 to Women Judges Fund for Justice (1989). To provide summer fellowships to encourage law school students interested in pursuing careers in civil and human rights, $50,000 to Columbia University Law School (1989). To enable a U.S. team to visit the Soviet Union to discuss judicial reforms, $3,000 to International Network of Resource Information Centers (1989). To establish the Orville H. Schell, Jr. Center for International Human Rights, $170,000 (final installment of a two-year $295,000 grant) to Yale University Law School (1989).

Eligibility/Limitations The fund does not make grants to individuals, but will provide support for an individual's project which is sponsored by a domestic or foreign educational, scientific, or charitable organization.

Fiscal Information In 1989 the fund awarded 74 grants totaling over $3 million.

Application Information The fund does not encourage the submission of unsolicited applications for grants. Instead, the trustees will request individuals to submit proposals for grants to support projects within their respective institutions.

Deadline(s) No deadlines are announced.

295. Metropolitan Life Foundation

One Madison Avenue
New York, NY 10010-3690
(212) 578-6272

Grants

Program Description The Metropolitan Life Foundation was created for the purpose of supporting various scientific, educational, health and welfare, and civic and cultural organizations. In the area of civic affairs and public policy, the foundation's goal is to help strengthen the social and economic fabric, to provide training and employment opportunities for specific groups that are presently at a disadvantage, and to improve the quality of the environment. Grants are made for programs to promote equal opportunity for socially or economically disadvantaged groups; efforts to improve the legal system; and business, economic, and public policy research organizations.

Sample Grants In support of the Institute for Law and Economics, $5,000 to the University of Pennsylvania (1989). To the American Judicature Society, $3,000 (1988).

Eligibility/Limitations The foundation limits its support to tax-exempt organizations in the areas of health, education, civic affairs, and culture. Grants are not made to private foundations; individuals; local chapters of national organizations; labor groups; organizations whose activities are mainly international; organizations primarily engaged in patient care or direct treatment, drug treatment centers and community clinics; elementary and secondary schools; or endowments.

Fiscal Information Foundation giving in 1989 totaled more than $10.4 million.

Application Information Metropolitan Life Foundation welcomes requests for support within the guidelines and program areas set forth. Requests must be made in writing and should include the following information: a brief description of the organization, including its legal name, history, activities, purpose, and governing board; the purpose for which the grant is requested; the amount requested and a list of other sources of financial support; a copy of the organization's most recent audited financial statement; a copy of the IRS determination letter indicating 501(c)(3) tax-exempt status as an organization that is not a private foundation; and a copy of the organization's most recent Form 990-Income Tax Return of Organization Exempt from Income Tax.

Deadline(s) Requests are accepted and reviewed throughout the year.

296. Mexican American Legal Defense and Educational Fund (MALDEF)

Law School Scholarship Program
634 South Spring Street, 11th Floor
Los Angeles, CA 90014
(213) 629-2512

Law School Scholarship Program

Program Description This program is designed to offset somewhat the high cost of attending law school. The program currently provides financial assistance through direct scholarships.

Eligibility/Limitations In selecting scholarship recipients, primary consideration is given to the following three factors: demonstrated involvement with and commitment to serve the Hispanic community; indebtedness and the finances necessary to complete law school; and academic achievement indicating the potential for successful completion of law school.

Fiscal Information Nineteen $1,000 scholarships and one $2,000 scholarship are awarded each year.

Application Information Contact the directory of the MALDEF Law School Scholarship Program at the address listed above to obtain an application.

Deadline(s) Applications must be completed and submitted to MALDEF prior to May 30.

297. The Eugene and Agnes E. Meyer Foundation

1400 16th Street, NW, Suite 360
Washington, DC 20036
(202) 483-8294

Grants

Program Description The Meyer Foundation is a general purpose grant maker and welcomes grant requests from organizations serving the Washington, DC metropolitan area. Foundation funding is concentrated in five broad program categories: community service, education, health and mental health, arts and humanities, and law and justice.

Sample Grants In support of a program working with low-literate juvenile offenders at the Oak Hill Youth Center, $30,000 to the American Bar Association-Juvenile Justice Center, Washington, DC (1988). In support of a project to improve DC's child support system and monitor implementation of recent amendments in the DC child support law, $25,000 to the Women's Legal Defense Fund, Washington, DC (1988). In support of a project to train volunteers to act as advocates for children appearing in court on alleged abuse and neglect cases, $10,000 to Stop Child Abuse Now, Northern Virginia (1988).

Eligibility/Limitations The foundation only funds programs that serve local constituencies. The foundation normally makes grants only to organizations that are tax-exempt under section 501(c)(3) of the Internal Revenue Code. The foundation does not make grants to individuals; does not generally support capital campaigns or endowment drives; and does not fund scientific or medical research.

Fiscal Information In 1988 the foundation authorized grants totaling over $1.9 million.

Application Information The foundation requests preproposal letters of inquiry. Include a short narrative about the nature of the proposed project and the amount of funding being sought.

Deadline(s) Submit the letter of inquiry approximately one or two months before proposals are due. The deadlines for receipt of proposals are April 1, August 1 and December 1.

298. Meyer Memorial Trust
1515 SW Fifth Avenue, Suite 500
Portland, OR 97201
(503) 228-5512

Grants

Program Description The trust operates three types of grant-making programs. One of these is a special purpose program of support for children, which invites proposals from qualified applicants in Alaska, Idaho, Montana, Oregon, and Washington. The other two grant programs, general purpose grants and small grants, respond to a wide variety of unsolicited requests and are restricted to Oregon and that part of Washington located in the greater Portland metropolitan area.

Sample Grants To produce a public television program, "Road from Runnymede," which chronicals the origin of the U.S. Constitution, and to distribute film and related curriculum materials to schools, $238,000 to the Constitution Project, Portland, OR (1988). For a seminar for Oregon judges on the changes needed in the judicial system to protect the rights of crime victims, $18,000 to the Judicial Foundation for Criminal Justice, Portland, OR (1987). To evaluate the effectiveness of court-annexed mediation and arbitration, $3,000 to the Oregon Commission on the Judicial Branch, Portland, OR (1987).

Eligibility/Limitations The trust will normally make grants only to organizations that are tax-exempt under Section 501(c)(3) of the Internal Revenue Code and are not "private foundations" as defined under Section 509(a) of the Code. At this time, applications are invited only from the state of Oregon. The trust generally will not favor proposals seeking funds for direct grants, scholarships, or fellowships to individuals; endowments; general fund drives or annual appeals; ongoing general operating budgets; indirect or overhead costs; debt retirement or operational deficits; projects of sectarian or religious organizations whose principal benefit is for their own members or adherents; or propagandizing or influencing elections or legislation.

Fiscal Information Grants awarded in fiscal 1989 totaled over $11.1 million. There are no limitations on the size of the grant that may be requested in general purpose grant proposals. Small grants range from $500-$8,000.

Application Information The trust does not use a standard application form, although an application summary form (available from the trust office) must be submitted as the cover sheet to a proposal. A proposal must contain a description of the proposed project; a project budget; a statement of the financial condition of the applicant organization; and copies of the applicant's 501(c)3 and 509(a) tax-exemption letters, or documentation of other basis for tax exemption. More specific application procedures are available upon request from the trust.

Deadline(s) Requests for small grants should be submitted by January 15, April 15, July 15, or October 15. Children at Risk grants should be submitted by April 1 or October 1. General purpose grants may be submitted at any time.

299. The Michigan Society of Fellows
3030 Rackham Building
The University of Michigan
Ann Arbor, MI 48109-1070
(313) 763-1259

Fellowships in the Arts, Sciences, and Professions

Program Description The Michigan Society of Fellows was founded for the purpose of promoting the highest degree of excellence in the arts, sciences, and professions. The objective of the program is to support individuals selected for scholarly accomplishment and professional promise. The society invites applications from qualified candidates for three-year postdoctoral fellowships at the University of Michigan. Fellows are appointed as Assistant Professors/Postdoctoral Scholars with departmental affiliations. They spend the equivalent of one academic year teaching; the balance of time is devoted to their own scholarly research and creative work.

Eligibility/Limitations Candidates should be at the beginning of their professional careers, not more than three years beyond completion of their degrees. The Ph.D. or comparable professional degree, received prior to appointment, is required.

Fiscal Information Four new fellows will be selected for three-year terms beginning September 1. The stipend will be $24,000 plus insurance benefits.

Application Information Application materials are available upon request.

Deadline(s) Completed applications are due by October 15.

300. Mobil Foundation, Inc.
3225 Gallows Road, Room 3D809
Fairfax, VA 22037-0001

Grants

Program Description Mobil Foundation, Inc., offers grants to civic, health, art and cultural organizations, hospitals and educational institutions.

Eligibility/Limitations Charitable, federally tax-exempt organizations who meet funding criteria are eligible to apply. Grants are not made to individuals.

Fiscal Information Contributions in 1989 totaled over $9.9 million.

Application Information Grant applications to the foundation must be in writing and include the following: a brief description of the organization and its goals; amount requested and the specific purpose for it; other sources of funding; a budget and audited financial statement; other pertinent supporting data, such as an annual report, if available; and a copy of the organization's most recent tax-exemption letter under Section 501(c)(3) of the Internal Revenue Code.

Deadline(s) The foundation has no application deadlines.

301. Charles Stewart Mott Foundation
1200 Mott Foundation Building
Flint, MI 48502-1851
(313) 238-5651

Program Description The purpose of the Mott Foundation is to identify, demonstrate, support, test and disseminate principles that, in application, strengthen and enrich the quality of living of individuals and their community. Foundation grantmaking is organized under six program missions: education, environment, Flint area, neighborhoods and economic development, philanthropy and volunteerism, and exploratory and special projects.

Sample Grants To provide technical assistance and information to local organizations in their efforts to channel energy-overcharge funds toward conservation and energy-related aid for low- and moderate-income households, $15,000 to the National Consumer Law Center, Inc., Boston, MA (1987). To provide partial support for a conference on airborne toxic pollution in the Great Lakes, $15,000 to the Center for Environmental Study, Grand Rapids, MI (1987).

Eligibility/Limitations The foundation does not make grants to individuals. Normally, the foundation makes grants only to organizations accorded a tax-exempt 501(c)(3) public charity status by the IRS. Grant programs should generally be practical rather than theoretical. Capital, research, and endowment grants will be made only when they are necessary to carry out or advance a program objective or for strengthening relevant public policy.

Fiscal Information Grants awarded in 1988 totaled over $23 million.

Application Information Application guidelines are available upon request. To apply for a grant, send a letter stating the proposal simply and clearly. Generally, the following information is needed for full consideration: what the project will accomplish; how the objective will be reached; what effect it will have on the community; why the proposal is innovative; why the applicant organization is the one best equipped to achieve the desired result; other qualifications of the organization including Internal Revenue Service public charity classification, record of accomplishment, and the track record of leadership; a line-item budget, the proposed starting and ending dates, and plans for postgrant funding; and plans to evaluate the result. The letter should be clearly marked GRANT PROPOSAL and should be sent to the Office of Proposal Entry.

Deadline(s) Proposals may be submitted at any time. The trustees meet quarterly to review proposals. Normally, about four months are required to process proposals, allowing for a possible site visit and for studying the proposal in relation to other programs of the foundation. Grantees requesting renewal should also take this time requirement into consideration.

302. M.J. Murdock Charitable Trust

P.O. Box 1618
Vancouver, WA 98668
(206) 694-8415

Grants

Program Description The trust focuses its attention in a few fields of activity and on certain priorities within those fields. Projects or programs aimed at solutions to or the prevention of important problems, either through research or the application of existing knowledge and capabilities, will be favored, rather than those which deal with the consequences of problems or merely react to needs. Also favored are proposals which address critical priorities of regional or national, rather than local significance. Of major concern are endeavors which expand people's knowledge of themselves and their world and which promote those values and activities of society leading to a happier, healthier, freer, and more productive life.

Eligibility/Limitations Applications for grants are considered only from organizations which have been ruled to be tax-exempt under Section 501(c)(3) of the Internal Revenue Code and which are not private foundations as defined in Section 509(a) of the code. Grants are not awarded to individuals or to conduit organizations. Priority is given to applications for support of projects and programs conducted within the states of Washington, Oregon, Idaho, Montana, and Alaska.

Fiscal Information The trusts primary function is provide "up-front" or venture capital, along with that of other donors and the applicant's own resources, in the testing and validation of promising concepts and in launching of well thought-out programs which have the potential to thrive beyond the stage of initial funding.

Application Information Grant proposal guidelines and additional information are available from the foundation. The foundation will review letters of inquiry summarizing the main elements of a proposed project to determine whether a formal application would be within the foundation's interests.

Deadline(s) There are no specific deadlines for proposals.

303. The Henry A. Murray Research Center of Radcliffe College

10 Garden Street
Cambridge, MA 02138
(617) 495-8140

The Radcliffe Research Support Program

Program Description The Radcliffe Research Support Program offers small grants to postdoctoral investigators for research drawing on the data resources of the Murray Center.

Eligibility/Limitations Postdoctoral scholars in appropriate fields are eligible to apply.

Fiscal Information Funds are provided for travel to the center, duplicating, computer time, assistance in coding data, and other research expenses. Grants of up to $5,000 are available.

Application Information Write to the center for complete program descriptions and application guidelines.

Deadline(s) Deadlines for application are October 15, February 15, and April 15.

Additional Information The center funds dissertation research by women doctoral candidates. Contact the center for additional information.

304. The Henry A. Murray Research Center of Radcliffe College

10 Garden Street
Cambridge, MA 02138
(617) 495-8140

Visiting Scholars

Program Description Each year the Murray Center hosts three to five visiting scholars who wish to investigate some aspect of women and social change or the study of lives. Researchers have come from a wide range of fields including psychology, sociology, anthropology, political science, psychiatry, economics, law, and history.

Sample Grants A visiting scholarship was awarded to an associate professor from the College of Criminal Justice at Northeastern University who will continue longitudinal research on criminal careers and crime control.

Eligibility/Limitations Researchers in appropriate fields are eligible to apply.

Fiscal Information The program includes office space and a formal appointment at Radcliffe College which allows for access to the facilities of Radcliffe and Harvard. The program does not include a stipend.

Application Information Researchers interested in applying may contact the Murray Center for more information.

Deadline(s) The application deadline for the following summer or academic year is February 1.

305. National Academy of Education

Stanford University School of Education
CERAS-507
Stanford, CA 94305-3084

Spencer Fellowship Program

Program Description Spencer Fellowships are designed to promote scholarship in the United States and abroad on matters relevant to the improvement of education in all its forms.

Sample Grants Spencer postdoctoral scholars in 1990-1991 studied: the search for racial justice in the post-Brown era—the case of Ravenswood High School; the many faces of equal educational opportunity; and separate but equal—a case study of "good" pre-integration schooling for African-American children.

Eligibility/Limitations Applicants must have received their Ph.D., Ed.D. or equivalent degree no earlier than January 1, 1985. Applicants from education, the humanities, or the social or behavioral sciences are eligible.

Fiscal Information Fellows will receive $30,000 for one academic year of research, or $15,000 for each of two contiguous years, working half-time.

Application Information Contact the academy for further information and application forms. Applications may be made either directly by the individual applying for the fellowship or by nomination from a senior scholar.

Deadline(s) Completed applications and all supporting materials must be received by January 2.

306. National Association for Public Interest Law

1666 Connecticut Avenue, NW, Suite 424
Washington, DC 20009
(202) 462-0120

Loan Repayment Assistance Programs

Program Description Loan Repayment Assistance Programs, LRAPs, are postgraduate financial aid programs which assist law school graduates pursuing low-paying public interest positions in repaying their loans. Loan assistance plans offer a more efficient allocation of scarce financial aid resources to those who are most severely burdened by their educational debts as a result of their career choice.

Eligibility/Limitations To participate in a loan assistance program a graduate must hold qualifying employment, generally designated as legal or law-related work for the government, legal services, or a nonprofit organization as defined in sections 501(c)(3)-(5) of the IRS Code. In addition, most loan assistance programs require that a participant's disposable income be below a specified amount. A few LRAPs also stipulate a minimum educational loan debt.

Fiscal Information LRAPs are different from other financial aid plans in three respects: aid begins after graduation; it is contingent on the type of employment pursued by the graduate; and it varies according to the graduate's total income.

Application Information NAPIL acts as a national clearinghouse on loan repayment assistance and forgiveness programs. For further information contact NAPIL at the address above.

Deadline(s) As long as the applicant is a graduate from an eligible law school class, he or she can usually enter the LRAP anytime after graduation.

Additional Information Fifty law schools are currently attempting to establish LRAPs, and 22 campuses have already succeeded. Contact NAPIL for additional information.

307. The National Council for Soviet and East European Research

1755 Massachusetts Avenue, NW, Suite 304
Washington, DC 20036
(202) 387-0168

Research Program

Program Description The council is an incorporated, nonprofit, autonomous academic body whose purpose is to develop and sustain high-quality research and related activities dealing with the social, political, economic, and historical development of the USSR and Eastern Europe. Scholars should be guided by the following subject matter in formulating proposals: the operation of, and long-term prospects for, the Soviet and East European economies, including the burden of defense; long-term developments in Soviet and East European foreign policies as they affect the United States; long-term trends in Soviet and East European societies; and Soviet and East European intentions, objectives, and policy options. In addition to basic research, the council invites proposals that may include the following: meetings, seminars, workshops, conferences, consultations, pilot studies, and such other activities as are appropriate to the design, stimulation, or facilitation of relevant research; provisions for research assistants, the acquisition of research skills, and other activities in support of research-related training; contact and cooperation among individual scholars, and between them and specialists in government and private enterprise; the acquisition, processing, and maintenance of research materials and the development of bibliographies, data banks, and other reference aids; and the dissemination of research data, methodology, and findings.

Eligibility/Limitations Eligibility for funding as principal investigator is limited to scholars at the postdoctoral level for academic participants and to an equivalent degree of maturity and professional achievement for those from other fields. These qualifications are not required of research assistants. The coun-

cil will consider proposals for both collaborative and individual projects, to be submitted through U.S. institutions only.

Fiscal Information The council will not normally make awards of more than $50,000 for any individual project. Projects should be limited in duration to not more than one academic year and two summers. Council contracts are public documents. The council has established the policy or reimbursing institutional indirect costs at a rate of not more than 20 percent of the council's share of the total direct costs of sponsored research projects. The difference between 20 percent and standard negotiated rates may be treated as cost-sharing, and the council will look with special favor on proposals which include cost-sharing of both direct and indirect costs. Cost-sharing at a minimum of 10 percent in any combination of direct and/or indirect costs is mandatory.

Application Information Before preparing an application, scholars should obtain current application guidelines from the council. Applications to the council should take the form of institutional (principally educational) proposals for a research contract. The council's contracts involve provisions comparable to those of federal research contracts, and applicant institutions should be prepared to administer that level of complexity. Detailed guidance is available in federal codifications pertaining to contract costs, principles and procedures, OMB Circulars A-21, A-110, A-122, and the Federal Acquisition Regulations in particular. Thus scholars should prepare their applications, and especially budgets, in consultation with institutional officers responsible for the administration of federal research contracts.

Deadline(s) The deadline for submission of proposals is November 1.

308. National Endowment for Democracy

1101 15th Street, NW, Suite 203
Washington, DC 20005
(202) 293-9072

Grants

Program Description The National Endowment for Democracy is a new U.S. initiative to strengthen democratic institutions throughout the world through private, nongovernmental efforts. Through its worldwide grant program, the endowment assists those abroad who are working for democratic goals. In this effort, it seeks to enlist the energies and talents of private citizens and groups in the United States to work in partnership with democrats abroad. The endowment is currently funding programs in five substantive areas. (1) Pluralism—the endowment encourages the development of strong, independent, private-sector organizations, especially trade unions and business associations. (2) Democratic Governance and Political Processes—the endowment seeks to promote strong, stable political parties committed to the democratic process. The endowment will support programs on the rule of law and the administration of justice. (3) Education, Culture and Communications—the endowment funds programs that nourish a strong democratic civic culture, including support for publications and other communications media and training programs for journalists; the production and dissemination of books and other materials to strengthen popular understanding and intellectual advocacy of democracy; and programs of democratic education. (4) Research and Scholarly Cooperation—a modest portion of endowment resources is reserved for research, including studies of particular regions or countries where the endowment has special interest, and evaluations of previous or existing efforts to promote democracy. (5) International Cooperation—the endowment seeks to encourage regional and international cooperation in promoting democracy, including programs that strengthen cohesion among democracies and enhance coordination among democratic forces.

Sample Grants To support the formation of a Lawyers Association of Free Afghanistan (LAFA) based in Peshawar, Pakistan, committed to the rule of law and pluralistic democracy, respect for human rights and a central role for the private sector in rebuilding Afghanistan, $25,000 to American Friends of Afghanistan (1989). To assist the Federation of Korean Trade

Unions (FKTU) and its affiliated unions in increasing their ability to influence government policies, the federation sponsors programs which disseminate its views on labor law reform and legitimize the participation of unions in the policital process, $66,000 to Free Trade Union Institute, Korea (1989).

Eligibility/Limitations Funding decisions are made by the board of directors on the basis of established selection criteria. In addition to evaluating how a program fits within the endowment's overall priorities, the board considers factors such as the urgency of a program, its relevance to specific needs and conditions in a particular country, and the democratic commitment and experience of the applicant. The endowment is especially interested in proposals that originate with indigenous democratic groups.

Fiscal Information The endowment awarded grants totaling over $10 million in 1989.

Application Information Endowment staff is happy to discuss proposal ideas and welcomes preliminary letters of inquiry prior to submission of a formal proposal. Additional information and application guidelines are available from the director of public affairs of the endowment.

Deadline(s) Contact the endowment for current deadline information.

309. National Endowment for the Humanities
Division of Education Programs, Room 302
1100 Pennsylvania Avenue, NW
Washington, DC 20506
(202) 786-0380

Institutes for College and University Faculty

Program Description Each year the endowment supports national and regional institutes in which college and university faculty study important humanities texts or topics under the guidance of leading scholars. Institutes focus on materials related to a theme, issue, genre, major figure, period, or cultural movement, and they must be broadly applicable to subjects frequently taught at the undergraduate level. The endowment particularly encourages proposals that will assist participants in offering strong core humanities courses in their home institutions.

Eligibility/Limitations Any college, university, or cultural organization with appropriate resources and facilities may propose an institute. Faculty may be drawn from other institutions and, if necessary, from abroad. Institutes are usually offered during the summer for four to six weeks, depending on the scope of the topic. Typically, institutes involve 20 to 30 participants chosen by the institute director. An individual institution or group of institutions may also employ the institute format for internal use in preparing their own faculty to teach an improved curriculum.

Fiscal Information The average cost of an institute is approximately $160,000 in NEH funds. Potential applicants should contact the program for additional information on budget preparation.

Application Information If you plan to seek a grant from the endowment, request guidelines and application forms for the program in which you are interested. Write or call the program. Guidelines and application forms are generally available two months in advance of an application deadline.

Deadline(s) Application postmark deadlines are October 1 and April 1.

Additional Information Each year the division supports a few special projects that are intended to address national or regional needs in higher education in the humanities. These projects should be the product of collaboration by eminent scholars in a field, and they should address issues or topics of major significance for undergraduate teaching. Contact the endowment for additional information. In addition, the division is currently soliciting proposals in two special initiative categories. (1) The Foundations of American Society: within its existing fellowships programs, the endowment continues to encourage study, re-search, and discussion about the history, culture, and principles of the founding period, an emphasis that began with the initiative on the bicentennial of the U.S. Constitution. (2) The Columbian Quincentenary: proposals that explore the ideas—political, religious, philosophical, scientific, technological, and aesthetic—that shaped the processes of exploration, settlement, and cultural conflict and transformation set into motion by Columbus's momentous voyage are invited.

310. National Endowment for the Humanities
Division of Fellowships and Seminars, Room 316
1100 Pennsylvania Avenue, NW
Washington, DC 20506
(202) 786-0466

Fellowships for College Teachers and Independent Scholars

CFDA Program Number 45.143

Program Description These fellowships provide opportunities for individuals to pursue independent study and research that will enhance their capacities as teachers, scholars, or interpreters of the humanities and that will enable them to make significant contributions to thought and knowledge in the humanities. Fellowships enable people to devote extended periods of uninterrupted time to investigation, reflection, and often writing. The program is intended for a range of people, from those who have made significant contributions to the humanities to those who stand at the beginning of their careers. Projects, too, may cover a range of activities from general study to specialized research.

Sample Grants Fellowships were awarded in 1989 for a history of federal civil rights policy, 1972-80; for study of alternative pluralism—a comparison of Israeli and American constitutionalism; and for research on concepts of justice in late Imperial China.

Eligibility/Limitations The program of Fellowships for College Teachers and Independent Scholars, including special NEH initiatives within this program, is open to faculty members, either full-time or part-time, of two-year, four-year, and five-year colleges; faculty members of university departments, interdepartmental programs, and central graduate schools that do not grant the Ph.D.; individuals affiliated with institutions other than colleges and universities; and scholars and writers working independently. Individuals who have such positions on terminating contracts are eligible for this program as long as they do not take appointments in departments or programs that grant the Ph.D. before the January following the application deadline. Retired faculty members who had such positions are also eligible for this program. Although applicants need not have advanced degrees, those whose professional training includes a degree program must have received their degrees or completed all official requirements for them by the June 1 application deadline. If a prospective applicant has completed all of the official requirements for the degree and is awaiting only the formal award, certification that all requirements for the degree have been met by the application deadline must be submitted by the dean of the school awarding the degree. Persons seeking support for work leading to a degree are not eligible to apply, nor are active candidates for degrees, even if they expect to have finished all work for their degree by the time they would begin tenure of the fellowship and the work proposed is not related to the degree program. Persons who have recently held major fellowships or grants are not eligible to apply for an NEH fellowship. Specifically, three years must have elapsed between the conclusion of tenure of the fellowship or grant and the proposed beginning date of tenure for an NEH fellowship. For the endowment, a "major fellowship or grant" is a postdoctoral award or its equivalent which provides a continuous period of released time covering at least one term of the academic year; which enables the recipient to pursue scholarly research, personal study, professional development, or writing; that is in the amount of $10,000 or more; and which comes from sources other than the recipient's employing institution. Thus, sabbaticals and grants from an individual's own institution are not considered major fellowships, nor are stipends and grants from other sources supporting study and research during the summer academic recess, such as NEH Summer Stipends and NEH Summer Seminar awards. An applicant for an NEH fellowship should be a U.S. citizen, a native resident of a U.S. territorial possession, or a foreign national who has been residing in the United States or its territories for at least the three years immediately preceding the application deadline.

Fiscal Information Fellowships normally support full-time work and are awarded for continuous periods of six to twelve full months of tenure. The stipend is intended primarily to replace salary lost through the taking of leave. The maximum amount of the NEH stipend for tenure periods of between nine and twelve months, which for teachers encompass the full academic year, is $27,500. The maximum for periods of between six and nine months is prorated by months or, for teachers, by academic year terms. Some assistance may be provided within the stipend limit to help defray the costs of necessary travel, but no allowance is given for any other expense. Fellows may supplement their awards with small grants from other sources but may not hold other major fellowships or grants during fellowship tenure, except sabbaticals and grants from their own institutions. Successful applicants who receive offers of fellowships from other foundations after June 1 must hold the NEH fellowship first. Part-time fellowships can be awarded under exceptional circumstances, such as job responsibilities that cannot be relinquished or the value that teaching a particular course would have for the work proposed for the fellowship. Part-time fellowships carry a maximum stipend of $27,500 and are awarded for any amount of released time between half-time and full-time.

Application Information Guidelines and application materials are available from the Division of Fellowships and Seminars. When contacting NEH, include the name of the program for which you are applying.

Deadline(s) Applications must be postmarked by June 1.

Additional Information The division is currently soliciting proposals in two special initiative categories. (1) The Foundations of American Society: within its existing fellowships programs, the endowment continues to encourage study, research, and discussion about the history, culture, and principles of the founding period, an emphasis that began with the initiative on the bicentennial of the U.S. Constitution. (2) The Columbian Quincentenary: proposals that explore the ideas—political, religious, philosophical, scientific, technological, and aesthetic—that shaped the processes of exploration, settlement, and cultural conflict and transformation set into motion by Columbus's momentous voyage are invited.

311. National Endowment for the Humanities
Division of Fellowships and Seminars, Room 316
1100 Pennsylvania Avenue, NW
Washington, DC 20506
(202) 786-0466

Fellowships for University Teachers

CFDA Program Number 45.142

Program Description These fellowships provide opportunities for individuals to pursue independent study and research that will enhance their capacities as teachers, scholars, or interpreters of the humanities and that will enable them to make significant contributions to thought and knowledge in the humanities. Fellowships enable people to devote extended periods of uninterrupted time to investigation, reflection, and often writing. The program is intended for a range of people, from those who have made significant contributions to the humanities to those who stand at the beginning of their careers. Projects, too, may cover a range of activities from general study to specialized research.

Sample Grants Fellowships were awarded in 1990 for a study of Simon Greenleaf, Republican legal culture, and the rise of the Harvard Law Schol in mid-19th-century America; for a study of the origins of modern legal theory: from communal justice to common law. Fellowships were awarded in 1989 for a reappraisal of the Sacco and Vanzetti case; for a study on the laws of the Book of the Covenant; for a study on the law's conscience: equitable constitutionalism in America; for a study on

the justices of metropolitan London in the 18th century; for a study of the libel trial of a woman surgeon; and for a critique of legal bioethics.

Eligibility/Limitations The program of fellowships for university faculty, including special NEH initiatives within this program, is open only to faculty members of departments in universities that grant the Ph.D., faculty members with appointments to interdepartmental programs and central graduate schools that grant the Ph.D., and faculty members of postgraduate professional schools. Individuals who have such appointments either part-time or full-time or on terminating contracts are eligible only for this program. Retired faculty members who had such positions are normally eligible for this program. Although applicants need not have advanced degrees, those whose professional training includes a degree program must have received their degrees or completed all official requirements for them by the June 1 application deadline. If a prospective applicant has completed all of the official requirements for the degree and is awaiting only the formal award, certification that all requirements for the degree have been met by the application deadline must be submitted by the dean of the school awarding the degree. Persons seeking support for work leading to a degree are not eligible to apply, nor are active candidates for degrees, even if they expect to have finished all work for their degree by the time they would begin tenure of the fellowship and the work proposed is not related to the degree program. Persons who have recently held major fellowships or grants are not eligible to apply for an NEH fellowship. Specifically, three years must have elapsed between the conclusion of tenure of the fellowship or grant and the proposed beginning date of tenure for an NEH fellowship. For the endowment, a "major fellowship or grant" is a postdoctoral award or its equivalent which provides a continuous period of released time covering at least one term of the academic year; which enables the recipient to pursue scholarly research, personal study, professional development, or writing; which provides a stipend of at least $6,000; and which comes from sources other than the recipient's employing institution. Thus, sabbaticals and grants from an individual's own institution are not considered major fellowships, nor are stipends and grants from other sources supporting study and research during the summer academic recess, such as NEH Summer Stipends and NEH Summer Seminar awards. An applicant for an NEH fellowship should be a U.S. citizen, a native resident of a U.S. territorial possession, or a foreign national who has been residing in the United States or its territories for at least the three years immediately preceding the application deadline.

Fiscal Information Fellowships normally support full-time work and are awarded for continuous periods of six to twelve full months of tenure. The stipend is intended primarily to replace salary lost through the taking of leave. The maximum amount of the NEH stipend for tenure periods of between nine and twelve months, which for teachers encompass the full academic year, is $27,500. The maximum for periods of between six and nine months is prorated by months or, for teachers, by academic year terms. Some assistance may be provided within the stipend limit to help defray the costs of necessary travel, but no allowance is given for any other expense. Fellows may supplement their awards with small grants from other sources but may not hold other major fellowships or grants during fellowship tenure, except sabbaticals and grants from their own institutions. Successful applicants who receive offers of fellowships from other foundations after June 1 must hold the NEH fellowship first. Part-time fellowships can be awarded under exceptional circumstances, such as job responsibilities that cannot be relinquished or the value that teaching a particular course would have for the work proposed for the fellowship. Part-time fellowships carry a maximum stipend of $27,500 and are awarded for any amount of released time between half-time and full-time.

Application Information Guidelines and application materials are available from the Division of Fellowships and Seminars. When contacting NEH include the name of the program for which you are applying.

Deadline(s) Applications must be postmarked by June 1.

Additional Information The division is currently soliciting proposals in two special initiative categories. (1) The Foundations of American Society: within its existing fellowships programs, the endowment continues to encourage study, research, and discussion about the history, culture, and principles of the founding period, an emphasis that began with the initiative on the bicentennial of the U.S. Constitution. (2) The Columbian Quincentenary: proposals that explore the ideas—political, religious, philosophical, scientific, technological, and aesthetic—that shaped the processes of exploration, settlement, and cultural conflict and transformation set into motion by Columbus's momentous voyage are invited.

312. National Endowment for the Humanities

Division of Fellowships and Seminars, Room 316
1100 Pennsylvania Avenue, NW
Washington, DC 20506
(202) 786-0463

Summer Seminars for College Teachers

CFDA Program Number 45.116

Program Description Summer seminars for college teachers are offered for teachers at undergraduate and two-year colleges who wish to deepen and enrich their knowledge of the subjects they teach. The purpose of the seminars is to provide college teachers with opportunities to work with distinguished scholars in their teaching or research fields; to work with other college teachers who share similar interests; and to undertake an individual project (e.g., intensive reading, scholarly research or writing) of their own choosing at institutions with libraries suitable for advanced work. The seminars offered in the program deal with significant works and subject matter of central concern to the humanities. Proposals to direct summer seminars for college teachers are encouraged from professors who are not only recognized scholars in their fields but who are also well qualified by virtue of their interest and ability in undergraduate teaching or the pertinence of their work to the interests of undergraduate teachers.

Sample Grants A summer seminar on "Liberal Ideals in American Law, 1870-1940," was held at Stanford University (1990). A summer seminar on "American Constitutionalism in Comparative Perspective" was held at the University of Notre Dame (1989). A summer seminar on "Anthropological Approaches to Law" was held at Princeton University (1989). A summer seminar on "Biblical Law in Historical Perspective" was held at the University of California, Berkeley (1988).

Eligibility/Limitations College teachers wishing to participate in the seminars should be persons who are well qualified to do the work of the seminar, who are able and committed teachers, and who can make significant contributions to the seminar. The program is intended primarily for individuals teaching undergraduate courses, full- or part-time, at two-year, four-year, or five-year colleges and universities, but other persons who are qualified to do the work of the seminar and make a contribution are also eligible to apply. Preference will be given to those who have been teaching at least three years and who have not recently had the resources of a major library readily available to them. Faculty members of departments with doctoral programs in the humanities are not eligible as participants in this program.

Fiscal Information Participation in each seminar is limited to twelve college teachers, each of whom receives a stipend of $3,500 for the eight-week seminar or $2,750 for the six-week seminar. The selection of participants and the awarding of stipends is the responsibility of seminar directors, acting in consultation with their selection committees and within the guidelines established by the endowment. Funds are officially awarded to the institution hosting the NEH summer seminar (in most instances the institution with which the selected seminar director is affiliated). The grant will include stipends for the participants, salary for the seminar director, secretarial support, and direct and indirect costs to the host institution. General grant provisions, narrative and financial reporting requirements and forms, payment information, and applicable conditions and special provisions are provided within the award notification.

Institutional fiscal personnel and the seminar director will be expected to comply with normal grant procedures.

Application Information After the decisions are made on the seminars to be offered, the complete list of seminars will be publicized by the endowment. College teachers wishing to participate in the seminars should apply directly to the seminar director. Potential directors should apply through institutions.

Deadline(s) The deadline for receipt of applications is March 1 for participants and directors.

Additional Information The division is currently soliciting proposals in two special initiative categories. (1) The Foundations of American Society: within its existing fellowships programs, the endowment continues to encourage study, research, and discussion about the history, culture, and principles of the founding period, an emphasis that began with the initiative on the bicentennial of the U.S. Constitution. (2) The Columbian Quincentenary: proposals that explore the ideas—political, religious, philosophical, scientific, technological, and aesthetic—that shaped the processes of exploration, settlement, and cultural conflict and transformation set into motion by Columbus's momentous voyage are invited.

313. National Endowment for the Humanities

Division of Fellowships and Seminars, Room 316
1100 Pennsylvania Avenue, NW
Washington, DC 20506
(202) 786-0463

Summer Seminars for School Teachers

Program Description Participants' grants provide support for full-time or regular part-time school teachers to participate in summer seminars focusing on significant texts in the humanities and directed by accomplished teachers and active scholars. Director's grants provide support for accomplished teachers and scholars to direct summer seminars at colleges, universities, museums, libraries, and similar institutions.

Sample Grants A summer seminar was held on "The Bill of Rights and American Liberty: Freedom of Expression" (1988).

Eligibility/Limitations Although seminars are designed primarily for full-time or regular part-time teachers at public, private or parochial schools, grades 7 through 12, other school personnel, K-12 are also eligible to apply. Applicants must be U.S. citizens, native residents of a U.S. territorial possession, or foreign nationals who have been residing in the United States for at least three years immediately preceding the application deadline.

Fiscal Information Teachers selected to participate in the program will receive a stipend of $2,000, $2,375, or $2,750, depending on the length of the seminar. The stipend is intended to cover travel costs to and from the seminar location, books and other research expenses, and living expenses for the tenure of the seminar.

Application Information Applicants must write to the seminar directors for application instructions and forms and for detailed information about the structure, special requirements, site, and housing of seminars. Applicants may apply only to one seminar. However, applicants may write to more than one seminar director for information. Applicants who apply to more than one seminar will not be eligible for a place in any seminar. The director and a selection committee will decide who will attend the seminar. Therefore, the complete application should be mailed directly to the seminar director. Potential directors may apply through institutions.

Deadline(s) Applications should be postmarked no later than March 1 for participants and April 1 for directors.

Additional Information The division is currently soliciting proposals in two special initiative categories. (1) The Foundations of American Society: within its existing fellowships programs, the endowment continues to encourage study, research, and discussion about the history, culture, and principles of the founding period, an emphasis that began with the initiative on the bicentennial of the U.S. Constitution. (2) The Columbian Quincentenary: proposals that explore the ideas—political, religious, philosophical, scientific, technological, and aesthetic—that shaped the processes of exploration, settlement, and cultural conflict and transformation set into motion by Columbus's momentous voyage are invited.

314. National Endowment for the Humanities

Division of Fellowships and Seminars, Room 316
1100 Pennsylvania Avenue, NW
Washington, DC 20506
(202) 786-0466

Summer Stipends

CFDA Program Number 45.121

Program Description The summer stipends program provides support for faculty members in universities and in two-year and four-year colleges, and for others working in the humanities so that they can devote two consecutive months of full-time study and research to a project. The proposed project should be not only an immediate contribution to learning in a particular field, but also a contribution to the advancement of knowledge in the humanities more generally, and to the applicant's development as a scholar, teacher, and interpreter of the humanities. Each college and university in the United States and its territorial possessions may nominate three members of its faculty for the Summer Stipend competition. No more than two of the nominees may be in the early stages of their careers, i.e., junior nominees; no more than two may be at a more advanced stage, i.e., senior nominees.

Sample Grants Summer stipends were awarded in 1990 for study of when cultural factors may be a legal defense in American courts; and for a study of law and modernization: the underground financial system in Taiwan. Summer stipends were awarded in 1989 for study of the revolution in the family: Soviet law and social change, 1917-1936, for study in legal guardianship over women in 13th- and 14th-century Flanders; for study of prostitution and the law: the formation of social policy in early Imperial Rome; and for study of the legal foundations of character in the 18th-century English novel.

Eligibility/Limitations An applicant for an endowment fellowship should be a U.S. citizen, a native resident of a U.S. territorial possession, or a foreign national who has been residing in the United States or its territories for at least the three years immediately preceding the application deadline. Although applicants need not have advanced degrees, those whose professional training includes a degree program must have received their degrees, or completed all official requirements for them by October 1. If a prospective applicant has completed all of the official requirements for the degree and is awaiting only the formal award, certification that all requirements have been met by the application deadline must be submitted by the dean of the school awarding the degree. Persons seeking support for work leading toward degrees are not eligible to apply, nor are active candidates for degrees, even if they expect to have finished all work for their degree by the time they would begin tenure of the summer stipend and the work proposed is not related to their degree program. Preference is given to persons who have not received major fellowships or other leave-providing grants, except sabbaticals or grants from their own institutions, within the last five years. The more recent the grant, the more heavily it weighs in the endowment's decision.

Fiscal Information Each summer stipend provides $3,500 for two consecutive summer months of full-time study or research. Recipients of summer stipends may not hold major fellowships or grants during the tenure of their awards, and they must devote full time to their projects for the two months of their tenure.

Application Information Application forms and additional information and guidelines are available from the Division of Fellowships and Seminars. When contacting NEH include the program for which you are applying.

Deadline(s) Applications must be postmarked by October 1.

Additional Information The division is currently soliciting proposals in two special initiative categories. (1) The Foundations of American Society: within its existing fellowships programs, the endowment continues to encourage study, research, and discussion about the history, culture, and principles of the founding period, an emphasis that began with the initiative on the bicentennial of the U.S. Constitution. (2) The Columbian Quincentenary: proposals that explore the ideas—political, religious, philosophical, scientific, technological, and aesthetic—that shaped the processes of exploration, settlement, and cultural conflict and transformation set into motion by Columbus's momentous voyage are invited.

315. National Endowment for the Humanities

Division of Fellowships and Seminars, Room 316
1100 Pennsylvania Avenue, NW
Washington, DC 20506
(202) 786-0463

Travel to Collections

CFDA Program Number 45.152

Program Description The purpose of the Travel to Collections program is to enable American scholars to travel to use the research collections of libraries, archives, museums, or other repositories to consult research materials of fundamental importance for the progress of their scholarly work. This grant program is intended to help scholars meet the costs associated with a research trip anywhere in the world. The research proposed must fall within the scope of the humanities. Projects in the social sciences which are historical or philosophical, or which attempt to cast light on questions of interpretation or criticism traditionally in the humanities, are eligible, as are historical or philosophical studies of the natural sciences. Projects that involve critical, historical, and theoretical studies of the arts are eligible for support. The program is designed for scholars whose research could not progress satisfactorily without consultation of materials at a specific location.

Sample Grants Travel to Collections grants were awarded in 1989 to support a study of crime and law in Guangdong Province, China, 1770-1840; a study of democratic crisis, American politics and election laws, 1870-1910; a study of the ritual trial of Trent, 1475-1478; a study of Justice Stephen J. Field and post-Civil War American law; and a study of a new edition of a Roman law on the water supply of Rome.

Eligibility/Limitations Applicants should be citizens of the United States, native residents of U.S. territorial possessions, or foreign nationals who have lived in the United States or its territories for three years immediately prior to submitting an application. Applicants need not have academic affiliations to be eligible. Although applicants need not have advanced degrees, candidates for degrees and persons seeking support for work leading to degrees are not eligible. Applications that are focused on pedagogical theory, research in educational methods, tests and measurements, or cognitive psychology, are not eligible.

Fiscal Information Applicants recommended for awards will receive an award of $750 in one payment. The award is to be used exclusively to help defray the scholar's expenses in undertaking the specific research trip, including travel costs, subsistence and lodging, reproduction and photoduplication costs, and other associated research expenses. Applications for research travel to locations easily accessible to the applicant on a regular basis will not be competitive. Applicants are expected to undertake the research travel during the period proposed in the application. The expenditures proposed may not include salary support or replacement or support for released time from the applicant's regular employment.

Application Information Application forms and additional information and guidelines are available from the Division of Fellowships and Seminars. When contacting NEH, include the program for which you are applying.

Deadline(s) To be eligible for consideration an application must be postmarked no later than July 16 or January 15.

Additional Information The division is currently soliciting proposals in two special initiative categories. (1) The Foundations of American Society: within its existing fellowships programs, the endowment continues to encourage study, research, and discussion about the history, culture, and principles of the founding period, an emphasis that began with the initiative on the bicentennial of the U.S. Constitution. (2) The Columbian Quincentenary: proposals that explore the ideas—political, religious, philosophical, scientific, technological, and aesthetic—that shaped the processes of exploration, settlement, and cultural conflict and transformation set into motion by Columbus's momentous voyage are invited.

316. National Endowment for the Humanities

Division of Fellowships and Seminars, Room 316
1100 Pennsylvania Avenue, NW
Washington, DC 20506
(202) 786-0463

Younger Scholars Program

CFDA Program Number 45.115

Program Description Awards for younger scholars provide the nation's students with opportunities to conduct noncredit independent research and writing projects during the summer months. Under the close supervision of advisers who are humanities scholars, individuals pursue their own humanities projects during a concentrated period of time not normally available during the school year. This program enables grantees to enhance their intellectual development by producing research papers on a specific humanities topic. In both subject matter and methodology, projects must be firmly grounded in one of the disciplines of the humanities. Applicants are expected to discuss the way in which their projects engage one or more of the following areas of emphasis: the interpretation of cultural works; the study of historical ideas, figures, and events; and understanding the disciplines of the humanities.

Sample Grants Grants to younger scholars have been awarded to support research on: "Rape Cases and Their Relation to Racial Attitudes in the Antebellum Era" (1990); "Racial Integration in Washington, DC: A Legal History" (1990); "Constraints on Judicial Freedom in Legal Interpretation" (1990); "Gerrymandering: A Legal and Political Study of Redistricting" (1989); "Individual Liberty and AIDS: A Milliam Perspective" (1989); "The Legal History of a California Town" (1988); and "Law and DeSoto's Expedition" (1988).

Eligibility/Limitations The program is intended for two groups of students. High-school younger scholar awards are made to secondary school students, and college younger scholars awards are made to undergraduates below the level of senior. These two competitions will be judged separately. Applicants must be 21 years of age or under throughout the entire calendar year in which the application is submitted; or, if they are over 21, they must be full-time college students pursuing an undergraduate degree at the time of application. Applicants must be either U.S. citizens or foreign nationals who have lived in the United States for at least three consecutive years at the time of application. Proposed projects require a project adviser with knowledge and qualifications in an appropriate humanities discipline and must result in a substantial research paper. Individuals who will have received or expect to receive a bachelor's degree by October 1 are not eligible to apply. No project activities may take place outside the United States during the grant period. Joint projects by two or more individuals may not be submitted.

Fiscal Information College students (or high-school graduates at the time of application) may apply for $2,200, of which $400 is allotted to the adviser. High-school students (at the time of application) may apply for $1,800, of which $400 is allotted to the adviser. All grants involve nine weeks of full-time work by an individual on a specific humanities project during the summer months. Grantees may not be enrolled in a credit course during the grant period, and projects may not be used for academic credit.

Application Information Application forms and additional information are available from the Division of Fellowships and Seminars. When contacting NEH, include the program for which you are applying.

Deadline(s) Applications should be received by November 1.

Additional Information The division is currently soliciting proposals in two special initiative categories. (1) The Foundations of American Society: within its existing fellowships programs, the endowment continues to encourage study, research, and discussion about the history, culture, and principles of the founding period, an emphasis that began with the initiative on the bicentennial of the U.S. Constitution. (2) The Columbian Quincentenary: proposals that explore the ideas—political, religious, philosophical, scientific, technological, and aesthetic—that shaped the processes of exploration, settlement, and cultural conflict and transformation set into motion by Columbus's momentous voyage are invited.

317. National Endowment for the Humanities

Division of General Programs
1100 Pennsylvania Avenue, NW, Room 420
Washington, DC 20506
(202) 786-0271

Humanities Projects in Libraries and Archives

CFDA Program Number 45.137

Program Description Through the Humanities Projects in Libraries and Archives, the endowment supports programs that are designed to increase public understanding of the humanities through the discovery, interpretation, and greater appreciation of books and other resources in library collections. Projects should involve the active collaboration of scholars from the appropriate disciplines of the humanities and the professional staff of libraries during both the planning and implementation of programs. The Humanities Projects in Libraries program encourages public, academic, or special libraries to plan and present programs in the humanities. The program also encourages the development of cooperative projects between public, academic, or special libraries, as well as between libraries, museums, historical societies, and other cultural institutions. Programs may also take place at locations other than a library, but the primary objective of using the resources of libraries to enhance the understanding and appreciation of the humanities must be evident in the design of any project. Applicants for these grants are expected to address the manner in which their projects deal with one or more of the following areas: the appreciation and interpretation of cultural works; the illumination of historical ideas, figures, and events; and an understanding of the disciplines of the humanities.

Eligibility/Limitations Eligible applicants include nonprofit public, academic, special, or institutional libraries; local, statewide or regional library systems; and state, regional, or national library associations. The following types of projects are not eligible for support: projects to create musical composition, dance, painting, sculpture, poetry, short stories or novels, and projects providing for performance or training in these arts; projects from profit-making organizations or institutions, or from individuals without an organizational or institutional base; projects whose primary function is to mount exhibitions from the collections of museums or historical societies; projects that have as their primary focus a media production; projects for renovation, restoration, rehabilitation, construction, establishment of historic markers and plaques or for historic preservation; projects that have as their primary focus organizing, cataloguing, indexing, microfilming, or preserving collections; projects that consist primarily of research activities; individual fellowships and stipends, support for graduate education, or projects that require participants to register for academic credit; projects for training of personnel or individual requests for travel to professional meetings; the publication or editorial costs of articles or monographs for scholarly audiences; and projects directed at persuading an audience to a particular political, philosophical, religious, or ideological point of view or that advocate a particular program of social action or change.

Fiscal Information Humanities Projects in Libraries offers planning and implementation grants. Planning grants are awarded to support the collaborative efforts of scholars and an institution's administrative staff to design programs. Planning grants generally last no longer than six months and usually range from $5,000 to $15,000. Support may occasionally exceed $15,000 if such activities are regional or national in scope or involve more than one type of institution. Requests for funds in excess of $15,000 should be discussed with the program's staff before an application is made. Implementation grants support the presentation of fully developed public programs in the humanities. Such grants are normally funded for periods of one to three years. These grants usually range from $15,000 to $200,000. Requests for funds in excess of $200,000 should be discussed with the program's staff before an application is submitted. Cost sharing of at least 20 percent of a project's total budget is recommended for an implementation grant.

Application Information Application forms and additional information are available from the Division of General Programs.

Deadline(s) The deadlines for receipt of application for planning projects are August 3, November 2, February 1, and May 3. The deadlines for receipt of applications for implementation grants are September 14 and March 15.

Additional Information Within its existing programs, the endowment continues to support study of the foundations of American society. This initiative encourages study, research, and discussion about the history, culture, and principles of the American founding, an emphasis that began with the NEH initiative on the bicentennial of the U.S. Constitution. Proposals may deal directly with the events and achievements of the founding, including the ratification of the new Constitution, the establishment of the federal government, and the works of philosophy, politics, literature, and art that were produced during this founding period.

318. National Endowment for the Humanities

Division of General Programs, Room 420
1100 Pennsylvania Avenue, NW
Washington, DC 20506
(202) 786-0278

Humanities Projects in Media

CFDA Program Number 45.104

Program Description Projects supported by the Media Program present—through television, film, and radio programming—the most important work in scholarship and learning in the humanities, and they engage the public in critical analysis and interpretation. The program expects high technical standards and intellectual depth and rigor; thus, projects must involve collaboration between humanities scholars and experienced producers, directors, and writers. Scholars participate in each project at every stage—planning, script preparation, and production—to ensure that the information presented is conceptually sound and factually accurate. Producers, directors, and writers work with the scholars to develop an intellectual and artistic approach and vision for the programs, shaping the material into attractive, imaginative, and intellectually stimulating programs. The program supports historical and cultural documentaries, dramatizations, talk shows, animation, or combinations of these formats. All television projects must have demonstrable value for a national audience, either adult or youth. Radio projects may be designed for local, regional, or national distribution. The program is especially interested in applications for television and radio biographies of people who have been important to our nation's history. Projects may be full-length biography, focus on a single aspect of an individual's life, or present a collective biography, thematically organized. Either the documentary or the dramatic format may be used.

Sample Grants To produce five one-hour television programs for a dramatic miniseries based on *Simple Justice*, Richard Kluger's history of the Supreme Court decision *Brown vs. Board*

of Education, $1,000,800 in outright funds and $500,000 in matching funds to New Images Productions, Berkeley, CA (1989).

Eligibility/Limitations Any private, nonprofit organization, college or university, or branch of state or local government may apply for a Media Program grant. In addition, any group of scholars or professionals with experience in media and the humanities may form their own nonprofit group to apply for funding. Applicants are not required to be incorporated or to have 501(c)(3) status with the Internal Revenue Service although obtaining such status is recommended, especially for larger projects. In any case, applicants must have the ability to administer the project in compliance with federal regulations as well as generally accepted accounting principles. The Media Program does not provide support for the following projects: projects to create musical composition, dance, painting, sculpture, poetry, short stories, novels, or projects providing for performance or training in these arts; projects directed at persuading an audience to a particular political, philosophical, religious, or ideological point of view or that advocate a particular program of social action or change; projects that are designed exclusively to preserve information for deposit in archives; projects that require the permanent acquisition of facilities or equipment or the establishment of training programs in film, radio, or television productions; projects aimed at technological experimentation in the development of electronic media; and instructional projects primarily designed for classroom use.

Fiscal Information The endowment provides three types of funding for projects: matching grants, outright grants, and a combination of the two. Endowment matching funds are awarded on an up to one-for-one basis. An outright grant is one in which the award of endowment funds is not contingent on the applicant's raising gifts for the project. Applicants may also request a combination of outright and matching funds from the endowment.

Application Information Early contact with Media Program staff can be helpful and is strongly recommended. Either a letter describing the project or a draft proposal may be submitted (no later than six weeks before the deadline to allow time for a response). A staff member will be able to determine if the basic idea fits within the general guidelines of the program and, if time permits, can help anticipate some questions that reviewers and panelists may later raise. In preparing the application, applicants should remember that it will be read by both authorities in the subject area and professionals in the broadcast industry. The more precise an applicant can be about a proposal's concept, its importance in the humanities, the way it will be developed, how the medium will be used to enhance it, and the roles of key participants, the more likely it is that evaluators will have confidence in the quality of the project, in the applicant's control of it and ability to carry it out.

Deadline(s) Applications should be received by March 15 and September 14.

Additional Information The Media Program has three funding categories—planning, scripting, and production—which are designed to help applicants produce high-quality programs, following appropriate stages and steps. However, the applicant may apply in any category depending on the status and needs of the project in question. In addition, the division is currently soliciting proposals in two special initiative categories. (1) The Foundations of American Society: within its existing fellowships programs, the endowment continues to encourage study, research, and discussion about the history, culture, and principles of the founding period, an emphasis that began with the initiative on the bicentennial of the U.S. Constitution. (2) The Columbian Quincentenary: proposals that explore the ideas—political, religious, philosophical, scientific, technological, and aesthetic—that shaped the processes of exploration, settlement, and cultural conflict and transformation set into motion by Columbus's momentous voyage are invited.

319. National Endowment for the Humanities

Division of General Programs, Room 420
1100 Pennsylvania Avenue, NW
Washington, DC 20506
(202) 786-0284

Humanities Projects in Museums and Historical Organizations

CFDA Program Number 45.125

Program Description The goal of this program is to help make possible exhibitions that "speak" to people today, exhibitions that give visitors an understanding and appreciation of an object itself and also of its relationship to ideas, events, and aesthetics. The endowment seeks to facilitate the groundwork of research and collections management that are the foundation for any intellectually substantial public exhibition, and it seeks to help in the planning and implementation of the exhibitions themselves. The spectrum of endowment support extends from an inventory of permanent collections to the preparation of catalogues, to the sharing of collections among several museums. The endowment supports projects designed especially for children as well as those designed for adults. It supports the preparation of publications related to permanent collections and to both temporary and permanent exhibitions. In addition, the endowment can assist in the conservation of objects used in an exhibition or, under some circumstances, objects that are part of the permanent collection.

Sample Grants To support an exhibition that will examine the critical issues our nation's government faced in the first year under the Constitution, $254,129 to the National Park Foundation, Washington, DC (1989).

Eligibility/Limitations Eligible applicants include museums, historical societies, and other nonprofit organizations and institutions.

Fiscal Information Project costs can be supported by (1) endowment funds and (2) cash and noncash contributions, such as donated services and goods, which are contributed to the project by the applicant and nonfederal third parties. Contributions from the applicant and third parties constitute the applicant organization's "cost sharing." While the program for museums and historical organizations does not have established requirements on levels of cost sharing, all applicants are encouraged to participate in the support of the expenses related to carrying out a project, especially for large projects. More specific information on cost sharing is available from the program. The endowment provides three types of funding for projects: matching grants, outright grants, and a combination of the two. The program for museums and historical organizations does not provide support for the following activities: projects in the creative or performing arts; establishment of a new institution; general operating expenses; architectural preservation; acquisition of artifacts, works of art, or documents; purchase of permanent equipment for general operation purposes (filing cabinets, office equipment or furniture); capital improvements of buildings; attendance at professional meetings; and projects that focus on current affairs or events for the purpose of eliciting a specific public response or advocating a particular program of social action or change.

Application Information Additional information and specific guidelines are available from the program.

Deadline(s) Applications should be received by June 7 and December 7.

320. National Endowment for the Humanities

Division of General Programs, Room 426
1100 Pennsylvania Avenue, NW
Washington, DC 20506
(202) 786-0271

Public Humanities Projects

CFDA Program Number 45.113

Program Description This program offers support to a wide variety of projects designed to increase public understanding of the humanities. Through this program the endowment recognizes exemplary public programs and promotes model projects that may have national significance. The program is especially interested in identifying new opportunities for calling the public's attention to the work of humanities scholars. This program does not restrict its grantmaking to any one type of project, and applicants may make use of a number of formats—including public symposia, community forums, debates, interpretive pamphlets, or audio-visual materials—to reach segments of the general public with humanities scholarship.

Sample Grants To support two conferences on the American judiciary and on religion and the U.S. Constitution, $75,000 to Georgetown University (1988).

Eligibility/Limitations Eligible applicants include colleges and universities, professional organizations or associations, cultural and community organizations, agencies of state and local governments, and various nonprofit community groups. In many cases, an applicant will be a consortium of such groups or an ad-hoc group formed to mount special, one-time events such as the commemoration of an anniversary. As a general rule, priority is given to applications which promise to reach a national and regional audience, but well-conceived local projects are frequently competitive. All projects should feature the participation of scholars from one or more disciplines of the humanities.

Fiscal Information The program offers both planning grants and implementation awards. Normally, planning grants range from $5,000 to $20,000 and last no longer than six months. Cost sharing is not required for planning grants. Implementation grants may range from $15,000 to $150,000 and are funded for periods of one to three years. Normally, the endowment will support no more than 80 percent of the total costs of an implementation project.

Application Information Applicants should submit a preliminary proposal six to eight weeks before a deadline, and this draft should include a tentative budget to enable the program staff to determine eligibility and competitiveness. Contact the program for guidelines and application forms.

Deadline(s) The program runs two competitions each year; deadlines are March 15 and September 14.

Additional Information The division is currently soliciting proposals in two special initiative categories. (1) The Foundations of American Society: within its existing fellowships programs, the endowment continues to encourage study, research, and discussion about the history, culture, and principles of the founding period, an emphasis that began with the initiative on the bicentennial of the U.S. Constitution. (2) The Columbian Quincentenary: proposals that explore the ideas—political, religious, philosophical, scientific, technological, and aesthetic—that shaped the processes of exploration, settlement, and cultural conflict and transformation set into motion by Columbus's momentous voyage are invited.

321. National Endowment for the Humanities

Division of Research Programs, Room 318
1100 Pennsylvania Avenue, NW
Washington, DC 20506
(202) 786-0204

Centers for Advanced Study

CFDA Program Number 45.122

Program Description Through grants in this category, the endowment supports coordinated research in well-defined subject areas at independent centers for advanced study, overseas research centers, independent research libraries, and research museums. In assessing an application from a center, the endowment emphasizes the intrinsic importance of the work to be undertaken at the center, the relation of this work to the center's collections and other facilities, and the degree to which arrangements at the center will promote collegial exchange. The regrants awarded by the centers enable individual scholars to pursue their own research for periods ranging from six to twelve months and to participate in the interchange of ideas among the center's scholars.

Eligibility/Limitations Awards are made to colleges and universities and to organizations such as learned societies, federations and committees of scholarly associations, and major independent research libraries and centers.

Application Information Centers, libraries, museums, or other appropriate institutions that wish to apply to this program should write to the endowment to request more detailed information and application instructions. Individuals interested in pursuing research at any of the centers receiving endowment support should apply directly to the centers themselves. A list of currently funded centers is available from the endowment on request.

Deadline(s) Applications should be received by December 1.

Additional Information The division is currently soliciting proposals in two special initiative categories. (1) The Foundations of American Society: within its existing fellowships programs, the endowment continues to encourage study, research, and discussion about the history, culture, and principles of the founding period, an emphasis that began with the initiative on the bicentennial of the U.S. Constitution. (2) The Columbian Quincentenary: proposals that explore the ideas—political, religious, philosophical, scientific, technological, and aesthetic—that shaped the processes of exploration, settlement, and cultural conflict and transformation set into motion by Columbus's momentous voyage are invited.

322. National Endowment for the Humanities
Division of Research Programs, Room 318
1100 Pennsylvania Avenue, NW
Washington, DC 20506
(202) 786-0204

Conferences
CFDA Program Number 45.134

Program Description Grants in this category support conferences that enable both American and foreign scholars to advance the current state of research on topics of major importance in the humanities. These conferences should be designed to accomplish objectives that cannot be achieved by other means. Normally, presenters at the conference number from 10 to 20 and include both junior and senior scholars. Other conference participants number from 30 to 200 and should draw junior and senior faculty from a wide range of institutions and fields of specialty.

Sample Grants To support an international conference on Montesquiew's influence on the formation of the U.S. Constitution, $25,000 to the Committee on Montesquiew and the American Constitution, Claremont, CA (1989).

Eligibility/Limitations Awards are made to colleges and universities and to organizations such as learned societies, federations and committees of scholarly associations, and major independent research libraries and centers.

Fiscal Information In addition to the costs of organizing and publicizing the conference itself, endowment funds awarded to the sponsoring institution or organization support travel and other expenses for the presenters as well as stipends to participants for partial travel and per diem expenses. Support is also available for the publication of conference results, but such publication costs are frequently contributed by the applicant as cost sharing. Normally, the endowment's contribution to the total costs of a conference will range from $6,000 to $40,000, depending upon the number of participants. All applicants are encouraged to seek full or partial support through federal matching funds.

Application Information Centers, libraries, museums, or other appropriate institutions that wish to apply to this program should write to the endowment to request more detailed information and application instructions.

Deadline(s) Applications should be received by January 15.

Additional Information The division is currently soliciting proposals in two special initiative categories. (1) The Foundations of American Society: within its existing fellowships programs,

the endowment continues to encourage study, research, and discussion about the history, culture, and principles of the founding period, an emphasis that began with the initiative on the bicentennial of the U.S. Constitution. (2) The Columbian Quincentenary: proposals that explore the ideas—political, religious, philosophical, scientific, technological, and aesthetic—that shaped the processes of exploration, settlement, and cultural conflict and transformation set into motion by Columbus's momentous voyage are invited.

323. National Endowment for the Humanities
Division of Research Programs, Room 318
1100 Pennsylvania Avenue, NW
Washington, DC 20506
(202) 786-0210

Interpretive Research: Humanities, Science, and Technology

CFDA Program Number 45.133

Program Description Grants in this program support research that brings to bear the knowledge, methods, and perspectives of the humanities on the subjects of science, technology, and medicine. Historical studies and studies of current topics are eligible. Studies of current science, technology, or medicine must deal with fundamental issues, and the humanities must play a central role. The endowment encourages studies that promote the collaboration of humanities scholars with scientists as well as projects that promise to improve interdisciplinary approaches to research. All projects are expected to lead to major publications. Support is available for collaborative or coordinated research in many areas of inquiry that include, but are not limited to, the form, content, and purposes of scientific knowledge; the processes through which scientific knowledge is developed; the invention, innovation, and transfer of technology; the social, moral, and legal meaning of specific scientific and technological innovations; the interaction among sciences, technology, and other elements of culture; and the methods and concepts that the humanities use to study science and technology. The endowment supports projects that involve historical and philosophical approaches to the social sciences, but does not support empirical social scientific research, specific policy studies, or technical impact assessments.

Sample Grants To support the research and writing of a book that will explore the philosophical questions of distributive justice raised by the AIDS epidemic, $120,000 to Tufts University, Medford, MA (1989). To support a study of urban growth in the United States from 1840 to 1980 that will focus on the environmental consequences and the political, legal, and civic responses to problems associated with the growth of cities, $165,065 to the University of Houston-University Park (1988).

Eligibility/Limitations Projects that require coordinated or collaborative efforts involving various combinations of individual researchers and consultants, research assistants, and clerical or technical support personnel are eligible for support. All applications for support of individual study and research for periods of a year or less normally should be submitted to the endowment's Division of Fellowships and Seminars.

Fiscal Information The endowment provides three types of funding: federal matching funds, outright funds, and a combination of the two. Endowment matching funds are awarded on an up to one-for-one basis. An outright grant is one in which the award of endowment funds is not contingent on the applicant's raising gifts for the project. Applicants may also request a combination of outright and matching funds from the endowment.

Application Information Program guidelines are available upon request. After reading these guidelines, the prospective applicant should draft a brief description (no more than five pages) of the proposed project. This description should be sent to the program officer. So that staff members have sufficient time to give the project thorough attention, this correspondence should begin at least two or three months prior to the formal application deadline. Applicants should not attempt to prepare a full proposal using only general guidelines. Upon receipt of the brief description, endowment staff will assess the eligibility and competitiveness of the project and will contact the applicant about the proposal. If the project is eligible, the endowment staff member will send application forms and instructions. If sufficient time before the deadline remains, the applicant may submit a draft of the proposal for further informal comment. After this additional consultation with the staff, the applicant should prepare a full application using the appropriate forms.

Deadline(s) Deadline for receipt of applications is October 15.

Additional Information The division is currently soliciting proposals in two special initiative categories. (1) The Foundations of American Society: within its existing fellowships programs, the endowment continues to encourage study, research, and discussion about the history, culture, and principles of the founding period, an emphasis that began with the initiative on the bicentennial of the U.S. Constitution. (2) The Columbian Quincentenary: proposals that explore the ideas—political, religious, philosophical, scientific, technological, and aesthetic—that shaped the processes of exploration, settlement, and cultural conflict and transformation set into motion by Columbus's momentous voyage are invited.

324. National Endowment for the Humanities
Division of Research Programs, Room 318
1100 Pennsylvania Avenue, NW
Washington, DC 20506
(202) 786-0210

Interpretive Research: Projects

CFDA Program Number 45.140

Program Description Grants in this category support coordinated or collaborative research that will be important for humanities scholarship. Projects supported in this category include biographies; historical and analytical studies in literature and the arts; research in history, philosophy, and other basic humanities disciplines; focused interdisciplinary studies; humanistic research in political science, sociology, and cultural anthropology; and other major collaborative or cooperative undertakings that promise to advance research methods or the means of interpretation in the humanities. Projects, both interdisciplinary and within single disciplines, that aim for more integrated approaches to understanding the humanities are particularly encouraged. All projects are expected to lead to major publications. Support is also available for institutions that want to establish a research center or similarly structured program for research on a single topic or a series of related topics in the humanities. Projects undertaken by such a center or program should lead to specific products, such as a series of essays or a series of monographs that would represent an important advance in the humanities discipline or disciplines involved.

Sample Grants To support the research and writing of a book on North American Indian formulations of international law and peace as laid down in their treaties and negotiations with European nations between 1600 and 1800, $40,000 to the University of Arizona (1989). To support an interdisciplanary project designed to understand, through comparison and analysis, the working of the American Constitution and other constitutions throughout the world, $15,000 to the University of Chicago (1989).

Eligibility/Limitations Research projects that require coordinated or collaborative efforts involving various combinations of researchers and consultants, research assistants, and clerical or technical support personnel are eligible for support in this category.

Fiscal Information The endowment provides three types of funding: federal matching funds, outright funds, and a combination of the two. Endowment matching funds are awarded on an up to one-to-one basis. An outright grant is one in which the award of endowment funds is not contingent on the applicant's raising gifts for the project. Applicants also may request a combination of outright and matching funds from the endowment.

Application Information Program guidelines are available upon request. After reading these guidelines, the prospective applicant should draft a brief description (no more than five pages) of the proposed project. This description should be sent to the program officer. So that staff members have sufficient time to give the project thorough attention, this correspondence should begin at least two or three months prior to the formal application deadline. Applicants should not attempt to prepare a full proposal using only general guidelines. Upon receipt of the brief description, endowment staff will assess the eligibility and competitiveness of the project and will contact the applicant about the proposal. If the project is eligible, the endowment staff member will send application forms and instructions. If sufficient time before the deadline remains, the applicant may submit a draft of the proposal for further informal comment. After this additional consultation with the staff, the applicant should prepare a full application using the appropriate forms.

Deadline(s) Deadline for receipt of applications is October 15.

Additional Information The division is currently soliciting proposals in two special initiative categories. (1) The Foundations of American Society: within its existing fellowships programs, the endowment continues to encourage study, research, and discussion about the history, culture, and principles of the founding period, an emphasis that began with the initiative on the bicentennial of the U.S. Constitution. (2) The Columbian Quincentenary: proposals that explore the ideas—political, religious, philosophical, scientific, technological, and aesthetic—that shaped the processes of exploration, settlement, and cultural conflict and transformation set into motion by Columbus's momentous voyage are invited.

325. National Endowment for the Humanities
Division of Research Programs, Room 318
1100 Pennsylvania Avenue, NW
Washington, DC 20506
(202) 786-0358

Reference Materials: Access

CFDA Program Number 45.124

Program Description In this category, the endowment supports projects that promise to increase the availability of important research collections and other significant source material in all fields of the humanities. Support is provided for such activities as archival arrangement and description projects; bibliographies; records surveys; cataloguing projects involving print, graphic, film, sound, and artifact collections; indices; and other guides to humanities documentation. Under certain circumstances, oral histories are also eligible. In addition, support is provided for the development of national standards for access to different types of scholarly resources and for projects that promise to improve significantly the ways in which libraries, archives, and other repositories make research documentation available. Archival arrangement and description projects that involve the microfilming of unique materials are also eligible for support in the access category, as are projects to microfilm important collections in foreign repositories that are largely inaccessible to American scholars. An applicant must demonstrate that the level and form of description proposed is an appropriate and cost-effective means of gaining bibliographic control over the collection or collections involved. In standard archival arrangement and description projects, support is normally limited to the preparation of finding aids to the box and folder level. Applicants who propose to organize nontextual collections are urged to employ minimal level cataloguing. Applications for projects to provide access to collections that remain in private hands or essentially under private control are ineligible for support. Also ineligible are proposals dealing with collections to which scholarly access is restricted to any significant degree.

Sample Grants To arrange and describe the Delaware State Archives' collection of court records, $90,000 to the Bureau of Archives and Records Management, Dover, DE (1989). To complete a three-year project to classify 40,000 manuscript fragments from Cairo Genizah and to prepare a catalogue of 8,000 fragments relating to rabbinic law and exegesis, $35,000 outright funds and $35,000 matching funds to the Jewish Theological Seminary of America, New York, NY (1989).

Eligibility/Limitations Institutions in the United States engaged in the humanities and individual U.S. citizens or foreign nationals who have been living in the United States or its territories for at least three years at the time of application are eligible to apply. Support may also be given to any individual or organization whose work promises significantly to advance knowledge and understanding of the humanities in the United States. Foreign nationals who do not meet the residence requirement may apply if they are formally affiliated with a U.S. educational institution and in these cases must apply through the institution. In exceptional circumstances, the endowment may also provide support to a foreign institution or foreign national not meeting the eligibility criteria mentioned above when a project promises to advance knowledge and understanding of the humanities in the United States to an unusually large extent. The endowment does not support research in pursuit of an academic degree.

Fiscal Information The endowment provides three types of funding: federal matching funds, outright funds, and a combination of the two. Endowment matching funds are awarded on an up to one-to-one basis. An outright grant is one in which the award of endowment funds is not contingent on the applicant's raising gifts for the project. Applicants also may request a combination of outright and matching funds from the endowment.

Application Information Program guidelines are available upon request. After reading these guidelines, the prospective applicant should draft a brief description (no more than five pages) of the proposed project. This description should be sent to the program officer. So that staff members have sufficient time to give the project thorough attention, this correspondence should begin at least two or three months prior to the formal application deadline. Applicants should not attempt to prepare a full proposal using only general guidelines. Upon receipt of the brief description, endowment staff will assess the eligibility and competitiveness of the project and will contact the applicant about the proposal. If the project is eligible, the endowment staff member will send application forms and instructions. If sufficient time before the deadline remains, the applicant may submit a draft of the proposal for further informal comment. After this additional consultation with the staff, the applicant should prepare a full application using the appropriate forms.

Deadline(s) Postmark deadline for applications is September 1.

Additional Information The division is currently soliciting proposals in two special initiative categories. (1) The Foundations of American Society: within its existing fellowships programs, the endowment continues to encourage study, research, and discussion about the history, culture, and principles of the founding period, an emphasis that began with the initiative on the bicentennial of the U.S. Constitution. (2) The Columbian Quincentenary: proposals that explore the ideas—political, religious, philosophical, scientific, technological, and aesthetic—that shaped the processes of exploration, settlement, and cultural conflict and transformation set into motion by Columbus's momentous voyage are invited.

326. National Endowment for the Humanities
Division of Research Programs, Room 318
1100 Pennsylvania Avenue, NW
Washington, DC 20506
(202) 786-0358

Reference Materials: Tools

CFDA Program Number 45.145

Program Description Grants in this category support the creation of dictionaries, historical or linguistic atlases, encyclopedias, concordances, *catalogues raisonnes*, linguistic grammars, descriptive catalogues, data bases, and other materials that serve to codify information essential to research in the humanities. Applicants must make a convincing case for the project's editorial

and administrative procedures and for the importance of the final product to scholars in several fields. In addition, applicants must demonstrate that the form chosen for the proposed research tool (printed volume, microform, on-line data base, etc.) represents the most effective means of disseminating the information.

Sample Grants To prepare a three-volume history of medieval canon law to the 16th century describing its development, sources, and literature, $144,128 outright funds and $50,000 matching funds to Syracuse University (1989).

Eligibility/Limitations Institutions in the United States engaged in the humanities and individual United States citizens or foreign nationals who have been living in the United States or its territories for at least three years at the time of application are eligible to apply. Support may also be given to any individual or organization whose work promises significantly to advance knowledge and understanding of the humanities in the United States. Foreign nationals who do not meet the residence requirement may apply if they are formally affiliated with a United States educational institution and in these cases must apply through the institution. In exceptional circumstances, the endowment may also provide support to a foreign institution or foreign national not meeting the eligibility criteria mentioned above when a project promises to advance knowledge and understanding of the humanities in the United States to an unusually large extent. The endowment does not support research in pursuit of an academic degree.

Fiscal Information The endowment provides three types of funding: federal matching funds, outright funds, and a combination of the two. Endowment matching funds are awarded on an up to one-to-one basis. An outright grant is one in which the award of endowment funds is not contingent on the applicant's raising gifts for the project. Applicants also may request a combination of outright and matching funds from the endowment.

Application Information Program guidelines are available upon request. After reading these guidelines, the prospective applicant should draft a brief description (no more than five pages) of the proposed project. This description should be sent to the program officer. So that staff members have sufficient time to give the project thorough attention, this correspondence should begin at least two or three months prior to the formal application deadline. Applicants should not attempt to prepare a full proposal using only general guidelines. Upon receipt of the brief description, endowment staff will assess the eligibility and competitiveness of the project and will contact the applicant about the proposal. If the project is eligible, the endowment staff member will send application forms and instructions. If sufficient time before the deadline remains, the applicant may submit a draft of the proposal for further informal comment. After this additional consultation with the staff, the applicant should prepare a full application using the appropriate forms.

Deadline(s) Postmark deadline for applications is September 1.

Additional Information The division is currently soliciting proposals in two special initiative categories. (1) The Foundations of American Society: within its existing fellowships programs, the endowment continues to encourage study, research, and discussion about the history, culture, and principles of the founding period, an emphasis that began with the initiative on the bicentennial of the U.S. Constitution. (2) The Columbian Quincentenary: proposals that explore the ideas—political, religious, philosophical, scientific, technological, and aesthetic—that shaped the processes of exploration, settlement, and cultural conflict and transformation set into motion by Columbus's momentous voyage are invited.

327. National Endowment for the Humanities
Division of Research Programs, Room 318
1100 Pennsylvania Avenue, NW
Washington, DC 20506
(202) 786-0204

Regrants for International Research

CFDA Program Number 45.148

Program Description Through this category, the endowment awards funds to national organizations and learned societies to enable American scholars to pursue research abroad, to attend or participate in international conferences, and to engage in collaborative work with foreign colleagues. The regranting organizations also sponsor international scholarly exchange and collaborative international research endeavors.

Eligibility/Limitations National organizations and learned societies are eligible to apply.

Application Information Organizations and societies that wish to apply to this program should write to the endowment to request more detailed information and application instructions. Individuals interested in applying for support should write directly to the funded organization or society; a list of currently funded organizations and societies is available from the endowment upon request.

Deadline(s) Applications should be received by April 1.

Additional Information The division is currently soliciting proposals in two special initiative categories. (1) The Foundations of American Society: within its existing fellowships programs, the endowment continues to encourage study, research, and discussion about the history, culture, and principles of the founding period, an emphasis that began with the initiative on the bicentennial of the U.S. Constitution. (2) The Columbian Quincentenary: proposals that explore the ideas—political, religious, philosophical, scientific, technological, and aesthetic—that shaped the processes of exploration, settlement, and cultural conflict and transformation set into motion by Columbus's momentous voyage are invited.

328. National Endowment for the Humanities

Division of Research Programs, Room 318
1100 Pennsylvania Avenue, NW
Washington, DC 20506
(202) 786-0207

Texts: Editions

CFDA Program Number 45.146

Program Description Grants in this category support various stages of the preparation of authoritative and annotated editions of sources of significant value to humanities scholars and general readers. Support is provided for projects that make available important texts and documents that have been either previously unavailable or accessible only in seriously flawed editions. All printed editions supported by the endowment are accompanied by critical introductions and annotations that provide essential information about the form, transmission, and historical and intellectual context of the texts and documents involved. Since complete editions in printed volumes are expensive to produce, endowment reviewers frequently recommend selected editions, microform editions, and editions that combine printed volumes and microform. Consequently, applicants must demonstrate that the form proposed for the edition represents the most effective means of disseminating the material involved. Applicants for microform editions must also demonstrate that the project will make available materials dispersed among a number of widely scattered repositories.

Sample Grants To support the preparation of a documentary history of the ratification of the Constitution and Bill of Rights, $100,000 in outright funds and $70,000 in matching funds to the University of Wisconsin (1989). To support work on a four-volume edition of sources that record the proceedings of the English Parliament of 1626 and work on editions of sources for the first House of Commons session during the Long Parliament 1640-41, $125,000 in outright funds and $70,000 in matching funds to Yale University (1989).

Eligibility/Limitations Institutions in the United States engaged in the humanities and individual U.S. citizens or foreign nationals who have been living in the United States or its territories for at least three years at the time of application are eligible to apply. Support may also be given to any individual or organization whose work promises significantly to advance knowledge and understanding of the humanities in the United States. Foreign nationals who do not meet the residence requirement may apply if they are formally affiliated with a U.S. educational institution and in these cases must apply through the institution. In exceptional circumstances, the endowment may also provide support to a foreign institution or foreign national not meeting the eligibility criteria mentioned above when a project promises to advance knowledge and understanding of the humanities in the United States to an unusually large extent.

Fiscal Information Awards in the editions category are made for up to three years and range from $25,000 to $100,000 per year, with the amount of the award dependent on the scope and importance of the project. Applicants whose projects are complex in organization or are likely to involve large budget requests should consult with a member of the program staff before a final application is submitted. Normally, the endowment's contribution to a project will not exceed 80 percent of the project's total costs. All applicants are encouraged to seek full or partial support through federal matching funds.

Application Information Program guidelines are available upon request. After reading these guidelines, the prospective applicant should draft a brief description (no more than five pages) of the proposed project. This description should be sent to the program officer. So that staff members have sufficient time to give the project thorough attention, this correspondence should begin at least two or three months prior to the formal application deadline. Applicants should not attempt to prepare a full proposal using only general guidelines. Upon receipt of the brief description, endowment staff will assess the eligibility and competitiveness of the project and will contact the applicant about the proposal. If the project is eligible, the endowment staff member will send application forms and instructions. If sufficient time before the deadline remains, the applicant may submit a draft of the proposal for further informal comment. After this additional consultation with the staff, the applicant should prepare a full application using the appropriate forms.

Deadline(s) Postmark deadline for application is June 1.

Additional Information The division is currently soliciting proposals in two special initiative categories. (1) The Foundations of American Society: within its existing fellowships programs, the endowment continues to encourage study, research, and discussion about the history, culture, and principles of the founding period, an emphasis that began with the initiative on the bicentennial of the U.S. Constitution. (2) The Columbian Quincentenary: proposals that explore the ideas—political, religious, philosophical, scientific, technological, and aesthetic—that shaped the processes of exploration, settlement, and cultural conflict and transformation set into motion by Columbus's momentous voyage are invited.

329. National Endowment for the Humanities

Division of Research Programs, Room 318
1100 Pennsylvania Avenue, NW
Washington, DC 20506
(202) 786-0207

Texts: Publication Subvention

CFDA Program Number 45.132

Program Description Grants in this category are intended to assist the publication and dissemination of distinguished scholarly works in all fields of the humanities. In all cases, the scholarly work for which an application is being made must have been formally accepted for publication by the appropriate editor or editorial board. All applications for subvention will be judged on the basis of the quality and scholarly importance of the work to be published as well as on the appropriateness of the budget and publishing plan. In this category, the endowment will also consider applications for projects designed to diminish the need for individual publication subventions by introducing cost-effective mechanisms, such as computerized typesetting machines, into the operation of a press.

Sample Grants To support the publication of a two-volume edition of the unpublished legal papers of Lord Mansfield, Chief Justice of King's Bench and close adviser to George III, $7,000 to the University of North Carolina Press, Chapel Hill, NC (1989).

Eligibility/Limitations Applicants must be established publishers or scholarly publishing entities; applications from individual scholars are not accepted.

Fiscal Information Awards in this category average $6,000 per volume; no award for a single volume will exceed $10,000 in outright funds. All applicants are encouraged to seek support through federal matching funds. In a federal fiscal year, a single publisher may not receive more than $50,000 in outright and federal matching funds or support for more than five works, whichever is less.

Application Information Program guidelines are available upon request. After reading these guidelines, the prospective applicant should draft a brief description (no more than five pages) of the proposed project. This description should be sent to the program officer. So that staff members have sufficient time to give the project thorough attention, this correspondence should begin at least two or three months prior to the formal application deadline. Applicants should not attempt to prepare a full proposal using only general guidelines. Upon receipt of the brief description, endowment staff will assess the eligibility and competitiveness of the project and will contact the applicant about the proposal. If the project is eligible, the endowment staff member will send application forms and instructions. If sufficient time before the deadline remains, the applicant may submit a draft of the proposal for further informal comment. After this additional consultation with the staff, the applicant should prepare a full application using the appropriate forms.

Deadline(s) Postmark deadline for application is April 1.

Additional Information The division is currently soliciting proposals in two special initiative categories. (1) The Foundations of American Society: within its existing fellowships programs, the endowment continues to encourage study, research, and discussion about the history, culture, and principles of the founding period, an emphasis that began with the initiative on the bicentennial of the U.S. Constitution. (2) The Columbian Quincentenary: proposals that explore the ideas—political, religious, philosophical, scientific, technological, and aesthetic—that shaped the processes of exploration, settlement, and cultural conflict and transformation set into motion by Columbus's momentous voyage are invited.

330. National Endowment for the Humanities
Division of Research Programs, Room 318
1100 Pennsylvania Avenue, NW
Washington, DC 20506
(202) 786-0207

Texts: Translations

CFDA Program Number 45.147

Program Description In this category the endowment supports the translation into English of works that will provide insight into the history, literature, philosophy, and artistic achievements of other cultures and that will make available the thought and learning of their civilizations. Applicants may propose to translate from any language, and the texts to be translated may be either primary sources or secondary works. Every applicant must make a convincing case for the importance of the translation to those scholars and general readers who do not command the language of the original text. All translations supported by the endowment provide critical introductions and explanatory annotations that clearly establish the historical and intellectual contexts of the work involved. Where an authoritative text in the original language does not exist, applicants may apply for support to establish one. Applicants proposing to retranslate works that already exist in English must provide a strong ar-

gument for a new version or for an emendation of the existing version.

Sample Grants To support the translation, with annotation, of the medieval laws of Hungary, which then included Czechoslovakia, Austria, Yugoslavia, Rumania, and part of the Soviet Union, $2,670 to an individual scholar (1988). To translate a selection of the basic law codes of the Ottoman Empire (1500-1800), $25,000 to the University of Chicago (1987).

Eligibility/Limitations Institutions in the United States engaged in the humanities and individual U.S. citizens or foreign nationals who have been living in the United States or its territories for at least three years at the time of application are eligible to apply. Support may also be given to any individual or organization whose work promises significantly to advance knowledge and understanding of the humanities in the United States. Foreign nationals who do not meet the residence requirement may apply if they are formally affiliated with a U.S. educational institution and in these cases must apply through the institution. In exceptional circumstances, the endowment may also provide support to a foreign institution or foreign national not meeting the eligibility criteria mentioned above when a project promises to advance knowledge and understanding of the humanities in the United States to an unusually large extent.

Fiscal Information Grant awards in this category usually range from $3,500 to $75,000, depending upon the scope and magnitude of the project. Applicants are encouraged to seek support from appropriate foreign governments and from foundations and are also encouraged to apply for federal matching funds.

Application Information Program guidelines are available upon request. After reading these guidelines, the prospective applicant should draft a brief description (no more than five pages) of the proposed project. This description should be sent to the program officer. So that staff members have sufficient time to give the project thorough attention, this correspondence should begin at least two or three months prior to the formal application deadline. Applicants should not attempt to prepare a full proposal using only general guidelines. Upon receipt of the brief description, endowment staff will assess the eligibility and competitiveness of the project and will contact the applicant about the proposal. If the project is eligible, the endowment staff member will send application forms and instructions. If sufficient time before the deadline remains, the applicant may submit a draft of the proposal for further informal comment. After this additional consultation with the staff, the applicant should prepare a full application using the appropriate forms. All translation applications must be accompanied by a seven-page sample of the translation to be undertaken during the course of the grant.

Deadline(s) Postmark deadline for application is June 1.

Additional Information The division is currently soliciting proposals in two special initiative categories. (1) The Foundations of American Society: within its existing fellowships programs, the endowment continues to encourage study, research, and discussion about the history, culture, and principles of the founding period, an emphasis that began with the initiative on the bicentennial of the U.S. Constitution. (2) The Columbian Quincentenary: proposals that explore the ideas—political, religious, philosophical, scientific, technological, and aesthetic—that shaped the processes of exploration, settlement, and cultural conflict and transformation set into motion by Columbus's momentous voyage are invited.

331. National Endowment for the Humanities
Office of Preservation, Room 802
1100 Pennsylvania Avenue, NW
Washington, DC 20506
(202) 786-0570

Preservation Projects

Program Description Grants in this category support projects that address the problem of the disintegration of significant humanities materials, particularly books and newspapers, but also other media such as journals, manuscripts, documents, maps, drawings, plans, photographs, film and tapes. Eligible activities include cooperative and selective microfilming, professional training in preservation management, and the improvement of preservation technology.

Sample Grants To microfilm volumes from its special collection of Soviet government documents, 1917-40, including laws, statutes, publications of ministries and people's commissariats, congress of Soviets, and publications of scholarly bodies, $266,402 to The Hoover Institution on War, Revolution, and Peace (1989). To microfilm 27,554 brittle volumes from subject collections relating to American history, Italian history, and pre-Soviet law, $1,848,360 to Harvard University (1989).

Eligibility/Limitations Eligible applicants include individuals and institutions. Any nonprofit institution or organization may apply. Such institutions include, but are not limited to, research or public libraries, historical societies, archives, museums, regional organizations, library consortia, and scholarly or professional societies.

Fiscal Information The endowment provides three types of funding: federal matching funds, outright funds, and a combination of the two. The program emphasizes the use of federal matching funds in making awards. Federal matching funds are awarded on a one-for-one basis when an applicant raises gifts from third parties that will be used to support project activities during the grant period. Most of the endowment's awards for preservation will be made on a matching basis. An outright grant is one in which the award of endowment funds is not contingent on the applicant's raising gifts for the project.

Application Information One of the major responsibilities of staff in the Office of Preservation is to counsel prospective applicants about the program and their proposals. Potential applicants are strongly encouraged to discuss their proposal plans with program staff before submitting a formal application. Program staff will review draft applications, and applicants are also strongly encouraged to submit a draft application for staff review well in advance of an application deadline. Program staff provide the majority of counsel by telephone or letter.

Deadline(s) Application deadlines are June 1 and December 1.

332. National Federation of the Blind
Scholarship Committee
814 Fourth Avenue, Grinnell State Bank Building, Suite 200
Grinnell, IA 50112
(515) 236-3366

Howard Brown Rickard Scholarship

Program Description This scholarship is available to a legally blind student who is studying or planning to study law, medicine, engineering, architecture, or the natural sciences.

Eligibility/Limitations Legally blind persons pursuing or planning to pursue full-time postsecondary study in law, medicine, engineering, architecture, or the natural sciences are eligible to apply. Scholarships are awarded on the basis of academic excellence, service to the community, and financial need.

Fiscal Information The scholarship carries an award of $2,500.

Application Information Application forms are available from the scholarship committee.

Deadline(s) Applications must be received by March 31 of the year in which the scholarship is to be awarded.

333. National Hispanic Scholarship Fund
Selection Committee
P.O. Box 748
San Francisco, CA 94101
(415) 892-9971

NHSF Scholarships

Program Description Hispanic Americans continue to be underrepresented in the nation's colleges and universities. The National Hispanic Scholarship Fund was established to help bridge the higher educational gap by providing financial resources to outstanding Hispanic American students so that they can complete a college or graduate school education.

Eligibility/Limitations The emphasis on awards is in areas where Hispanics are underrepresented. Recent successful NHSF scholars have come predominately from the fields of engineering, business, science, medicine and law. Eligible applicants must be U.S. citizens or permanent residents of Hispanic-American background; students enrolled and attending college on a full-time basis; students presently enrolled and attending a college or university in one of the 50 states; and students who have completed a minimum of 15 units of college work prior to submission of an application.

Fiscal Information Since 1976, NHSF has awarded $3.6 million in scholarships to over 6,000 National Hispanic Scholarship Fund scholars. Awards range from $500 to $1,000.

Application Information Applications must include a complete NHSF application form; an official transcript of college grades; evidence of financial need; a high-quality typed personal statement; and a letter of recommendation, preferably from a school official.

Deadline(s) The annual NHSF application period is from August 5 to October 5 of each year. Postmark by October 5 satisfies deadline date requirements.

334. National Historical Publications and Records Commission
National Archives Building
Washington, DC 20408
(202) 724-1090

Publications Program

CFDA Program Number 89.003

Program Description The publications program is intended to ensure the dissemination and more general availability of documentary source material important to the study and understanding of U.S. history. Projects should therefore be based upon material of widespread interest among scholars, students, and informed citizens. Documents should have historical value and interest that transcend local and state boundaries. Grants in the program include: (1) book publication projects that reproduce in print the text of the papers of outstanding U.S. citizens and other documents that may be important for an understanding and appreciation of U.S. history (projects involve collecting, compiling, editing, and publishing such papers or documents); and (2) microfilm publications projects that involve the arrangement and microcopying (in roll microfilm, microfiche, etc.) of papers of national significance.

Eligibility/Limitations Nonprofit organizations and institutions and federal, state, and local government agencies may apply to the commission for assistance in funding appropriate publications projects. Grants are made only to institutional sponsors of projects. Private scholars are eligible for support if a sponsoring institution agrees to submit the grant application and administer the grant funds.

Fiscal Information An application for an outright grant requests the commission to recommend support for the entire cost of a project, minus the share of costs borne by the sponsoring institution. Any direct or indirect costs relating to the project that are contributed by the applicant's institution may be included as cost-sharing. As a rule, the institution's share of the costs should be at least one-half of the entire cost. A matching grant may be awarded as a supplement to an outright grant or as the sole form of commission support. When a matching grant is offered, the grantee is authorized to raise gifts up to a level approved by the NHPRC and have that amount matched by the commission. For example, a $50,000 matching offer means that a grantee must raise $25,000 in nonfederal funds to secure the maximum match. Gifts cannot be submitted from an applicant's immediate family or academic institution nor from another federal agency. Matching funds are not to be confused with the cost-sharing requirement noted above.

Application Information Application information and guidelines are available upon request.

Deadline(s) The commission usually meets in February, June, and October to consider grant applications. Except for certain types of microfilm proposals that must meet earlier records program deadlines, new publications program proposals should reach the commission offices by November 15, March 15, and July 15, in order to be considered at the next commission meeting.

Additional Information The commission considers applications from university and other nonprofit presses for subvention for printing and manufacturing costs in book publications that have been formally endorsed by the commission. Grants not exceeding $10,000 per volume are recommended in order to reduce the amount of financial losses anticipated by the presses in publishing volumes considered essential to the commission's programs. The granting of a subvention is intended to encourage the highest standards in the production of volumes, particularly the quality of paper and binding materials. Only a limited number of subvention grants are available annually. Applications for subvention should be submitted by the press. The applications should include the press estimate of editorial, design, manufacturing, warehousing, and distribution costs, as well as anticipated sales price and income. The difference between costs and projected income is the amount eligible for subvention support.

335. National Historical Publications and Records Commission

National Archives Building
7th & Pennsylvania Avenue, NW
Washington, DC 20408
(202) 523-5386

Records Program

CFDA Program Number 89.003

Program Description The program is intended to help preserve important historical documents. Funds may be used for the collection, preservation, arrangement, and description of records of historical interest.

Sample Grants To help publish *The Lincoln Legal Papers: A Documentary History of the Law Practice of Abraham Lincoln, 1836-1861*, $30,000 to the Illinois Historic Preservation Agency (1990). To develop four units of a comprehensive series of training modules in archival and records management theory, methodology, and law, $40,900 to the New Jersey Division of Archives and Records Management, Trenton, NJ (1989).

Eligibility/Limitations State and local government, and U.S. territorial agencies and federally and state recognized Indian tribes, educational and other nonprofit institutions (e.g., universities, colleges, libraries, historical societies, museums, university presses, archives, etc.) are eligible to apply. Applicants must be legally established and located within the United States, its territories, and the District of Columbia. In some cases individuals may also apply.

Fiscal Information Grants in 1989 ranged from $450 to $386,000 with an average award of $33,849. The commission makes funds available as outright or matching grants or as grants combining these two types of funding.

Application Information Request detailed brochures for records preservation grants or publication grants from the executive director of the commission. Special guidelines and policies have been prepared for the following grants and project activities: historical photograph projects; microform projects; projects included in the commision's Native American Initiative; grants to individuals; regrant projects sponsored by state boards; state assessment and reporting projects; and projects involving the hiring of consultants.

Deadline(s) Deadlines for application are June 1, October 1 and February 1.

Additional Information The commission's education program includes fellowships in advanced historical editing, fellowships in archival administration, and an annual editing institute.

336. National Humanities Center

7 Alexander Drive, P.O. Box 12256
Research Triangle Park, NC 27709
(919) 549-0661

Fellowships

Program Description The National Humanities Center supports advanced study in history, philosophy, literature, and other fields of the humanities. The center admits a company of 40 fellows annually who pursue research and writing in residence at the center. In addition to scholars from fields normally associated with the humanities, representatives of the natural and social sciences, the arts, the professions, and public life are welcome.

Sample Grants Fellows named to study at the center during the 1989-1990 academic year include a professor of history whose research project is law, politics, and society in England, 1485-1660; a professor of law, whose research project is agents and their ends—prolegomena to a doctrine of the good.

Eligibility/Limitations The competition for fellowships is open to humanistic scholars from all nations. In addition to supporting scholars of recognized accomplishment, the center awards fellowships to promising young scholars who are no more than 10 years beyond graduate study and are undertaking projects significantly beyond their dissertation research.

Fiscal Information The amount of fellowship stipend is based on a scholar's usual academic salary. Many fellows have partial funding in the form of sabbatical salaries or grants from other sources and receive from the center the difference between that funding and their usual salaries. All fellows are given travel expenses to and from the center for themselves and their families. Most fellowships at the center are awarded for the full academic year. The center does not cover fringe benefits.

Application Information For information and application material, write to the assistant director.

Deadline(s) Applications and letters of recommendation must be postmarked no later that October 15.

337. National Institute for Dispute Resolution

1901 L Street, NW, Suite 600
Washington, DC 20036
(202) 466-4764

Courts

Program Description The National Institute for Dispute Resolution has inaugurated a three-year program that is designed to encourage state courts to test and use various dispute resolution methods. The program seeks to introduce, test, and evaluate several dispute resolutions methods (other than court-ordered arbitration) in at least five state court systems and to integrate those methods in a comprehensive way into the standard operations of state courts. The program's other goals are to expand significantly the number and percentage of cases settled through these court-based methods and increase understanding of the effectiveness and fairness of court-annexed dispute resolution.

Eligibility/Limitations State court systems, bar associations, judiciary task forces, dispute resolution organizations, and other groups interested in court improvement are encouraged to apply under the program. The institute welcomes proposals for grants and requests for technical assistance.

Application Information Submit a letter of inquiry, rather than a fully developed proposal, for either a grant or for technical assistance. Grant seekers should describe their objectives, approach, partners, and participants in their project, budget, and additional sources of funding. Applicants for technical assistance should outline their needs and objectives. Applicants whose letters most closely meet the goals of the court-annexed dispute resolution program will be invited to submit a more detailed request.

Deadline(s) Applicants may submit a letter at any time, and there are no fixed deadlines for submission.

338. National Institute for Dispute Resolution
1901 L Street, NW, Suite 600
Washington, DC 20036
(202) 466-4764

Higher and Professional Education

Program Description The program awards matching grants to faculty to develop teaching materials for traditional courses in law schools and graduate schools of business, planning, public administration and public policy.

Eligibility/Limitations Faculty at appropriate insitutions are eligible to apply.

Application Information Contact the foundation for additional information and application guidelines.

Deadline(s) No deadlines are announced.

339. National Institute for Dispute Resolution
1901 L Street, NW, Suite 600
Washington, DC 20036
(202) 466-4764

Innovation Fund Grants

Program Description The National Institute for Dispute Resolution is the only grantmaker in the United States devoted solely to conflict resolution. It seeks to enhance the fairness, effectiveness and efficiency of the ways Americans resolve disputes. The purpose of the innovation fund is discovery. The institute seeks to discover new ways for using these processes in settling conflicts and solving problems. For this reason, the institute is interested in funding innovations where dispute resolution efforts have yet to be applied; where potential benefits from innovations will likely serve an important segment of society; and where persons and groups, due to lack of financial resources or access to appropriate forums, typically have difficulty in resolving disputes. Grants, usually nonrenewable, will be awarded in three categories: (1) projects that test innovative uses of dispute resolution methods in both familiar and untried settings; (2) projects that develop a new project concept; and (3) projects that document the innovative use of dispute resolution.

Sample Grants To develop a computer-based model of the thought processes a mediator uses in resolving disputes, $9,293 to Ohio State University Research Foundation (1989). To design a model for using an empowering style of mediation in settling medical malpractice disputes among physicians, insurance companies, and plaintiffs, $9,969, to The Center for the Study of Dispute Resolution, University of Missouri Law School (1989). To determine whether disputes involving emerging high-tech companies can be resolved outside the court system, $10,000 to Albany Law School (1989). To document the Case Status Conference, a procedure that five Connecticut family division courts used experimentally during 1988 in 1,800 child protection hearings, $8,948 to the Institute for Judicial Administration, New York, NY (1989).

Eligibility/Limitations The institute welcomes applications from both organizations and individuals with an interest in dispute resolution and its uses. All grants will serve charitable purposes. The institute will consider proposals in all areas except those involving labor-management collective bargaining, international affairs and proposals that are eligible for funding under other institute programs.

Fiscal Information The fund will provide up to $200,000 in 1990 and 1991 in grants to support promising dispute resolution initiatives that are ineligible for funding under the institute's other grant-making programs.

Application Information Applicants must submit a concept paper which will be reviewed in competition with other submissions. Applicants whose concept papers most closely meet selection criteria will be invited to submit full proposals. Concept papers should describe the critical problems that are to be addressed; summarize the key objectives; identify the grant category under which the concept paper falls; describe the methodology and desired results; provide a brief work plan and schedule which include planned starting and completion dates; describe how the project will be evaluated; provide a budget summary; be signed by an official with authority to commit the applicant in business and financial matters. The concept paper should be no more than 10 double-spaced typewritten pages; submit one original and six copies. Attach a cover page that includes a one paragraph executive summary. Attach seven copies of resumes, vitae, letters of support from individuals and organizations whose participation in the project is required for its completion, and, in the case of nonprofit organizations, a copy of the most recent Internal Revenue Service section 501(c)(3) determination or ruling letter.

Deadline(s) Concept papers are due November 16.

340. National Institute for Dispute Resolution
1901 L Street, NW, Suite 600
Washington, DC 20036
(202) 466-4764

Public Policy

Program Description The purpose of the institute's program in public policy is to build the institutions and improve the methods for resolving public disputes. The program provides support for: establishing statewide offices of mediation; regulatory negotiation; and a fund for public interest mediation.

Eligibility/Limitations State agencies, court systems, and nonprofit dispute resolution organizations may apply for grants and technical assistance under statewide offices of mediation and regulatory negotiation.

Application Information There is no formal application process for projects proposing statewide offices of mediation. The institute invites concept papers that propose developing and testing the state-level use of regulatory negotiation. Applications are not yet being accepted for the fund for public interest mediation.

Deadline(s) There are no fixed deadlines.

341. National Institute for Juvenile Justice and Delinquency Prevention
Office of Juvenile Justice and Delinquency Prevention
633 Indiana Avenue, NW
Washington, DC 20531
(202) 724-7560

Project Grants

CFDA Program Number 16.542

Program Description The objectives of this program are to encourage, coordinate and conduct research and evaluation of juvenile justice and delinquency prevention activities; to provide for public and private agencies, institutions, justice system agencies, and a clearinghouse and information center for collecting, disseminating, publishing, and distributing information on juvenile delinquency; to conduct national training programs for juvenile-related issues, and provide technical assistance and training assistance to federal, state, and local governments, courts, public and private agencies, institutions, and individuals, in the planning, establishment, funding, operation, or evaluation of juvenile justice programs.

Sample Grants Projects funded during fiscal year 1988 included training of juvenile court judges and other personnel.

Eligibility/Limitations Public or private agencies, organizations, or individuals are eligible to apply.

Fiscal Information Grants are awarded in amounts consistent with the institute's plans, priorities, and levels of financing.

Application Information Applicants must submit proposals on Standard Form 424. This program is subject to the provisions of OMB Circular Nos. A-110 and A-102. Proposals must be prepared and submitted in accordance with program announcements published in the Federal Register.

Deadline(s) Deadlines are published in the Federal Register.

Additional Information The institute also awards State Formula Grants (CFDA 16.540) designed to increase the capacity of state and local governments to support the development of more effective education, training, research, prevention, diversion, treatment and rehabilitation programs in the area of juvenile delinquency and programs to improve the juvenile justice system. Contact the institute for additional information.

342. National Institute for Juvenile Justice and Delinquency Prevention

Office of Juvenile Justice and Delinquency Prevention
633 Indiana Avenue, NW
Washington, DC 20531
(202) 724-5914

Special Emphasis

CFDA Program Number 16.541

Program Description The objectives of the program are to develop and implement programs that design, test, and demonstrate effective approaches, techniques, and methods for preventing and controlling juvenile delinquency through development and testing selected approaches; for developing and maintaining community-based alternatives; developing and implementing effective means of diverting juveniles from the traditional juvenile justice and correctional system; developing and supporting programs stressing advocacy activities aimed at improving services to youth impacted by the juvenile justice system; developing model programs to strengthen and maintain the family unit; developing and implementing special emphasis prevention and treatment programs relating to juveniles who commit serious crimes; and developing and implementing further a coordinated, national, law-related education program of delinquency prevention.

Eligibility/Limitations Special Emphasis funds are available to public and private nonprofit agencies, organizations, individuals, state and local units of government, combinations of state or local units.

Fiscal Information Contact the program to determine if it was refunded for the current fiscal year.

Application Information Contact the program for preapplication and application information.

Deadline(s) Deadlines are announced in the Federal Register.

Additional Information The institute also awards State Formula Grants (CFDA 16.540) designed to increase the capacity of state and local governments to support the development of more effective education, training, research, prevention, diversion, treatment, and rehabilitation programs in the area of juvenile delinquency and programs to improve the juvenile justice system. Contact the institute for additional information.

343. National Institute of Justice

Center for Crime Control Research
633 Indiana Avenue, NW, Room 900
Washington, DC 20531
(202) 724-7636

Criminal Careers and the Control of Crime

CFDA Program Number 15.560

Program Description The broad mandate of this program is to support an accumulation of sound research on the crime control effectiveness of official sanctions. The following list of project classes, while not intended to be complete in its coverage, illustrates the scope and variety of the program's interests: crime career research directed toward a thorough understanding of the participation in, rate of criminal activity, seriousness, and length of criminal careers; neighborhood and community-level studies building on an extensive research tradition which has estimated such things as the relative gains in crime reduction generated by different sanction levels; perceptions research investigating why the assessment of sanction risk or sanction cost differs greatly among various subpopulations, and whether the criminal justice system can communicate sanction threats more effectively; and measuring crime.

Eligibility/Limitations State and local governments, private nonprofit organizations, public nonprofit organizations, profit organizations, nonprofit organizations, institutions of higher education, and qualified individuals are eligible to apply. Applicants from the territories of the United States and federally recognized Indian tribal governments are also eligible to participate in this program.

Fiscal Information The total amount requests must include the full amount of NIJ funding for a project. Grant awards are in amounts consistent with the institute's plans, priorities, and levels of financing.

Application Information Prior to expending the effort necessary to develop a competitive proposal, prospective applicants are strongly encouraged to contact the program to discuss the appropriateness of possible research topics under their program area.

Deadline(s) The deadline for this program is February 23.

344. National Institute of Justice

Center for Crime Control Research
633 Indiana Avenue, NW, Room 900
Washington, DC 20531
(202) 724-7631

Drugs, Alcohol, and Crime Research Program

CFDA Program Number 15.560

Program Description This research program has two major objectives: increasing knowledge and understanding of the nature and extent of drug- and alcohol-related crimes and the factors which affect them, and applying such knowledge to support the development of informed public policies aimed at control of drug and alcohol abuse and related criminality. Priority areas include: informing state and local drug control strategies; drug gangs and violent drug crime; assessing drug usage and drug-related crime; and drug-crime linkages, treatment, and prevention.

Eligibility/Limitations State and local governments, private nonprofit organizations, public nonprofit organizations, profit organizations, nonprofit organizations, institutions of higher education, and qualified individuals are eligible to apply. Applicants from the territories of the United States and federally recognized Indian tribal governments are also eligible to participate in this program.

Fiscal Information The total amount requests must include the full amount of NIJ funding for a project. Grant awards are in amounts consistent with the institute's plans, priorities, and levels of financing.

Application Information Prior to expending the effort necessary to develop a competitive proposal, prospective applicants are strongly encouraged to contact the program to discuss the appropriateness of possible research topics under their program area.

Deadline(s) The deadlines for submission of proposals are 5 p.m., January 10 for cycle 1, and May 9 for cycle 2.

345. National Institute of Justice

Center for Crime Control Research
633 Indiana Avenue, NW, Room 900
Washington, DC 20531
(202) 724-7636

Ethnographies of Property Offenders

CFDA Program Number 15.560

Program Description The goal of this program is to gain information on how property-crime offenders become involved in and continue their criminal careers. The long-range goal of this program is to develop methods that will help law enforcement and other criminal justice officials change patterns of criminal careers to aid in the reduction of property crime. Projects awarded through this program must have an ethnographic orientation.

Eligibility/Limitations State and local governments, private nonprofit organizations, public nonprofit organizations, profit organizations, nonprofit organizations, institutions of higher education, and qualified individuals are eligible to apply. Applicants from the territories of the United States and federally recognized Indian tribal governments are also eligible to participate in this program.

Fiscal Information The total amount requests must include the full amount of NIJ funding for a project. Grant awards are in amounts consistent with the institute's plans, priorities, and levels of financing.

Application Information Prior to expending the effort necessary to develop a competitive proposal, prospective applicants are strongly encouraged to contact the program to discuss the appropriateness of possible research topics under their program area.

Deadline(s) Completed proposals must be received at NIJ no later than 5 p.m., April 20.

346. National Institute of Justice

Center for Crime Control Research
633 Indiana Avenue, NW, Room 900
Washington, DC 20531
(202) 724-7631

Forensic Sciences and Criminal Justice Technology

CFDA Program Number 15.560

Program Description The institute supports research in the physical and biological sciences and their technologies, addressing advances in the forensic sciences and developments of equipment or techniques which will aid in crime prevention, crime detection, investigation, and adjudication.

Eligibility/Limitations State and local governments, private nonprofit organizations, public nonprofit organizations, profit organizations, nonprofit organizations, institutions of higher education, and qualified individuals are eligible to apply. Applicants from the territories of the United States and federally recognized Indian tribal governments are also eligible to participate in this program.

Fiscal Information The total amount requests must include the full amount of NIJ funding for a project. Grant awards are in amounts consistent with the institute's plans, priorities, and levels of financing.

Application Information Prior to expending the effort necessary to develop a competitive proposal, prospective applicants are strongly encouraged to contact the program to discuss the appropriateness of possible research topics under their program area.

Deadline(s) Completed proposals must be received at NIJ no later than 5 p.m., March 16.

347. National Institute of Justice

Center for Crime Control Research
633 Indiana Avenue, NW, Room 900
Washington, DC 20531
(202) 724-7631

Offender Classification and Prediction of Criminal Behavior

CFDA Program Number 15.560

Program Description This program is designed to support the accumulation of a body of research on the classification of offenders and the prediction of future dangerousness. Research results from this program have had, and will continue to have, direct policy impact upon many criminal justice practices—jail and prison construction needs, pretrial release decisions, the management of jails and prisons, the management of probation and parole, the timing and conditions of parole, and in some jurisdictions, the selection of cases for early release.

Eligibility/Limitations State and local governments, private nonprofit organizations, public nonprofit organizations, profit organizations, nonprofit organizations, institutions of higher education, and qualified individuals are eligible to apply. Applicants from the territories of the United States and federally recognized Indian tribal governments are also eligible to participate in this program.

Fiscal Information The total amount requests must include the full amount of NIJ funding for a project. Grant awards are in amounts consistent with the institute's plans, priorities, and levels of financing.

Application Information Prior to expending the effort necessary to develop a competitive proposal, prospective applicants are strongly encouraged to contact the program to discuss the appropriateness of possible research topics under their program area.

Deadline(s) Completed proposals must be received at NIJ no later than 5 p.m., January 12 to be considered for the first cycle, and May 2 for the second.

348. National Institute of Justice

Center for Crime Control Research
633 Indiana Avenue, NW, Room 900
Washington, DC 20531
(202) 724-7631

Violence Prevention and Control

CFDA Program Number 15.560

Program Description This program seeks research that could improve criminal justice practices to prevent, control, or treat violence. The unifying theme of the program is that the research should point toward criminal justice policies or practices that could reduce levels of violence.

Eligibility/Limitations State and local governments, private nonprofit organizations, public nonprofit organizations, profit organizations, nonprofit organizations, institutions of higher education, and qualified individuals are eligible to apply. Applicants from the territories of the United States and federally recognized Indian tribal governments are also eligible to participate in this program.

Fiscal Information The total amount requests must include the full amount of NIJ funding for a project. Grant awards are in amounts consistent with the institute's plans, priorities, and levels of financing.

Application Information Prior to expending the effort necessary to develop a competitive proposal, prospective applicants are strongly encouraged to contact the program to discuss the appropriateness of possible research topics under their program area.

Deadline(s) Completed proposals must be received at NIJ no later than 5 p.m., January 19 to be considered for the first cycle, and April 27 for the second.

349. National Institute of Justice

Office of Justice Programs, Office of Crime Prevention
   and Criminal Justice Research
633 Indiana Avenue, NW
Washington, DC 20531
(202) 724-2952

Apprehension, Prosecution, and Adjudication Program

CFDA Program Number 16.560

Program Description The following topic areas, although not intended to be complete in their coverage, are presented as examples of research themes that would fall within the general scope of this program. Other areas and issues of relevance to criminal apprehension, prosecution, adjudication, and sanctioning may also be addressed. Experimental and descriptive studies are encouraged and the projected utility and generalizability of the proposed research are of major interest. A variety of apprehension and prosecution programs and policies have been inaugurated, aimed at removing from the community offenders who pose the greatest threat in terms of the frequency and seriousness of their crimes. Research and evaluation interests include: (1) efforts that target investigations and prosecutions to individuals who fit established criteria as "career criminals" or "repeat offenders;" (2) studies directed toward increasing the apprehension rates for serious criminal offenders and increasing the probability of convicting guilty defendants through more conclusive physical, documentary, and testimonial evidence; (3) coordination efforts between state and local agencies and the federal government; and (4) coordination within a criminal justice system—among police, prosecutors, and the court—to realize the common goals of justice and societal safety. Innovative practices and policies have been instituted in some jurisdictions. These have included improved decision-making in regard to pretrial release, improvements in the trial process, and sentencing reforms. Areas of research interest include the following: (1) the conflicting theories about the function of the bail system; (2) the trial process, including methods for improving juror decision making through such mechanisms as juror notetaking and judicial management of certain cases by separating them from others by way of specialized courts; and (3) the impact of sentencing policy and practice, including sentencing guidelines for community service, the expanded use of fines, examination of a lower age of majority for felony offenses, and the sentencing of special populations such as the mentally retarded.

Eligibility/Limitations State and local governments, private nonprofit organizations, public nonprofit organizations, profit organizations, nonprofit organizations, institutions of higher education, and qualified individuals are eligible to apply. Applicants from the territories of the United States and federally recognized Indian tribal governments are also eligible to participate in this program.

Fiscal Information The total amount requests must include the full amount of NIJ funding for a project. Grant awards are in amounts consistent with the institute's plans, priorities, and levels of financing.

Application Information Prior to expending the effort necessary to develop a competitive proposal, prospective applicants are strongly encouraged to contact the program to discuss the appropriateness of possible research topics under their program area. To obtain further information about this program, researchers may write to Bernard Auchter, Program Manager, Apprehension, Prosecution, and Adjudication Program, at the above address.

Deadline(s) Proposals must be received before 5 p.m. January 19 for cycle 1, and before 5 p.m. May 11 for cycle 2. These deadlines will not be extended.

350. National Institute of Justice

Office of Justice Programs, Office of Crime Prevention and Criminal Justice Research
633 Indiana Avenue, NW
Washington, DC 20531
(202) 724-7460

Drug Testing in Community Corrections

CFDA Program Number 16.560

Program Description The purpose of this program is to support research that studies the effectiveness of urine testing, alone or in combination with criminal justice interventions, treatment interventions, or both, in reducing drug use, criminal behavior, or both by offenders under community supervision.

Eligibility/Limitations State and local governments, private nonprofit organizations, public nonprofit organizations, profit organizations, nonprofit organizations, institutions of higher education, and qualified individuals are eligible to apply. Applicants

from the territories of the United States and federally recognized Indian tribal governments are also eligible to participate in this program.

Fiscal Information The total amount requests must include the full amount of NIJ funding for a project. Grant awards are in amounts consistent with the institute's plans, priorities, and levels of financing.

Application Information Prior to expending the effort necessary to develop a competitive proposal, prospective applicants are strongly encouraged to contact the program to discuss the appropriateness of possible research topics under their program area.

Deadline(s) Completed proposals must be received at NIJ no later than 5 p.m., March 30.

351. National Institute of Justice

Office of Justice Programs, Office of Crime Prevention and Criminal Justice Research
633 Indiana Avenue, NW
Washington, DC 20531
(202) 724-2956

Public Safety and Security

CFDA Program Number 15.560

Program Description This program supports projects that will develop models to integrate police, citizens, and private sector resources in a more effective manner. Problems of drugs and drug-related crimes are a priority concern. In addition, there is interest in improving the effectiveness and efficiency of police services and operations that impact on public safety. Experiments, case studies, observational research, and ethnographies are specifically encouraged.

Eligibility/Limitations State and local governments, private nonprofit organizations, public nonprofit organizations, profit organizations, nonprofit organizations, institutions of higher education, and qualified individuals are eligible to apply. Applicants from the territories of the United States and federally recognized Indian tribal governments are also eligible to participate in this program.

Fiscal Information The total amount requests must include the full amount of NIJ funding for a project. Grant awards are in amounts consistent with the institute's plans, priorities, and levels of financing.

Application Information Prior to expending the effort necessary to develop a competitive proposal, prospective applicants are strongly encouraged to contact the program to discuss the appropriateness of possible research topics under their program area.

Deadline(s) Completed proposals must be received at NIJ no later than 5 p.m., on the dates specified by each cycle. The first cycle deadline is January 26; the second cycle deadline is May 25.

352. National Institute of Justice

Office of Justice Programs, Office of Crime Prevention and Criminal Justice Research
633 Indiana Avenue, NW
Washington, DC 20531
(202) 724-2951

Punishment and Control of Offenders

CFDA Program Number 15.560

Program Description The problems caused by prison and jail crowding affect both community and institutional corrections, creating opportunities for innovation at both the operational and administrative levels. This program supports research in community corrections, institutional corrections, management of correctional systems, application of technology, specific measures of correctional performance, costs of alternative programs, and an new initiative: female offenders.

Eligibility/Limitations State and local governments, private nonprofit organizations, public nonprofit organizations, profit organizations, nonprofit organizations, institutions of higher education, and qualified individuals are eligible to apply. Applicants from the territories of the United States and federally recognized Indian tribal governments are also eligible to participate in this program.

Fiscal Information The total amount requests must include the full amount of NIJ funding for a project. Grant awards are in amounts consistent with the institute's plans, priorities, and levels of financing.

Application Information Prior to expending the effort necessary to develop a competitive proposal, prospective applicants are strongly encouraged to contact the program to discuss the appropriateness of possible research topics under their program area.

Deadline(s) Completed proposals must be received at NIJ no later than 5 p.m., February 1 for cycle 1, and June 1 for cycle 2.

353. National Institute of Justice

Office of Justice Programs, Office of Crime Prevention
and Criminal Justice Research
633 Indiana Avenue, NW
Washington, DC 20531
(202) 724-7686

Victims of Crime

CFDA Program Number 15.560

Program Description In its research on victims of crime, the institute plans to continue its efforts to better understand the process of how and why criminal victimization occurs and what measures can be taken to assist victims and secure their rights. The aim is to reduce the level of victimization in the first instance, as well as to restore the victim to wholeness, a sense of justice, and a life of contributing to society as much as possible. Research is supported in the following areas: studies of the causes of victimization; studies to determine how to develop better measures of aggregate costs of criminal victimization; studies of more effective ways to provide services to victims, system changes and responses that could support victims; studies of the nature and amount of victimization by drugs and violent crime and the financial, emotional, and social costs to the individuals and communities; and studies of victimization by consumer fraud, white-collar crime, and burglary and other property offenses.

Eligibility/Limitations State and local governments, private nonprofit organizations, public nonprofit organizations, profit organizations, nonprofit organizations, institutions of higher education, and qualified individuals are eligible to apply. Applicants from the territories of the United States and federally recognized Indian tribal governments are also eligible to participate in this program.

Fiscal Information The total amount requests must include the full amount of NIJ funding for a project. Grant awards are in amounts consistent with the institute's plans, priorities, and levels of financing.

Application Information Prior to expending the effort necessary to develop a competitive proposal, prospective applicants are strongly encouraged to contact the program to discuss the appropriateness of possible research topics under their program area.

Deadline(s) Completed proposals must be received at NIJ no later than 5 p.m., February 2 for cycle 1, and May 25 for cycle 2.

354. National Institute of Justice

Office of Justice Programs, Office of Crime Prevention
and Criminal Justice Research
633 Indiana Avenue, NW
Washington, DC 20531
(202) 724-7684

White Collar and Organized Crime

CFDA Program Number 15.560

Program Description This program supports projects that will build on previous research to develop new, more effective approaches to white-collar crime and organized crime prevention and control. The ultimate goals of the program are to reduce victimization and decrease the costs of these complex corruptive crimes to individuals, businesses, the criminal justice system, and society as a whole. Some white-collar crime issues of particular interest are: research on strategies to prevent and control fraud and insider abuse in financial institutions and other major commercial and industrial corporations; studies aimed at the prevention and control of public corruption; research aimed at the prevention and control of money laundering; and studies focusing on computer crime. Policy-relevant research on organized crime is also of particular interest, including studies of major drug-trafficking groups and operations and development of strategies for improved detection, interdiction, and control; examination of the impact of criminal and civil RICO legislation on organized criminal groups and their operations, as well as on criminal justice policies and procedures; broadening of organized crime enforcement efforts beyond their traditional Cosa Nostra syndicate targets to include the wide range of organized criminal groups which have emerged more recently; enhancement of enforcement efforts by identifying reliable direct and indirect measures to detect the presence, types, and levels of organized crime activity; and development and promotion of effective intelligence data collection and analysis techniques.

Eligibility/Limitations State and local governments, private nonprofit organizations, public nonprofit organizations, profit organizations, nonprofit organizations, institutions of higher education, and qualified individuals are eligible to apply. Applicants from the territories of the United States and federally recognized Indian tribal governments are also eligible to participate in this program.

Fiscal Information The total amount requests must include the full amount of NIJ funding for a project. Grant awards are in amounts consistent with the institute's plans, priorities, and levels of financing.

Application Information Prior to expending the effort necessary to develop a competitive proposal, prospective applicants are strongly encouraged to contact the program to discuss the appropriateness of possible research topics under their program area.

Deadline(s) Completed proposals must be received at NIJ no later than 5 p.m., February 16 for cycle 1, and June 8 for cycle 2.

355. National Institute of Justice

Visiting Fellowships Program
633 Indiana Avenue, NW, Room 900
Washington, DC 20531
(202) 724-7635

Graduate Research Fellowships

CFDA Program Number 15.562

Program Description The purpose of the program is to encourage scholars to undertake research in criminal justice or directly related fields and to develop a continuing and capable cadre of individuals who can conduct research, as well as operations, directed at resolving critical issues in the criminal justice system.

Eligibility/Limitations Fellowships are awarded to sponsoring universities on behalf of eligible students. Eligible students are doctoral candidates engaged in dissertation research and writing on a problem related to law enforcement, crime, or criminal justice.

Fiscal Information Fellowships carry stipends of up to $11,000 to support the completion of the dissertation.

Application Information Applicants are encouraged to contact the institute to discuss topic viability or proposal content before submitting proposals.

Deadline(s) Completed proposals must be received at the NIJ no later than 5 p.m. on February 16. Extensions will not be granted.

356. National Institute of Justice
Visiting Fellowships Program
633 Indiana Avenue, NW, Room 900
Washington, DC 20531
(202) 724-7636

Summer Research Fellowships

Program Description This program is aimed at the re-analysis of existing research data, particularly of data sets resulting from NIJ-sponsored research.

Eligibility/Limitations The program is intended for both senior researchers, relatively new Ph.D.s, and those in-between.

Fiscal Information The award is $10,000.

Application Information Because this award is not a grant but a small contract, the application procedures are different from other NIJ fellowship programs. Applicants are encouraged to contact the program for application information, to discuss topic viability, data availability, or proposal content.

Deadline(s) Completed proposals must by received at NIJ no later than 5 p.m. on February 2. Extensions will not be granted.

357. National Institute of Justice
Visiting Fellowships Program
633 Indiana Avenue, NW, Room 900
Washington, DC 20531
(202) 724-7631

Visiting Fellowships Program

CFDA Program Number 15.561

Program Description The program offers criminal justice practitioners and researchers an opportunity to undertake independent research on policy-relevant issues in the criminal justice area.

Eligibility/Limitations Fellowship grants are awarded to individuals or to their parent agencies or organizations. Generally, professionals working in the criminal justice field, including university or college-based academic researchers and upper-level managers in criminal justice agencies, are eligible.

Fiscal Information NIJ support will cover: fellow's salary, fringe benefits, reasonable relocation costs, travel essential to the project, supplementary expenses (some special equipment), and office costs (telephone, computers, supplies, furniture). Projects can run from six to eighteen months.

Application Information Applicants are encouraged to contact the institute to discuss topic viability or proposal content before submitting proposals.

Deadline(s) Completed proposals must be received at the NIJ no later than 5 p.m. on February 16. Extensions will not be granted.

358. National Institute of Mental Health
5600 Fishers Lane
Rockville, MD 20857
(301) 443-3683

Mental Health Research Grants

CFDA Program Number 13.242

Program Description The objectives of this program are to increase knowledge and improve research methods on mental and behavioral disorders; to generate information regarding basic biological and behavioral disorders; to generate information regarding basic biological and behavioral processes underlying these disorders and the maintenance of mental health; and to improve mental health services.

Sample Grants Research funded includes studies of fertility agreement and conflict resolution; the evolution of mental health policy in the United States; management and treatment of insanity acquittees in Oregon; and assessing the impact of insanity defense reforms.

Eligibility/Limitations Public, private, profit or nonprofit agencies (including state and local government agencies), eligible federal agencies, universities, colleges, hospitals, and academic or research institutions may apply for research grants.

Fiscal Information Grant awards range from $10,000 to $1,095,000 with an average award of $156,000.

Application Information The standard application forms, as furnished by PHS and required by 45 CFR, Part 92, must be used for applicants that are state and local governments. Application kits, containing the necessary forms and instructions, may be obtained from the Grants Management Branch, NIMH at the address listed above.

Deadline(s) Deadlines for application are February 1, June 1, and October 1.

359. National Institute on Aging
National Institutes of Health
9000 Rockville Pike, Building 31
Bethesda, MD 20892
(301) 496-4996

Aging Research

CFDA Program Number 13.866

Program Description The National Institute on Aging has established programs to encourage biomedical, social, and behavioral research and research directed toward greater understanding of the aging process and the diseases, special problems, and needs of people as they age. The behavioral and social research program supports research that will lead to greater understanding of the social, cultural, economic, and psychological factors that affect both the process of growing old and the place of older people in society.

Sample Grants Research supported includes a study on private pensions, implicit contracts and older workers, and on the ADEA amendment and public support for older workers.

Eligibility/Limitations Universities, colleges, medical, dental, and nursing schools, schools of public health, laboratories, hospitals, state and local health departments and other public or private institutions (both for-profit and nonprofit), and individuals are eligible to apply.

Fiscal Information Grant awards in 1990 range from $15,800 to $1.2 million, with an average award of $170,280.

Application Information A research grant application, PHS 398, must be submitted to the Division of Research Grants, NIH, Bethesda, MD 20892. Application kits are available on request.

Deadline(s) The deadlines for research grants are February 1, June 1, and October 1.

360. National Institute on Alcohol Abuse and Alcoholism
Public Health Service
5600 Fishers Lane
Rockville, MD 20857
(301) 443-2530

Alcohol Research Programs

CFDA Program Number 13.273

Program Description The objectives of this program are to develop a sound fundamental knowledge base which can be applied to the development of improved methods of treatment and more effective strategies for preventing alcoholism and alcohol-related problems. The National Institute on Alcohol Abuse and Alcoholism (NIAAA) supports research in a broad range of discipline and subject areas related to biomedical and genetic factors, psychological and environmental factors, and alcohol-related problems and medical disorders.

Sample Grants Funded research includes studies of the role of alcohol use in breaches-of-the-peace; the impact of minimum drinking age laws on American youth; effects of legal restrictions on alcohol consumption; and effects of legal drinking age on fatal injuries.

Eligibility/Limitations Public or private profit and nonprofit agencies, including state, local, or regional government agencies, universities, colleges, hospitals, academic or research institutions may apply for research grants.

Fiscal Information Grant awards range from $19,000 to $789,000 with an average award of $135,000.

Application Information The standard application forms, as furnished by PHS and required by 45 CFR, Part 92 must be used for grant applicants that are state and local governments. Application kits containing the necessary forms and instructions may be obtained from NIAAA.

Deadline(s) Deadlines for application are February 1, June 1, and October 1.

361. National Institutes of Health
National Center for Human Genome Research, Ethical,
  Legal and Social Implications Program
Building 38A, Room 613
Bethesda, MD 20894
(301) 496-7531

Ethical, Legal and Social Implications Program

Program Description The National Institutes of Health (NIH) invite applications for research grants and conference grants addressing ethical, legal, and social issues that may arise from the application of knowledge gained as a result of the Human Genome Initiative. The capabilities that arise out of the Human Genome Initiative are expected to have a profound impact on individuals and society. Knowing the entire sequence of the human genome will raise questions about how this information should be used. The NIH will give high priority to studies that address social, legal, and ethical implications of the project and develop options for policies or programs that minimize the possibilities of adverse impact. Areas of special interest include, but are not limited to: questions of fairness in the use of genetic information; the privacy and confidentiality of genetic information, including questions of ownership and control of genetic information and consent to disclosure and use of genetic information; issues raised by reproductive decisions influenced by genetic information; issues raised by the introduction of increased genetic information into mainstream medical practice; the uses and misuses of genetics in the past and their relevance to the current situation; questions raised by the commercialization of the products from the Human Genome Initiative including, intellectual property rights, property rights, impact on scientific collaboration and candor, and accessibility of data and materials; and conceptual and philosophical implications raised by the initiative.

Eligibility/Limitations Support for conferences will be limited to those that are highly focused and produce a specific product, such as recommendations or policy options. Research should be appropriate to the nature of the projects proposed and the disciplines involved, but priority will be given to studies that address the normative problems of social policy, professional ethics, and jurisprudence raised by the topics above. Thus, projects that use the interpretive methods traditional to humanities, law and the social sciences are particularly encouraged. General surveys for purposes of information gathering will not be supported at this time. The program is interested in attracting individuals with varied backgrounds to consider studies in this area. However, individuals must show that they either have or will obtain a sound working knowledge of the underlying biology so that relevance to the human genome program can be assured.

Fiscal Information Although there is no set-aside of funds for this area of research, the human genome program is prepared to spend at least 3 percent of its resources in addressing these issues, provided a sufficient number of high-quality applications is received.

Application Information Applications should be submitted on the new PHS 398 (Rev. 10/88). Application kits are available at most institutional business offices and from: Office of Grants Inquiries, Division of Research Grants, Westwood Building, Room 449, National Institutes of Health, Bethesda, MD, 20892.

Deadline(s) Applications for research grants and conference grants will be accepted in accordance with the usual NIH receipt dates for new applications—October 1, February 1, and June 1.

Additional Information Postdoctoral fellowships will be provided to scientists trained in biomedical disciplines relevant to the human genome project to receive training in ethics, law or other topics that will enable those scientists to contribute to studies of the ethical, legal or social implications of the genome project. Conversely, individuals with doctoral degrees in disciplines traditional to the humanities and social sciences can receive support for postdoctoral training in genomics research in order to enhance their abilities to study problems related to the Human Genome Initiative. Applications for individual postdoctoral fellowships will be accepted September 10, January 10, and May 10.

362. National Italian American Foundation
666 11th Street, NW, Suite 800
Washington, DC 20001
(202) 638-0220

Law Fellowship

Program Description This fellowship is offered to support law students.

Eligibility/Limitations All graduate law students are eligible.

Fiscal Information The fellowship carries a stipend of $1,000.

Application Information Application information is available from the foundation.

Deadline(s) Contact the foundation for deadlines.

363. National Lawyers Guild
NLG Summer Projects
1205 Smith Tower
Seattle, WA 98104
(206) 622-5151

Summer Projects

Program Description The Summer Projects Program sends interns to work with community and legal organizations from Florida to Washington state. The program helps organizations working for peace and justice meet the legal and educational needs of the people they serve. The program provides law students with direct experiences in progressive legal work, encouraging careers in fields of law dedicated to using the legal system in the service of justice.

Eligibility/Limitations Law students are eligible to apply for a maximum of three projects.

Fiscal Information All Summer Projects interns receive a $2,000 stipend. All applicants are strongly encouraged to seek other funding sources, including law school work-study and fellowship programs, to supplement their stipend up to a ceiling of $2,800. Interns are required to work full-time for 10 weeks. Starting and ending dates of the internship are negotiated with the project coordinator.

Application Information Contact the NLG for application forms and instructions, and for a listing of available summer projects.

Deadline(s) Applications must be postmarked by February 1.

Additional Information In the past, interns have worked with groups to provide legal, political, and educational support on a wide variety of issues, including voting rights, union democracy, workplace health and safety, Native American treaty rights, the death penalty and prison reform, Asian-American women seeking decent wages, working conditions and housing, Central American refugees, and illegal governmental spying.

364. National Library of Medicine

Extramural Programs, National Institutes of Health
8600 Rockville Pike, Building 38
Bethesda, MD 20894
(301) 496-6131

Medical Library Assistance

CFDA Program Number 13.879

Program Description The objective of this program is to improve health information services by providing funds to train professional personnel, strengthen library and information services, support biomedical publications, and conduct research in information science and in medical information.

Sample Grants Research funded includes a study of mental health law—clinical and legal issues for clinicians.

Eligibility/Limitations Institutions or organizations with research capabilities in the health science information fields or in medical informatics are eligible to apply for research grants. Fellowships are limited to individuals at the postdoctoral level who are citizens or noncitizen nationals of the United States or have been lawfully admitted to the United States for permanent residence.

Fiscal Information Grant awards in 1989 ranged from $12,000 to $1 million, with an average award of $167,000.

Application Information The standard application forms, as furnished by PHS and required by 45 PHS, Part 92 for state and local governments, must be used for this program. Additional application information is available from the program.

Deadline(s) The deadlines for new applications are February 1, June 1, and October 1. The deadlines for fellowships are January 10, May 10, and September 10.

365. National Research Council

The Fellowship Office
2101 Constitution Avenue, NW
Washington, DC 20418
(202) 334-2860

Ford Foundation Postdoctoral Fellowships for Minorities

Program Description The National Research Council awards Ford Foundation Postdoctoral Fellowships for Minorities to provide opportunities for continued education and experience in research for American Indians and Alaskan Natives (Eskimo and Aleut), Black Americans, Mexican Americans/Chicanos, and Puerto Ricans. Fellows are selected from among scientists, engineers, and scholars in the humanities who show promise of future achievement in academic research and scholarship in higher education. Awards are made in the behavioral and social sciences, humanities, engineering, mathematics, physical sciences, and biological sciences, and for interdisciplinary programs comprised of two or more eligible disciplines. Awards are not made in professions such as medicine, law, social work, library science, and such areas as business administration and management, educational administration, curriculum development and supervision, teacher training, and personnel and guidance.

Eligibility/Limitations Citizens or nationals of the United States who are members of one of the designated minority groups, who are preparing for or are already engaged in college or university teaching, and who hold doctoral or other terminal degrees may apply for a one-year fellowship. Fellowships are awarded for research at an appropriate not-for-profit institution of higher education or research, primarily in the United States. Appropriate institutions include universities, museums, libraries, government or national laboratories, privately sponsored not-for-profit institutes, government chartered not-for-profit research organizations, and centers for advanced study.

Fiscal Information The stipend for fellows at the regular postdoctoral level is $25,000 per year. No dependency allowance is available. In addition to the stipend, the fellow will receive a travel and relocation allowance up to a maximum of $3,000. Each fellow's employing institution will be provided a $2,500 grant-in-aid for the fellow's use once the fellowship tenure is completed. The employing institution will be asked to match the grant. These funds are designated to be used for the fellow's research expenditures. Fellowship recipients are required to choose for affiliation an institution other than that from which they apply.

Application Information Application materials and information is available from the Fellowship Office, National Research Council.

Deadline(s) Application postmark deadline is January 12.

366. National Research Council

The Fellowship Office
2101 Constitution Avenue, NW
Washington, DC 20418
(202) 334-2860

Ford Foundation Predoctoral and Dissertation Fellowships for Minorities

Program Description The National Research Council administers the Ford Foundation Doctoral Fellowships for Minorities, which offers 40 three-year predoctoral fellowships and 10 one-year dissertation fellowships to American Indians or Alaskan Natives (Eskimo or Aleut), Black Americans, Mexican Americans/Chicanos, and Puerto Ricans. These fellowships provide higher education opportunities for members of minority groups that are most severely underrepresented in the nation's Ph.D. population, the pool from which colleges and universities draw their faculties. Fellowships will be awarded in research-based doctoral programs in the behavioral and social sciences, humanities, engineering, mathematics, physical sciences, and biological sciences, and for interdisciplinary programs comprised of two or more eligible disciplines. Awards will not be made in such areas as business administration and management, communications, health sciences, journalism, library science, educational administration, curriculum development and supervision, teacher training, or personnel and guidance. In addition, awards will not be made for work leading to terminal master's degrees, Doctor of Education (Ed.D.) degrees, Doctor of Fine Arts (D.F.A.) degrees, or practice-oriented professional degrees in areas such as medicine, law, or social work.

Eligibility/Limitations Citizens of the United States who are members of one of the designated minority groups, who are beginning graduate students or who are within one year of completing the dissertation, and who expect to work toward the Ph.D. or Sc.D. degree may apply for a fellowship award.

Fiscal Information Fellowships will be tenable at any accredited nonprofit U.S. institution of higher learning offering the Ph.D. or Sc.D. in the fields eligible for support in this program. Each predoctoral fellowship will include an annual stipend of $11,000 to the fellow, and an annual institutional grant of $6,000 to the fellowship institution in lieu of tuition and fees. Dissertation fellows will receive a stipend of $18,000 for the twelve-month tenure with no institutional grant.

Application Information All inquiries concerning application materials and program administration should be addressed to the Fellowship Office of the NRC.

Deadline(s) The postmark deadline for submission of the preliminary application is November 9. The postmark deadline for submission of the fellowship application is December 8.

367. National Science Foundation

Directorate for Science and Engineering Education,
  Division of Research Career Development
1800 G Street, NW
Washington, DC 20550

Graduate Fellowships

CFDA Program Number 47.009

Program Description This program promotes the future strength of the nation's scientific and technological base by providing recognition and support for advanced study to outstanding graduate students. Fellowships are awarded for study or work leading to master's or doctoral degrees in the mathematical, physical, biological, engineering and social sciences, and the history and philosophy of science. Fellows are selected in a national competition on the basis of actual and potential achievements in their chosen disciplines. They may pursue their studies at any appropriate U.S. or foreign institution of higher learning.

Eligibility/Limitations Applicants must be U.S. citizens or nationals. Persons who hold permanent resident status are not eligible to apply. Applicants must not have completed, by the beginning of the fall term, more than 20 semester hours, 30 quarter hours, or the equivalent, of study in the science and engineering fields listed above following completion of their first baccalaureate degree in science or engineering, or its equivalent. Individuals who, at the time of application, have earned an advanced degree in science or engineering are ineligible. Awards are not made in clinical or business fields, in other education programs of any kind, or in history or social work, for work leading to medical, dental, law or public health degrees, or for study in joint science-professional degree programs.

Fiscal Information Each fellowship gives up to three years of support for full-time graduate study. The stipend is $12,900 for a twelve-month tenure, prorated monthly for lesser periods. A $1,000 special international research travel allowance is available. There are no dependency allowances. In addition, NSF will provide fellowship institutions, on behalf of each fellow, with a cost-of-education allowance ($6,000) in lieu of all tuition costs and assessed fees.

Application Information For information and application materials write to The Fellowship Office, National Research Council, 2101 Constitution Avenue, Washington, DC 20418 or telephone (202) 334-2872. A detailed program description and guidelines for application are in the brochure "Graduate Fellowships Announcement" available from NSF.

Deadline(s) The deadline for filing part one of the application is November 9; for filing part two, December 8.

368. National Science Foundation

Directorate for Science and Engineering Education,
  Division of Research Career Development
1800 G Street, NW
Washington, DC 20550

Minority Graduate Fellowships

CFDA Program Number 47.009

Program Description This program gives fellowship support to members of ethnic minority groups whose abilities traditionally have been untapped in the advanced levels of the nation's science talent pool. Under this program, support goes to outstanding minority graduate students for study or work toward master's or doctoral degrees in the mathematical, physical, biological, engineering, and social sciences, and in the history and philosophy of science.

Eligibility/Limitations Applicants must be U.S. citizens or nationals who are members of one of the following ethnic minority groups: American Indian, Black, Hispanic, Native Alaskan (Eskimo or Aleut), or Native Pacific Islander (Polynesian or Micronesian). Applicants must not have completed, by the beginning of the fall term, more than 30 semester hours, 45 quarter hours, or the equivalent, of study in the science and engineering fields listed above following completion

of their first baccalaureate degree in science or engineering, or its equivalent. Individuals who, at the time of application, have earned an advanced degree in science or engineering are ineligible. Awards are not made in clinical or business fields, in other education programs of any kind, or in history or social work, for work leading to medical, dental, law, or public health degrees, or for study in joint science-professional degree programs.

Fiscal Information Each award provides up to three years of support for full-time graduate study. The stipend is $12,900 for a 12-month tenure, prorated monthly at $1,075 for lesser periods. A $1,000 special international research travel allowance is available. There are no dependency allowances. In addition, NSF will provide fellowship institutions, on behalf of each fellow, with a cost-of-education allowance ($6,000) in lieu of all tuition costs and assessed fees.

Application Information For information and application materials write to The Fellowship Office, National Research Council, 2101 Constitution Avenue, Washington, DC 20418 or telephone (202) 334-2872. A detailed program description and guidelines for application are in the brochure "Graduate Fellowships Announcement" available from NSF.

Deadline(s) The postmark deadline for filing part one of the application is November 9; the postmark deadline for filing part two of the application is December 8.

369. National Science Foundation

Law and Social Science Program
1800 G Street, NW
Washington, DC 20550
(202) 357-9567

Law and Social Science Program

Program Description The program supports social scientific studies of law and law-like systems of rules. These can include, but are not limited to, research on processes affecting compliance and the impact of law; causes and consequences of variations and changes in legal institutions; personal, social, economic, and cultural conditions affecting use of and responses to law; dynamics of disputing and dispute resolution; determinants of legal decision making; effects of and factors accounting for administrative rule making and regulating behaviors; patterns of social control and deterence; and processes that influence the development of law and explain the relationship between legal processes and other social processes. The primary consideration is that the research shows promise of advancing a scientific understanding of law and legal process. Within this framework, the program has an "open window" for diverse theoretical perspectives, methods, and contexts for study.

Sample Grants For a study of the impact of lawsuits against public participation, $175,000 to the University of Denver, CO (1988). For a study of organizational response to legal change, $64,175 to the University of Wisconsin, Madison (1988). For a study of patent law, competition and the advancement of social knowledge, $52,682 to NBER, MA (1988). For a study of political authority, social change, and legal evolution in Indonesia, $25,929 to the University of Washington, Seattle (1988).

Eligibility/Limitations The most frequent recipients of support for research are academic institutions and nonprofit research groups. In special circumstances, grants are also awarded to other types of institutions and to individuals. In these cases, preliminary inquiry should be made to the appropriate program officer before a proposal is submitted. Support may be provided for projects involving a single scientist or a number of scientists. Awards are made for projects confined to a single disciplinary area and for those that cross or merge disciplinary interests.

Fiscal Information Level of support varies from project to project. Grant awards in 1988 ranged from $1,000 to $175,000. Although most grants are for much shorter periods, up to five years of support may be requested. Grant funds may be used for paying direct and indirect costs necessary to conduct research or studies. Institutions are required to share in the cost of each research project. This may be accomplished by a contribution to any cost element, direct or indirect.

Application Information Address inquiries to the program director. Guidelines are contained in the publication "Grants for Scientific and Engineering Research."

Deadline(s) The target dates for the submission of proposals are January 15 and August 15.

Additional Information Proposals for doctoral dissertation support, research conferences, the acquisition of specialized research and computation equipment, group international travel, and data resource development will be considered.

370. National Wildlife Federation
1400 16th Street, NW
Washington, DC 20036-2266
(703) 790-4484

Environmental Conservation Fellowships

Program Description These fellowships for graduate students are offered annually to encourage advanced study in fields relating to wildlife, natural resource management, and protection of environmental quality. Proposals addressing the following topics are especially encouraged: the impact of livestock and highway fences on western migratory wildlife; the impacts to sea turtles from domestic and international shrimping operations with an emphasis on trawl entanglement and release; the impacts of shoreline development on wildlife habitat; the impacts to marine ecosystems from finfish and shellfish by catch and discard by commercial fisherman; the impacts of military use in public lands; and the use in constructed wetlands for treating agricultural waste water.

Sample Grants Fellowships in 1988-1989 were awarded for study of criteria influencing support of strong conservation legislation and mitigation of wetland loss: policy issues, ecological issues, and evaluation of examples.

Eligibility/Limitations Applications will be accepted from individuals who are pursuing degrees in a college or university graduate program or law school and have been accepted for the fall semester following the awarding of the grant. Applicants must be principally engaged in research, rather than in course work, during the period for which support is given. First-year graduate students engaged primarily in course work should not apply.

Fiscal Information Grants up to $10,000 are made for a one-year period, however, recipients may apply in subsequent years for additional funding.

Application Information Application for the fellowships must be made on official forms which are available from April through July of each year from the executive vice president of the federation.

Deadline(s) Completed applications must be received by July 15.

371. National Wildlife Federation
1400 16th Street, NW
Washington, DC 20036-2266
(703) 790-4484

Resources Conservation Internships

Program Description The NWF offers a program for interns to work in Washington, DC in its Resources Conservation Department. Much of an intern's time is spent in researching environmental policy issues and covering Congressional activity. The federation seeks interns with experience and academic backgrounds in the areas of energy, fisheries and wildlife, international issues, pollution and toxics, public lands, and water resources, as well as economics, environmental conservation, and natural resource management.

Eligibility/Limitations The internship program is designed for college graduates and graduate students with a special interest in environmental issues.

Fiscal Information Internships are for a 24-week period beginning in early July and early January. A stipend totaling $5,400 is paid in biweekly increments.

Application Information Application forms are not required. An application consists of a personal letter indicating the applicant's special interests, a complete resume, including a list of three to five references, and a short, nontechnical writing sample.

Deadline(s) Applications for January must be received by November 16; for July, by April 9.

372. The Needmor Fund
1730 15th Street
Boulder, CO 80302
(303) 449-5801

Program Description The primary interest of the fund is to assist groups of people working together to overcome problems: those forces and events which have an adverse and profound effect upon their lives as individuals, as families, and as members of a community. The fund recognizes that the nature of the problem faced will vary from group to group, and thus, does not specify certain areas of concern, only that people have joined forces to take control over their own lives.

Sample Grants To assist in amassing documentary and testimonial evidence for use in all Guatemalan Indian asylum claims raised in the United States, $30,000 to Corn Mayas, Florida Rural Legal Services, Bartow, FL (1987).

Eligibility/Limitations The fund looks for grass-roots, member-controlled organizations, capable of setting out and implementing realistic strategies and goals. A clear preference is given to organizations whose membership represents traditionally disenfranchised populations. Organizations which are tax-exempt under Section 501(c)(3) of the Internal Revenue Service Code are eligible to apply. The fund does not award grants to individuals.

Fiscal Information The average grant size is $15,000.

Application Information Initial contact with the fund should be a telephone call or letter describing the history and goals of the organization, the nature of the project to be funded, and the amount which will be requested from the fund. If it is determined that the activity falls within the fund's guidelines, submission of a written proposal will be invited.

Deadline(s) The deadlines for receipt of proposals are January 10 and July 10.

373. The New World Foundation
100 East 85th Street
New York, NY 10028
(212) 249-1023

Grants

Program Description The foundation attempts to be responsive to the needs and aspirations of neglected segments of our society, and to support programs which have creative and innovative individuals working with them. The principal areas of current interest for the foundation's consideration of grant applications are equal rights and opportunities, public education, public health, community initiatives, and avoidance of war.

Sample Grants To support their law reform project, $15,000 to the Indian Law Resource Center, Washington, DC (1986). To sponsor a continuing series of meetings and joint papers between Soviet and U.S. lawyers on the subject of nuclear arms control, $3,000 to Lawyers Alliance for Nuclear Arms Control, Boston, MA (1986).

Eligibility/Limitations The foundation ordinarily makes grants only to tax-exempt organizations or to projects administered by a tax-exempt organization. It does not make grants to individuals, nor does it support scholarships, academic research, films, publications, media and arts projects, or direct social service delivery programs.

Fiscal Information Grants awarded in 1987 totaled over $1.9 million.

Application Information The foundation has no standard application form. A concise proposal, addressed to the president, should contain the following information as applicable: a cover letter which briefly summarizes the proposal and states the amount requested; a description of the specific project; objectives, a timetable for their achievement, and the strategies and methods by which they will be attained; a brief description of the sponsoring organization; the organization's budget for the fiscal year for which funds are being sought and a budget for the specific project being proposed; if possible, an audited report for the previous fiscal year or, if an audit is not available, a financial statement for the prior period; the current sources of support and amount of income, and a list of sources from which additional funds are being solicited; and a copy of the ruling granting federal tax exemption.

Deadline(s) The foundation has no deadlines for application.

374. The New York Community Trust

415 Madison Avenue
New York, NY 10017
(212) 758-0100

Grants

Program Description As the trust is a community foundation for the greater New York City area, the distribution committee gives priority with many of its funds to grant proposals which deal with the problems of this metropolitan region. Giving categories fall into four major program areas: children, youth and families; community development and environment; education, arts and humanities; and health and people with special needs.

Sample Grants To support research in support of efforts to protect the civil rights of Hispanics in New York City, $30,000 to the Puerto Rican Legal Defense and Education Fund, New York (1990).

Eligibility/Limitations Grants are not awarded to individuals. The trust rarely makes grants for endowments, building campaigns, deficit financing, films, general operating support or religious purposes. Grants are concentrated in the New York City area.

Fiscal Information Grants awarded in 1988 totaled over $42.7 million.

Application Information Specific grant-making guidelines are available for each category of funding. Contact the trust in writing for these guidelines and additional information.

Deadline(s) The foundation reviews proposals throughout the year.

375. The New York Times Company Foundation, Inc.

229 West 43rd Street
New York, NY 10036
(212) 556-1091

Grants

Program Description The major areas in which the foundation entertains applications for grants are education, journalism, cultural affairs, community services, and environmental concerns.

Eligibility/Limitations Grants are not made to individuals, to sectarian religious institutions, or for health, drug or alcohol-related purposes. Although urban affairs rank high among the foundation's interests, grants are not usually made on the neighborhood level. Some national and international activities receive contributions, but the majority of grants are concentrated in the Greater New York area and localities served by affiliates of The New York Times Company.

Fiscal Information In 1988 the foundation made grants totaling over $4.8 million.

Application Information Appeals for grants should be addressed to the president of the foundation. The foundation discourages

investment of excessive time and money in the preparation of requests and proposals. A letter describing the purpose for which funds are requested and providing information concerning the funds involved in the specific venture, including details of other potential sources of support, is sufficient. Submission of a copy of a determination by the IRS that the applicant enjoys tax-exempt status under the Internal Revenue Code is required.

Deadline(s) The board meets at least twice annually, within the first and third quarter of each calendar year, to review the president's recommendations and authorize grants to be disbursed. In extraordinary circumstances, decisions may be made outside that schedule.

376. The Newberry Library

Committee on Awards
60 West Walton Street
Chicago, IL 60610
(312) 943-9090

American Society for Eighteenth-Century Studies Fellowships

Program Description The Newberry Library, founded in 1887, is a privately endowed, independent research library located on the near north side of Chicago. Comprising more than one million volumes and five million manuscripts, it has a strong general collection embracing history and the humanities within Western Civilization from the late Middle Ages to the early 20th century. Bibliographic holdings are extensive, and certain special collections are internationally noted. ASECS/Newberry Library Fellowships are available for one to three months in residence at the Newberry for studies in the period 1660-1815.

Eligibility/Limitations Applicants must be postdoctoral scholars no more than 10 years from receipt of the Ph.D.

Fiscal Information Stipends are $800 per month.

Application Information For additional information and application forms, write to the Committee on Awards, The Newberry Library.

Deadline(s) Completed applications are due by March 1 or October 15.

377. The Newberry Library

Committee on Awards
60 West Walton Street
Chicago, IL 60610
(312) 943-9090

Joint Fellowships with the American Antiquarian Society

Program Description The Newberry Library, founded in 1887, is a privately endowed, independent research library located on the near north side of Chicago. Comprising more than one million volumes and five million manuscripts, it has a strong general collection embracing history and the humanities within Western Civilization from the late Middle Ages to the early 20th century. Bibliographic holdings are extensive, and certain special collections are internationally noted. Scholars who desire to use collections both at the Newberry and the American Antiquarian Society may apply for a joint fellowship via a single application.

Eligibility/Limitations Applicants must have the Ph.D. or have completed all requirements except the dissertation.

Fiscal Information Awards are available for up to two months at the Newberry, and from one to three months at the American Antiquarian Society. Stipends at the Newberry are $800 per month.

Application Information For additional information and application forms, write to the Committee on Awards, The Newberry Library.

Deadline(s) Completed applications are due January 31 or October 15.

378. The Newberry Library
Committee on Awards
60 West Walton Street
Chicago, IL 60610
(312) 943-9090

Lloyd Lewis Fellowships in American History

Program Description These fellowships are available for established scholars in any field of American history appropriate to the Newberry's collections. The library's collections in American history are especially strong on the discovery, exploration, and settlement of the New World; the American Indian; the American West; local history, genealogy, and census records; family and social history; the Midwest; and colonial Latin America, especially Mexico and Brazil. In addition, the library houses the archives of the Illinois Central and the Chicago, Burlington, and Quincy Railroads, and the Pullman Company.

Eligibility/Limitations Applicants must hold the Ph.D., or its equivalent, at the time of the application, and must have demonstrated, through their publications, particular excellence in the field.

Fiscal Information The award carries a maximum stipend of $40,000 for periods of six to eleven months.

Application Information For further information and application forms, contact the library.

Deadline(s) Applications are due January 10.

379. The Newberry Library
Committee on Awards
60 West Walton Street
Chicago, IL 60610
(312) 943-9090, ext. 267

D'Arcy McNickle Center for the History of the American Indian Fellowships: Frances C. Allen Fellowships

Program Description These fellowships are available to scholars working in any graduate or preprofessional field, but the particular purpose of the fellowship is to encourage study in the humanities and social sciences.

Eligibility/Limitations Women of Indian heritage who are pursuing a graduate academic program are eligible to apply.

Fiscal Information Stipend varies according to need. Fellows are expected to spend a significant amount of their fellowship term in residence at the McNickle Center.

Application Information Contact the center for further information and application materials.

Deadline(s) Applications are due August 1 and February 1 of each year.

380. The Newberry Library
Committee on Awards
60 West Walton Street
Chicago, IL 60610
(312) 943-9090

Monticello College Foundation Fellowship for Women

Program Description The Newberry Library, founded in 1887, is a privately endowed, independent research library located on the near north side of Chicago. Comprising more than one million volumes and five million manuscripts, it has a strong general collection embracing history and the humanities within Western Civilization from the late Middle Ages to the early 20th century. Bibliographic holdings are extensive, and certain special collections are internationally noted. The Monticello College Foundation Fellowship is designed primarily for women at an early stage in their professional careers whose work gives clear promise of scholarly productivity and whose career would be significantly enhanced by six months of research and writing. Preference will be given to applicants whose scholarship is particularly concerned with the study of women, but study may

be proposed in any field appropriate to the Newberry's collections.

Eligibility/Limitations Applicants must have the Ph.D. at the time of application, and must be U.S. citizens or permanent residents.

Fiscal Information The six-month fellowship for work in residence at the Newberry carries a stipend of $10,000.

Application Information For additional information and application forms, write to the Committee on Awards, The Newberry Library.

Deadline(s) Completed applications are due by January 15.

381. The Newberry Library
Committee on Awards
60 West Walton Street
Chicago, IL 60610
(312) 943-9090

National Endowment for the Humanities Fellowships

Program Description The Newberry Library, founded in 1887, is a privately endowed, independent research library located on the near north side of Chicago. Comprising more than one million volumes and five million manuscripts, it has a strong general collection embracing history and the humanities within Western Civilization from the late Middle Ages to the early 20th century. Bibliographic holdings are extensive, and certain special collections are internationally noted. NEH/Newberry Fellowships are designed not only to encourage the individual scholar's research, but also to deepen and enrich the opportunities for serious intellectual exchange through the active participation of fellows in the Newberry community. Fellowships are available for research in residence in any field appropriate to the Newberry's collections.

Eligibility/Limitations These grants are for established scholars at the postdoctoral level, or its equivalent. Awards are open to U.S. citizens or nationals, and to foreign nationals who have been living in the United States for at least three years. Preference is given to applicants who have not held major fellowships or grants for three years preceding the proposed period of residency.

Fiscal Information Fellowships are available for six to eleven months' research and are for up to $30,000.

Application Information For additional information and application forms, write to the Committee on Awards, The Newberry Library.

Deadline(s) Completed applications are due by January 10.

382. The Newberry Library
Committee on Awards
60 West Walton Street
Chicago, IL 60610
(312) 943-9090

Newberry-British Academy Fellowship for Study in Great Britian

Program Description The Newberry Library offers an exchange fellowship for three months' study in Great Britian in any field in the humanities in which the Newberry's collections are strong.

Eligibility/Limitations Applicants must be established scholars at the postdoctoral level, or its equivalent. Preference is given to readers and staff of the Newberry and to scholars who have previously used the Newberry.

Fiscal Information The stipend is £30 per day while the fellow is in Great Britian. The fellow's home institution is expected to continue to pay his/her salary.

Application Information For additional information and application forms write the library.

Deadline(s) Completed applications are due by March 1.

383. The Newberry Library
Committee on Awards
60 West Walton Street
Chicago, IL 60610
(312) 943-9090

Resident Fellowships for Unaffiliated Scholars

Program Description The Newberry Library, founded in 1887, is a privately endowed, independent research library located on the near north side of Chicago. Comprising more than one million volumes and five million manuscripts, it has a strong general collection embracing history and the humanities within Western Civilization from the late Middle Ages to the early 20th century. Bibliographic holdings are extensive, and certain special collections are internationally noted. These fellowships support unaffiliated scholars working on a specific research project in a field appropriate to the Newberry's collections.

Eligibility/Limitations Applicants must have held the Ph.D. at least two years and not be employed professionally as scholars. Applicants must anticipate spending at least six to eight hours a week in residence and participating fully in the intellectual life of the Newberry.

Fiscal Information The fellowships carry stipends of $250 per calendar quarter. Stipends may be renewed quarterly up to one year; after the first year, fellowship status may be renewed annually, but without stipend.

Application Information For additional information and application forms, write to the Committee on Awards, The Newberry Library.

Deadline(s) Completed applications are due March 1 or October 15.

384. The Newberry Library
Committee on Awards
60 West Walton Street
Chicago, IL 60610
(312) 943-9090

Short-Term Resident Fellowships for Individual Research

Program Description The Newberry Library, founded in 1887, is a privately endowed, independent research library located on the near north side of Chicago. Comprising more than one million volumes and five million manuscripts, it has a strong general collection embracing history and the humanities within Western Civilization from the late Middle Ages to the early 20th century. Bibliographic holdings are extensive, and certain special collections are internationally noted. Short-term fellowships are designed primarily to help provide access to Newberry resources for people who live beyond commuting distance. Preference is given accordingly to applicants from outside the greater Chicago area.

Eligibility/Limitations Applicants must have the Ph.D. or have completed all requirements except the dissertation.

Fiscal Information Fellowships carry stipends of $800 per month, for periods of up to two months, or when travel from a foreign country is involved, three months.

Application Information For additional information and application forms, write to the Committee on Awards, The Newberry Library.

Deadline(s) Completed applications are due by March 1 or October 15.

385. Northwest Area Foundation
West 975 First National Bank Building
St. Paul, MN 55101-1373
(612) 224-9635

Grants

Program Description The foundation targets its resources to achieve two major goals: to focus, deepen, and enhance the public dialogue so that the region's citizenry may make more effective decisions concerning important regional issues, and to build individual and organizational capacity to address those issues even after foundation support terminates. Funding is provided in the areas of regional economic development, basic human needs, natural resource conservation and management, and the arts.

Sample Grants To explore the potential of mediation as a means of resolving environmental conflicts in the eastern half of the foundation's region, $18,390 to the Median Center for Dispute Resolution, St. Paul, MN (1990). For public policy education and research on the potential impact of international environmental regulations on agriculture in the foundation's region, $295,000 to the Center for International Food and Agricultural Policy, University of Minnesota (1990). To develop formal policies for land-use planning and regulation and environmental protection between federally recognized Indian tribes in Washington and the counties in which their reservations are located, $265,000 to Northwest Renewable Resources Center, Seattle, WA (1990).

Eligibility/Limitations Grants are restricted to nonprofit organizations located and operating in Minnesota, Iowa, North Dakota, South Dakota, Montana, Idaho, Washington, and Oregon. The foundation does not approve grants for equipment or endowments, and will not approve grants for scholarships, fellowships, travel, publication, or films, except in special circumstances.

Fiscal Information The foundation is willing to consider proposals requesting several years of support. In general, the foundation limits grants to a maximum of $300,000.

Application Information The foundation urges prospective applicants to request a copy of its brochure that describes in detail the foundation's funding interests, policies, and procedures. The brochure also includes an application cover sheet and an outline of the information that should be included in a grant application.

Deadline(s) Applications are accepted throughout the year.

386. The Norwegian Information Service
825 Third Avenue, 17th Floor
New York, NY 10022-7584
(212) 421-7333

The Norwegian Emigration Fund of 1975

Program Description In 1975 Norway's Parliament, as part of the observation of the 150th anniversary of organized Norwegian emigration to the United States, voted to establish this fund with a capital of one million kroner. The purpose of the fund is to award scholarships to Americans for advanced or specialized studies in Norway of subjects dealing with emigration history and relations between the United States and Norway.

Eligibility/Limitations Scholarships can be awarded to citizens and residents of the United States. Awards may also be given to institutions in the United States whose activities are primarily centered on the subjects mentioned.

Fiscal Information The scholarships and grants usually range from Nok 5,000 to Nok 30,000.

Application Information Requests for application forms should be addressed to either the Royal Norwegian Embassy, 2720 34th Street, NW, Washington, DC 20008, telephone (303) 333-6000 or to the Norwegian Information Service.

Deadline(s) Application deadline is July 1.

387. The Norwegian Information Service

825 Third Avenue, 17th Floor
New York, NY 10022-7584
(212) 421-7333

The Norwegian Marshall Fund

Program Description The Norwegian Marshall Fund was established in 1977 as a token of Norway's gratitude to the United States. Its objective is to promote scientific research in fields of importance to both countries. The fund seeks to support primarily research projects in Norway by American researchers. The fund will also support projects at Norwegian universities and institutions of higher learning where participation of American researchers seems desirable.

Eligibility/Limitations American and Norwegian citizens are eligible to apply.

Fiscal Information The awards granted will depend upon the nature of the project. Awards larger than $5,000 will normally not be granted.

Application Information Application forms may be obtained from The Norway-America Association, Drammensveien 20 C, 0255 Oslo 2, Norway, telephone (02) 44 76 83 44 77 16.

Deadline(s) The annual grants are announced by the fund directly to Norwegian institutions of higher learning which in turn make the grants known to similar institutions and possible qualified candidates in the United States.

388. The Norwegian Information Service

825 Third Avenue, 17th Floor
New York, NY 10022-7584
(212) 421-7333

Travel Grants

Program Description The Norwegian Ministry of Foreign Affairs and the Norwegian Information Service in the United States are offering travel grants to members of the Society for the Advancement of Scandinavian Study. The awards are meant as a financial assistance for teachers and students visiting Norway for study and research purposes.

Eligibility/Limitations Applicants should be citizens and residents of the United States who are members of the SASS. They must be university or college teachers of Norwegian or other courses in Norwegian culture or society, or graduate students who have passed their preliminary examinations in these fields.

Fiscal Information The awards range from $750 to $1,500, and are meant as a financial assistance for students and teachers visiting Norway for study and research purposes.

Application Information Application forms may be obtained from the Norwegian Information Service in the United States.

Deadline(s) Applications should be sent by April 15.

389. Jessie Smith Noyes Foundation

16 East 34th Street
New York, NY 10016
(212) 684-6577

Grants

Program Description The Jessie Smith Noyes Foundation is committed to two goals: preventing irreversible damage to the natural systems upon which all life depends; and strengthening individuals and institutions committed to protecting natural systems and ensuring a sustainable society. The foundation makes grants primarily in the interrelated areas of environment and population. The components of the program are population and reproductive rights, tropical ecology, water resources, and sustainable agriculture.

Sample Grants To support a law fellow who will conduct legal and policy analysis related to groundwater protection and sustainable agriculture, $25,000 to Tulane University Law School, New Orleans, LA (1989). To support continuing work on the

international aspects of the Reproductive Freedom Project, $40,000 to the American Civil Liberties Union, New York, NY (1989). To support the council's activities, including statewide policy formulation concerning groundwater and solid and hazardous waste management and waste reduction, $20,000 to Kentucky Resources Council, Frankfort, KY (1989). To support the development of a handbook that will educate citizens, environmental activists, and government officials to effectively assess solid waste management alternatives, $30,000 to Environmental Defense Fund, New York, NY (1988). In support of a survey of current approaches to coordinating water quality and water use for both ground and surface water in key western states and develop case studies and provide analyses to illustrate the opportunities for integrated and comprehensive water management, $40,000 to the University of Colorado School of Law, Natural Resources Law Center, Boulder, CO (1988).

Eligibility/Limitations The foundation only makes grants to tax-exempt organizations with 501(c)(3) classification from the Internal Revenue Service or the equivalent for organizations outside the United States. The foundation will not consider requests for endowments, capital construction, general fund-raising, deficit financing, or loans and grants to individuals. The foundation no longer provides scholarship or fellowship support to individuals except within broader program activities. The foundation does not ordinarily consider projects that are primarily of local interest. It rarely makes grants for research projects or supports conferences, seminars, or workshops unless they are an integral part of a broader program. The foundation does not usually provide support for the production and development of television and radio programming.

Fiscal Information Grants awarded in 1989 totaled over $4.5 million.

Application Information The first step in applying to the foundation is a short, two-page letter of inquiry. The following information should be included: a brief statement of the issues to be addressed and the organization's involvement with these issues; a brief summary of the activities for which support is requested, including an outline of objectives and anticipated outcomes and implications; the approximate starting date and duration of the proposed activities; and the total amount of funding needed, the amount requested from the foundation, and information about other sources of support, both assured and requested. The foundation reviews letters to determine if they fall within the foundation's program guidelines. When a letter of inquiry reflects most closely the foundation's program priorities, the foundation will request a full proposal.

Deadline(s) The foundation reviews letters of inquiry on a continuous basis. Once the foundation requests a proposal, it is scheduled for discussion at one of the foundation's three board meetings during the year, which usually take place in March, July, and December. Applicants are urged to send their letters of inquiry well in advance of the proposed starting date of their project.

390. Office of Technology Assessment

Congress of the United States, Congressional
  Fellowships, Personnel Office
600 Pennsylvania Avenue, SE
Washington, DC 20510-8025
(202) 224-8713

OTA Congressional Fellowship Program

Program Description The program provides an opportunity for individuals of proven ability to gain a better understanding of science and technology issues facing Congress and the ways in which Congress establishes national policy related to these issues. Assessments are conducted in such areas as economic competitiveness, international security, energy, advanced materials, biotechnology, neuroscience, agriculture, advanced medical technologies and services, information technologies and policy, environment, education, and science policy.

Eligibility/Limitations The program is open to individuals who have demonstrated exceptional ability in such areas as the physical or biological sciences, engineering, law, economics, environmental and social sciences, and public policy. Candidates must have significant experience in technical fields or management or have completed research at the doctoral level. Applicants must have the ability to perform objective, comprehensive analyses; to work cooperatively with individuals of diverse backgrounds, experience, and training; and to present reports in clear and concise language.

Fiscal Information The stipend range is from $28,000 to $45,000 per year, based on the fellow's current salary and/or training and experience. In some instances a fellow may accept a salary supplement from his or her parent organization.

Application Information Applicants for the fellowships are required to submit the following: a resume limited to two pages, including education, experience, area(s) of special interest; and a one page listing of most recent published works; three letters of reference, including telephone numbers, from individuals who know the applicant well enough to write about his or her professional competence; and a statement of up to 1,000 word describing the applicants interests, significant attributes, and potential contributions to national policy.

Deadline(s) Applications and letters of reference must be postmarked by January 31.

391. John M. Olin Foundation, Inc.
100 Park Avenue, Suite 2701
New York, NY 10017
(212) 661-2670

Program Description The general purpose of the John M. Olin Foundation is to provide support for projects that reflect or are intended to strengthen the economic, political, and cultural institutions upon which the American heritage of constitutional government and private enterprise is based. The foundation also seeks to promote a general understanding of these institutions by encouraging the thoughtful study of the interactions between economic and political freedoms, and the cultural heritage that sustains them. Within the context of the foundation's general purposes, the board of trustees has authorized grants in the following areas: research on the formulation, implementation, and evaluation of public policy in the economic and social fields, including grants in such areas as regulatory policy, tax policy, fiscal policy, monetary policy, and welfare policy; projects that address the relationship between American institutions and the international context within which they operate, including studies of American foreign policy; studies of the American Constitution, the operation of American political institutions, and the moral and cultural principles underlying these institutions; and public interest law and studies related to the judicial system, jurisprudence, and the relationship between law and economics. In each of these four areas, the foundation attempts to advance its objectives through support of the following kinds of activities: research, institutional support, fellowships, professorships, lectures and lecture series, books, scholarly journals, journals of opinion, conferences and seminars, and, on occasion, television and radio programs.

Sample Grants To support a book on the state constitutional ratification debates of 1787 and 1788, $10,000 to the Freedom of Expression Foundation, Long Beach, CA (1989). To support work in the field of government natural resources regulation, $25,000 (of $50,000 grants authorized) to East Hampton Beach Preservation Society, East Hampton, NY (1989). To support *Benchmark*, a bimonthly journal of opinion on the Constitution and the courts, $25,000; to support the 1987 Resident Scholars program, $26,500 to the Center for Judicial Studies, Washington, DC (1987). To support the John M. Olin Chair in Legal Studies held by Judge Robert H. Bork, $162,750 to the American Enterprise Institute, Washington, DC (1988). To support a book on governmental liability, $25,000 to the Center for Policy Studies, Clemson University (1988). To support the 1987 Law and Economics Institute for Federal Judges, $100,000 to George Mason University, Law and Economics Center, Fairfax, VA (1987). To support the John M. Olin Program in Law and Economics, 1985-89, $917,000 ($603,000 paid prior to 1987) to

Harvard Law School, Cambridge, MA (1987). To support public interest law activities concerning regional issues, $100,000 to the Pacific Legal Foundation, Sacramento, CA (1987). To support research on hazardous waste policy, 1987-90, $75,000 to The Rand Corporation, Santa Monica, CA (1987).

Eligibility/Limitations The guidelines established by the board of trustees normally preclude funding for administrative overhead costs. In addition, grants will not be considered for endowment or building programs, annual giving programs, direct support for individuals or programs without significant impact on national affairs. Grants will be made only to institutions that provide a responsible fiscal agent and that are tax exempt under Section 501(c)(3) of the Internal Revenue Code.

Fiscal Information Grant authorized in 1988 totaled over $55 million.

Application Information Applicants should prepare a letter which gives a brief and concise description of the project, its objectives and significance, and the qualifications of the organizations and individuals involved. Included with the letter should be a project budget, the amount of the grant sought from the foundation, and mention of other sources of support. To ensure eligibility for a grant, the applicant should also submit a copy of the IRS letter confirming the organizations's tax-exempt status under Section 501(c)(3) of the Internal Revenue Code.

Deadline(s) Final authority for making grants rests with the board of trustees which meets five times a year.

392. Ottinger Foundation
1601 Connecticut Avenue, NW, Suite 803
Washington, DC 20009
(202) 232-7333

Grants

Program Description The Ottinger Foundation supports projects which aim to promote democracy, economic justice, environmental preservation, energy conservation, and world peace. The foundation encourages submission of innovative proposals which seek to address causes rather than the symptoms of problems. Most projects supported by the foundation include a strong component of citizen activism.

Eligibility/Limitations The foundation contributes to tax-exempt organizations in the United States. The foundation does not make grants to organizations that traditionally enjoy popular support such as universities, museums, or hospitals. It does not support academic research, film or video projects, construction or restoration projects, books, or local programs without national significance.

Fiscal Information Grant expenditures in 1987/1988 totaled $610,489.

Application Information Proposals should not exceed 10 pages and should include the following information: a statement of the need for support, the project's goals, and an action plan for achieving those goals; a certificate of tax-exempt status; staff and organizational qualifications for carrying out the program; lists of other sources of financial support already committed and sources to whom proposals have been sent; project and organizational line item budget(s); and a list of other organizations involved in similar programs and how the proposed project is different.

Deadline(s) There are no application deadlines. All grants are awarded by a board of directors that meets twice a year.

393. Pacific Telesis Foundation
Pacific Telesis Center
130 Kearny Street, Room 3351
San Francisco, CA 94108
(415) 394-3693

Grants

Program Description Contributions are made in the areas of education, human services, community and civic programs, and arts and culture. Community and civic programs support organizations which seek to resolve common-interest community problems, and give priority to programs that improve the quality of life for individuals who have limited access to social and economic opportunities; help build the technical and organizational capabilities of community-based groups and small businesses; and promote skills and independence in individuals who are not fully empowered to help themselves.

Sample Grants To equip four teaching/seminar rooms at the Center for Continuing Judicial Education with state-of-the-art audiovisual equipment, $25,000 to the National Council of Juvenile and Family Court Judges, Reno, NV (1987). For Communications Law Program, $7,500 to the School of Law, University of California at Los Angeles, CA (1987).

Eligibility/Limitations It is the policy of the foundation not to make grants to organizations that do not have current 501(c)(3) tax-exempt status; to private foundations; to "flow-through" organizations; for endowment funds; to individuals; for general operating purposes; to organizations that practice discrimination; for emergencies; or for special occasion goodwill advertising in the form of products and services.

Fiscal Information Grants awarded in 1988 totaled over $5.8 million.

Application Information Requests should include a description of the organization's purpose and scope, as well as its short-term and long-range objectives; evidence of how the request fits foundation guidelines; standards by which the success of the program will be evaluated; the current total budget of the organization; a budget for the specific project for which support is requested; current IRS documentation of tax-exempt status; a copy of the most recent audited financial statement and the most recent federal tax return; a list of members of the board of directors, including their business, governmental or educational affiliations; a list of current corporate and foundation funders and funding levels; and evidence of strategies to develop earned income and to avoid over-dependence on any single source of contributed income.

Deadline(s) There is no specific deadline for submission of grant requests. However, because of the high volume of grant requests considered by the foundation, grant seekers should allow six to eight weeks for a decision.

Additional Information In addition to the Pacific Telesis Foundation, two of Pacific Telesis Group's subsidiaries, Pacific Bell and Nevada Bell, manage their own separate local contributions programs under the direction of community relations organizations throughout California and Nevada. Inquiries about these giving programs should be directed to area managers.

394. The David and Lucile Packard Foundation
300 Second Street, Suite 200
Los Altos, CA 94022
(415) 948-7658

Grants

Program Description Grants are made for national and international programs in science and education; population, and conservation, including land-use planning and the protection of wildlife and wildlife habitat; children; and local communities. Most community-oriented grants are made to organizations that serve the people of San Mateo, Santa Clara, Santa Cruz, and Monterey counties of California.

Sample Grants To help support a research project intended to develop a model which will result in better coordination and less fragmentation of services to children and families in crises who are involved in public welfare systems, $25,000 to the Youth Law Center, San Francisco, CA (1988). To assist a research project to examine the impacts of the current budgeting and appropriations process on the National Forest Management Act, $20,000 to the Conservation Foundation, Washington, DC (1988).

Eligibility/Limitations Applications for grants are accepted only from qualified tax-exempt charitable organizations. Applications

cannot be accepted for the benefit of individuals or religious purposes.

Fiscal Information In 1988 the foundation authorized grants totaling $131 million.

Application Information Foundation staff is willing, whenever possible, to offer assistance through advice and contacts, in addition to the review of proposals. Additional information and application guidelines are available on request.

Deadline(s) Although proposals shall be accepted throughout the year, applicants wishing to be considered at quarterly board meetings should forward their proposals by the following deadlines: January 1 for the March meeting; April 1 for the June meeting; July 1 for the September meeting; and October 1 for the December meeting.

395. William Penn Foundation
1630 Locust Street
Philadelphia, PA 19103-6305
(215) 732-5114

Grants

Program Description The foundation awards grants in the following categories: culture, environment, human development, community fabric, national and policy grants, international peace, and international development.

Sample Grants For "Eyes on the Prize: Part II," an eight-part television documentary on the Civil Rights Movement from the 1960s to the early 1980s, $250,000 to the Civil Rights Project, Boston, MA (1988). For international conflict resolution work, $25,000 to the International Peace Academy, New York, NY (1986). A three-year grant to help disseminate its work in the area of medical ethics, $75,000 to the Hastings Center, Inc., Hastings-on-Hudson, NY (1986).

Eligibility/Limitations Grants are limited to organizations which are defined as tax exempt under Section 501(c)(3) of the Internal Revenue Code and which are not private foundations. Foundation grants are almost always limited to organizations in the five southeastern Pennsylvania counties and Camden County, New Jersey. In the case of grants made to protect the environment, the foundation will consider proposals from a geographic area which encompasses a radius of approximately 50 miles from Philadelphia. Grants will not be made to institutions which, in policy or practice, unfairly discriminate. The foundation does not fund grants to individuals or for scholarships, fellowships, or travel; nor to organizations wishing to distribute funds at their own discretion; or for recreational programs and films.

Fiscal Information Grant payments in 1988 totaled over $23 million.

Application Information The foundation has no standard application form. Only proposals submitted in writing will be considered. Proposals for grants should include a complete and detailed narrative statement. Brevity is appreciated. A complete application should have the following elements: a one-page summary outline; information about the agency making the request; complete description of the project proposed; a copy of the IRS letter stating tax-exempt status; a list of officers and directors of the organization making application; a copy of the organization's most recent annual program report; and a copy of the most recent financial statement.

Deadline(s) The foundation accepts and reviews written requests for grants throughout the year. There are no formal deadlines.

396. The Pew Charitable Trusts
Three Parkway, Suite 501
Philadelphia, PA 19102-1305
(215) 587-4045

Conservation and Environment Grants

Program Description Conservation and environment grants are made to advance the field of conservation through development of its human and information resources and support of critical research issues. Support is given for education, development, and training which will help strengthen the field's infrastructure and enhance its capacity to cope with the changing and complex challenges of managing finite resources. Support is given to encourage multidisciplinary applied and policy research that directly contributes to environmental preservation and resource management.

Sample Grants In support of the International Environmental Policy Project, over two years, $150,000 to Environmental and Energy Study Institute, Washington, DC (1987). In support of research for the National Forest Policy Papers, over two years, $160,000 to The Wilderness Society, Washington, DC (1987).

Eligibility/Limitations The trusts make grants to nonprofit organizations that are not classified as private foundations under section 509(a) of the IRS Code. Grants are made to individuals only as part of specific programs initiated by the trusts.

Fiscal Information Conservation grants totaled $5.9 million in 1987.

Application Information There are no application forms, and only one copy of a proposal with supporting documents is required. Before submitting a formal proposal, organizations may wish to contact a member of the trusts' staff or submit a brief summary of their project for initial review and discussion. Those who wish to send in full proposals without prior contact may do so; however, they should be sure to include all the information set out in the proposal checklist, available from the trusts.

Deadline(s) Requests for funding are reviewed throughout the year. Grants are awarded five times a year in February, April, June, September, and December.

397. The Pew Charitable Trusts

Three Parkway, Suite 501
Philadelphia, PA 19102-1305
(215) 587-4050

Education

Program Description Grants in education are made nationally to encourage and maintain academic excellence, to strengthen the liberal arts and sciences, to support diversity among colleges and universities, to make higher education more accessible to disadvantaged populations, and to encourage better understanding of major issues that affect the quality of education.

Eligibility/Limitations The trusts make grants to nonprofit organizations that are not classified as private foundations under section 509(a) of the IRS Code. Grants are made primarily to four-year, private, liberal arts colleges and universities, selected secondary schools, and educational support groups. Grants are made to individuals only as part of specific programs initiated by the trusts.

Fiscal Information Education grants totaled $38 million in 1987.

Application Information There are no application forms, and only one copy of a proposal with supporting documents is required. Before submitting a formal proposal, organizations may wish to contact a member of the trusts' staff or submit a brief summary of their project for initial review and discussion. Those who wish to send in full proposals without prior contact may do so; however, they should be sure to include all the information set out in the proposal checklist, available from the trusts.

Deadline(s) Requests for funding are reviewed throughout the year. Grants are awarded five times a year in February, April, June, September, and December.

398. The Pew Charitable Trusts

Three Parkway, Suite 501
Philadelphia, PA 19102-1305
(215) 587-4022

Public Policy Grants

Program Description Grants are made to promote a better understanding of the free enterprise system and the need to maintain and preserve a limited form of government in the United States as expressed in the Constitution and the Bill of Rights. Support is also given to promote a better understanding of the U.S. role in maintaining international peace and security, and to encourage critical analytical research and debate on contemporary policy concerns as they affect government, industry, international relations, and the development of traditional American values. The trusts also fund programs to promote distinguished scholarship in policy studies. Special consideration will be given to collaborative and interdisciplinary projects.

Sample Grants In support of the Oral History Project, over two years (partial matching grant), $470,000 to The Fletcher School of Law and Diplomacy, Tufts University, Medford, MA (1987).

Eligibility/Limitations The trusts make grants to nonprofit organizations that are not classified as private foundations under section 509(a) of the IRS Code. Grants are made primarily to four-year, private, liberal arts colleges and universities, selected secondary schools, and educational support groups. Grants are made to individuals only as part of specific programs initiated by the trusts.

Fiscal Information Public policy grants totaled $7.6 million in 1987.

Application Information There are no application forms, and only one copy of a proposal with supporting documents is required. Before submitting a formal proposal, organizations may wish to contact a member of the trusts staff or submit a brief summary of their project for initial review and discussion. Those who wish to send in full proposals without prior contact may do so; however, they should be sure to include all the information set out in the proposal checklist, available from the trusts.

Deadline(s) Requests for funding are reviewed throughout the year. Grants are awarded five times a year in February, April, June, September, and December.

399. The Pillsbury Company Foundation

Community Relations, M.S. 3775
200 South Sixth Street, Pillsbury Center
Minneapolis, MN 55402-1464
(612) 330-4629

Grants

Program Description The Pillsbury Company seeks to respond to needs, in communities where it does business, with creative problem-solving in partnership with those who seek it. In addition to supporting health and welfare, educational, cultural, art and civic organizations, the company focuses its foundation resources on the most urgent needs of particular interest to the company: hunger and youth.

Eligibility/Limitations The company does not fund: organizations operating for profit; support of individuals; endowment campaigns; capital campaigns, with limited exceptions; appeals for product donations; projects of religious denominations or sects; propaganda or lobbying efforts to influence legislation; fund-raising events or advertising associated with such events; or support of travel for individuals or groups.

Fiscal Information During fiscal 1989, the company and the company foundation contributed $8.1 million, addressing the needs of local communities and a broad spectrum of social and economic issues.

Application Information All proposals should be typewritten and include a brief description of the requesting organization's history of service and a statement of its purpose and objectives; a definition of the project, including an explanation of community need and the specific goals and objectives which the project is designed to meet; specific activities or methods to reach the project goals and a plan of evaluation; an itemized budget and a list of sources of financial support, both committed and pending; and a request for a specific amount of money, date by which the funds are needed and timeline of the project. The proposal should also include: a copy of the IRS ruling of the organization's tax-exempt status under Section 501(c)(3); a copy of the most recent audited financial statements; a detailed organizational budget for the current operating year; a donor's list, showing private, corporate and foundation support during the past 12 months; a list of the board of directors, officers and their affiliations; and a copy of Form 990-Income Tax Return.

Deadline(s) Applications are accepted throughout the year. Pillsbury tries to acknowledge proposals within 30 days of receipt. For careful investigation and assessment of proposals, however, notification of final action may take up to 120 days.

400. PPG Industries Foundation
One PPG Place
Pittsburgh, PA 15272
(412) 434-2962

Grants

Program Description The objectives of the foundation continue to be the enhancement of the quality of life in those communities within the United States where PPG Industries has a major presence, and the development of human potential. In fulfillment of these objectives, five areas receive nearly all of the foundation's grants: human services, health and safety, education, civic and community affairs, and culture. The foundation recognizes its commitment to public policy and economic education through support for selected organizations and issues of national, state, and local interest. National public policy organizations dealing with subjects such as science and health, justice and law, international concerns, and environmental affairs are included.

Eligibility/Limitations Normally, only organizations that are designated as public foundations or charities by the IRS are eligible to be considered for funds. Private operating foundations may qualify under certain conditions. In general, the foundation gives priority to applications from local organizations dedicated to enhancing the welfare in communities where PPG operates, as well as to those organizations whose activities either enhance individual opportunities or help to strengthen the nation's human services, educational or economic systems on a regional or nationwide basis. In general, the foundation will not award grants to individuals. The foundation will not consider grant applications for less than $100.

Fiscal Information Grants awarded in 1988 totaled over $4.4 million.

Application Information Specific application form is not required. Initial inquiries about foundation interest are normally made in the form of a one- or two-page letter that briefly outlines the purpose of the organization, the population it serves, and how the requested funds will be used. Organizations located in the Pittsburgh area and organizations of national scope should direct their inquiries to the executive director of the foundation. Organizations serving communities where PPG facilities are located should direct their initial inquiries to the local PPG Industries Foundation agent in their area. If the response to an initial inquiry is favorable, a formal proposal will be invited.

Deadline(s) The foundation does not have an application deadline, although proposals to be considered for the following calendar year's budget must be received by September 1.

401. President's Commission on White House Fellowships
712 Jackson Place, NW
Washington, DC 20503
(202) 395-4522

White House Fellowship

Program Description The White House Fellowships are a highly competitive opportunity to participate in and learn about the federal government from a unique perspective. For one year, fellows are full-time Schedule A employees of the federal government working in the Executive Office of the President or in an Executive Branch department or agency. Rather than fit the fellows to their prefellowship specialties, the program aims at utilizing their abilities and developing their skills in the broadest sense possible.

Eligibility/Limitations U.S. citizens are eligible to apply during the early and formative years of their careers or professions. There are no basic educational requirements and no special career or professional categories. Applicants may not be a civilian employee of the federal government. There are no restrictions as to specific age, sex, race, creed or national origin, nor any physical requirements. Fellows may not retain an official state or local office during their fellowship. In the previous 25 classes of fellows there have been lawyers, physicians, academicians, businesspeople, engineers, military officers, journalists, farmers, police officers, an orchestra conductor, and former state legislators.

Fiscal Information As a government employee, each fellow is paid by his or her agency at an appropriate level based on experience and education. Fellows may not be paid at a rate higher than a GS-15, step 3, which, at this time, is $60,000. Moving and relocation expenses are not funded by the government and fellows and their families are responsible for seeking their own housing and accommodations in the Washington area.

Application Information Application forms and additional information are available on request.

Deadline(s) Applications must be postmarked on or before December 15.

402. The Prospect Hill Foundation
420 Lexington Avenue, Suite 3020
New York, NY 10170
(212) 370-1144

Grants

Program Description The foundation has a broad range of philanthropic interests. Grants primarily address arms control, environmental conservation, family planning, and youth and social services issues and support selected arts, cultural, and educational institutions. The foundation's environmental grantmaking promotes the conservation of natural resources and concern for environmental equality. Grants are made primarily to organizations that focus on environmentally significant public and private lands and efforts advocating improved air and water quality. The foundation encourages proposals that offer strategies for the preservation of such public and private lands; promote public understanding of these critical environmental issues; and strengthen regulatory and legislative frameworks for environmental protection.

Sample Grants Toward the scholarship fund, $20,000 to Columbia University School of Law, New York, NY (1987). Toward preparation and publication of "Chemical Contamination of New England's Fish and Shellfish: A Report to the Governors and the Public," $7,500 to Conservation Law Foundation of New England, Inc., Boston, MA (1986).

Eligibility/Limitations The foundation does not consider grants for individuals, scholarly research, or sectarian religious activities. The foundation favors project support over general support requests. Only a limited number of new applications for grant requests from arts, cultural, and educational institutions receive favorable consideration and such institutions are cautioned that applications for grants should be made only upon invitation.

Fiscal Information Grants in 1988 totaled over $1.6 million.

Application Information Grants requests may be in the form of a letter (three pages maximum) that summarizes the applicant organization's history and goals; the project for which funding is sought; the contribution of the project to other work in the field or to the organization's own development; the organization's total budget and staff size; the project budget; the organization's board of directors. All material is reviewed by the executive director and one or more members of the board. If there is interest in the proposal, more detailed information will be requested.

Deadline(s) Applicants may submit grant requests to the executive at any time of the year.

403. The Prudential Foundation
751 Broad Street, 15th Floor
Newark, NJ 07102-3777
(201) 802-7354

Grants

Program Description The Prudential Foundation makes grants in the following categories: health and human services, education, urban and community development, business and civic affairs, and culture and the arts. Business and civic affairs grants support the examination and development of effective public policy, particularly as it affects the efficiency and accountability of government. Special emphasis is given to the civil justice system and to the development of alternative methods for the resolution of disputes that might otherwise result in litigation.

Sample Grants For tort liability reform, $17,500 to the Manhattan Institute for Policy Research, Inc., New York, NY (1987). For evaluation of effectiveness of dispute resolution programs, $25,000 to National Institute for Dispute Resolution, Washington, DC (1987). For tort liability research, $25,000 to Yale University School of Law, New Haven, CT (1987). For civil justice system research, $150,000 to the Institute for Civil Justice, Santa Monica, CA (1987).

Eligibility/Limitations Priority will be assigned to programs with potential impact in those areas in which the company has a major economic presence, with a special emphasis on Newark, NJ. Awards are not generally made to organizations that are not tax-exempt under section 501(c)(3) of the Internal Revenue Code, or to individuals as direct grants or scholarships.

Fiscal Information Grants awarded in 1989 totaled over $14.3 million.

Application Information Initial contact with the foundation should consist of a letter or brief abstract of the funding proposal. If the foundation subsequently requires additional information, it will be requested.

Deadline(s) Proposals are accepted and reviewed on a continuing basis. The board meets three times a year, in April, August, and December.

404. Public Welfare Foundation
2600 Virginia Avenue, NW, Suite 505
Washington, DC 20037-1977
(202) 965-1800

Grants

Program Description The basic philosophy of the foundation has always been to provide support to organizations that serve low-income or otherwise seriously disadvantaged people, primarily through direct services. All funding occurs in three general program areas: health, education, and community support. Within these general areas, the foundation has identified five priorities for funding: the environment, population, criminal justice, disadvantaged youth, and the elderly. Within the criminal justice area, seven topics are the focus of interest: prison overcrowding and alternatives to incarceration, improvement of

the conditions of confinement toward enhanced effectiveness of rehabilitation, female offenders, victim assistance, drugs, public education and other community concerns, and crime control.

Sample Grants To promote international law as a means of protecting the oceans, $35,000 to Council on Ocean Law, Washington DC (1989). For work with Native Alaskans to develop proposals for hunting regulations which do not conflict with traditional practices of native subsistence hunting, $32,000 to Rural Alaska Community Action Program, Inc, Anchorage, AK (1989). To provide a database of case law and other legal documents to victim advocates, attorneys, and victims of violent crimes, $25,000 to National Victim Center, Virginia Beach, VA (1989).

Eligibility/Limitations The foundation has an interest in funding nationally and internationally; foreign grants are usually designated for developing countries.

Fiscal Information Grants awarded in 1989 totaled over $12 million.

Application Information Additional information and a suggested proposal outline are available upon request. The foundation prefers concise, written proposals of not more than 10 pages (in English). If additional supporting material is needed, it will be requested. Do not submit letters of inquiry or request exploratory meetings.

Deadline(s) Requests for grants may be submitted at any time. Generally, it takes three or more months to complete investigation of proposals under consideration.

405. Resources for the Future
1616 P Street, NW
Washington, DC 20036
(202) 328-5022

The RFF Small Grants Program

Program Description Each year Resources for the Future (RFF) awards several small grants for the support of research on issues related to the environment, natural resources, or energy. The program is intended to address a need that is not now being met by most funding agencies, which tend to emphasize large projects and require complex lengthy applications. Currently, RFF is particularly interested in proposals having to do with experimental economics or other innovative techniques that address the problems of managing common property resources or natural monopolies; alternative legal or other arrangements that reduce transactions costs in cases involving toxic torts or natural resource damage claims; and policies to facilitate sustained economic growth consistent with the protection of natural resources and the environment.

Eligibility/Limitations Researchers of all nationalities are eligible for grants, but grants can only be made through tax-exempt institutions. The program provides start-up funding for new projects or supplementary support to complete specific aspects of ongoing projects. Proposals for RFF small grants may deal with theoretical or applied topics but they must be focused on research. Proposals for community action projects, litigation, or political activities will not be considered.

Fiscal Information The maximum grant will be $30,000 including overhead, but most grants will be for smaller amounts. The maximum allowable overhead rate will be 10 percent.

Application Information For further information and application forms, write RFF.

Deadline(s) The deadline for receipt of applications is March 1.

406. Resources for the Future

1616 P Street, NW
Washington, DC 20036
(202) 328-5022

Gilbert F. White Postdoctoral Fellowship Program

Program Description These fellowships are intended for two postdoctoral researchers who wish to devote a year to scholarly work on social science or public policy problems in areas of natural resources, energy, or the environment.

Sample Grants Recipients of fellowships for 1989-90 conducted research on the efficiency of alternative policies for taxing petroleum; and institutional structures for resource management: public lands and common property.

Eligibility/Limitations The award is open to individuals in any discipline who will have completed their doctoral requirements by the beginning of the academic year in which the application is made.

Fiscal Information Fellowships will be awarded for a minimum of nine and a maximum of twelve months. Fellows will receive an annual stipend of $27,000 plus research support, office facilities at Resources for the Future, and an allowance of up to $1,000 for moving or living expenses. This stipend may be supplemented from other sources if the supplement does not divert the fellow from the research project. Fellowships do not provide medical insurance or other RFF fringe benefits. Neither Social Security nor tax payments will be deducted from the stipend.

Application Information For further information and application forms, write to RFF.

Deadline(s) Applications must be received by March 1.

407. The Retirement Research Foundation

1300 West Higgins Road, Suite 214
Park Ridge, IL 60068
(312) 823-4133

Program Description The Retirement Research Foundation has four major objectives which seek to improve the quality of life for older persons: to maintain older adults in independent living environments; to improve nursing home care; to encourage employment and volunteer opportunities; and to support selected basic, applied, and policy research which seeks causes and solutions to significant problems of the aged. The foundation is particularly interested in innovative programs which have the potential for national and regional impact.

Sample Grants To support the Education for Justice Program, $10,000 to the 8th Day Center for Justice, Chicago, IL (1989). To develop a training and advocacy project to reduce inappropriate guardianship and to improve the guardianship process through closer liaison with ABA, training of elders in management, and training of guardians, $35,130 over two years to Alternatives for the Older Adult, Moline, IL (1989). To develop, produce, and distribute a handbook outlining eligibility rules and estate planning devices for prospective long-term care Medicaid patients and their families, $12,000 to Cook County Legal Assistance Foundation, Oak Park, IL (1988). To complete development of the country's first network of lawyers committed to providing pension assistance to older workers and retirees, $170,000 over two years to the Pension Rights Center, Washington, DC (1988). To support a program to educate the private bar, the judiciary, and senior citizens in a 17-county area of Illinois on the preservation of assets and Medicaid assistance for the payment of long-term nursing home care, $50,000 to Senior Citizen's Legal Services, Effingham, IL (1988).

Eligibility/Limitations To be eligible for support, organizations and institutions must qualify under the regulations of the Internal Revenue Service. The foundation normally does not provide support for construction of facilities; general operating expenses of established organizations; endowment or developmental campaigns; scholarships or loans; grants to individuals; projects outside the United States; dissertation research; or conferences, publications, and travel unless components of other larger foundation projects. The foundation has strong interest in serving the Chicago metropolitan area. Where projects of equal significance are being considered, priority will be given to organizations serving this geographic area.

Fiscal Information Generally, support of projects beyond a three-year period will not be provided. Second- and third-year support of an approved project is dependent upon progress of the first year.

Application Information The foundation does not have a standard application form. Additional information and application procedures are available on request.

Deadline(s) The foundation considers grant applications three times each year. Deadlines for receipt of applications are February 1, May 1, and August 1.

408. Smith Richardson Foundation, Inc.

210 East 86th Street
New York, NY 10028
(212) 861-8181

Public Policy Grants

Program Description The public policy grants program of the Smith Richardson Foundation funds projects directly or indirectly dealing with the foreign policies of the United States and projects in domestic public policy.

Sample Grants To support instruction on legal dispute resolution, $44,000 to Duke University School of Law, Durham, NC (1988). To provide renewed support of an educational program on religious freedom and human rights, $85,000 to Puebla Institute, Washington, DC (1988). To provide general support, $50,000 to The Federalist Society for Law and Public Policy Studies, Washington, DC (1988).

Eligibility/Limitations Grants are normally made to organizations which are tax-exempt under the Internal Revenue Code. The foundation does not make grants directly to individuals.

Fiscal Information Grants paid in 1988 in the public policy program totaled over $3.9 million.

Application Information The foundation has no specific forms for requesting grants nor requires a specific presentation format. A letter of application is sufficient and should include the following: a brief statement of the purpose and desirability of the project; a brief description of the applicant organization; a detailed schedule of work and budget for the project; evidence that the proposed project has not been earlier and adequately carried out; and a description of the audience for which the project is intended. All requests should be submitted to the coordinator.

Deadline(s) Grants are normally approved quarterly.

409. Rockefeller Archive Center

15 Dayton Avenue, Pocantico Hills
North Tarrytown, NY 10591
(914) 631-4505

Research Grant Program

Program Description The Research Grant Program awards grants to scholars engaged in projects based substantially on the holdings of the center. The center's collections are outstanding resources for the study of philanthropy, education, medicine, science, black history, agriculture, labor, social welfare and the social sciences, politics, religion, women's history, population, international relations and economic development, and the arts.

Sample Grants Support for a Ph.D. candidate in history from The University of Chicago to research, "A New Faith: the Growth of Administrative Law and the American Legal Order, 1887-1960" (1990).

Eligibility/Limitations Applicants of any discipline, usually graduate students or postdoctoral scholars, who are engaged in projects that require substantial use of collections at the center are eligible.

Fiscal Information Grants carry awards up to $1,500. The exact size of the grant is dependent upon the travel and research needs of the applicants.

Application Information Additional information and application guidelines are available on request.

Deadline(s) The deadline for applications is December 31 of each year.

410. Rockefeller Brothers Fund
1290 Avenue of the Americas
New York, NY 10104
(212) 373-4200

Grants

Program Description The Rockefeller Brothers Fund seeks to achieve its major objective of improving the well-being of all people through support of efforts in the United States and abroad that contribute ideas, develop leaders, and encourage institutions in the transition to global interdependence and that counter world trends of resource depletion, militarization, protectionism, and isolation which now threaten to move humankind everywhere further away from cooperation, trade and economic growth, arms restraint, and conservation. The basic theme of interdependence presupposes a global outlook and, hence, internationally oriented activity. Although U.S. problems and grantees will receive considerable attention, this will be in the context of global concerns and not simply national ones. The fund makes grants in four general areas. The first, "One World," is made up of two components, Sustainable Resource Use and World Security, which will receive the major portion of grant funds. The other three areas are New York City, Nonprofit Sector, and Special Concerns.

Sample Grants Toward its new East European and Soviet Program, $120,000 over three years, to the Environmental Law Institute, Washington, DC (1988). For its legal research project to secure enhanced tax deductibility for U.S. donations of publications and supplies to East European countries, $15,000 to the Sabre Foundation, New York, NY (1988). Toward a project investigating successful conflict mediation efforts in East Africa for insights on the use of this aspect of international law for reducing global tensions, $20,000 to Friends of the Hague Academy of International Law, New York, NY (1987).

Eligibility/Limitations To qualify for a grant from RBF, a prospective grantee must be either a tax-exempt organization or an organization seeking support for a project that would qualify as tax-exempt. A grantee must also be engaged in work that fits generally within the fund's new program, Global Interdependence. The fund does not make grants to individuals, nor does it, as a general rule, support research, graduate study, or the writing of books or dissertations by individuals.

Fiscal Information Although the RBF has made substantial gifts to organizations and programs in which it has considerable interest, most grants run between $10,000 and $75,000, the average between $25,000 and $35,000. Grant payments and matching gifts during 1988 amounted to over $7.9 million.

Application Information A preliminary letter of inquiry is recommended for an initial approach to the fund, although the submission of detailed proposals is also appropriate. Additional information and application guidelines are available on request.

Deadline(s) Grants are awarded by the trustees, who meet regularly throughout the year.

411. The Rockefeller Foundation
1133 Avenue of the Americas
New York, NY 10036
(212) 869-8500

Agricultural Sciences Grants

Program Description Agricultural sciences grants support work that uses biotechnology to improve crops that are developing-country staples, improve family food production systems in Africa, and enhance international collaboration in agricultural research. Although the program is science-based, it also emphasizes other factors—local culture and values, equitable policymaking, competent management, and production capability—that can determine whether science and technology effectively contribute to the well-being of people in the developing world. As a result, the foundation encourages work that connects the products of research with adopting strategies that are both effective and equitable.

Sample Grants Toward the costs of a workshop on equitable patent protection for the developing world, $10,800 to Cornell University, Ithaca, NY (1989). For use by a professor of law for an analysis of the regulatory and intellectual property issues significant to developing countries' plant biotechnology research, $21,750 to Stanford University, CA (1988). Toward the development of the International Policy Council on Agriculture and Trade, $50,000 to Resources for the Future, Washington, DC (1988). To establish a small grants program conducted by developing-country specialists that will support forest policy studies and related field research, $1 million to World Wildlife Fund, Washington, DC (1988).

Eligibility/Limitations As a matter of policy, the foundation does not give or lend money for personal aid to individuals; contribute to the establishment of local hospitals, churches, schools, libraries, or welfare agencies, or to their building and operating funds; finance altruistic movements involving private profit; or support attempts to influence legislation. The foundation does not normally provide general institutional support or endowment.

Fiscal Information Expenditures in this program division totaled over $14.3 million in 1989.

Application Information No special form is required in making a request for foundation aid, but the proposal or application should include a description of the proposed project or fellowship activity, with clearly stated plans and objectives; a comprehensive plan for total funding during and, where applicable, after the proposed grant period; and a listing of the applicant's qualifications and accomplishments.

Deadline(s) Grant appropriations are approved by an independent board of trustees which meets three times a year, in April, September, and December.

Additional Information The foundation offers fellowships for training and to assist in the production of a piece of work. Advanced training fellowships, biotechnology career fellowships, and social science research fellowships are given to help prepare outstanding younger scholars and scientists, primarily from the developing world, to make significant contributions to research and training or to public service.

412. The Rockefeller Foundation
1133 Avenue of the Americas
New York, NY 10036
(212) 869-8500

Arts and Humanities Grants

Program Description Arts and humanities grants seek to encourage international and intercultural understanding in the United States. The program supports activities extending international and intercultural scholarship, increasing artistic experimentation across cultures, and improving international perspectives in American public schools.

Sample Grants Toward the costs of a study entitled "Black Americans and International Law," $25,000 (joint grant with Equal Opportunity, for a total of $75,000) to the Joint Center for Political Studies, Washington, DC (1988).

Eligibility/Limitations Creative artists and scholars and teachers in the humanities whose work can advance international and intercultural understanding in the United States are eligible to apply.

Fiscal Information Expenditures in this program division totaled over $13.5 million in 1989.

Application Information A special form is not required in making a request for foundation aid, but the proposal or application should include a description of the proposed project or fellowship activity, with clearly stated plans and objectives; a comprehensive plan for total funding during and, where applicable, after the proposed grant period; and a listing of the applicant's qualifications and accomplishments.

Deadline(s) Grant appropriations are approved by an independent board of trustees which meets three times a year, in April, September, and December.

413. The Rockefeller Foundation
1133 Avenue of the Americas
New York, NY 10036
(212) 869-8500

Equal Opportunity Grants

Program Description Equal opportunity grants seek to assure full participation of minorities in American life. It supports three approaches attacking persistent poverty in urban America: program of planning and action in a few selected cities, research and policy analysis, and research and action to strengthen basic skills and family support. To protect basic rights, the program supports litigation and advocacy, voter registration and education, and related research in policy analysis.

Sample Grants Toward the costs of a study entitled "Black Americans and International Law," $48,800 to the Joint Center for Political Studies, Washington, DC (1989). For an in-depth survey of racial attitudes in the United States, $75,000 to NAACP Legal Defense and Educational Fund, New York, NY (1988). Toward the cost of a symposium entitled "Afro-Americans and the Evolution of a Living Constitution," $15,000 to the Smithsonian Institution, Washington, DC (1988).

Eligibility/Limitations As a matter of policy, the foundation does not give or lend money for personal aid to individuals; contribute to the establishment of local hospitals, churches, schools, libraries, or welfare agencies, or to their building and operating funds; finance altruistic movements involving private profit; or support attempts to influence legislation. The foundation does not normally provide general institutional support or endowment.

Fiscal Information Expenditures in this program division totaled over $13.5 million in 1989.

Application Information A special form is not required in making a request for foundation aid, but the proposal or application should include a description of the proposed project or fellowship activity, with clearly stated plans and objectives; a comprehensive plan for total funding during and, where applicable, after the proposed grant period; and a listing of the applicant's qualifications and accomplishments.

Deadline(s) Grant appropriations are approved by an independent board of trustees which meets three times a year, in April, September, and December.

414. The Rockefeller Foundation
1133 Avenue of the Americas
New York, NY 10036
(212) 869-8500

Global Environmental Program

Program Description The Global Environmental Program gives initial emphasis to assisting developing countries to advance environmentally sound development in their own countries and participate fully in international responses to environmental challenges. There are four broad areas of interest for grant and fellowship activity. First is the creation of a cadre of young environmental scientists, analysts, policymakers and community leaders who can be architects of future policy in development and the environment. Second is the training of environmental economists in the developing world and the development of economic research applied to environmental decision making,

resources accounting and monitoring, and global bargaining and scorekeeping. The third area of interest centers around the relationships, cultural perspectives, and institutional changes required to foster global and regional accords on such subjects as energy generation and use, forest preservation, ozone layer depletion, hazardous waste generation and disposal, greenhouse emission, and preservation of clean water and arable land. And finally, there are the attitudes and processes which will shape how the United States undertakes its share of global adjustments necessary to protect the environment and promote a more equitable sharing of the earth's resources. The foundation will not be considering funding requests in this final area until preliminary explorations on possible initial activities are completed.

Sample Grants To undertake a study of emerging Soviet policy toward international cooperation on protection of the environment, $43,000 to the American Committee on U.S.-Soviet Relations, Washington, DC (1989). Toward its 1989 program activities, $45,000 to the Council on Ocean Law, Washington, DC (1989).

Eligibility/Limitations As a matter of policy, the foundation does not give or lend money for personal aid to individuals; contribute to the establishment of local hospitals, churches, schools, libraries, or welfare agencies, or to their building and operating funds; finance altruistic movements involving private profit; or support attempts to influence legislation. The foundation does not normally provide general institutional support or endowment.

Fiscal Information Expenditures in this program division totaled over $400,000 in 1989.

Application Information No special form is required in making a request for foundation aid, but the proposal or application should include: a description of the proposed project or fellowship activity, with clearly stated plans and objectives; a comprehensive plan for total funding during and, where applicable, after the proposed grant period; and a listing of the applicant's qualifications and accomplishments.

Deadline(s) Grant appropriations are approved by an independent board of trustees which meets three times a year, in April, September, and December.

415. The Rockefeller Foundation
1133 Avenue of the Americas
New York, NY 10036
(212) 869-8500

Other Interests and Initiatives

Program Description Although most of the foundation's work is done through established programs, a special interests and explorations fund is available to support a very small number of projects of exceptional merit that do not fall within these programs.

Sample Grants In support of the second phase of its Reproductive Laws for the 1990s project, $100,000 for the Center for Women Policy Studies, Washington, DC (1989). Toward the costs of providing negotiation training for South Africans at Harvard Law School and at the Salzburg Seminar in Austria, $10,000 to the Conflict Management Fund, Cambridge MA (1988).

Eligibility/Limitations As a matter of policy, the foundation does not give or lend money for personal aid to individuals; contribute to the establishment of local hospitals, churches, schools, libraries, or welfare agencies, or to their building and operating funds; finance altruistic movements involving private profit; or support attempts to influence legislation. The foundation does not normally provide general institutional support or endowment.

Fiscal Information Expenditures in this program division totaled over $4.5 million in 1989.

Application Information A special form is not required in making a request for foundation aid, but the proposal or application should include a description of the proposed project or fellowship activity, with clearly stated plans and objectives; a comprehensive plan for total funding during and, where applicable, after the proposed grant period; and a listing of the applicant's qualifications and accomplishments.

Deadline(s) Grant appropriations are approved by an independent board of trustees which meets three times a year, in April, September, and December.

416. The Rockefeller Foundation
1133 Avenue of the Americas
New York, NY 10036
(212) 869-8500

Population Sciences Grants

Program Description Population sciences grants seek to enhance reproductive choice in the developing world by supporting work to develop new contraceptive technologies, increase the availability of existing technologies, and identify the constraints, risks, and barriers that affect contraceptive use. Although the program is science-based, it also emphasizes other factors—local culture and values, equitable policymaking, competent management, and production capability—that can determine whether science and technology effectively contribute to the well-being of people in the developing world. As a result, the foundation encourages work that connects the products of research with adopting strategies that are both effective and equitable.

Sample Grants For a judicial conference on the impact of reproductive technology on law, $25,000 to the Women Judges' Fund for Justice, Washington, DC (1989). For a project to study reproductive rights law and policy, $8,000 to Rutgers University, New Brunswick, NJ (1988). For a symposium on politics and population policies in developing countries, $60,000 to University of Michigan, Ann Arbor, MI (1988).

Eligibility/Limitations As a matter of policy, the foundation does not give or lend money for personal aid to individuals; contribute to the establishment of local hospitals, churches, schools, libraries, or welfare agencies, or to their building and operating funds; finance altruistic movements involving private profit; or support attempts to influence legislation. The foundation does not normally provide general institutional support or endowment.

Fiscal Information Expenditures in this program division totaled over $8.5 million in 1989.

Application Information A special form is not required in making a request for foundation aid, but the proposal or application should include a description of the proposed project or fellowship activity, with clearly stated plans and objectives; a comprehensive plan for total funding during and, where applicable, after the proposed grant period; and a listing of the applicant's qualifications and accomplishments.

Deadline(s) Grant appropriations are approved by an independent board of trustees which meets three times a year, in April, September, and December.

Additional Information The foundation offers fellowships for training and to assist in the production of a piece of work. Advanced training fellowships, biotechnology career fellowships, and social science research fellowships are given to help prepare outstanding younger scholars and scientists, primarily from the developing world, to make significant contributions to research and training or to public service.

417. The Rockefeller Foundation
1133 Avenue of the Americas
New York, NY 10036
(212) 869-8500

Special Programming Grants in Science-Based Development

Program Description Special programming supports a small number of projects in science-based development that cross the traditional boundaries of the agriculture, health, and population divisions of the foundation. Although the program is science-based, it also emphasizes other factors—local culture and values, equitable policy-making, competent management, and production capability—that can determine whether science and technology effectively contribute to the well-being of people in the developing world. As a result, the foundation encourages work that connects the products of research with adopting strategies that are both effective and equitable.

Sample Grants Toward the costs of a research project on credit and rural development policy in India, $20,000 to Massachusetts Institute of Technology, Cambridge, MA (1989). Toward the costs of presenting a course for Chinese policymakers on the interactions of law, science, and technology, $25,000 to the American Association for the Advancement of Science, Washington, DC (1988). Toward the costs of a project on conflict resolution within Islam, $15,000 to the Ethics and Public Policy Center, Washington, DC (1988).

Eligibility/Limitations As a matter of policy, the foundation does not give or lend money for personal aid to individuals; contribute to the establishment of local hospitals, churches, schools, libraries, or welfare agencies, or to their building and operating funds; finance altruistic movements involving private profit; or support attempts to influence legislation. The foundation does not normally provide general institutional support or endowment.

Fiscal Information Awards in this program division totaled over $2.9 million in 1988.

Application Information A special form is not required in making a request for foundation aid, but the proposal or application should include a description of the proposed project or fellowship activity, with clearly stated plans and objectives; a comprehensive plan for total funding during and, where applicable, after the proposed grant period; and a listing of the applicant's qualifications and accomplishments.

Deadline(s) Grant appropriations are approved by an independent board of trustees which meets three times a year, in April, September, and December.

Additional Information The foundation also supports a series of fellowship programs in science-based development: advanced training fellowships, biotechnology career fellowships, social science research fellowships, and an African dissertation internship program.

418. Rosenberg Foundation
210 Post Street
San Francisco, CA 94108-5172
(415) 421-6105

Grants

Program Description The Rosenberg Foundation makes grants in four major fields. In early childhood development, it supports new programs which appear to have unusual promise of encouraging the normal, healthy development of young children both as individuals and as members of a diverse society. For adolescent and older youth, it supports new programs in which young people have joint responsibility for planning and implementation and which will strengthen their relationship with the community. In rural development, it supports programs designed to enhance the quality of life for children and their families in rural areas of California. In immigration policy, it supports projects which identify and address policy issues in the immigration field with particular emphasis on migration from Mexico and its consequences for both children and their families in both countries.

Sample Grants To promulgate regulations under the Immigration Reform and Control Act, $25,000 to the Farmworker Justice Fund, Washington, DC (1988).

Eligibility/Limitations The foundation does not make grants for programs outside California. Support is given to tax-exempt groups or organizations, public or private. Grants are not made to individuals, for construction, scholarships, operating expenses of ongoing programs, or for support of basic research.

Fiscal Information The foundation's policies preclude grants to continue or expand projects started with funds from other sources or to match grants from other sources. The foundation made grants for over $1.5 million in 1988.

Application Information The foundation does not use application forms but prefers brief letters of inquiry which describe the proposed project, the applicant agency, and the estimated budget. If, after preliminary review, the proposal appears to fall within the foundation's narrow program priorities, the foundation will request an application.

Deadline(s) Grants are authorized by the foundation board at monthly meetings. Because of the large number of requests, there is usually a waiting period of two to three months before an application can be considered by the board.

419. Samuel Rubin Foundation

777 United Nations Plaza
New York, NY 10017-3521
(212) 697-8945

Grants

Program Description The foundation's general purpose is to carry on the vision of its founder, Samuel Rubin, whose life was dedicated to the pursuit of peace and justice and the search for an equitable reallocation of the world's resources. The foundation believes that these objectives can be achieved only through the fullest implementation of the social, economic, political, civil, and cultural rights for all the world's people.

Eligibility/Limitations Tax-exempt organizations are eligible to apply.

Fiscal Information Limited funds and recurring commitments restrict the foundation's grant-making ability.

Application Information Contact the foundation for additional information and application guidelines.

Deadline(s) Applications may be made at any time.

420. Helena Rubinstein Foundation

405 Lexington Avenue
New York, NY 10174
(212) 986-0806

Grants

Program Description The foundation supports programs in education, the arts, community services, health care, and medical research, with an emphasis on projects that benefit women and children. The largest percentage of the grants, particularly for the arts and community services, is made to organizations in New York City.

Sample Grants To provide scholarships for older women returning to law school, $10,000 to Barbara Aronstein Black Endowment Fund, Columbia University, School of Law, New York, NY (1989). For internships for women law students, $8,000 to NOW Legal Defense and Education Fund, New York, NY (1989). In support of a Congressional fellowship for a woman graduate student, $13,000 to Women's Research and Education Institute, Washington, DC (1988).

Eligibility/Limitations Grants are made only to federally tax-exempt, nonprofit organizations. Grants are not offered to individuals or for film or video projects. Grants are rarely made to endowment funds and capital campaigns.

Fiscal Information Grants awarded in 1989 totaled over $5 million.

Application Information There is no application form. Organizations seeking funds are asked not to make telephone inquiries, but to submit a brief letter outlining the project, its aims, budget, amount requested, other funding sources, and a short history of the organization. If the proposal is one the foundation is able to consider, more detailed information will be requested.

Deadline(s) Proposals are accepted throughout the year.

421. Russell Sage Foundation

112 East 64th Street
New York, NY 10021
(212) 750-6000

Social Science Research Support

Program Description The Russell Sage Foundation is the principal American foundation devoted exclusively to research in the social sciences. The foundation is dedicated to support of social science research as a means of improved social policies. Although its support of scholars has tended to reflect this broad view of social research, its limited resources require that it give special attention to a few research topics at a time. These topics change from time to time and the foundation makes a strong effort to ensure that the attention given to these special research problems does not prevent it from seeing and supporting promising work in other areas of social research. The foundation now pursues three principal programs: (1) the program in the social analysis of poverty supports research designed to improve understanding of the social, economic, and institutional processes that allow the persistently poor to escape from poverty; (2) the behavioral economics program is an interdisciplinary effort to examine the consequences of introducing into economics information from neighboring social sciences about the nature of human motivation and decision making, as well as the complexities of economic institutions; and (3) the research synthesis program provides financial support and technical assistance designed to encourage effective use of statistical methods for detecting the significant generalizations that can be derived from multiple studies of the same social problem or program.

Eligibility/Limitations Grants are not made for the support of undergraduate or graduate degree work, or for institutional support. Grantees are generally expected to produce, and to offer to the foundation first refusal rights on, book-length research reports.

Fiscal Information Grant awards and program expenditures totaled over $4 million in 1987. Individual grant awards vary depending on the project proposed.

Application Information There is no application form; a brief letter of inquiry is advisable to determine whether the foundation's present interests and funds permit consideration of a proposal for research or residence at the foundation. Grant applications should summarize the project's objectives, the work plan, the qualifications of persons engaged in the work, and an estimated budget. After consideration of this letter, the foundation will indicate whether or not a detailed proposal should be submitted.

Deadline(s) Applications are considered throughout the year.

Additional Information At its headquarters in New York City, the foundation has established a small center for advanced study, where scholars can pursue their research. This professional community consists of full-time resident scholars, social scientists who engage in their own research and help administer foundation policies and projects; visiting scholars, who work in fields of interest to the foundation for periods ranging from a few months to two years, continuing their own research and writing and occasionally helping the foundation with its activities; visiting postdoctoral fellows, young social scientists selected in a national competition and appointed for one year to pursue a program of research on topics of their own choosing; and a few social scientists who are affiliated with nearby universities and who serve part-time as advisors and consultants. Contact the foundation for information about the Visiting Fellows Program.

422. Santa Fe Southern Pacific Foundation

224 South Michigan Avenue
Chicago, IL 60604-2401
(312) 786-6204

Grants

Program Description The foundation provides financial support for nonprofit organizations dedicated to improving the quality of life in the territory Santa Fe Pacific Corporation companies serve and in the communities where their employees live. The foundation contributes to educational, health, and human services, cultural, civic and other charitable organizations. Within the funding area of civic and community affairs, contributions are made to good citizenship, legal aid and minority assistance organizations, and to organizations devoted to research and educational programs that address public policy issues. The foundation also supports organizations dedicated to the preservation of the private enterprise system and the principles of economic freedom.

Eligibility/Limitations Most contributions are made to nonprofit organizations in communities served by the company and its operating components. Grants to culture and art organizations that are national in scope are rarely considered. The foundation generally will not contribute to individuals; tax-supported educational institutions or governmental agencies; tours, conferences, seminars, or workshops; purchase of tables, tickets or advertisements; endowment funds; or programs beyond stated geographic areas of interest.

Fiscal Information Grants awarded in 1987 totaled over $3.1 million.

Application Information Initial inquiries and proposals should be handled by mail. Proposals should include a brief covering letter that describes the organization, summarizes the proposal and specifies the amount requested; a copy of IRS tax-exempt letter; a current audited financial statement and budget data; other sources of support during the most recent year; a list of the organization's officers and directors; a narrative explaining the organization's history, purpose, geographic area of concern and accomplishments; and the kind and amount of grant requested and how it will be used. When funds are requested for special programs, indicate the program's objectives and how they will be accomplished and evaluated. Plans for future funding of ongoing projects should be outlined.

Deadline(s) Proposals will be accepted and reviewed continuously, except that major requests in excess of $20,000 will be reviewed annually in the fall, if received prior to September 1. All proposals received after September 1 will be considered in the following year.

423. Sara Lee Foundation

Three First National Plaza
Chicago, IL 60602-4206
(312) 558-8448

Grants

Program Description Sara Lee has developed general principles that guide its efforts in the area of employee and public responsibility. To provide a focus for giving, corporate contributions concentrate on programs affecting the disadvantaged and on those supporting cultural activities. To emphasize involvement with local communities, contributions programs support projects in the areas of company operations. To maximize resources and improve expertise, programs stress not only financial support, but also the personal involvement of company employees.

Sample Grants For the Women's Law Project, which addresses the legal problems of indigent women, $2,000 to the Legal Assistance Foundation of Chicago, Chicago, IL (1988). For the Leadership Training Program, which prepares emerging Hispanic leaders for greater participation in civic affairs, $5,000 to Mexican American Legal Defense and Educational Fund, Chicago, IL (1988). For advocacy, research and technical assistance for policymakers, parents, and school personnel to improve the Chicago Public School system, $3,000 to Chicago Panel on Public School Policy and Finance, Chicago, IL (1988).

Eligibility/Limitations Organizations must be duly certified by the state in which they operate and be in receipt of an IRS ruling that they are classified as a 501(c)(3) organization. The following are not eligible for grants: capital and endowment campaigns; individuals; organizations with a limited constituency; organizations which limit their services to members of one religious group or those whose purpose is to propagate a particu-

lar religious faith or creed; and political organizations. In general, contributions reflect the geographic mix of company operations. The foundation's cash grants are used primarily to support organizations in the greater Chicago area.

Fiscal Information The foundation awarded over $1.9 million in cash grants in fiscal year 1988.

Application Information Application forms and additional information on any foundation program can be obtained by writing the foundation at the address listed above. Application forms must be accompanied by the organization's most recent audited financial statement; current operating budget; annual report or other materials summarizing programs; list of current board of directors and their affiliations; IRS letter of tax-exempt certification; and a list of public and private grants of $500 or more received during the most recently completed fiscal year.

Deadline(s) Applications must be received by the first working day of March, June, September, or December to be considered during that quarter. Applications received after these dates will be held for a subsequent meeting. The foundation's fiscal year begins July 1.

424. Sarah Scaife Foundation

P.O. Box 268
Pittsburgh, PA 15230
(412) 392-2900

Grants

Program Description The foundation's grant program is directed primarily toward public policy programs that address major domestic and international issues. The foundation provides assistance to groups engaged in public policy research, as well as to publications that examine areas of national concern.

Sample Grants For general operating support, $130,000 to the American Bar Association Fund for Justice and Education, Chicago, IL (1988). For general operating support, $60,000 to The Federalist Society for Law and Public Policy Studies, Washington, DC (1988). For the International Security Affairs Program, $135,000 to Tufts University, The Fletcher School of Law and Diplomacy, Medford, MA (1987). For the Center for Law and National Security, $200,000 to the University of Virginia Law School Foundation, Charlottesville, VA (1989).

Eligibility/Limitations The foundation does not make grants to individuals for any purpose or to nationally organized fundraising groups. There are no geographical restrictions.

Fiscal Information In 1989 a total of over $7.8 million was awarded.

Application Information Initial inquiries to the foundation should be in letter form and signed by the organization's chief executive officer or authorized representative and have the approval of the organization's board of directors. The letter should include a concise description of the purpose for which funds are requested, along with the related budget. Accompanying information should include: latest audited financial statements and annual report; current annual budget; list of officers and directors and their major affiliations; and a copy of current determination letter from the IRS evidencing tax-exempt status under section 501(c)(3) of the IRS Code. Additional information may be requested for further evaluation.

Deadline(s) The foundation meets in February, May, September, and November to consider grants. Requests, however, may be submitted at any time.

425. Dr. Scholl Foundation

11 South LaSalle Street, Suite 2100
Chicago, IL 60603
(312) 782-5210

Grants

Program Description The foundation supports private education at all levels, general charitable programs, and civic, cultural, social welfare service, economic, and religious activities.

Sample Grants For seminars on current national and international issues, $100,000 to the American Bar Association, Chicago, IL (1987). For a criminal justice internship program, $15,000 to the Chicago Crime Commission (1987).

Eligibility/Limitations Generally, the foundation does not consider for funding organizations not eligible for tax-deductible support, public education, or grants to individuals.

Fiscal Information Grants awarded in 1987 totaled over $6.9 million.

Application Information An application form is required and can be obtained by written request from the foundation office.

Deadline(s) To be eligible for consideration in the current calendar year, the application form together with related materials must be received by May 15.

426. The School of American Research
Resident Fellowship Program
P.O. Box 2188
Santa Fe, NM 87504

Resident Scholar Fellowship Program

Program Description These fellowships provide support to scholars working in any world area on any topic within anthropology and related disciplines in the humanities and social sciences.

Eligibility/Limitations There are two fellowship programs available: the Weatherhead Fellowship supports doctoral candidates and postdoctoral individuals in all areas of anthropology; the National Endowment for the Humanities Fellowship supports postdoctoral individuals in areas related to the humanities. Preference in both these fellowship programs will be given to those applicants whose field work and analysis are complete and who need time to write up their results.

Fiscal Information Scholars are provided apartments on or near the school's campus, have offices on the school grounds, and receive the assistance of a librarian in obtaining interlibrary loans to supplement the school's limited collection. The length of tenure is usually 11 months.

Application Information Additional information and application forms are available from the school.

Deadline(s) The deadline for receipt of applications is December 1.

427. The Florence and John Schumann Foundation
33 Park Street
Montclair, NJ 07042
(201) 783-6660

Grants

Program Description The Schumann Foundation limits its support to three distinct areas of concern: environment, international relations, and effective governance.

Sample Grants To support a study of national energy policy and alternative energy sources, $25,000 to Natural Resources Defense Council, San Francisco, CA (1988). To support activities of a program to monitor important social policy decisions, $50,000 to Center for Community Change, Washington, DC (1988). To support an organization striving to promote citizen reassessment of the U.S. Constitution, $60,000 (two years) to The Jefferson Foundation, Washington, DC (1988).

Eligibility/Limitations The foundation does not encourage applications for capital campaigns, annual giving, endowment, or direct support of individuals.

Fiscal Information Grants awarded in 1987 totaled over $3.1 million.

Application Information There is no standard application form to be used in presenting a request to the foundation. It is requested that a written proposal be submitted which includes a description of the organization's objectives and activities, its leadership, and a description in some detail of the purpose for which assistance is desired and the plan for accomplishment. The proposal should be accompanied by a copy of the organization's latest audited financial statement; an expense budget which also specifically identifies all sources of income; the time frame and future funding plans; and IRS documents confirming the organization's status as tax-exempt and not a private foundation.

Deadline(s) Proposals should reach the foundation before January 15, April 15, August 15, or October 15.

428. Scoville Peace Fellowship Program
110 Maryland Avenue, NE, Room 211
Washington, DC 20002
(202) 543-4100

Nuclear Arms Control Fellowships

Program Description The fellowship provides the opportunity to work on several issues, including disarmament, nuclear and conventional arms control, the military budget, and U.S.-Soviet relations.

Eligibility/Limitations College graduates are eligible to apply.

Fiscal Information The fellowship carries a stipend of $1,200 a month for four to six months, plus travel expenses.

Application Information For further information, program description, and application requirements, contact the program at the address listed above.

Deadline(s) The deadlines for completed action are October 15 for the spring semester and March 15 for the fall semester.

429. Gardiner Howland Shaw Foundation
45 School Street
Boston, MA 02108
(617) 451-9206

Contributions

Program Description The Shaw Foundation was established for the study, prevention, correction and alleviation of crime and delinquency, and the rehabilitation of adult and juvenile offenders. The foundation has established three priority categories for contributions. Fifty percent of available grant funds are awarded to special programs in the courts; 30 percent of the available funds are awarded to former recipients with outstanding community programs for offenders; and 20 percent of available grant funds are awarded to programs exploring new ideas or approaches to criminal justice problems, and attracting new resources into the criminal justice field.

Sample Grants To fund a one-day conference to explore the concept of court accreditation in the Commonwealth, $2,500 to the Court Accreditation Conference, Massachusetts Bar Association, Boston, MA (1989).

Eligibility/Limitations The foundation cannot fund substance abuse or mental health counseling programs, capital requests, the arts, endowments, proposals from individuals, or requests from programs operating outside Massachusetts.

Fiscal Information Grants awarded in 1989 totalled over $500,000.

Application Information Additional information and application guidelines are available on request from the foundation.

Deadline(s) Application deadlines are January 2, May 1, and September 1. Mail proposals to Executive Directory, 95 Berkeley Street, Boston, MA, 02116.

430. Shell Oil Company Foundation

Two Shell Plaza, P.O. Box 2099
Houston, TX 77252
(713) 241-3617

Contributions

Program Description The foundation makes contributions for worthwhile charitable, scientific, educational, religious, or literary purposes. Within these broad guidelines, the foundation gives to programs and projects focusing on the environment and the disadvantaged; health and welfare, culture and the arts; and aid to education.

Sample Grants Shell Graduate Grants were given to University Houston Law Center, Louisiana State University and A&M College Law Center, University of Mississippi School of Law, Tulane University School of Law, the University of Texas at Austin Law School (1989).

Eligibility/Limitations Most of the foundation's contributions are made through planned, continuing programs in support of education and charitable activities in communities where Shell people are located. The foundation prefers not to contribute in certain areas, including: capital campaigns of national organizations; endowment or development funds and special requests of colleges and universities; college fund-raising associations; direct donations to individuals and individual community organizations; and hospital operating expenses.

Fiscal Information In 1989 support totaled more than $16.4 million.

Application Information There is no formal application procedure. Requests may be made by letter and should include the following information: a description of the structure, purpose, history, and program of the organization; a summary of the need for support and how it will be used; detailed financial data on the organization such as an independent financial audit, budget, sources of income, breakdown of expenditures by program, administration, and fund raising; and a copy of the IRS rule, dated after 1969, classifying the organization as tax-exempt under section 501(c)(3) and not a private foundation under section 509(a) of the code; a copy of the organization's most recent Form 990; and a list of corporate donors and their level of support.

Deadline(s) Contributions are planned a year in advance and based on a calendar-year budget. Interim donations are rarely made.

431. Skadden Fellowship Program

919 Third Avenue
New York, NY 10022

Skadden Fellowships

Program Description These fellowships provide support for law school graduates and outgoing judicial law clerks who want to work in the public interest.

Eligibility/Limitations Grants are made to sponsoring organizations. Before final application, a public interest organization that will sponsor the applicant must be identified. The sponsor must be a 501(c)(3) organization that provides legal services to the poor, the homeless, the disabled, or those deprived of their civil or human rights. The fellow cannot receive any other fellowship funds or prize monies for the duration of the Skadden Fellowship.

Fiscal Information The duration of the fellowship is one year and may be renewed for a second year if requested and approved by the grant-making panel.

Application Information Fellowship application forms and additional information are available upon request.

Deadline(s) Applications must be received by October 16.

432. The L.J. Skaggs and Mary C. Skaggs Foundation

1221 Broadway, 21st Floor
Oakland, CA 94612-1837
(415) 451-3300

Grants

Program Description The foundation presently makes grants under seven program categories: performing arts, social concerns, projects of historic interest, folklore/folklife, international grants, visual arts, and special projects. Where necessary, as new program areas arise, new funding categories may be opened.

Sample Grants For a campaign of public awareness around the 200th anniversary of the Constitution, $10,000 to the Center for Constitutional Rights, New York, NY (1987). For support of a conference on gender bias in the courts, the interpretation of rape laws, the economic consequences of divorce for the female, family law, child abuse law, and other issues which concern women, $4,000 to the National Judicial Education Program, New York, NY (1987). For general support for workplace fundraising program for social justice issues in Appalachia, $5,000 to Community Shares, Knoxville, TN (1987). For support of a publication of work on judicial activism with reference to the interpretation of the U.S. Constitution, $10,000 to the Washington Legal Foundation, Washington, DC (1988). To support the International Women's Rights Action Watch to monitor the law and public policy reforms to improve the status of women in 91 countries which were ratified at the United Nations Convention on the elimination of all forms of discrimination against women, $7,500 to the Hubert Humphrey Institute of Public Affairs, Minneapolis, MN (1988).

Eligibility/Limitations The foundation makes grants to qualified tax-exempt charitable organizations. Grants are not made to individuals, or for capital fund, endowment fund or annual fund drives for sectarian or religious purposes. With very special exceptions, grants to programs in the social and community concerns category will only be made in Northern California.

Fiscal Information In 1989 the foundation awarded grants totaling over $2.3 million.

Application Information Telephone inquiries regarding program eligibility are not encouraged. Requests for grants are initiated by a brief letter of intent to apply for funding during the following calendar year. This letter should briefly describe the applying organization and the purpose for which funds are sought. Information concerning the organization's income and expenses, and material outlining the experience and expertise of key personnel should also be included. When a letter of intent is received, the foundation's staff determines whether the proposed project meets current guidelines and interests. The foundation then invites a full proposal.

Deadline(s) Letters of intent must be received by the foundation no later than June 1; full proposals, if invited, must be received by the foundation no later than September 1.

433. The Skillman Foundation

333 West Fort Street, Suite 1350
Detroit, MI 48226
(313) 961-8850

Grants

Program Description The foundation is interested in the needs of young persons and the elderly and in particular the disadvantaged within these groups. The foundation intends to fulfill its purpose through grantmaking in five program areas: children, youth and young persons; education; basic human needs; culture and arts; and communitywide collaborative efforts.

Sample Grants In support of a street law program for high school students, $15,000 to Wayne County Neighborhood Legal Services, Detroit, MI (1987)

Eligibility/Limitations The foundation emphasizes grants affecting the metropolitan Detroit area. Agencies and organizations serving southeastern Michigan and the State of Michigan are also eligible for grants. Grant requests for organizations located elsewhere in the United States will be considered, but are assigned a lower priority. The foundation does not grant support directly to individuals, for basic research or legislative activities, or for less than $5,000.

Fiscal Information Grants approved in 1988 totaled over $10.9 million.

Application Information The foundation does not have a set form for applications or proposals. Requests should be concise, and include a history and description of the organization; the purpose and amount of the request; an explanation of the need for the program; other sources of support; an evaluation of the process by which the success or failure of the program will be measured; the names and qualifications of the staff; authorization for the request; a current list of the organization's board of directors or trustees; and a detailed cost budget of the program for which funding is requested.

Deadline(s) Trustees of the foundation review grant requests five times each year, generally in February, April, June, September, and November.

434. Alfred P. Sloan Foundation

630 Fifth Avenue, Suite 2550
New York, NY 10111
(212) 649-1649

Grants

Program Description The main interests of the foundation are science and technology; education in science, technology, and management; competitiveness/economics; and other national problems.

Sample Grants In support of a research conference to evaluate the impact of the Tax Reform Act of 1986, $20,000 to the University of Michigan, Ann Arbor, MI (1989). For costs of data processing required to complete research on equitable property distribution at divorce, $10,000 to a professor of law, Brooklyn Law School, Brooklyn, NY (1989). To plan a Center for Space Policy, $26,000 to Center for Space and Geosciences Policy, University of Colorado Foundation, Boulder, CO (1987). For research on American divorce law, $79,500 to Brooklyn Law School, Brooklyn, NY (1989). To develop legislative options concerning the AIDS epidemic, $30,000 to the School of Public Health, Harvard University, Cambridge, MA (1988). For research on the effects of the Immigration Reform and Control Act of 1986: Mexican immigration to the United States, $104,535 to the National Opinion Research Center, Chicago, IL (1989).

Eligibility/Limitations Recognized institutions of higher education and other tax-exempt organizations are eligible to apply.

Fiscal Information Grants and appropriations authorized in 1989 totaled over $21 million. Grants may not include any overhead charge.

Application Information The foundation has no standard application forms. Often a brief letter of inquiry rather than a fully developed proposal is an advisable first step. Letters of application should include, in addition to details about the applicant and the proposed project, information about the cost and duration of the project.

Deadline(s) Applications can be made at any time. Grants of $30,000 or less are made throughout the year by the officers of the foundation; grants over that amount are made by the trustees, who meet five times a year for that purpose.

435. Social Science Research Council

605 Third Avenue
New York, NY 10158
(212) 661-0280

Japan: Doctoral Dissertation Research Fellowships

Program Description Fellowships are offered to support advanced graduate students during the writing of their dissertations in the United States.

Eligibility/Limitations Applications will be accepted from graduate students working towards the Ph.D. who have completed research on a Japanese topic and who are now writing their dissertations, as well as from students who will have completed such research and will have begun writing their dissertations by the time they propose to begin the fellowship. Citizens and permanent residents of the United States, and noncitizens and nonpermanent residents who are working toward a doctorate at a university in the United States, are eligible to apply.

Application Information Application forms for area studies programs are mailed in response to written requests from applicants. In requesting forms, an applicant should give the following information: a brief statement of the proposed research project; geographical area or areas of interest; proposed site of research; occupation or current activity, university or other affiliation; academic degrees held, specifying disciplines or fields of study; if currently working for a doctoral degree, the date of completion of all requirements except the dissertation; proposed date for beginning tenure of the award and the duration requested; and if requesting forms for a collaborative grant, the academic qualifications of the collaborator. Application forms will be sent after preliminary determination of eligibility by the council staff. Application forms are available in September.

Deadline(s) The deadline for applications is November 1.

436. Social Science Research Council

605 Third Avenue
New York, NY 10158
(212) 661-0280

Korea: Doctoral Dissertation Research Fellowships

Program Description Fellowships are awarded for doctoral dissertation research on Korea in the social sciences and humanities.

Eligibility/Limitations Applicants must be enrolled in full-time graduate study for an advanced degree at a university in the United States, or be U.S. citizens similarly enrolled in a foreign university. Applicants are expected to be proficient in Korean.

Fiscal Information In general, dissertation fellowships support nine to eighteen consecutive months of field research in the relevant area. They normally include maintenance stipends and transportation expenses for the fellow and financial dependents, health insurance for the fellow and dependents, and a research allowance.

Application Information Application forms for area studies programs are mailed in response to written requests from applicants. In requesting forms, an applicant should give the following information: a brief statement of the proposed research project; geographical area or areas of interest; proposed site of research; occupation or current activity, university or other affiliation; academic degrees held, specifying disciplines or fields of study; if currently working for a doctoral degree, the date of completion of all requirements except the dissertation; proposed date for beginning tenure of the award and the duration requested; and if requesting forms for a collaborative grant, the academic qualifications of the collaborator. Application forms will be sent after preliminary determination of eligibility by the council staff. Application forms are available in September.

Deadline(s) The deadline for applications is February 1.

437. Social Science Research Council
605 Third Avenue
New York, NY 10158
(212) 661-0280

Latin America and the Caribbean: Doctoral Dissertation Research Fellowships

Program Description Fellowships are offered for doctoral dissertation research in the social sciences and humanities. Proposals on any topic are eligible for support, including projects comparing Latin American or Caribbean countries to others located outside the region.

Eligibility/Limitations There are no citizenship requirements. However, applicants must be enrolled in full-time graduate study at a university in the United States, and have completed all Ph.D. requirements, except the dissertation, before going into the field. While abroad, fellows are required to affiliate with a university, research institute, or another appropriate insitution in the country where they will be conducting research.

Fiscal Information Recipients of fellowships are expected to devote a minimum of nine and a maximum of eighteen months to field research in the country or countries relevant to their proposals. Support for dissertation write-up is available for up to six months after return from the field.

Application Information Application forms for area studies programs are mailed in response to written requests from applicants. In requesting forms, an applicant should give the following information: a brief statement of the proposed research project; geographical area or areas of interest; proposed site of research; occupation or current activity, university or other affiliation; academic degrees held, specifying disciplines or fields of study; if currently working for a doctoral degree, the date of completion of all requirements except the dissertation; proposed date for beginning tenure of the award and the duration requested; and if requesting forms for a collaborative grant, the academic qualifications of the collaborator. Application forms will be sent after preliminary determination of eligibility by the council staff. Application forms are available in September.

Deadline(s) The deadline for applications is November 1.

Additional Information Support for this program is contingent upon funding. Contact the SSRC for current information.

438. Social Science Research Council
605 Third Avenue
New York, NY 10158
(212) 661-0280

Near and Middle East: Doctoral Dissertation Research Fellowships

Program Description Fellowships are awarded for doctoral dissertation research in the Near and Middle East in the humanities and social sciences. The area is defined to include North Africa, the Middle East, Afghanistan, Iran and Turkey. Research projects must be concerned with the period since the beginning of Islam.

Eligibility/Limitations There are no citizenship requirements for full-time students enrolled in doctoral programs in the United States. American citizens or permanent residents of the United States who are similarly enrolled at accredited foreign universities are also eligible to apply.

Fiscal Information Recipients of fellowships are expected to devote a minimum of nine and a maximum of eighteen months to field research in the country or countries relevant to their proposals. Support for dissertation write-up is available for up to six months after return from the field.

Application Information Application forms for area studies programs are mailed in response to written requests from applicants. In requesting forms, an applicant should give the following information: a brief statement of the proposed research project; geographical area or areas of interest; proposed site of research; occupation or current activity, university or other affiliation; academic degrees held, specifying disciplines or fields

of study; if currently working for a doctoral degree, the date of completion of all requirements except the dissertation; proposed date for beginning tenure of the award and the duration requested; and if requesting forms for a collaborative grant, the academic qualifications of the collaborator. Application forms will be sent after preliminary determination of eligibility by the council staff. Application forms are available in September.

Deadline(s) The deadline for applications is November 1.

439. Social Science Research Council
605 Third Avenue
New York, NY 10158
(212) 661-0280

Russia and the Soviet Union: Dissertation Fellowships

Program Description Fellowships are offered to attract promising scholars in the social sciences and the humanities to enter graduate work in Russian and Soviet studies; to support further study by students who have already completed the initial stages of graduate work in their disciplines; and to support the completion of Ph.D. dissertations. The awards provide two-year fellowships for graduate training in Russian and Soviet studies and dissertation fellowships.

Sample Grants A fellowship was awarded to a graduate student from the Department of Law, Emory University, for training in preparation for dissertation research on Soviet law and legal regulation (1988-89).

Eligibility/Limitations Applicants must be U.S. citizens.

Fiscal Information The awards provide annual stipends of up to $15,000.

Application Information Application forms for area studies programs are mailed in response to written requests from applicants. In requesting forms, an applicant should give the following information: a brief statement of the proposed research project; geographical area or areas of interest; proposed site of research; occupation or current activity, university or other affiliation; academic degrees held, specifying disciplines or fields of study; if currently working for a doctoral degree, the date of completion of all requirements except the dissertation; proposed date for beginning tenure of the award and the duration requested; and if requesting forms for a collaborative grant, the academic qualifications of the collaborator. Application forms will be sent after preliminary determination of eligibility by the council staff. Application forms are available in September.

Deadline(s) The deadline for application is December 1.

440. Social Science Research Council
605 Third Avenue
New York, NY 10158
(212) 661-0280

South Asia: Doctoral Dissertation Research Fellowships

Program Description Fellowships are awarded for doctoral dissertation research in the humanities and social sciences, and for the advanced research of students in programs in which the doctoral degree is not usually offered, such as law, architecture, and urban or regional planning. Fellowships may be used for research to be carried out in Bangladesh, Nepal, and Sri Lanka, but not in India or Pakistan. Fellowships are available for support of dissertation research on India and Pakistan. However, applicants for such support must apply for and obtain at least nine months' support for field research in India or Pakistan from an organization other than the SSRC.

Eligibility/Limitations There are no citizenship requirements. However, applicants must be enrolled in full-time graduate study for an advanced degree in the United States, or be U.S. citizens similarly enrolled at an accredited foreign university. Applicants are expected to be proficient in a major South Asian language, but may request support for study of a local language while in the region.

Fiscal Information The total period of support for additional language training and field research normally cannot exceed 18 months.

Application Information Application forms for area studies programs are mailed in response to written requests from applicants. In requesting forms, an applicant should give the following information: a brief statement of the proposed research project; geographical area or areas of interest; proposed site of research; occupation or current activity, university or other affiliation; academic degrees held, specifying disciplines or fields of study; if currently working for a doctoral degree, the date of completion of all requirements except the dissertation; proposed date for beginning tenure of the award and the duration requested; and if requesting forms for a collaborative grant, the academic qualifications of the collaborator. Application forms will be sent after preliminary determination of eligibility by the council staff. Application forms are available in September.

Deadline(s) The deadline for applications is November 1.

441. Social Science Research Council
605 Third Avenue
New York, NY 10158
(212) 661-0280

Southeast Asia: Doctoral Dissertation Research Fellowships

Program Description Fellowships are awarded for doctoral dissertation research in the humanities and social sciences in one or more countries of Southeast Asia. Applications will also be considered for the advanced research of students in programs in which the doctoral degree is not usually offered, such as law, public health, and urban/regional planning. Fellowships are available for support of dissertation research in Southeast Asian, including Brunei, Myanmar, Indonesia, Cambodia, Laos, Malaysia, the Philippines, Thailand, Singapore, and Vietnam. Support for archival research (not in the United States) will also be considered.

Eligibility/Limitations There are no citizenship requirements. However, applicants must be enrolled in full-time graduate study for an advanced degree in the United States, or be U.S. citizens similarly enrolled at an accredited foreign university. Applicants are expected to be proficient in a major Southeast Asian language, but may request support for study of a local language while in the region.

Fiscal Information The total period of support for additional language training and field research normally cannot exceed 18 months. Support for research write-up cannot exceed six months.

Application Information Application forms for area studies programs are mailed in response to written requests from applicants. In requesting forms, an applicant should give the following information: a brief statement of the proposed research project; geographical area or areas of interest; proposed site of research; occupation or current activity, university or other affiliation; academic degrees held, specifying disciplines or fields of study; if currently working for a doctoral degree, the date of completion of all requirements except the dissertation; proposed date for beginning tenure of the award and the duration requested; and if requesting forms for a collaborative grant, the academic qualifications of the collaborator. Application forms will be sent after preliminary determination of eligibility by the council staff. Application forms are available in September.

Deadline(s) The deadline for applications is November 1.

442. Social Science Research Council
605 Third Avenue
New York, NY 10158
(212) 661-0280

Western Europe: Dissertation Fellowships

Program Description Fellowships are awarded for doctoral dissertation research in Western Europe in the social sciences and humanities. Particularly encouraged are applications from disciplines in which relatively less attention has been devoted to Western Europe, such as economics, social psychology, and sociology. Applications will also be accepted for research involving both Europe and the United States if required by the comparative nature of the project.

Eligibility/Limitations There are no citizenship requirements for full-time students enrolled in doctoral programs in the United States. American citizens or permanent residents of the United States who are similarly enrolled at accredited foreign universities are also eligible to apply. Applicants are expected to devote a minimum of nine and a maximum of eighteen months to field research. They should be prepared to commence research within the year following the date the awards are made. Support for dissertation write-up cannot exceed six months.

Application Information Application forms for area studies programs are mailed in response to written requests from applicants. In requesting forms, an applicant should give the following information: a brief statement of the proposed research project; geographical area or areas of interest; proposed site of research; occupation or current activity, university or other affiliation; academic degrees held, specifying disciplines or fields of study; if currently working for a doctoral degree, the date of completion of all requirements except the dissertation; proposed date for beginning tenure of the award and the duration requested; and if requesting forms for a collaborative grant, the academic qualifications of the collaborator. Application forms will be sent after preliminary determination of eligibility by the council staff. Application forms are available in September.

Deadline(s) The deadline for the application is November 1.

443. Social Science Research Council
Africa Program
605 Third Avenue
New York, NY 10158
(212) 661-0280

Africa: Doctoral Dissertation Research Fellowships

Program Description Fellowships are offered for doctoral dissertation research in the social sciences and the humanities to be carried out in Africa south of the Sahara. Doctoral Dissertation Research Fellowships support research in the social sciences and humanities in Africa in disciplines which have been underrepresented in African studies, such as sociology and economics, as well as innovative proposals in the humanities.

Sample Grants A dissertation fellowship was awarded to a Ph.D. candidate in political science for research on the relationship between nongovernmental organizations and the state in the implementation of development programs in Kenya (1988-89). A dissertation fellowship was awarded to a Ph.D. candidate in economics for research on the nature and importance of dynamic and interlinked contracts in Sudan (1988-89). A dissertation fellowship was awarded to a Ph.D. candidate in geography for research on the origins and meanings of land-use conflict in Arusha National Park in Tanzania.

Eligibility/Limitations All full-time students enrolled in a doctoral program in the United States are eligible to apply for Doctoral Dissertation Research Fellowships; citizens and permanent residents of the United States who are enrolled in doctoral programs abroad are also eligible.

Application Information Application forms for area studies programs are mailed in response to written requests from applicants. In requesting forms, an applicant should give the following information: a brief statement of the proposed research project; geographical area or areas of interest; proposed site of research; occupation or current activity, university or other affiliation; academic degrees held, specifying disciplines or fields of study; if currently working for a doctoral degree, the date of completion of all requirements except the dissertation; proposed date for beginning tenure of the award and the duration requested; and if requesting forms for a collaborative grant, the academic qualifications of the collaborator. Application forms will be sent after preliminary determination of eligibility by the council staff. Application forms are available in September.

Deadline(s) The deadline for applications is November 1.

444. Social Science Research Council
Africa Program
605 Third Avenue
New York, NY 10158
(212) 661-0280

Africa: Fellowships for Training and Dissertation Research on Agriculture and Health

Program Description Fellowships are offered for doctoral dissertation research in the social sciences and the humanities to be carried out in Africa. Fellowships for Training and Dissertation Research on Agriculture and Health provides natural or technical science training along with support for dissertation research for social science Ph.D. candidates whose research topics address issues of African agriculture and health.

Sample Grants A dissertation fellowship was awarded to a Ph.D. candidate in law, policy and society, for training in marine biology in Abidjan and for research on policy planning and fisheries development in Cote d'Ivoire, (1988-89).

Eligibility/Limitations Social science Ph.D. candidates of any nationality who are enrolled in a U.S. university, and social science Ph.D. candidates who are U.S. citizens enrolled in a university abroad, are eligible to apply. Applicants are expected to have a topic, a research site, and preliminary plans for their training.

Application Information Application forms for area studies programs are mailed in response to written requests from applicants. In requesting forms, an applicant should give the following information: a brief statement of the proposed research project; geographical area or areas of interest; proposed site of research; occupation or current activity, university or other affiliation; academic degrees held, specifying disciplines or fields of study; if currently working for a doctoral degree, the date of completion of all requirements except the dissertation; proposed date for beginning tenure of the award and the duration requested; and if requesting forms for a collaborative grant, the academic qualifications of the collaborator. Application forms will be sent after preliminary determination of eligibility by the council staff. Application forms are available in September.

Deadline(s) The deadline for applications is November 1.

445. Social Science Research Council
Africa Program
605 Third Avenue
New York, NY 10158
(212) 661-0280

Africa: Predissertation Fellowships

Program Description Fellowships are offered for doctoral dissertation research in the social sciences and the humanities to be carried out in Africa. Predissertation Fellowships support short-term field trips to encourage preliminary field activities and planning for students preparing for dissertation research on Africa.

Eligibility/Limitations Predissertation Fellowship applicants must have completed one year of graduate study in the social sciences or humanities at a U.S. university at the time of application, or be a U.S. citizen or permanent resident who has completed this study abroad, and be accepted into a full-time Ph.D. program. Applications are especially encouraged from two groups of students: Africanists in disciplines that traditionally have been underrepresented in African studies, such as economics, the humanities, psychology, and sociology; and non-Africanist students in any discipline who might be encouraged by the period of preliminary research support by these fellowships to plan dissertation field research in Africa, perhaps as part of a comparative project.

Fiscal Information The fellowships provide support of up to $2,000.

Application Information Application forms for area studies programs are mailed in response to written requests from applicants. In requesting forms, an applicant should give the following information: a brief statement of the proposed research project; geographical area or areas of interest; proposed site of research; occupation or current activity, university or other affiliation; academic degrees held, specifying disciplines or fields of study; if currently working for a doctoral degree, the date of completion of all requirements except the dissertation; proposed date for beginning tenure of the award and the duration requested; and if requesting forms for a collaborative grant, the academic qualifications of the collaborator. Application forms will be sent after preliminary determination of eligibility by the council staff. Application forms are available in September.

Deadline(s) The application deadline is December 1.

446. Social Science Research Council
Berlin Program for Advanced German and European Studies
605 Third Avenue
New York, NY 10158
(212) 661-0280

Berlin Program for Advanced German and European Studies

Program Description The purpose of this program is to encourage the comparative and interdisciplinary study of the economic, political, and social aspects of modern and contemporary German and European affairs.

Eligibility/Limitations The program supports anthropologists, economists, political scientists, sociologists, and all scholars in germane fields, including historians working on the period since the mid-19th century. Citizens and permanent residents of the United States are eligible to apply. At the dissertation level, applicants must have completed all requirements except the dissertation for the Ph.D. at the time the fellowship begins. At the postdoctoral level, the program is open to scholars who have received the Ph.D. degree or its equivalent in the last two years.

Fiscal Information Awards are for a minimum of nine and a maximum of 24 months.

Application Information When requesting application forms, provide: the date on which you will/did receive your Ph.D.; your citizenship; and a brief summary of your proposed research.

Deadline(s) Application deadline is January 15.

447. Social Science Research Council
Fellowships and Grants
605 Third Avenue
New York, NY 10158
(212) 661-0280

Grants for Advanced Area Research

Program Description This program is designed to support research in one country, comparative research between countries in an area, and comparative research between areas. Research will be supported in Africa, Japan, Korea, Latin America and the Caribbean, the Near and Middle East, Russia and the Soviet Union, South Asia and Southeast Asia. Comparative studies of Muslim societies are also eligible for support.

Sample Grants For research on law and change in contemporary Japan, a study of the Equal Employment Opportunity Act, a fellowship to a professor of political science (1988-89).

Eligibility/Limitations These grants are offered to scholars whose competence for research in the social sciences or humanities has been demonstrated by their previous work and who hold the Ph.D. or have equivalent research experience. Candidates for academic degrees are not eligible. Some area studies awards require the researcher to be a citizen or permanent resident of the United States. Contact the council for more complete information.

Fiscal Information Grant amounts vary from country to country. Grants are normally made for periods of two months to one year. Budgetary limitations may make it impossible, however, to provide full maintenance for the duration of the award.

Application Information Application forms for area studies programs are mailed in response to written requests from applicants. In requesting forms, an applicant should give the following information: a brief statement of the proposed research project; geographical area or areas of interest; proposed site of research; occupation or current activity, university or other affiliation; academic degrees held, specifying disciplines or fields of study; for advanced research grants, the approximate amount of support needed; proposed date for beginning tenure of the award and the duration requested; and if requesting forms for a collaborative grant, the academic qualifications of the collaborator. Application forms will be sent after preliminary determination of eligibility by the council staff. Application forms are available in September.

Deadline(s) Deadline for receipt of application is December 1.

448. Social Science Research Council
Indochina Scholarly Exchange Program (ISEP)
605 Third Avenue
New York, NY 10158
(212) 661-0280

Indochina Scholarly Exchange Program

Program Description This program is intended to encourage and support research in the social sciences and humanities relating to Cambodia, Laos, and Vietnam, and to develop projects of scholarly cooperation within Southeast Asia and internationally.

Eligibility/Limitations The program welcomes inquiries from scholars and other professionals about projects involving research, exchange of faculty and students, or training and institutional support in the three countries. Preference will be given to projects which involve collaboration between scholars and institutions in Indochina and other countries. There are no citizenship requirements.

Application Information Persons interested in the program are urged to submit a two- or three-page letter in English describing the nature and significance of the proposed projects; the kinds of methods and materials to be utilized; the researcher's qualifications for conducting the project, including a curriculum vitae if possible; and a preliminary timetable and budget. On the basis of review of these initial letters of inquiry, a small number of applicants will be encouraged to develop detailed projects and formal application materials will be forwarded to them.

Deadline(s) The deadline for completed applications is December 1.

449. Social Science Research Council
Program in Foreign Policy Studies
605 Third Avenue
New York, NY 10158
(212) 661-0280

Foreign Policy Studies Advanced Research Fellowships

Program Description The purpose of this program is to encourage research on foreign policy making processes that takes account the complex interplay of political, economic, social, and international forces believed to influence policy making. Fellowships are intended to support research that compares the making of contemporary U.S. foreign policy to the making of policy in different countries or across historical periods; analyzes the making of foreign policy on economic or social issues; investigates how foreign nations or extragovernmental institutions such as ethnic or industry lobbies attempt to affect the making of U.S. foreign policy; explores the role of the media in the making of U.S. foreign policy; or connects the study of Congressional elections and policy-making process with the study of foreign policy making generally. The program does not support studies of the impacts of U.S. policies on other countries or regions or studies that investigate what U.S. policy toward a particular issue or country should be.

Eligibility/Limitations The program supports empirical research that applies theories and insights from diverse social science disciplines, including anthropology, economics, history, political science, psychology, sociology, and foreign area studies. The fellowship is open to individual researchers who hold the doctoral degree (Ph.D. or its equivalent) or to others with professional backgrounds in law, journalism, or government. Applicants should have demonstrated their ability to contribute to the research literature through the publication of books or articles. Some preference will be given to researchers in the early stages of their careers. Applications are welcome without regard to the prospective fellow's citizenship or country of residence.

Fiscal Information These fellowships support one to two years of research. Awards include a stipend, as well as limited funds to cover research expenses and travel outside the United States. The size of the stipend depends on the fellow's current salary or level of experience. Total awards are expected to average $30,000 per year, and in no case can the award exceed $35,000 per year. The program permits fellows to acquire additional training if it contributes to their proposed research. Fellows are required to devote full time to research during the award period.

Application Information For further information and application materials contact the council.

Deadline(s) Completed applications must be received at the council by December 1.

450. Social Science Research Council
Program in International Peace and Security
605 Third Avenue
New York, NY 10158
(212) 661-0280

SSRC-MacArthur Foundation Fellowships in International Peace and Security

Program Description The council offers dissertation and postdoctoral fellowships for training and research in international peace and security. The fellowships are intended to support research on the implications for security issues of worldwide cultural, social, economic, and political changes. Many assumptions about world affairs, the future of states, and the relations of states with one another have been called into question as a result of changes in China, the Soviet Union, Southern Africa, Latin America and Eastern Europe during 1989 and 1990. In addition to previous questions of concern, a new range of issues has come to the fore. These issues include the effect of demographic trends; increased pressure on the natural environment; massive patterns of migration; the altered nature of economic ties; ethnic, racial, and national conflicts; the economic and social effects of decreased levels of military spending; and the impact of large arsenals of nuclear weapons on political change and stability.

Sample Grants In support of research aimed at developing a process for negotiating an equitable resolution to the Arab-Israeli conflict over Jerusalem, a dissertation fellowship to a Ph.D. candidate in international relations (1988-89).

Eligibility/Limitations The competition is open to researchers in the social and behavioral sciences (including history and area studies), the humanities, or the physical and biological sciences. An academic appointment is not a requirement, nor is an academic affiliation during the term of the fellowships always expected. Dissertation fellowships are open to researchers who are finishing course work, examinations, or similar requirements for the Ph.D. or its equivalent. Postdoctoral fellowships are open to researchers who, in most cases, hold the Ph.D. or its equivalent. However, possession of that degree is not a requirement for lawyers, public servants, journalists, or others who can demonstrate comparable research experience and an ability to contribute to the research literature. The postdoctoral fellowship is designed for researchers in the first 10 years of their postdoctoral careers; most senior researchers are discouraged from applying. There are no citizenship or nationality requirements.

Fiscal Information Dissertation fellowships pay a stipend appropriate for the cost of living in the area where the fellow will be working. The stipend will rarely exceed $17,500 per year, but it will not be less than $12,500 per year. Postdoctoral fellowships pay a stipend appropriate for the fellow's current salary and the cost of living in the area where the fellow will be working. The stipend will rarely exceed $35,000 per year, but it will not be less than $25,000 per year.

Application Information For further information and application materials contact the Program in International Peace and Security, SSRC.

Deadline(s) Applications are due December 1.

Additional Information At the time of application, both dissertation and postdoctoral applicants who are already qualified as area studies researchers may request a three- to twelve-month extension of the term of the fellowships for field work in the nation or region of their expertise.

451. Social Science Research Council
Public Policy Research on Contemporary Hispanic Issues
605 Third Avenue
New York, NY 10158
(212) 661-0280

Public Policy Research on Contemporary Hispanic Issues

Program Description The purposes of the program are to encourage the development of theory and research on the Hispanic population, to strengthen the capability of Hispanic scholars to engage in policy relevant research, and to increase collaboration between Hispanic and non-Hispanic scholars.

Eligibility/Limitations The program offers advanced research grants to support scholars engaged in research on the Hispanic population that can inform public policy. Postdoctoral fellowships support young Hispanic scholars engaged in basic research on the Hispanic population who have received their Ph.D. in the last seven years. Public policy fellowships support Hispanic scholars engaged in policy-relevant research for a one-year, full-time research term at a policy institute in Washington, DC. All applicants must be citizens or permanent residents of the United States.

Fiscal Information Advanced research grants are for a maximum of $35,000. Postdoctoral fellowships provide a stipend of $24,000 for two years of research and writing. Public policy fellowships provide a $24,000 stipend for one year of research.

Application Information For further information contact the council.

Deadline(s) The deadline for receipt of application is January 16.

452. Social Science Research Council
Research on the Urban Underclass
605 Third Avenue
New York, NY 10158
(212) 661-0280

Research on the Urban Underclass

Program Description The aim of the program is to encourage research on the structures and processes that generate, maintain, and overcome the conditions and consequences of persistent and concentrated urban poverty. The program is designed to develop and improve understanding of the urban underclass.

Eligibility/Limitations The program offers undergraduate, dissertation, and postdoctoral awards for research on the urban underclass. University or college faculty may apply for the support of undergraduate research assistants who conduct research in collaboration with faculty. Applicants for dissertation fellowships should have completed all requirements for the

Ph.D., except the dissertation, within one year after the announcement of the award. Special emphasis is placed on the recruitment of minority students and scholars. Postdoctoral grants provide support for advanced research.

Fiscal Information Support is provided for individual or group-based research projects through stipends to undergraduates of up to $4,000 per student and through additional resources for research-related expenses of up to $1,000 per student. A maximum of five students may be supported by one grant. Dissertation fellowships provide financial support to graduate students for up to eighteen months of research. Fellowships provide a stipend of up to $1,000 per month and up to an additional $4,000 for research expenses incurred during the fellowship period. Postdoctoral grants offer a stipend of up to $30,000 and an additional $7,500 for research-related expenses.

Application Information For further information contact the council.

Deadline(s) Application deadline is January 10.

453. Society of Fellows in the Humanities
Heyman Center for the Humanities, Columbia
   University
Box 100 Central Mail Room
New York, NY 10027

Fellowships

Program Description The society seeks to enhance the role of the humanities in the university by exploring and clarifying the interrelationships within the humanities, as well as their relationship to the natural and social sciences and the several professions. The program is designed to strengthen the intellectual and academic qualifications of the fellows, first, by associating them individually and collectively with some of the finest teaching scholars in the university; second by involving them in interdisciplinary programs of general education and in innovative and renovative courses of their own design; and third, by affording them time and resources to develop independent scholarship within a broadening educational and professional context.

Eligibility/Limitations Fellows must have received the Ph.D. within three years of appointment.

Fiscal Information The appointment as fellow, considered as equivalent to the rank of lecturer, is for one year. The appointment is ordinarily renewed for a second year. The stipend is for $31,000, one half for independent research and one half for teaching. Additional funds are available to support research.

Application Information Additional information and application forms are available from the society.

Deadline(s) The deadline for applications is October 15.

454. The Sophia Fund
53 West Jackson Boulevard
Chicago, IL 60604
(312) 663-1552

Grants

Program Description The fund makes grants to organizations and projects that advocate for social change for women, especially in the issues of violence against women, economic justice, reproductive rights, and women's philanthropy.

Sample Grants For the Women and Child Care project for coalition-building and advocacy on child care, $2,000 to National Women's Law Center, Washington, DC (1988). For the Women's Economic Justice Center for organizing, research, and advocacy on women's issues, $4,000 to National Center for Policy Alternatives, Washington, DC (1988). To evaluate federal judge appointments, especially their records on women's rights, $3,000 to the Federation of Women Lawyers Judicial Screening Panel, Washington, DC (1988). For research on the judicial court system's impact on woman, $3,500 to Task Force on Gender Bias in the Courts, Chicago (1988).

Eligibility/Limitations The fund does not award grants to individuals, or for scholarships or fellowships, medical research, or to religious organizations for religious purposes. Contributions are restricted to nonprofit organizations whose efforts are directed solely or primarily toward women, and who are working in advocacy, community awareness and education, public policy areas, research, or, on rare occasions, in pilot service projects.

Fiscal Information The fund contributes to general operating expenses or to special projects. Grants are usually under $10,000. Grants awarded in 1988 totaled over $221,000.

Application Information To apply for a grant, write a proposal, not more than five-pages long, and include the following: a description of the sponsoring agency and the populations it serves; an explanation of the issue the organization is addressing; the method of addressing the issue; accomplishments of the organization, or history of its work in the community; an itemized budget of project and organization; list of current and projected foundation and corporate support; a list of staff members and board of directors, and resumes of those responsible for the project or program; the latest audited financial statement, if available; a completed IRS 990 form; and an IRS ruling on nonprofit status, which includes nonprofit identification number.

Deadline(s) Proposals will be reviewed twice a year and must be received by March 1 and September 1. The deadline will be extended to the first workday after these days if the first of the month falls on a weekend or holiday.

455. The Space Foundation
P.O. Box 58501
Houston, TX 77258
(713) 332-0779

Space Industrial Fellowship

Program Description This fellowship is designed to reward and encourage innovative thinking in disciplines related to the peaceful use of space resources through commercialization. New frontiers are opening in microgravity, remote sensing, biotechnology, materials processing, space robotics, solar power, satellite engineering, heat transfer, artificial intelligence, space transport, and many other space-oriented research areas. Applicants are solicited not only from the sciences and engineering, but from business, law, economics, social sciences, environmental studies, and the humanities.

Eligibility/Limitations Outstanding graduate students from accredited universities whose research work expands a frontier area will be encouraged to apply. Applicants should hold bachelor degrees and intend to devote their careers to further practical space research, engineering, business, or other application ventures.

Fiscal Information The fellowship carries a $5,000 stipend.

Application Information Additional information and application materials are available from the executive director of the foundation.

Deadline(s) Deadline for receipt of applications is November 15.

456. The Spencer Foundation
875 North Michigan Avenue
Chicago, IL 60611
(312) 337-7000

Grants

Program Description The Spencer Foundation supports research that gives promise of yielding new knowledge about education. The foundation is interested in a wide variety of disciplinary and interdisciplinary approaches, though by direction of its charter it gives emphasis to the behavioral sciences, and it defines education broadly to include all the situations and institutions in which education proceeds, across the entire life span, in the United States and around the world. The foundation is also interested in a wide variety of research areas, including what the anthropologist might call cultural knowledge, what the political scientist might call socialization, and what the economist might call the production and distribution of knowledge. Finally, the foundation is interested in a wide variety of research formats, from relatively low-cost individual efforts extending over a few months to more expensive collaborative efforts extending over several years.

Sample Grants For a study of the constraints imposed by immigration laws on colleges and universities regarding their treatment of undocumented and immigrant students and the institutions' understanding of these constraints, $100,000 over two years to the University of Houston Law Center, Houston, TX (1989).

Eligibility/Limitations The principal investigator must have an earned doctorate in an academic discipline or in the field of education and must have an affiliation with a college or university, a research facility, or a cultural institution.

Fiscal Information Grants awarded during the 1989 fiscal year totaled over $8.9 million.

Application Information An informal letter of inquiry or a brief preliminary proposal is usually sufficient for the foundation to determine whether a proposed study falls within the foundation's scope. A curriculum vitae of the principal investigator is expected with the initial inquiry to inform the foundation staff concerning the individual's qualifications for conducting the research suggested. If the proposed research appears to be of potential interest, three copies of a more detailed proposal will be requested.

Deadline(s) Inquiries and proposals are welcome at any time.

Additional Information The foundation also conducts a small grants program within the domains of its concerns, which is intended to facilitate scholars in pursuing exploratory research, problem-finding research, pilot research, modest research projects, and the initial phases of larger investigations. Grants made under the program may range from $1,000 to $7,500. The principal investigator must have an earned doctorate in an academic discipline or in the field of education and must hold an appointment in a college or university, a research facility, or a cultural institution; and the research topic must be clearly relevant to the field of education. Projects under the Small Grants Program may not extend beyond a year in duration. Inquiries concerning this program should be addressed to the administrator of the Small Grants Program and The Spencer Foundation.

457. Stanford Humanities Center
Stanford University
Mariposa House
Stanford, CA 94305-8630
(415) 723-3052

External Faculty Fellowships

Program Description The general aims of the Stanford Humanities Center are to promote humanistic studies and interests in three main ways: by operating a fellowship program mainly concerned with research; by supplementing and otherwise strengthening humanistic teaching at Stanford; and by conducting studies of problems in the area of the humanities broadly defined, and of their relationships to other disciplines. The fellowship program is primarily concerned with offering research opportunities both for members of humanities departments as traditionally defined and for all other scholars seriously interested in humanistic issues.

Sample Grants A fellowship was awarded in support of research on the structure of nationalist and judicial discourse: the riot at Chauri Chaura as metaphor and event (1990). A fellowship was awarded in support of research on the economics of patronage, intellectual property, and the historical roots of the institutions of open science (1990). A fellowship was awarded in support of research on the political experience and thought in the making of the Constitution (1988-89).

Eligibility/Limitations External fellowships are awarded in three categories: (1) fellowships for already well-established and usually tenured scholars; (2) fellowships for junior, usually untenured, scholars who teach at colleges or universities which do not have major graduate schools or do not have doctoral programs in their own departments; and (3) fellowships for U.S. ethnic minority scholars (Blacks, Chicanos/Mexican-Americans, Native Americans, Puerto Rican Americans) and for scholars from Third World countries who either now reside in a Third World nation or who intend to return and resume their professional careers there. Persons on temporary teaching appointments or without academic affiliation may apply, but their applications can only be considered under category (1). The external fellowship is not intended either for students who are now finishing, or who, with the exception of those who might qualify under category (3), have recently completed, their doctorates.

Fiscal Information Fellows will receive stipends based on their expected academic salary for the coming year. The funding at the center, however, is limited. Applicants are expected to seek supplementary financial support. External Fellows will also receive necessary travel allowances for themselves and their families.

Application Information Forms of application and further information are available from the center.

Deadline(s) The deadline for applications is December 1.

458. The Starr Foundation
70 Pine Street
New York, NY 10270
(212) 770-6882

Grants

Program Description The foundation awards scholarships to individuals and grants to educational and charitable organizations.

Sample Grants For renewed support of programs and activities, $50,000 to the Institute for Civil Justice, The Rand Corporation, Santa Monica, CA (1988). In support of Project on Civil Justice Reform, $50,000 to Manhattan Institute for Policy Research, New York, NY (1988).

Eligibility/Limitations Nonprofit educational and charitable organizations are eligible to apply.

Fiscal Information Grants awarded in 1988 totaled over $10.9 million.

Application Information Applications should be submitted in writing. There are no application forms. A letter setting forth basic information on the request is satisfactory.

Deadline(s) There are no submission deadlines.

459. State Justice Institute
120 South Fairfax Street
Alexandria, VA 22314
(703) 684-6100

Grants

Program Description The State Justice Institute was established to improve the administration of justice in state courts of the United States. Through the award of grants, contracts, and cooperative agreements, the institute is authorized to perform the following activities: support research, demonstrations, special projects, technical assistance, and training to improve the administration of justice in the state courts; provide for the preparation, publication, and dissemination of information regarding state judicial systems; participate in joint projects with federal agencies and other private grantors; evaluate or provide for the evaluation of programs and projects funded by the institute; encourage and assist in furthering judicial education; encourage, assist, and serve in a consulting capacity to state and local justice system agencies in the development, maintenance, and coordination of criminal, civil, and juvenile justice programs and services; and be responsible for the certification of national

programs that are intended to aid and improve state judicial systems.

Eligibility/Limitations The institute is authorized to award grants, contracts, and cooperative agreements to state and local courts and their agencies; national nonprofit organizations controlled by, operating in conjunction with, and serving the judicial branch of state governments; and national nonprofit organizations for the education and training of judges and support personnel of the judicial branch of state governments. The institute may also award funds to other nonprofit organizations with expertise in judicial administration; institutions of higher education; individuals, partnerships, firms, or corporations; and private agencies with expertise in judicial administration if the objectives of the funded program can be better served by such an entity.

Fiscal Information Applications for new projects and applications for continuation grants may request funding in amounts up to $300,000, although awards in excess of $200,000 are likely to be rare and to be made, if at all, only for highly promising proposals that will have a significant impact nationally. A project addressing the needs of the largest urban courts may receive support of up to $500,000. Applications for ongoing support grants may request funding in amounts up to $600,000.

Application Information The institute requires applicants to submit concept papers prior to submitting a formal grant application. Contact the institute for concept paper requirements and formal grant application guidelines.

Deadline(s) Confirm deadlines with the institute or as announced in the Federal Register.

460. Philip M. Stern Family Fund
1601 Connecticut Avenue, NW, Suite 803
Washington, DC 20009
(202) 232-7333

Grants

Program Description The Philip M. Stern Family Fund supports organizations working for systemic structural changes aimed at empowering the powerless, alleviating injustice, increasing government accountability, and strengthening the workings of American democracy. Areas of special interest include: campaign finance reform; election law reforms aimed at simplifying and encouraging voter participation; alleviating special problems faced by women, particularly women of color; fostering government accountability, open government, and the efforts of whistleblowers; providing technical assistance to progressive nonprofit groups to enable them to perform more effectively; and promoting corporate accountability and socially responsible corporate behavior.

Eligibility/Limitations The fund does not make grants to organizations that traditionally enjoy popular support such as universities, museums, or hospitals. It seldom supports projects with budgets over $500,000, capital campaigns, research projects, conferences, or films.

Fiscal Information Grants awarded in 1987-88 totaled over $600,000.

Application Information The fund has no standard application forms, procedures, or deadlines. A proposal accompanied by a short cover letter should be submitted to the executive director. Preference is given to proposals that do not exceed 10 pages. Every proposal should include a clear statement of the need for support, the project's goals, and an action plan for achieving those goals; a certificate of tax-exempt status; staff and organizational qualifications for carrying out the program; lists of other sources of financial support already committed and sources to whom proposals have been sent; project and organizational line item budget(s); a list of other organizations involved in similar programs and how the proposed project is different; and the hopes and/or expectations of achievement from the project, stated in as quantifiable terms as possible.

Deadline(s) The fund meets approximately six times a year.

461. Sun Company, Inc.
Director, Social Investment
100 Matsonford Road
Radnor, PA 19087-4597
(215) 293-6192

Corporate Contributions Program

Program Description Sun Company believes that its contributions program is a key part of the company's response to the public's economic and social needs. The purpose of the program, then, is to help improve the intellectual, economic, social, and cultural environments in those communities within the continental United States where the corporation has a major presence. Sun Company prioritizes its contributions efforts into five program areas, each with specific attributes: education; civic, economic development, and employment opportunities; health and human services; arts and culture; and public information and policy research. In the arts and culture program, support is available to museums, symphonies, and other visual and performing arts programs and institutions that have established community acceptance and support; and to other organizations that broaden the cultural experiences available to the public in Sun's communities.

Eligibility/Limitations Sun Company supports nonprofit organizations and institutions which meet the corporation's contributions guidelines. Company contributions programs are primarily local in scope and are focused on those areas where the corporation has a major presence, by virtue of a major installation or large concentration of employees. At the national level, Sun directs its contributions activities to limited program areas which fall within the company's priority funding areas and which are determined to help improve the economic, educational, and social climate throughout the nation in general. Contributions are not directed toward political parties or political candidates; organizations that are not tax exempt; or individuals. Generally, funds are not expended to veterans, religious, or athletic groups; goodwill advertising or benefit fund-raisers; or funding to cover continuing operating deficits.

Fiscal Information Grant contributions in 1989 totaled over $4.5 million.

Application Information All requests must be submitted in writing. Proposals should be brief, but concise, and should include a description of the organization as follows: brief history of the organization; copy of tax-exempt status; latest audited financial report; current operating budget and sources of income; listing of the organization's key management and board of directors; annual report or update of activities; and number of employees (paid and volunteer). Information regarding the particular program for which funding is being sought should include: purpose and objective of the program; needs to be addressed; population served; plan of action and time frame for proposed program; qualifications of program's administrators; total funding required and projected sources; amount of funds requested; methods of evaluation; and utilization of results.

Deadline(s) No deadlines are announced.

462. Supreme Court of the United States
Judicial Fellows Program
Washington, DC 20543

Judicial Fellows Program

Program Description The Judicial Fellows Program seeks outstanding individuals from diverse fields to spend one year working with top officials in the judicial branch of government.

Eligibility/Limitations The program is designed for professionals in the early stages of their career development who will receive long-term benefits from the experience and who will contribute to improvement of the judicial process both during and after the fellowship. Candidates should have one or more postgraduate degrees and at least two years of professional experience with a record of high performance. Multidisciplinary training and experience is highly desirable. Backgrounds of fellows have included political science, public and business administration, eco-

nomics, the behavioral sciences, operations research and system analysis, journalism, as well as law.

Fiscal Information The fellowship is ordinarily for one year. Salary is negotiable, based on the fellow's education, experience, and salary history, not to exceed the then-prevailing rate of pay for a GS-15, step 3.

Application Information Applicants should send the following to the above address: a resume highlighting specific academic, professional and personal accomplishments; an essay of not more than 700 words explaining the applicant's interest in the program, his or her major relevant qualifications, and the contributions he or she might make as a fellow; copies of no more than two publications or other writing samples; and letters forwarded directly by three references, focusing on the candidate's personal character and professional qualifications and emphasizing the criteria described above.

Deadline(s) The complete application should be received by November 15 to ensure consideration.

463. Texaco Philanthropic Foundation Inc.
2000 Westchester Avenue
White Planes, NY 10650
(914) 253-4150

Grants

Program Description The purpose of the Texaco Philanthropic Foundation Inc. is to enhance the quality of life in the United States by providing financial support to selected, nonprofit, tax-exempt organizations in the areas of education, health and hospitals, social welfare, arts and culture, civic and public interest, environmental protection, and other deserving charitable needs. In general, the foundation will make contributions to national organizations that serve a large segment of the population and to local organizations in areas where Texaco has a significant presence.

Eligibility/Limitations In general, the foundation will not consider a contribution to the following: individuals; private foundations; organizations not tax-exempt under the Internal Revenue Code; social functions, commemorative journals, or meetings; religious, fraternal, social or veterans' organizations; endowments; political or partisan organizations or candidates; organizations established to carry on propaganda or to attempt to influence legislation; organizations established to influence the outcome of any specific public election or to carry on any voter registration drives.

Fiscal Information Grant contributions in 1988 totaled over $6.6 million.

Application Information Applications should include the following: description of the overall purpose and objectives of the organization; description of the project or event for which funds are requested, including specific objectives and purposes of the project; specific reason(s) why Texaco Foundation is an appropriate donor; budget for the project or event; size and composition of the population to be served by the project; explanation of how the project does not duplicate the efforts of other agencies/institutions in the same or related fields; timetable of the project; method of measuring success of the project, and by whom; names of officers and key staff members; list of names and primary professional affiliations of members of the board of trustees; proof of tax-exempt status and certification as a 501(c)(3) charitable organization; most recent audited financial statements; funding sources by category for the organization and, if available, a listing of contributors and the size of gifts; and a description of how Texaco Foundation support will be acknowledged.

Deadline(s) No deadlines are announced.

464. The Tinker Foundation Incorporated

55 East 59th Street
New York, NY 10022
(212) 421-6858

Field Research Grants

Program Description These grants are intended to provide individuals of ability with the opportunity to acquire as comprehensive a knowledge as possible of language and culture, to gather research data and to develop contacts with scholars and institutions in their field.

Eligibility/Limitations These awards are available to all recognized centers or institutes of Ibero-American or Latin America studies with graduate doctoral programs at accredited U.S. universities, and are to be used only for brief periods of individual research in Iberia or Latin America. Latin America here is defined as the Spanish- and Portuguese-speaking countries of the Western Hemisphere. Field Research Grants are awarded to individuals by the appropriate university institutes/centers and should reflect primarily the major interests of the foundation, i.e., social sciences, natural resource development and international relations. They are intended to be used by graduate students and junior faculty (instructors and assistant professors). Graduate students and junior faculty from Latin American and Iberian countries may use the award to conduct research in their home countries.

Fiscal Information Grants carry awards of up to $15,000 per year. These grants must be matched by the university in the amount of $10,000.

Application Information Interested institutions should contact the foundation for complete application instructions and forms.

Deadline(s) Applications must be received by the foundation before October 1.

465. The Tinker Foundation Incorporated

55 East 59th Street
New York, NY 10022
(212) 421-6858

Institutional Grants

Program Description In order to qualify for consideration by the Tinker Foundation, proposals must be concerned with topics or activities related to Iberia, Central or South America or Antarctica. Emphasis is place on those activities that have strong public policy implications, offer innovative solutions to many of the problems facing these regions today, and incorporate new mechanisms for addressing environmental, economic, political and social issues. Such activities may include, but are not limited to, research projects, conferences and workshops, and the training of specialists at the postgraduate level. The foundation also promotes collaboration between and among organizations in the United States, Latin America, Spain and Portugal.

Sample Grants For partial support for a conference on the Antarctic treaty system in world politics, $30,000 to Fridtjof Nansens Institutt, Lysaker, Norway (1989). For the first payment of a three-year grant of $100,000 in partial support of a project on natural resources, poverty and public policy in Central America, $40,000 to Overseas Development Council, Washington, DC (1989). For a study which focuses on the economic, social, political, legal and international dimensions of narco-trafficking between the United States and Colombia in an attempt to develop new policies and approaches to the problem, $50,000 to Universidad de los Andes, Bogota, Colombia (1989).

Eligibility/Limitations Proposals must be written in English. The foundation will not consider requests for annual fund-raising appeals, the construction of buildings, requests from private individuals, proposals concerned with health/medical issues, production costs for films, television and radio projects, funding for arts and humanities projects, endowments, or general operating support.

Fiscal Information Grant awards range from $3,000 to $135,000 for one year of support. Grants may be renewable for up to

three years. In 1989 a total of over $2.3 million was paid for grants and fellowships by the foundation.

Application Information Additional information and application guidelines are available from the foundation.

Deadline(s) Applications are considered biannually by the board of directors. The deadline for receipt of proposals for the summer meeting is March 1; for the winter meeting it is October 1.

466. The Travelers Companies Foundation

One Tower Square
Hartford, CT 06115
(203) 277-0111

Grants

Program Description Current priority areas of funding include the following: health care and economic security for older Americans; jobs, education and training programs for youth in the Hartford area; small business development; higher education; community and civic affairs; arts and culture; and alternative dispute resolution and civil justice.

Eligibility/Limitations Grants will not be considered for organizations which are not tax-exempt under Section 501(c)(3) of the Internal Revenue Code; mass mail appeals, political organizations, testimonial dinners or memberships in associations; or for individuals.

Fiscal Information Contributions expended in 1987 totaled over $4.6 million

Application Information Organizations should initially submit a "Request for Consideration." This should include: brief history of the organization, its goals and objectives, and the purpose for which the grant is requested. Additional information will be requested if the application falls within the foundation's areas of interest.

Deadline(s) No deadlines are announced.

467. The Harry S Truman Library Institute

Independence, MO 64050
(816) 833-1400

Awards for Advanced Scholars

Program Description The institute offers two awards to be given to persons who are engaged in a study of either the public career of Harry S Truman or some aspect of the history of the Truman Administration.

Eligibility/Limitations Applicants are usually postdoctoral scholars. A Senior Scholar Award is intended for individuals having a well-established publications record. The other award, the Scholar's Development Award, is intended primarily for younger postdoctoral scholars who have completed their dissertation and are working on their second book.

Fiscal Information The size of the awards will be based primarily on a proposed budget submitted by the applicant and may amount to as much as one-half of the applicant's academic-year salary.

Application Information Application forms and further information concerning the fellowship may be obtained by writing to the secretary of the institute.

Deadline(s) Applications must be submitted by December 15.

468. The Harry S Truman Library Institute

Independence, MO 64050
(816) 833-1400

Dissertation-Year Fellowships

Program Description The institute offers fellowships to individuals who have completed their dissertation research and are ready to begin writing on the public career of Harry S Truman and on the history of the Truman Administration.

Eligibility/Limitations Doctoral candidates who have completed their dissertation research and are ready to begin writing are eligible to apply.

Fiscal Information The grant carries an award in the amount of $16,000 for one academic year.

Application Information Application forms may be obtained from the secretary of the institute.

Deadline(s) Applications should be mailed to the secretary by February 1.

469. The Harry S Truman Library Institute
Independence, MO 64050
(816) 833-1400

Research Grants

Program Description The institute offers research grants to enable applicants to spend one to three weeks conducting research at the library. Applicants must be working on a project pertaining to the public career of Harry S Truman or to some facet of the history of the Truman Administration.

Eligibility/Limitations Graduate students and postdoctoral scholars are eligible to apply.

Fiscal Information The grant carries an award of up to $2,000.

Application Information Prospective applicants should submit a proposal describing the scope of their project and how it relates to material already published to the Committee on Research and Education at the institute.

Deadline(s) Qualified applicants may submit proposals to the committee at any time, but always at least 90 days before grant funds would be needed.

470. United States Arms Control and Disarmament Agency
Office of Public Affairs
320 21st Street NW
Washington, DC 20451
(202) 647-8677

Hubert H. Humphrey Fellowship

Program Description The U.S. Arms Control and Disarmament Agency offers fellowships in support of doctoral dissertation research in arms control and disarmament.

Eligibility/Limitations Ph.D. candidates and law candidates for the Juris Doctor or any higher degree are also eligible if they are writing a substantial paper in partial fulfillment of degree requirements.

Fiscal Information The stipend for Ph.D. candidates is $5,000 plus tuition and fees up to a maximum of $3,400. Stipends and tuition for law candidates will be prorated according to the credits given for the research paper.

Application Information For information and application materials write the program.

Deadline(s) The application deadline for awards is March 15.

Additional Information The William C. Foster Fellows Visiting Scholars Program provides scholars with an opportunity for active participation in the arms control and disarmament activities of the agency. Contact the agency for additional information.

471. United States Information Agency
Bureau of Educational and Cultural Affairs, Office of
   Private Sector Programs
301 4th Street, SW
Washington, DC 20547
(202) 485-7319

Grants Program for Private, Nonprofit Organizations in Support of International Educational and Cultural Activities

Program Description The primary purpose of this program is to support international public diplomacy objectives of the United States by stimulating and encouraging increased private sector commitment, activity, and resources. The office gives high priority to project proposals that establish or promote linkages between American and foreign professional organizations. Projects must include an international people-to-people component, have an educational or cultural focus, and demonstrate a substantial contribution to long-term communication and understanding between the United States and other countries. Proposals involving any area of the world are welcome, with special attention given to projects involving regions and countries which have participated less frequently in exchanges, such as Africa, Eastern Europe, the Near East, South and Southeast Asia.

Eligibility/Limitations The office works with U.S. not-for-profit organizations on cooperative international group projects which introduce American and foreign participants to one another's traditions, arts, social, economic, political structures, and international interests.

Fiscal Information Grant assistance constitutes only a portion of total project funding. Most funding assistance is limited to participant travel and per diem requirements with modest contributions to cover administrative costs. Grants are not ordinarily given to support performing arts tours, film festivals, plastic arts exhibitions, research projects or professional training, or youth or youth-related activities, or to fund publications.

Application Information Contact the Office of Private Sector Programs for application guidelines and additional information.

Deadline(s) The office accepts proposals from July 1 through September 30, for projects whose activities will begin between January 1 and June 30 of the following year.

472. United States Institute of Peace
1550 M Street, NW, Suite 700
Washington, DC 20005-1708
(202) 457-1706

Fellowships

CFDA Program Number 91.001

Program Description These fellowships enable outstanding professionals and scholars to undertake research and education projects that will increase knowledge and spread awareness among the public and policymakers regarding the nature of violent international conflict and the full range of ways to deal with it peacefully. Individuals from a wide range of backgrounds—higher education, government, diplomacy, international affairs, military service, law, the media, business, labor, religion, humanitarian affairs and others—are encouraged to propose innovative, carefully conceived fellowship projects reflecting diverse interests, project approaches, and communication mediums.

Eligibility/Limitations The competition for fellowships is open to persons from any country. Professionals and scholars in international peace and conflict management and students in recognized doctoral programs in American universities who have completed all required work toward their doctoral degrees except their dissertations are eligible to apply.

Fiscal Information Awards for Distinguished Fellows will not exceed $78,200; for Peace Fellows, $59,216; and for Peace Scholars (graduate students), $12,000 for one-year fellowships.

Application Information To obtain further information, contact the institute.

Deadline(s) The postmark deadline for Peace Scholar application is November 15. Postmark deadline for Distinguished Fellow and Peace Fellow applications is October 15.

473. United States Institute of Peace

1550 M Street, NW, Suite 700
Washington, DC 20005-1708
(202) 457-1706

Unsolicited Grants Program

CFDA Program Number 91.001

Program Description The United States Institute of Peace is an independent, nonpartisan federal institution created and wholly funded by Congress to strengthen the nation's capacity to promote the peaceful resolution of international conflict. The broad purposes for which the institute will consider grants include, but are not restricted to: research on the relationship between adherence to international human rights standards and international peace; research on perceptions of peace across political systems and ideologies; research on negotiations; research on the relationship between domestic political systems and the aggressive use of force; research on the mediation of political change; developing curricula and materials; assisting media programming; and developing library programs. Through its grants program, the institute funds research projects which address a broad range of topics on international conflict including the future of the NATO alliance; the role of third-party negotiators in the resolution of regional conflicts; international humanitarian law as it applies to armed conflict at sea; religious and ethical questions in war and peace; and the use of nonviolent sanctions in confronting political violence.

Sample Grants Support for research of regime-type in relation to success or failure of international arbitration and mediation, $10,000 to Boise State University, Boise ID (1990).

Eligibility/Limitations The institute provides support to nonprofit organizations, official public institutions, and individuals. Where applicants are employed by an eligible institution, such as a college or university, the institute prefers that grants be made through the institution rather than to the individual. There is no citizenship requirement.

Fiscal Information Most grants are one to two years in duration. While the average award is in the $25,000 to $35,000 range, grants as low as $3,000 and as large as $200,000 have been made. The actual amount of a grant is based on the proposed budget and subsequent negotiations with successful applicants.

Application Information For additional information and application forms contact the institute.

Deadline(s) The deadlines for receipt of applications are April 1 and October 1.

Additional Information In addition to its practice of providing support for unsolicited grant proposals, the institute solicits proposals that focus attention on certain themes and topics of special interest. Solicited grants topics are announced annually. The annual deadline for applications in the solicited grants competition is April 1. A separate brochure describing the solicited grants procedures and identifying current topics of interest may be obtained from the institute.

474. United States-Japan Foundation

145 East 32nd Street
New York, NY 10016
(212) 481-8753

Program Grants

Program Description The foundation carries out its mission through programs that create networks of Japanese and Americans working together on problems of common interest, that stimulate dialogue on the major policy issues in the bilateral relationship, and that enhance understanding of the cultural differences, as well as the shared values between our two democratic societies. The foundation's program interests are focused on the exchange of people and ideas, the creation and support of core groups, and pre-college education. In each of these areas, emphasis is given to projects that have national rather than local implications.

Sample Grants To support the third year of a joint study on the foreign policy of the Soviet Union by Japanese and American specialists, $125,817 to the Research Institute for Peace and Security, Tokyo, Japan (1988).

Eligibility/Limitations As a rule, grants cannot be made to individuals applying on their own behalf for independent study, research, travel, or participation in meetings. The foundation will, however, consider proposals consistent with its program interests from organizations which support the collective activities of individuals.

Fiscal Information Grants authorized in 1989 totaled over $4.4 million.

Application Information There are no formal grant application forms. Requests for grants are made in two stages, the first of which is a request for consideration. This request should be contained in a letter no longer than three pages. It should provide a description of the applicant organization; a summary of the proposed project; present sources of funds; and the amount of the proposed grant. If the foundation decides that it has an interest in the proposal, the proposer will then be asked to submit a detailed prospectus of the project.

Deadline(s) Requests for grants may be initiated at any time. Experience suggests that the amount of time required to adequately review a proposal prior to awarding a grant is six months to a year.

475. University of Pennsylvania

Coordinating Official, Humanities Coordinating
　Committee
16 College Hall
Philadelphia, PA 19104-6378
(215) 898-4940

Mellon Fellowships in the Humanities

Program Description No particular topic is designated as the focus for the Mellon Fellowships at the University of Pennsylvania. Proposals may represent any aspect of humanistic study and research except for educational curriculum building and performing arts. Preference is given to proposals that are interdisciplinary and that represent areas falling outside of the established boundaries of disciplines and departments.

Eligibility/Limitations Applications are invited from scholars who, by the time the fellowship commences, will have held the Ph.D. for not fewer than three and not more than eight years. Preference is given to candidates who have not previously utilized the resources of the University of Pennsylvania.

Fiscal Information Fellowships carry stipends in the amount of $28,500.

Application Information Application forms and additional information are available from the Humanities Coordinating Committee.

Deadline(s) Postmark deadline for applications is October 15 and nominations from deans, department chairs, or administrators must be received by August 1.

476. University of Pittsburgh

Director of Graduate Programs
910 Cathedral of Learning
Pittsburgh, PA 15269
(412) 624-6094

Andrew Mellon Postdoctoral Fellowships

Program Description These fellowships support advanced research and study in anthropology, astronomy, the biological sciences, economics, history, the humanities, mathematics and statistics, political science, physics, and sociology.

Eligibility/Limitations Young scholars in appropriate disciplines are eligible to apply.

Fiscal Information Awards carry a stipend of $21,000 for eleven months, with a supplement for travel and research expenses.

Academic year (nine-month) appointments are also available and carry a stipend of $17,200 plus supplement.

Application Information Additional information is available on request.

Deadline(s) The deadline for application is January 15.

477. W.E. Upjohn Institute for Employment Research
300 South Westnedge Avenue
Kalamazoo, MI 49007
(616) 343-5541

Grant Program

Program Description The W.E. Upjohn Institute for Employment Research has a grant program aimed at supporting policy-relevant research on employment and unemployment at the national, state, and local levels. The institute is particularly interested in receiving applications for study in the following categories: income replacement and social insurance programs; worker adjustment; labor-management relations; labor market dynamics and demographic change; international comparative research in labor markets; education's role in the labor market; and regional economic growth and development policy.

Sample Grants Support for a study on "An Analysis of Causes of Litigation in Worker's Compensation," University of Delaware (1989).

Fiscal Information The maximum grant is $45,000, although most grants will be for less. An additional amount, up to $25,000, may be awarded to conduct surveys or assemble new analytic data from administrative sources. The institute will not provide funds for overhead support.

Application Information Prospective applicants are encouraged to submit brief letters of inquiry so that the institute can determine the extent of its interest in the proposed study.

Deadline(s) There are two review cycles, with application closing dates of March 26 and September 24.

478. The Urban Institute
2100 M Street, NW
Washington, DC 20037
(202) 833-7200

Research Fellows Program

Program Description The purpose of the program is to expand the pool of public policy researchers in general and to increase the number of minority researchers. Successful candidates will work collaboratively with institute researchers on studies of social and economic issues such as: poverty and the urban underclass; immigration and the adaptation of immigrants to U.S. society; health care for uninsured workers and the poor; physician payment reform; long-term care; employment and training programs for welfare recipients; low-income housing and the homeless; education policies for a competitive work force; and child care and family policy.

Eligibility/Limitations Appointments will generally be made for 12 months in the following categories based on the successful candidates' research qualifications: research scholar—junior faculty members or other candidates with a Ph.D. with at least two years of relevant research experience; postdoctoral research fellow—candidates who have completed a Ph.D. within two years prior to beginning the fellowship; and research fellow—candidates with the master's degree.

Fiscal Information Salaries will be commensurate with qualifications and experience; full benefits will be provided.

Application Information Applications should include the following: resume; letter describing your experience and the research areas in which you are most interested; names, addresses, and telephones numbers of three individuals who are willing to provide recommendations; and undergraduate and graduate transcripts.

Deadline(s) Applications will be reviewed as they are received.

479. U.S. General Accounting Office
Doctoral Research Program, Training Institute
441 G Street, NW, Room 7822
Washington, DC 20548
(202) 275-8673

Doctoral Research Program

Program Description The U.S. General Accounting Office (GAO) is an independent agency in the legislative branch of the federal government. Each year GAO funds a few research opportunities for doctoral students. This program allows students to become actively involved in GAO work directly related to their research topic while they are gathering data for their dissertations.

Sample Grants Support for doctoral dissertation research on assessing decision making and dispute resolution in environmental policy, Vanderbilt University (1989). Support for doctoral dissertation research on inputs and outputs of the federal government's anticrime policies, University of Washington (1989).

Eligibility/Limitations To become eligible, an applicant must do the following: complete all course work leading to a doctoral degree, including any comprehensives that are prerequisites to doctoral candidacy, by the date of selection; be a U.S. citizen; be willing to work in Washington, DC area for the period of employment.

Fiscal Information Students will receive temporary appointments at the GS-9, step 1, level ($24,705 per year). A student with sufficient relevant work experience may receive a GS-11, step 1, appointment ($29,891 per year).

Application Information There are no application forms in this program. Students should contact the program coordinator who will refer them to a REAP member through whom they should apply.

Deadline(s) Completed applications must be received by REAP nominator by February 2.

480. USX Foundation Inc.
USX Tower
600 Grant Street, Room 2649
Pittsburgh, PA 15219-4776
(412) 433-5237

Grants

Program Description The USX Foundation provides financial support in a planned and balanced manner to a variety of selected organizations and projects of benefit to educational, scientific, civic, medical/health, cultural, and charitable activities.

Eligibility/Limitations Grants are generally awarded to tax-exempt organizations in areas where USX Corporation and its divisions and subsidiaries operate. The foundation does not make grants to individuals. Additionally, grants are not generally awarded for conferences, seminars, symposia, travel purposes, or for the publishing of books, magazines, films, or television productions.

Fiscal Information Grants awarded in 1988 totaled over $5.9 million.

Application Information There is no standard form which must be used to apply for a grant from the foundation. Requests, however, must be made in writing. A one- to two-page letter should be submitted which concisely and completely explains the request, with all appropriate documentation attached. Requests must include a copy of the IRS notification of tax-exempt status as a public foundation under section 501(c)(3) of the Internal Revenue Code. Requests for grants must include a copy of the requesting organization's current budget and the most recent audited financial report. To be given full and prompt consideration, requests should include the following information: a description of the project and its goals; the amount requested and the estimated cost of the project with a full and complete explanation of the necessity of funds requested in relation to the total requirements and resources; a statement of other sources of aid in hand (if any) and the amounts of such aid; a statement of other sources of anticipated aid where requests are pending or have yet to be made and the amounts requested; the name of the executive in charge of the organization's activities and the names of the members of the board of directors or trustees; the request prepared and signed by an authorized executive of the tax-exempt organization; and a statement of approval prepared and signed by the individual in charge of the parent organization, if the application originates in a subdivision of such entity.

Deadline(s) While requests are received throughout the year, it is strongly recommended that requests in the aid to education category be received by April 15 to be considered during the current fiscal year.

481. Vatican Film Library
Saint Louis University, The Pius XII Memorial Library
3650 Lindell Boulevard
Saint Louis, MO 63108

The Andrew W. Mellon Fellowship Program

Program Description The Andrew W. Mellon Foundation has made available a grant for a continuing postdoctoral fellowship program to assist scholars wishing to conduct research in the manuscript collections in the Vatican Film Library at Saint Louis University. Projects proposed for support under the fellowship program can be in such areas as classical languages and literature, paleography, scriptural and patristic studies, history, philosophy and sciences in the Middle Ages and the Renaissance, and Romance literature. There are also opportunities for supported research in the history of music manuscript illumination, mathematics and technology, theology, liturgy, Roman and canon law, and political theory.

Eligibility/Limitations Scholars with well-defined research projects which require the collections of the library are eligible to apply.

Fiscal Information The program provides travel expenses and a reasonable per diem for periods of research at the library ranging from two to eight weeks.

Application Information Applications should be submitted in the form of a project description including a precise statement of the project, an account of current research, a bibliography of the applicant's publications in areas related to the project, a curriculum vitae, a statement of the length of time for which support is requested, and letters from three persons qualified to judge the applicant's manuscript research skills in the project area.

Deadline(s) Fellowship projects can be scheduled only within one of the following periods: January 15 to May 15, June 1 to July 31, and September 1 to December 22. Persons wishing to apply for research support within one of these periods should first write to indicate the exact dates during which support is desired. These persons will be notified about the availability of facilities for the desired dates; and if facilities are available, these persons will be given a deadline by which project descriptions must be submitted.

482. The Earl Warren Legal Training Program, Inc.
99 Hudson Street, Suite 1600
New York, NY 10013
(212) 219-1900

Scholarships for Black Law Students

Program Description The goal of these scholarships is to increase the number of black lawyers in the United States.

Eligibility/Limitations Applicants must be citizens of the United States, must have taken the LSAT, and must be unconditionally

accepted at an accredited law school. The program prefers applicants under 35 years of age, those who have financial need, those who expect to practice where there are few black lawyers, those interested in public interest law, and those who plan to enroll in southern law schools. Successful applicants must attend law school full time and expect to graduate in three years.

Fiscal Information Scholarships are for one year and may be renewed based on academic performance.

Application Information Application forms are available by written request.

Deadline(s) Deadline for application is March 15.

483. Wayne State University
Archives of Labor and Urban Affairs
Walter P. Reuther Library
Detroit, MI 48202
(313) 577-4024

Travel Support Program

Program Description This program supports travel and expenses related to research scholars using the Walther P. Reuther Archives of Labor and Urban Affairs. The holdings of the archives include the papers of nine major unions, worker organizations and social reform organizations, as well as individuals active in these groups. In addition there is extensive material relating to urban affairs, women's history, international affairs, radical movements, ethnic minorities, blacks, and civil rights.

Eligibility/Limitations The grant program is intended primarily to aid graduate students working on their doctoral dissertations and younger faculty members who need financial assistance to undertake research projects.

Fiscal Information Awards of up to $700 are available.

Application Information For further information on the program and for application forms contact the archives.

484. Wenner-Gren Foundation for Anthropological Research
220 Fifth Avenue, 16th Floor
New York, NY 10001
(212) 683-5000

Richard Carley Hunt Memorial Postdoctoral Fellowships

Program Description Wenner-Gren's sphere of interest is the support of research in all branches of anthropology and in related disciplines pertaining to the sciences of man. Projects supported use cross-cultural, historical, biological, and linguistic approaches towards understanding man's origins, development, and variation. Special consideration is give to projects integrating two or more subfields of anthropology or related disciplines, particularly when combined with theoretical or methodological issues. Small grants are available to accredited scholars and to students enrolled for an advanced degree and to cover research expenses contemplated by the applicant. Small grants are geared to seeding innovative or untried approaches and ideas and provide material support to encourage aid from other funding agencies. The Richard Carley Hunt Memorial Postdoctoral Fellowships are awarded to aid completion of specific studies or for preparation for publication of field manuals.

Eligibility/Limitations Postdoctoral scholars may apply.

Fiscal Information The fellowship carries a stipend of no more than $5,000 and is nonrenewable. Foundation aid does not support large-scale projects, salary and/or fringe benefits, tuition, nonproject personnel, travel to national meetings, dissertation publication, institutional overhead, intermediary funding agencies, or building material and construction.

Application Information Applicants are required to submit project description forms, which are available on request. Project description forms will be accepted only in accordance with the current deadline schedule, available from the foundation. Applicants may submit a brief description of the proposed project, including anticipated starting date and required funding. If a project is considered eligible, a formal application will be invited and the appropriate forms and guidelines supplied.

Deadline(s) May 1 and November 1 for applications for funding during the calendar year following.

485. Wenner-Gren Foundation for Anthropological Research

220 Fifth Avenue, 16th Floor
New York, NY 10001
(212) 683-5000

Predoctoral Grants

Program Description Wenner-Gren's sphere of interest is the support of research in all branches of anthropology and in related disciplines pertaining to the sciences of man. Projects supported use cross-cultural, historical, biological, and linguistic approaches towards understanding man's origins, development, and variation. Special consideration is give to projects integrating two or more subfields of anthropology or related disciplines, particularly when combined with theoretical or methodological issues. Predoctoral grants are awarded to individuals to aid doctoral dissertation or thesis research.

Sample Grants For research on land rights and community definitions among Campa, Peru, $3,500 (1985). For research on customary law and land management in Swaziland, $1,300 (1985).

Eligibility/Limitations Applicants must be enrolled in a doctoral degree program. Qualified students of all nationalities are eligible.

Fiscal Information Fellowships carry an award of up to $10,000. Foundation aid does not support large-scale projects, salary and/or fringe benefits, tuition, nonproject personnel, travel to national meetings, dissertation publication, institutional overhead, intermediary funding agencies, or building material and construction.

Application Information Application must be made jointly with a senior scholar who will undertake responsibility for supervising the project. Application materials for fellowships are mailed on request. Applicants may submit a brief description of the proposed project, including anticipated starting date and required funding. If a project is considered eligible, a formal application will be invited and the appropriate forms and guidelines supplied.

Deadline(s) May 1 and November 1 for applications for funding during the calendar year following.

486. Wenner-Gren Foundation for Anthropological Research

220 Fifth Avenue, 16th Floor
New York, NY 10001
(212) 683-5000

Research Grants

Program Description Wenner-Gren's sphere of interest is the support of research in all branches of anthropology and in related disciplines pertaining to the sciences of man. Projects supported use cross-cultural, historical, biological, and linguistic approaches towards understanding man's origins, development, and variation. Special consideration is give to projects integrating two or more subfields of anthropology or related disciplines, particularly when combined with theoretical or methodological issues.

Sample Grants For research in Philippine law, $8,150 (1985).

Eligibility/Limitations Scholars holding the doctorate or equivalent qualification in anthropology or a related discipline who have established records of research and publication may apply.

Fiscal Information Grants are for amounts up to $10,000. Foundation aid does not support large-scale projects, salary and/or fringe benefits, tuition, nonproject personnel, travel to national

meetings, dissertation publication, institutional overhead, intermediary funding agencies, or building material and construction.

Application Information Application materials for senior scholar research stipends are mailed on request. Applicants may submit a brief description of the proposed project, including anticipated starting date and required funding. If a project is considered eligible, a formal application will be invited and the appropriate forms and guidelines supplied.

Deadline(s) May 1 and November 1 for applications for funding during the calendar year following.

Additional Information The foundation also provides conference support.

487. Woodrow Wilson International Center for Scholars

Smithsonian Institution Building
Washington, DC 20560
(202) 357-2841

American Society and Politics

Program Description The center seeks to commemorate through its residential fellowship program of advanced research both the scholarly depth and the public concerns of Woodrow Wilson. The center welcomes from individuals throughout the world outstanding project proposals representing a wide diversity of scholarly interests and approaches. Projects are encouraged from the whole range of the humanities and social sciences. Through the American Society and Politics Program the center seeks projects that develop new perspectives on the evolution of modern American society and that emphasize the interplay of ideas, values, and institutions in the emergence or our present civic culture. The program is particularly interested in research that makes use of historical perspective and that treats public issues within the context of changes in the patterns of American society as a whole.

Sample Grants Support to a professor of political science for research on the two foundings: republicanism and federalism in the American constitutional order (1989). Support to a professor of law for research toward a general theory of family law, Georgetown University (1989). Support to an associate director of public affairs for research on the philosophic dimension of constitutional interpretation, U.S. Department of Justice (1988).

Eligibility/Limitations Applicants from any country are eligible. Individuals with outstanding capabilities and experience from a wide variety of backgrounds (such as academia, journalism, government, labor, business, and the professions) are eligible for support. For academic participants, eligibility is limited to the postdoctoral level, and normally it is expected that academic candidates will have demonstrated their scholarly development by the publication of some major work beyond the Ph.D. dissertation. For participants from other fields, an equivalent degree or professional achievement is expected. Although English is the working language of the center, research and writing may be pursued in any language. The center's program is residential in character and fellows are expected to devote full time to the major research project proposed in the application.

Fiscal Information Because the center has a limited amount of fellowship support it strongly encourages applicants to seek concurrent sources of funding (i.e., other fellowships, foundation grants, sabbaticals, or other funding from their home institutions). Within this limitation and under a ceiling established by the board of trustees, the center attempts to meet a fellow's previous year's earned income. For scholars from abroad, the center attempts to approximate, but does not exceed, the salaries of U.S. scholars of comparable experience and position. Certain travel expenses for a fellow and accompanying spouse and younger children may also be provided. Appointments normally extend from four months to a year.

Application Information Additional information and application procedures are available from the center.

Deadline(s) The center holds one round of competitive selection per year. The deadline for receipt of applications and all supporting materials is October 1.

488. Woodrow Wilson International Center for Scholars

Smithsonian Institution Building
Washington, DC 20560
(202) 357-2841

Asia Program

Program Description The center seeks to commemorate through its residential fellowship program of advanced research both the scholarly depth and the public concerns of Woodrow Wilson. The center welcomes from individuals throughout the world outstanding project proposals representing a wide diversity of scholarly interests and approaches. Projects are encouraged from the whole range of the humanities and social sciences. The Asia program supports advanced research on Asian culture, history, politics, and society, and on America's relations with Asia. While the primary focus is on China and Japan, proposals on other countries of Northeast and Southeast Asia are welcomed as well. The program is interested in research that will both make a significant contribution to scholarship on Asia and simultaneously place important contemporary issues in a broader historical, cultural, philosophical, or strategic context.

Sample Grants Support to a professor of political science and Japanese studies for research on advisory bodies in Japan: the institutionalization of policy learning, equity, and consensus building (1989).

Eligibility/Limitations Applicants from any country are eligible. Individuals with outstanding capabilities and experience from a wide variety of backgrounds (such as academia, journalism, government, labor, business, and the professions) are eligible for support. For academic participants, eligibility is limited to the postdoctoral level, and normally it is expected that academic candidates will have demonstrated their scholarly development by the publication of some major work beyond the Ph.D. dissertation. For participants from other fields, an equivalent degree or professional achievement is expected. Although English is the working language of the center, research and writing may be pursued in any language. The center's program is residential in character and fellows are expected to devote full time to the major research project proposed in the application.

Fiscal Information Because the center has a limited amount of fellowship support it strongly encourages applicants to seek concurrent sources of funding (i.e., other fellowships, foundation grants, sabbaticals, or other funding from their home institutions). Within this limitation and under a ceiling established by the Board of Trustees, the center attempts to meet a fellow's previous year's earned income. For scholars from abroad, the center attempts to approximate, but does not exceed, the salaries of U.S. scholars of comparable experience and position. Certain travel expenses for a fellow and accompanying spouse and younger children may also be provided. Appointments normally extend from four months to a year.

Application Information Additional information and application procedures are available from the center.

Deadline(s) The center holds one round of competitive selection per year. The deadline for receipt of applications and all supporting materials is October 1.

489. Woodrow Wilson International Center for Scholars

Smithsonian Institution Building
Washington, DC 20560
(202) 357-2841

History, Culture, and Society

Program Description In this program—the largest and most diversified—the center accommodates fellows who work on geographical regions not represented by other programs (e.g., Africa, Europe, the Middle East, and South Asia), on comparative studies that cut across several global areas, or on international relations. The program is also receptive to projects that study the distant as well as the recent past and to those with theoretical, philosophical, or theological dimensions. It particularly welcomes projects that promise to make a major contribution to our understanding of the human condition or attempt broad synthesis involving different fields or different cultures.

Sample Grants Support to an associate professor of law for research on the modern application of Islamic public law and its implications for human rights and international relations, University of Khartoum (1988). Support to an international radio broadcaster, voice of America, for research on Berber nationalism in North Africa: ethnic identity, regional instability, and the rights of people (1988).

Eligibility/Limitations Projects are encouraged from the whole range of the humanities and social sciences. Applicants from any country are eligible. Individuals with outstanding capabilities and experience from a wide variety of backgrounds (such as academia, journalism, government, labor, business, and the professions) are eligible for support. For academic participants, eligibility is limited to the postdoctoral level, and normally it is expected that academic candidates will have demonstrated their scholarly development by the publication of some major work beyond the Ph.D. dissertation. For participants from other fields, an equivalent degree or professional achievement is expected. Although English is the working language of the center, research and writing may be pursued in any language. The center's program is residential in character and fellows are expected to devote full time to the major research project proposed in the application.

Fiscal Information Because the center has a limited amount of fellowship support it strongly encourages applicants to seek concurrent sources of funding (i.e., other fellowships, foundation grants, sabbaticals, or other funding from their home institutions). Within this limitation and under a ceiling established by the board of trustees, the center attempts to meet a fellow's previous year's earned income. Historically, stipends have been limited to $36,000 of center funds for the academic year. For scholars from abroad, the center attempts to approximate, but does not exceed, the salaries of U.S. scholars of comparable experience and position. Certain travel expenses for a fellow and accompanying spouse and younger children may also be provided. Appointments normally extend from four months to a year.

Application Information Additional information and application procedures are available from the center.

Deadline(s) The center holds one round of competitive selection per year. The deadline for receipt of applications and all supporting materials is October 1.

490. Woodrow Wilson International Center for Scholars

Smithsonian Institution Building
Washington, DC 20560
(202) 357-2841

International Security Studies Program

Program Description The center seeks to commemorate through its residential fellowship program of advanced research both the scholarly depth and the public concerns of Woodrow Wilson. The center welcomes from individuals throughout the world outstanding project proposals representing a wide diversity of scholarly interests and approaches. Projects are encouraged from the whole range of the humanities and social sciences. This program concentrates on fundamental security issues especially those involving the United States, Western Europe, and the Middle East. The program encourages projects that integrate different elements of policy, compare national or regional approaches, or apply historical perspective to questions of contemporary importance. Proposals including psychological or economic analysis are of special interest.

Sample Grants Support to a professor from Cambridge University, U.K., for research on the rise of the secret world: intelligence communities in the 20th century (1987).

Eligibility/Limitations Applicants from any country are eligible. Individuals with outstanding capabilities and experience from a wide variety of backgrounds (such as academia, journalism, government, labor, business, and the professions) are eligible for support. For academic participants, eligibility is limited to the postdoctoral level, and normally it is expected that academic candidates will have demonstrated their scholarly development by the publication of some major work beyond the Ph.D. dissertation. For participants from other fields, an equivalent degree or professional achievement is expected. Although English is the working language of the center, research and writing may be pursued in any language. The center's program is residential in character and fellows are expected to devote full time to the major research project proposed in the application.

Fiscal Information Because the center has a limited amount of fellowship support it strongly encourages applicants to seek concurrent sources of funding (i.e., other fellowships, foundation grants, sabbaticals, or other funding from their home institutions). Within this limitation and under a ceiling established by the board of trustees, the center attempts to meet a fellow's previous year's earned income. Historically, stipends have been limited to $36,000 of center funds for the academic year. For scholars from abroad, the center attempts to approximate, but does not exceed, the salaries of U.S. scholars of comparable experience and position. Certain travel expenses for a fellow and accompanying spouse and younger children may also be provided. Appointments normally extend from four months to a year.

Application Information Additional information and application procedures are available from the center.

Deadline(s) The center holds one round of competitive selection per year. The deadline for receipt of applications and all supporting materials is October 1.

491. Woodrow Wilson International Center for Scholars
Smithsonian Institution Building
Washington, DC 20560
(202) 357-2841

Kennan Institute for Advanced Russian Studies

Program Description The center seeks to commemorate through its residential fellowship program of advanced research both the scholarly depth and the public concerns of Woodrow Wilson. The center welcomes from individuals throughout the world outstanding project proposals representing a wide diversity of scholarly interests and approaches. Projects are encouraged from the whole range of the humanities and social sciences. This program supports advanced research on both contemporary and historical subjects on Russia and the U.S.S.R.

Sample Grants Support for a professor of history.

Eligibility/Limitations Applicants from any country are eligible. Individuals with outstanding capabilities and experience from a wide variety of backgrounds (such as academia, journalism, government, labor, business, and the professions) are eligible for support. For academic participants, eligibility is limited to the postdoctoral level, and normally it is expected that academic candidates will have demonstrated their scholarly development by the publication of some major work beyond the Ph.D. dissertation. For participants from other fields, an equivalent degree or professional achievement is expected. Although English is the working language of the center, research and writing may be pursued in any language. The center's program is residential in character and fellows are expected to devote full time to the major research project proposed in the application.

Fiscal Information Because the center has a limited amount of fellowship support it strongly encourages applicants to seek concurrent sources of funding (i.e., other fellowships, foundation grants, sabbaticals, or other funding from their home institu-

tions). Within this limitation and under a ceiling established by the board of trustees, the center attempts to meet a fellow's previous year's earned income. Historically, stipends have been limited to $36,000 of center funds for an academic year. For scholars from abroad, the center attempts to approximate, but does not exceed, the salaries of U.S. scholars of comparable experience and position. Certain travel expenses for a fellow and accompanying spouse and younger children may also be provided. Appointments normally extend from four months to a year.

Application Information Additional information and application procedures are available from the center.

Deadline(s) The center holds one round of competitive selection per year. The deadline for receipt of applications and all supporting materials is October 1.

Additional Information In addition to this program of fellowships, the Kennan Institute each year offers visiting grants that provide per diem support for up to one month for scholars in Russian/Soviet studies. In the awarding of visiting grants, preference is given to scholars who have recently completed their Ph.D.s and to those who have particular need for the resources of a major research library.

492. Woodrow Wilson International Center for Scholars
Smithsonian Institution Building
Washington, DC 20560
(202) 357-2841

Latin American Program

Program Description This program supports advanced research by social scientists and humanists in Latin America, the Caribbean, and inter-American affairs. Proposals on any subject will be carefully reviewed, and particular attention will be given to projects examining the interplay between cultural traditions and political institutions, the history of ideas, and the evolution of U.S.-Latin American relations. The process and prospects for redemocratization and the consequences of international economic policies for Latin America are continuing interests of the program.

Sample Grants Support for a professor of political science for research on community in Latin America: contract, property, and taxation, Oregon State University (1989).

Eligibility/Limitations Projects are encouraged from the whole range of the humanities and social sciences. Applicants from any country are eligible. Individuals with outstanding capabilities and experience from a wide variety of backgrounds (such as academia, journalism, government, labor, business, and the professions) are eligible for support. For academic participants, eligibility is limited to the postdoctoral level, and normally it is expected that academic candidates will have demonstrated their scholarly development by the publication of some major work beyond the Ph.D. dissertation. For participants from other fields, an equivalent degree or professional achievement is expected. Although English is the working language of the center, research and writing may be pursued in any language. The center's program is residential in character and fellows are expected to devote full time to the major research project proposed in the application.

Fiscal Information Because the center has a limited amount of fellowship support it strongly encourages applicants to seek concurrent sources of funding (i.e., other fellowships, foundation grants, sabbaticals, or other funding from their home institutions). Within this limitation and under a ceiling established by the board of trustees, the center attempts to meet a fellow's previous year's earned income. Historically, stipends have been limited to $36,000 of center funds for the academic year. For scholars from abroad, the center attempts to approximate, but does not exceed, the salaries of U.S. scholars of comparable experience and position. Certain travel expenses for a fellow and accompanying spouse and younger children may also be provided. Appointments normally extend from four months to a year.

Application Information Additional information and application procedures are available from the center.

Deadline(s) The center holds one round of competitive selection per year. The deadline for receipt of applications and all supporting materials is October 1.

493. The Woodrow Wilson International Center for Scholars

Smithsonian Institute Building
Washington, DC 20560
(202) 357-2841

East European Program

Program Description This program sponsors advanced research on Albania, Bulgaria, Czechoslovakia, Germany, Hungary, Poland, Romania and Yugoslavia. Particularly welcome are projects in the humanities and social sciences that are broad in scope: comparing cultures and institutions in the region and exploring the underlying historical patterns of political, national, social, cultural and economic development. The program seeks to advance scholarship on questions regarding the nature of East European identity and on those beliefs and values common to the European tradition as a whole.

Eligibility/Limitations Applications from any country are welcome. Individuals with outstanding capabilities and experience from a wide variety of backgrounds (including government, the corporate world, and the professions, as well as academia) are eligible for appointment. For academic participants, eligibility is limited to the postdoctoral level, and normally it is expected that academic candidates will have demonstrated their scholarly development by the publication of some major work beyond the Ph.D. dissertation. For other applicants, an equivalent degree of professional achievement is expected. Fellows do not pursue contract work.

Fiscal Information In no case can the center's stipend exceed $50,000; the average yearly stipend is approximately $36,000. Travel expenses for fellows, their spouses, and dependent children are also provided.

Application Information Additional information and application forms are available from the center.

Deadline(s) The deadline for receipt of applications is October 1.

Additional Information Under a separate application procedure, the East European program also offers a small number of short-term grants. Contact the center for additional information.

494. The Woodrow Wilson International Center for Scholars

Smithsonian Institute Building
Washington, DC 20560
(202) 357-2841

West European Program

Program Description This program seeks to examine in depth the values and traditions common to Western Europe. There is a preference for research that is broad and comparative rather than narrow and national. This program supports advanced research by scholars and practitioners in the humanities and social sciences on the 12 countries of the European Community, plus Austria, Finland, Norway, Sweden and Switzerland.

Sample Grants Support to a senior research fellow, Australian National University, for research on "From Natural Law to the Rights of Man" (1988). Support to a professor of comparative law for research on constitutional problems in the creation of a European monetary fund (1988).

Eligibility/Limitations Applications from any country are welcome. Individuals with outstanding capabilities and experience from a wide variety of backgrounds (including government, the corporate world, and the professions, as well as academia) are eligible for appointment. For academic participants, eligibility is limited to the postdoctoral level, and normally it is expected

that academic candidates will have demonstrated their scholarly development by the publication of some major work beyond the Ph.D. dissertation. For other applicants, an equivalent degree of professional achievement is expected. Fellows do not pursue contract work.

Fiscal Information In no case can the center's stipend exceed $50,000; the average yearly stipend is approximately $36,000. Travel expenses for fellows, their spouses, and dependent children are also provided.

Application Information Additional information and application forms are available from the center.

Deadline(s) The deadline for receipt of applications is October 1.

495. Woodrow Wilson National Fellowship Foundation

Newcombe Dissertation Fellowships
P.O. Box 642
Princeton, NJ 08542

Charlotte W. Newcombe Doctoral Dissertation Fellowships

Program Description These fellowships are designed to encourage original and significant study of ethical or religious values in all fields. In addition to topics in philosophy and religion, dissertations might consider the ethical implications of foreign policy, the values determining political decisions, the moral modes of other cultures, and religious or ethical values as reflected in history or literature.

Sample Grants For study of trials of conscience, trials of ambivalence—law storytelling and identity in the Republic of Ireland, a fellowship was awarded (1990). For study of religion and law in colonial New England, 1620-1730, a fellowship was awarded (1989).

Eligibility/Limitations An applicant must be a candidate for a Ph.D., Th.D. or Ed.D. degree at a graduate school in the United States. These awards are not designed to finance field work, but rather the last full year of research and writing.

Fiscal Information Fellows will receive $10,000 for 12 months of full-time dissertation research and writing.

Application Information Additional information and application forms are available from the foundation.

Deadline(s) Applications must be requested by December 11. Completed applications must be postmarked by January 1.

Additional Information The foundation also funds women's studies research grants for doctoral candidates to encourage original and significant research about women, and Spencer Dissertation-Year Fellowships in research related to education. Contact the foundation for additional information.

496. Women's Research and Education Institute (WREI)

1700 18th Street, NW, Suite 400
Washington, DC 20009
(202) 328-7070

Congressional Fellowships on Women and Public Policy

Program Description The fellowships are designed to train women as potential leaders in public policy formation and to examine issues from the perspective of the experiences and needs of women.

Eligibility/Limitations Any student in a graduate program anywhere in the United States is eligible. Applicants must have the approval of their academic adviser to register for six hours of fellowship credit at the home institution.

Fiscal Information Fellows receive a stipend of $9,000 for the academic year, from August through April. An additional sum of $500 is provided for the purchase of health insurance. FREI will also reimburse fellows up to a maximum of $1,500 for the cost of six hours of tuition at their home institutions.

Application Information Applications can be obtained only by written request from WREI and will be available after November 1.

Deadline(s) Three copies of applications and supporting materials are due by February 16.

497. Woods Hole Oceanographic Institution
Marine Policy Center
Woods Hole, MA 02543
(508) 548-1400, ext. 2449

Research Fellowships in Marine Policy and Ocean Management

Program Description The Woods Hole Oceanographic Institution offers fellowships to individuals in social sciences, law, the humanities, or natural sciences to apply their training to the legal, political, social, or economic problems or issues involved with the use of the oceans. Present research in the center includes marine policy problems and opportunities in developing countries; policy and management issues concerning fisheries, marine minerals, and coastal zone use; implications of the Law of the Sea Treaty for ocean activities; Arctic and Antarctic resource issues; and the use of scientific information in decision making and policy planning. Other research topics are also appropriate. Previous policy fellows have been trained in fields such as law, economics, anthropology, political science, sociology, international relations, engineering, marine science, and geography. The objective of the fellowship program is to provide an opportunity for research in marine policy problems which may require the interdisciplinary application of natural science, technology, and social science.

Eligibility/Limitations Applicants to the center must have completed a doctoral level degree or possess equivalent professional qualifications through career experience. The center also welcomes experienced professionals who can arrange a leave or sabbatical.

Fiscal Information Recent doctorates will receive a stipend for a period of one year and are eligible for group health insurance. In addition, modest research and travel funds will be made available. Recipients are initially appointed for one year; however, depending upon the nature and scope of the recipient's effort, opportunities may be available to continue their professional affiliation with MPOM/WHOI.

Application Information A complete application consists of an application form, transcripts of college and university records, at least three personal references, and a preliminary but precise proposal for the research project to be undertaken while in residence in Woods Hole.

Deadline(s) Applications should be made no later than January 15.

Additional Information Undergraduates who have completed their junior year and beginning graduate students may apply for Summer Student Fellowships in chemistry, engineering, geology, geophysics, mathematics, meteorology, physics, biology, oceanography, or marine policy. Contact the institution for additional information.

Subject Index

Sponsor Type Index

Listing of Sponsoring Organizations

AARP Andrus Foundation
1909 K Street, NW
Washington, DC 20049

ABA IOLTA Clearinghouse
750 North Lake Shore Drive
Chicago, IL 60611

Administrative Conference of the United States
2120 L Street, NW, Suite 500
Washington, DC 20037

Aetna Life & Casualty Foundation
151 Farmington Avenue
Hartford, CT 06156

The Ahmanson Foundation
9215 Wilshire Boulevard
Beverly Hills, CA 90210

Alcoa Foundation
1501 Alcoa Building
Pittsburgh, PA 15219-1850

American Anthropological Association
1703 New Hampshire Avenue, NW
Washington, DC 20009

American Antiquarian Society
185 Salisbury Street
Worcester, MA 01609-1634

American Association for State and Local History
172 Second Avenue North, Suite 102
Nashville, TN 37201

American Association of Law Libraries
53 West Jackson Boulevard, Suite 940
Chicago, IL 60604

American Association of University Women Educational Foundation
2401 Virginia Avenue, NW
Washington, DC 20037

American Bar Association
750 North Lake Shore Drive
Chicago, IL 60611

American Bar Foundation
750 North Lake Shore Drive
Chicago, IL 60611

American Conservation Association, Inc.
30 Rockefeller Plaza, Room 5402
New York, NY 10112

American Council of Learned Societies
228 East 45th Street
New York, NY 10017-3398

American Defense Institute
214 Massachusetts Avenue, NE, P.O. Box 2497
Washington, DC 20013-2497

American Express Philanthropic Program
American Express Plaza Tower
New York, NY 10285-4710

American Historical Association
400 A Street, SE
Washington, DC 20003

American Indian Graduate Center
4520 Montgomery Boulevard, NE
Albuquerque, NM 87109

American Institute of Indian Studies
1130 East 59th Street
Chicago, IL 60637

American Institute of Pakistan Studies
P.O. Box 7568
Winston-Salem, NC 27109

American Jewish Archives
3101 Clifton Avenue
Cincinnati, OH 45220

American Philosophical Society
104 South Fifth Street
Philadelphia, PA 19106-3387

The American Research Center in Egypt
50 Washington Square South
New York, NY 10003

American Research Institute in Turkey
33rd and Spruce Streets
Philadelphia, PA 19105

American Water Foundation
P.O. Box 15577
Denver, CO 80215

Ameritech Foundation
30 South Wacker Drive, 34th Floor
Chicago, IL 60606

Amoco Foundation Inc.
200 East Randolph Drive
Chicago, IL 60601

The Annenberg/CPB Project
901 E Street, NW
Washington, DC 20004

The Arca Foundation
1425 21st Street, NW
Washington, DC 20036

ARCO Foundation
515 South Flower Street
Los Angeles, CA 90071

The Asia Foundation
465 California Street
San Francisco, CA 94104

AT&T Foundation
550 Madison Avenue, Room 2700
New York, NY 10022

Mary Reynolds Babcock Foundation
102 Reynolda Village
Winston-Salem, NC 27106-5123

BankAmerica Foundation
P.O. Box 37000
San Francisco, CA 94137

Benton Foundation
1776 K Street, NW, Suite 605
Washington, DC 20006

The William Bingham Foundation
1250 Leader Building
Cleveland, OH 44114

Boehm Foundation
500 Fifth Avenue
New York, NY 10110-0296

Booth Ferris Foundation
30 Broad Street
New York, NY 10004

Borg-Warner Foundation
200 South Michigan Avenue
Chicago, IL 60604

The Robert Bosch Foundation
330 Seventh Avenue, 19th Floor
New York, NY 10001

The Boston Foundation Inc.
60 State Street, Sixth Floor
Boston, MA 02109

The Boston Globe Foundation
135 Morrissey Boulevard
Boston, MA 02107

The Lynde and Harry Bradley Foundation, Inc.
777 East Wisconsin Avenue, Suite 2285
Milwaukee, WI 53202

The Brookings Institution
1775 Massachusetts Avenue, NW
Washington, DC 20036

John Carter Brown Library
Box 1894
Providence, RI 02912

Mary Ingraham Bunting Institute of Radcliffe College
34 Concord Avenue
Cambridge, MA 02138

Florence V. Burden Foundation
630 Fifth Avenue, Suite 2900
New York, NY 10111

Bureau of Justice Statistics
Washington, DC 20531

Business and Professional Women's Foundation
2021 Massachusetts Avenue, NW
Washington, DC 20036

The Bydale Foundation
299 Park Avenue, 17th Floor
New York, NY 10171

Canadian Embassy
501 Pennsylvania Avenue, NW
Washington, DC 20001

Carnegie Corporation of New York
437 Madison Avenue
New York, NY 10022

The Carthage Foundation
P. O. Box 268
Pittsburgh, PA 15230

Mary Flagler Cary Charitable Trust
350 Fifth Avenue, Room 6622
New York, NY 10118

Center for Defense Information
1500 Massachusetts Avenue, NW
Washington, DC 20005

Center for International Affairs
1737 Cambridge Street, Room 416
Cambridge, MA 02138

Center for International Security and Arms Control
320 Galvez Street
Stanford, CA 94305-6165

Center for Italian Renaissance Studies
401 Boylston Hall
Cambridge, MA 02138

Center for Medieval and Renaissance Studies
405 Hilgard Avenue
Los Angeles, CA 90024-1485

Center for the Humanities
The Center for the Humanities
Middletown, CT 06457

Center for the Study of Human Rights
1108 International Affairs Building
New York, NY 10027

Center for Women in Government
1400 Washington Avenue, Draper Hall, Room 302
Albany, NY 12222

Chevron U.S.A. Inc.
P.O. Box 7753
San Francisco, CA 94120-7753

The Edna McConnell Clark Foundation
250 Park Avenue
New York, NY 10017

Robert Sterling Clark Foundation, Inc.
112 East 64th Street
New York, NY 10021

The Cleveland Foundation
1400 Hanna Building
Cleveland, OH 44115

College of William and Mary
Marshall-Wythe School of Law
Williamsburg, VA 23185

Columbia Foundation
1090 Sansome Street
San Francisco, CA 94111

Committee on International Security
1737 Cambridge Street
Cambridge, MA 02138

Committee on Scholarly Communication with the People's Republic of China
2101 Constitution Avenue, NW
Washington, DC 20418

Compton Foundation
10 Hanover Square
New York, NY 10005

The Conservation and Research Foundation
Connecticut College, Foundation Call Box
New London, CT 06320

Consulate General of Japan
250 East First Street, Suite 1507
Los Angeles, CA 90012

Corporation for Public Broadcasting
901 E Street, NW
Washington, DC 20004-2006

Council for European Studies
Box 44 Schermerhorn
New York, NY 10027

Council for International Exchange of Scholars
3400 International Drive, NW, Suite M-500
Washington, DC 20008-3097

Council on Foreign Relations
58 East 68th Street
New York, NY 10021

Council on Legal Education Opportunity
1800 M Street, NW, Suite 290, North Lobby
Washington, DC 20036

Council on Library Resources
1785 Massachusetts Avenue, NW, Suite 313
Washington, DC 20036

William Nelson Cromwell Foundation
250 Park Avenue
New York, NY 10177

The Charles E. Culpeper Foundation, Inc.
Ten Stamford Forum, Suite 800
Stamford, CT 06901

Cummins Engine Foundation
Mail Code 60814, Box 3005
Columbus, IN 47202-3005

Charles and Margaret Hall Cushwa Center
Room 614, Memorial Library
Notre Dame, IN 46556

The Danforth Foundation
231 South Bemiston Avenue, Suite 580
St. Louis, MO 63105-1903

Shelby Cullom Davis Center for Historical Studies
129 Dickinson Hall
Princeton, NJ 08544-1017

Dayton Hudson Foundation
777 Nicollet Mall
Minneapolis, MN 55402-2055

Deer Creek Foundation
818 Olive Street, Suite 949
St. Louis, MO 63101

The Gladys Krieble Delmas Foundation
40 West 57th Street, 27th Floor
New York, NY 10019

Department of Education
7th & D Streets, SW
Washington, DC 20202

The Dirksen Congressional Center
Broadway & Fourth Street
Pekin, IL 61554

Geraldine R. Dodge Foundation, Inc.
95 Madison Avenue, P.O. Box 1239
Morristown, NJ 07962-1239

The William H. Donner Foundation, Inc.
500 Fifth Avenue, Suite 1230
New York, NY 10110

Earhart Foundation
2929 Plymouth Road, Plymouth Building, Suite 204
Ann Arbor, MI 48105

The Educational Foundation of America
23161 Ventura Boulevard, Suite 201
Woodland Hills, CA 91364

Environmental Law Institute
1616 P Street, NW
Washington, DC 20036

Ernst & Young Foundation
227 Park Avenue
New York, NY 10172

Exxon Corporation
225 East John W. Carpenter Freeway
Irving, TX 75062

Exxon Education Foundation
P.O. Box 101
Florham Park, NJ 07932-1198

The FERIS Foundation of America
34 South Oak Ridge Road
Mount Kisco, NY 10549

Firestone Trust Fund
205 North Michigan Avenue, Suite 3800
Chicago, IL 60601-5965

The Fluor Foundation
3333 Michelson Drive
Irvine, CA 92730

Folger Shakespeare Library
201 East Capitol Street, SE
Washington, DC 20003

The Ford Foundation
320 East 43rd Street
New York, NY 10017

Ford Motor Company Fund
The American Road, P.O. Box 1899
Dearborn, MI 48121-1899

Foreign Policy Research Institute
3615 Chestnut Street
Philadelphia, PA 19104

Foundation for Child Development
345 East 46th Street
New York, NY 10017

The Frost Foundation, Ltd.
650 South Cherry Street, Suite 205
Denver, CO 80222

Lloyd A. Fry Foundation
135 South LaSalle Street, Suite 1910
Chicago, IL 60603

Fund for Research on Dispute Resolution
1901 L Street, NW, Suite 600
Washington, DC 20036

Gates Foundation
3200 Cherry Creek South Drive, Suite 630
Denver, CO 80209-3247

General Electric Foundations
3135 Easton Turnpike
Fairfield, CT 06431

General Foods
250 North Street
White Plains, NY 10625

General Mills Foundation
P.O. Box 1113
Minneapolis, MN 55440

General Motors Foundation, Inc.
3044 West Grand Boulevard
Detroit, MI 48202-3091

General Semantics Foundation
14 Charcoal Hill
Westport, CT 06880

General Service Foundation
P.O. Box 4659
Boulder, CO 80306

The Wallace Alexander Gerbode Foundation
470 Columbus Avenue, Suite 209
San Francisco, CA 94133

German Academic Exchange Service (DAAD)
950 Third Avenue, 19th Floor
New York, NY 10022

The German Marshall Fund of the United States
11 Dupont Circle, NW, Suite 750
Washington, DC 20036

William T. Grant Foundation
515 Madison Avenue
New York, NY 10022-5403

The Daniel and Florence Guggenheim Foundation
950 Third Avenue
New York, NY 10022

The Harry Frank Guggenheim Foundation
527 Madison Avenue
New York, NY 10022-4301

John Simon Guggenheim Memorial Foundation
90 Park Avenue
New York, NY 10016

The George Gund Foundation
One Erieview Plaza
Cleveland, OH 44114-1773

Hagley Museum and Library
P.O. Box 3630
Wilmington, DE 19807

The Hague Academy of International Law
Peace Palace
Carnegieplein 2, 2517 KJ, The Hague
the Netherlands

Harvard University Mellon Faculty Fellowships
Lamont Library 202
Cambridge, MA 02138

The Hastings Center
255 Elm Road
Briarcliff Manor, NY 10510

The Hearst Foundations
90 New Montgomery Street, Suite 1212
San Francisco, CA 94105

The William R. and Flora L. Hewlett Foundation
525 Middlefield Road
Menlo Park, CA 94025-3495

The Hitachi Foundation
1509 22nd Street, NW
Washington, DC 20037

The Honor Society of Phi Kappa Phi
P.O. Box 16000
Baton Rouge, LA 70893

Hoover Institution on War, Revolution and Peace
Stanford University
Stanford, CA 94305-6010

Hoover Presidential Library Association, Inc.
P.O. Box 696
West Branch, IA 52358

Houston Endowment, Inc.
P.O. Box 52338
Houston, TX 77052

Hudson River Foundation
40 West 20th Street, 9th Floor
New York, NY 10011

The S.S. Huebner Foundation for Insurance Education
3641 Locust Walk
Philadelphia, PA 19104

Immigration History Research Center
826 Berry Street
St. Paul, MN 55114

The Institute for Advanced Study
Olden Lane
Princeton, NJ 08540

Institute for Humane Studies
4400 University Drive
Fairfax, VA 22030

Institute for Research on Poverty
1180 Observatory Drive, 3412 Social Science Building
Madison, WI 53706

Institute for the Study of World Politics
1755 Massachusetts Avenue, NW, Suite 500
Washington, DC 20036

Institute of Current World Affairs—The Crane-Rogers Foundation
Wheelock House, 4 West Wheelock Street
Hanover, NH 03755

Institute of International Education
809 United Nations Plaza
New York, NY 10017-3580

Institute of World Affairs
375 Twin Lakes Road
Salisbury, CT 06068

Inter-American Bar Foundation
1819 H Street, NW, Suite 310
Washington, DC 20006

Inter-American Foundation
P.O. Box 9486
Arlington, VA 22209-0486

International Foundation of Employee Benefit Plans
18700 West Bluemound Road, P.O. Box 69
Brookfield, WI 53008-0069

International Research & Exchanges Board
126 Alexander Street
Princeton, NJ 08540-7102

The International Society for General Semantics
P.O. Box 2469
San Francisco, CA 94126

The James Irvine Foundation
One Market Plaza, Spear Tower, Suite 1715
San Francisco, CA 94105

Ittleson Foundation
645 Madison Avenue, 16th Floor
New York, NY 10022

The Japan Foundation
142 West 57th Street, 6th Floor
New York, NY 10019

Japan-United States Friendship Commission
1200 Pennsylvania Avenue, NW, Room 3416
Washington, DC 20004

The J.M. Foundation
60 East 42nd Street, Room 1651
New York, NY 10165

The Lyndon Baines Johnson Foundation
2313 Red River
Austin, TX 78705

The Robert Wood Johnson Foundation
College Road, P.O. Box 2316
Princeton, NJ 08543

The Fletcher Jones Foundation
One Wilshire Building, Suite 1210, 624 South Grand Avenue
Los Angeles, CA 90017

W. Alton Jones Foundation
433 Park Street
Charlottesville, VA 22901

The Joyce Foundation
135 South LaSalle Street, Suite 4010
Chicago, IL 60603-4886

Judicial Conference of the United States
231 West Lafayette Boulevard, Room 240
Detroit, MI 48226

The J.M. Kaplan Fund, Inc.
330 Madison Avenue
New York, NY 10017

The Helen Kellogg Institute for International Studies
University of Notre Dame
Notre Dame, IN 46556

W. K. Kellogg Foundation
400 North Avenue
Battle Creek, MI 49017-3398

The Joseph P. Kennedy, Jr. Foundation
1350 New York Avenue, NW, Suite 500
Washington, DC 20005

Josiah W. and Bessie H. Kline Foundation, Inc.
42 Kline Village
Harrisburg, PA 17104

KPMG Peat Marwick Foundation
Three Chestnut Ridge Road
Montvale, NJ 07645-0435

Kraft Foundation
Kraft Court
Glenview, IL 60025

The Kresge Foundation
3215 West Big Beaver Road, P.O. Box 3151
Troy, MI 48007-3151

Legal Services Corporation
400 Virginia Avenue, SW
Washington, DC 20024-2751

The Max and Anna Levinson Foundation
P.O. Box 125
Costilla, NM 87524

Library Company of Philadelphia
1314 Locust Street
Philadelphia, PA 19107

Lilly Endowment, Inc.
2801 North Meridian Street, P.O. Box 88068
Indianapolis, IN 46208

The Charles A. Lindbergh Fund, Inc.
P.O. Box O
Summit, NJ 07901

The Henry Luce Foundation, Inc.
111 West 50th Street
New York, NY 10020

J. Roderick MacArthur Foundation
9333 North Milwaukee Avenue
Niles, IL 60648

The John D. and Catherine T. MacArthur Foundation
140 South Dearborn Street
Chicago, IL 60603

The John and Mary R. Markle Foundation
75 Rockefeller Plaza
New York, NY 10019-6908

McDonnell Douglas Foundation
P.O. Box 516
St. Louis, MO 63166-0516

James S. McDonnell Foundation
1034 South Brentwood Boulevard, Suite 1610
St. Louis, MO 63117

The Andrew W. Mellon Foundation
140 East 62nd Street
New York, NY 10021

Richard King Mellon Foundation
525 William Penn Place, 39th Floor
Pittsburgh, PA 15219

The John Merck Fund
11 Beacon Street, Suite 600
Boston, MA 02108

Metropolitan Life Foundation
One Madison Avenue
New York, NY 10010-3690

Mexican American Legal Defense and Educational Fund (MALDEF)
634 South Spring Street, 11th Floor
Los Angeles, CA 90014

The Eugene and Agnes E. Meyer Foundation
1400 16th Street, NW, Suite 360
Washington, DC 20036

Meyer Memorial Trust
1515 SW Fifth Avenue, Suite 500
Portland, OR 97201

The Michigan Society of Fellows
The University of Michigan
Ann Arbor, MI 48109-1070

Mobil Foundation, Inc.
3225 Gallows Road, Room 3D809
Fairfax, VA 22037-0001

Charles Stewart Mott Foundation
1200 Mott Foundation Building
Flint, MI 48502-1851

M.J. Murdock Charitable Trust
P.O. Box 1618
Vancouver, WA 98668

The Henry A. Murray Research Center of Radcliffe College
10 Garden Street
Cambridge, MA 02138

National Academy of Education
CERAS-507
Stanford, CA 94305-3084

National Association for Public Interest Law
1666 Connecticut Avenue, NW, Suite 424
Washington, DC 20009

The National Council for Soviet and East European Research
1755 Massachusetts Avenue, NW, Suite 304
Washington, DC 20036

National Endowment for Democracy
1101 15th Street, NW, Suite 203
Washington, DC 20005

National Endowment for the Humanities
1100 Pennsylvania Avenue, NW
Washington, DC 20506

National Federation of the Blind
814 Fourth Avenue, Grinnell State Bank Building, Suite 200
Grinnell, IA 50112

National Hispanic Scholarship Fund
P.O. Box 748
San Francisco, CA 94101

National Historical Publications and Records Commission
National Archives Building
Washington, DC 20408

National Humanities Center
7 Alexander Drive, P.O. Box 12256
Research Triangle Park, NC 27709

National Institute for Dispute Resolution
1901 L Street, NW, Suite 600
Washington, DC 20036

National Institute for Juvenile Justice and Delinquency Prevention
633 Indiana Avenue, NW
Washington, DC 20531

National Institute of Justice
633 Indiana Avenue, NW, Room 900
Washington, DC 20531

National Institute of Mental Health
5600 Fishers Lane
Rockville, MD 20857

National Institute on Aging
9000 Rockville Pike, Building 31
Bethesda, MD 20892

National Institute on Alcohol Abuse and Alcoholism
5600 Fishers Lane
Rockville, MD 20857

National Institutes of Health
Building 38A, Room 613
Bethesda, MD 20894

National Italian American Foundation
666 11th Street, NW, Suite #800
Washington, DC 20001

National Lawyers Guild
1205 Smith Tower
Seattle, WA 98104

National Library of Medicine
8600 Rockville Pike, Building 38
Bethesda, MD 20894

National Research Council
2101 Constitution Avenue, NW
Washington, DC 20418

National Science Foundation
1800 G Street, NW
Washington, DC 20550

National Wildlife Federation
1400 16th Street, NW
Washington, DC 20036-2266

The Needmor Fund
1730 15th Street
Boulder, CO 80302

The New World Foundation
100 East 85th Street
New York, NY 10028

The New York Community Trust
415 Madison Avenue
New York, NY 10017

The New York Times Company Foundation, Inc.
229 West 43rd Street
New York, NY 10036

The Newberry Library
60 West Walton Street
Chicago, IL 60610

Northwest Area Foundation
West 975 First National Bank Building
St. Paul, MN 55101-1373

The Norwegian Information Service
825 Third Avenue, 17th Floor
New York, NY 10022-7584

Jessie Smith Noyes Foundation
16 East 34th Street
New York, NY 10016

Office of Technology Assessment
600 Pennsylvania Avenue, SE
Washington, DC 20510-8025

John M. Olin Foundation, Inc.
100 Park Avenue, Suite 2701
New York, NY 10017

Ottinger Foundation
1601 Connecticut Avenue, NW, Suite 803
Washington, DC 20009

Pacific Telesis Foundation
130 Kearny Street, Room 3351
San Francisco, CA 94108

The David and Lucile Packard Foundation
300 Second Street, Suite 200
Los Altos, CA 94022

William Penn Foundation
1630 Locust Street
Philadelphia, PA 19103-6305

The Pew Charitable Trusts
Three Parkway, Suite 501
Philadelphia, PA 19102-1305

The Pillsbury Company Foundation
200 South Sixth Street, Pillsbury Center
Minneapolis, MN 55402-1464

PPG Industries Foundation
One PPG Place
Pittsburgh, PA 15272

President's Commission on White House Fellowships
712 Jackson Place, NW
Washington, DC 20503

The Prospect Hill Foundation
420 Lexington Avenue, Suite 3020
New York, NY 10170

The Prudential Foundation
751 Broad Street, 15th Floor
Newark, NJ 07102-3777

Public Welfare Foundation
2600 Virginia Avenue, NW, Suite 505
Washington, DC 20037-1977

Resources for the Future
1616 P Street, NW
Washington, DC 20036

The Retirement Research Foundation
1300 West Higgins Road, Suite #214
Park Ridge, IL 60068

Smith Richardson Foundation, Inc.
210 East 86th Street
New York, NY 10028

Rockefeller Archive Center
15 Dayton Avenue, Pocantico Hills
North Tarrytown, NY 10591

Rockefeller Brothers Fund
1290 Avenue of the Americas
New York, NY 10104

The Rockefeller Foundation
1133 Avenue of the Americas
New York, NY 10036

Rosenberg Foundation
210 Post Street
San Francisco, CA 94108-5172

Samuel Rubin Foundation
777 United Nations Plaza
New York, NY 10017-3521

Helena Rubinstein Foundation
405 Lexington Avenue
New York, NY 10174

Russell Sage Foundation
112 East 64th Street
New York, NY 10021

Santa Fe Southern Pacific Foundation
224 South Michigan Avenue
Chicago, IL 60604-2401

Sara Lee Foundation
Three First National Plaza
Chicago, IL 60602-4206

Sarah Scaife Foundation
P.O. Box 268
Pittsburgh, PA 15230

Dr. Scholl Foundation
11 South LaSalle Street, Suite 2100
Chicago, IL 60603

The School of American Research
P.O. Box 2188
Santa Fe, NM 87504

The Florence and John Schumann Foundation
33 Park Street
Montclair, NJ 07042

Scoville Peace Fellowship Program
110 Maryland Avenue, NE, Room 211
Washington, DC 20002

Gardiner Howland Shaw Foundation
45 School Street
Boston, MA 02108

Shell Oil Company Foundation
Two Shell Plaza, P.O. Box 2099
Houston, TX 77252

Skadden Fellowship Program
919 Third Avenue
New York, NY 10022

The L.J. Skaggs and Mary C. Skaggs Foundation
1221 Broadway, 21st Floor
Oakland, CA 94612-1837

The Skillman Foundation
333 West Fort Street, Suite 1350
Detroit, MI 48226

Alfred P. Sloan Foundation
630 Fifth Avenue, Suite 2550
New York, NY 10111

Social Science Research Council
605 Third Avenue
New York, NY 10158

Society of Fellows in the Humanities
Box 100 Central Mail Room
New York, NY 10027

The Sophia Fund
53 West Jackson Boulevard
Chicago, IL 60604

The Space Foundation
P.O. Box 58501
Houston, TX 77258

The Spencer Foundation
875 North Michigan Avenue
Chicago, IL 60611

Stanford Humanities Center
Mariposa House
Stanford, CA 94305-8630

The Starr Foundation
70 Pine Street
New York, NY 10270

State Justice Institute
120 South Fairfax Street
Alexandria, VA 22314

Philip M. Stern Family Fund
1601 Connecticut Avenue, NW, Suite 803
Washington, DC 20009

Sun Company, Inc.
100 Matsonford Road
Radnor, PA 19087-4597

Supreme Court of the United States
Washington, DC 20543

Texaco Philanthropic Foundation Inc.
2000 Westchester Avenue
White Planes, NY 10650

The Tinker Foundation Incorporated
55 East 59th Street
New York, NY 10022

The Travelers Companies Foundation
One Tower Square
Hartford, CT 06115

The Harry S Truman Library Institute
Independence, MO 64050

United States Arms Control and Disarmament Agency
320 21st Street NW
Washington, DC 20451

United States Information Agency
301 4th Street, SW
Washington, DC 20547

United States Institute of Peace
1550 M Street, NW, Suite 700
Washington, DC 20005-1708

United States-Japan Foundation
145 East 32nd Street
New York, NY 10016

University of Pennsylvania
16 College Hall
Philadelphia, PA 19104-6378

University of Pittsburgh
910 Cathedral of Learning
Pittsburgh, PA 15269

W.E. Upjohn Institute for Employment Research
300 South Westnedge Avenue
Kalamazoo, MI 49007

The Urban Institute
2100 M Street, NW
Washington, DC 20037

U.S. General Accounting Office
441 G Street, NW, Room 7822
Washington, DC 20548

USX Foundation Inc.
600 Grant Street, Room 2649
Pittsburgh, PA 15219-4776

Vatican Film Library
3650 Lindell Boulevard
Saint Louis, MO 63108

The Earl Warren Legal Training Program, Inc.
99 Hudson Street, Suite 1600
New York, NY 10013

Wayne State University
Walter P. Reuther Library
Detroit, MI 48202

Wenner-Gren Foundation for Anthropological Research
220 Fifth Avenue, 16th Floor
New York, NY 10001

Woodrow Wilson International Center for Scholars
Smithsonian Institution Building
Washington, DC 20560

Woodrow Wilson National Fellowship Foundation
P.O. Box 642
Princeton, NJ 08542

Women's Research and Education Institute (WREI)
1700 18th Street, NW, Suite 400
Washington, DC 20009

Woods Hole Oceanographic Institution
Marine Policy Center
Woods Hole, MA 02543

Selected Bibliography

Printed Materials

Academic Research Information Service (ARIS). San Francisco: Academic Research Information System. Monthly newsletters (*Biomedical Sciences Report, Creative Arts and Humanities Report, Social and Natural Sciences Report*) detailing grant information and deadlines of federal programs, foundations, associations, organizations, and universities.

America's Newest Foundations. 2nd ed. Washington, DC: The Taft Group, 1988. A listing of new and emerging foundations.

Annual Register of Grant Support, 1991. 24th ed. Wilmette, IL: National Register Publishing Co., 1990. An annual publication listing over 2,800 programs sponsored by foundations, the federal government, and professional and educational associations/organizations.

Catalog of Federal Domestic Assistance. 24th ed. Washington, DC: U.S. Office of Management and Budget, 1990. An annual publication, plus semi-annual update, of federal grants, programs, technical assistance support, and services.

The Chronicle of Higher Education. Washington, DC: The Chronicle of Higher Education, Inc. A weekly publication which includes grant and fellowship information and deadlines.

The College Blue Book: Scholarships, Fellowships, Grants and Loans. 22nd ed. New York: MacMillan Publishing Company, 1989. A compilation of sources of financial support for a college education.

Commerce Business Daily. Washington, DC: Superintendent of Documents, U.S. Government Printing Office. A daily publication, Monday through Friday, which includes information about grants and contracts from the federal government.

Corporate 500: The Directory of Corporate Philanthropy. 8th ed. San Francisco, CA: Public Management Institute, 1989. An annual publication listing corporations with direct-giving programs and foundations.

Corporate Foundation Profiles. 6th ed. New York: The Foundation Center, 1990. A publication listing approximately 250 corporate foundation profiles.

Directory of Financial Aid for Minorities, 1989-1990. Gail Ann Schlachter, ed. Redwood City, CA: Reference Service Press, 1989. A compilation of funding sources for Native Americans, Hispanic Americans, Asian Americans, African Americans, and other minorities.

Directory of Financial Aid for Women, 1989-1990. Gail Ann Schlachter, ed. Redwood City, CA: Reference Service Press, 1987. A listing of funding sources for women.

Directory of Grants in the Humanities, 1990/91. Phoenix, AZ: The Oryx Press, 1990. An annual publication listing over 3,500 humanities-related funding sources.

Directory of Research Grants, 1991. Phoenix, AZ: The Oryx Press, 1991. An annual publication listing over 5,500 funding sources including foundations, the federal government, and other private-sector monies.

Federal Grants & Contracts Weekly. Arlington, VA: Capitol Publications, Inc. Published weekly; lists grant and contract announcements, RFPs and RFAs of the federal government of interest to the academic community.

Federal Register. Washington, DC: Superintendent of Documents, U.S. Government Printing Office. Published daily and includes public regulations and legal notices issued by federal agencies, as well as RFPs and RFAs.

Federal Research Report. Silver Spring, MD: Business Publishers, Inc. Published weekly; lists federal contract and grant opportunities.

Foundation Directory. 13th ed. New York: The Foundation Center, 1990. An annual publication listing over 7,600 foundations in the million-dollar asset range or above.

Foundation Grants Index. 19th ed. New York: The Foundation Center, 1990. An annual publication listing over 45,000 foundation grant disbursements of $5,000 or more awarded by more than 450 major U.S. foundations.

Foundation Grants to Individuals. 6th ed. New York: The Foundation Center, 1988. A listing of foundation funding sources designed for individual applicants including unaffiliated scholars.

Funding for Anthropological Research. Karen Cantrell and Denise Wallen, eds. Phoenix, AZ: The Oryx Press, 1986. A compilation of over 700 sources of support for anthropological research, broadly defined.

Funding for Research, Study and Travel: Latin America and the Caribbean. Karen Cantrell and Denise Wallen, eds. Phoenix, AZ: The Oryx Press, 1987. A listing of approximately 400 sources of support for research, study and travel in or concerning Latin America or the Caribbean.

Funding for Research, Study and Travel: The People's Republic of China. Denise Wallen and Karen Cantrell, eds. Phoenix, AZ: The Oryx Press, 1987. A listing of over 300 sources of support for research, study, and travel in or concerning the PRC.

The Grant Advisor. Arlington, VA: Toft Consulting. Published monthly; lists grant opportunity information on federal and nonfederal sources of support.

Grant Seekers Guide. 3rd ed. Jill R. Shellow, ed. Mount Kisco, NY: Moyer Bell Ltd., 1989. A listing of change-oriented foundations which support projects and programs.

Grants and Fellowships of Interest to Historians. David Ransel, ed. Washington, DC: American Historical Association, 1989. A listing of over 300 funding sources in support of historical research.

Grants for Graduate Students, 1989-1990. 2nd ed. John H. Wells and Amy J. Goldstein, eds. Princeton, NJ: Peterson's Guides, Inc., 1989. A compilation of 695 fellowships, grants, and other programs that provide support to graduate students.

Grants Magazine. New York: Plenum Publishing Corporation. Quarterly publication containing information on corporation, foundation, and government grants, and information on current funding trends and programs.

The Grants Register, 1991-1993. Craig Lerner, ed. New York: St. Martins Press, 1990. A biannual publication listing sources of support from international and national government agencies, foundations, associations, and organizations.

Humanities. Washington, DC: Superintendent of Documents, U.S. Government Printing Office. A bimonthly review of National Endowment for the Humanities programs and deadlines.

The International Foundation Directory. 4th ed. H.V. Hodson, consultant ed. Detroit, MI: Gale Research Co., 1986. A listing of over 700 foundations which provide transnational support.

National Data Book. 14th ed. New York: The Foundation Center, 1990. A listing of over 24,000 foundation names, addresses, and principal officers in the United States.

National Directory of Corporate Giving. Suzanne W. Hale, ed. New York: The Foundation Center, 1989. This first edition profiles over 1,500 companies making contributions to nonprofit organizations.

National Guide to Foundation Funding in Higher Education. Stan Olson and Ruth Kovacs, eds. New York: The Foundation Center, 1989. A listing of 2,905 foundations that hold assets of $1 million or more or whose annual giving totals at least $100,000 that have a stated interest or report grant activity in higher education.

NIH Guide. Bethesda, MD: National Institutes of Health. A sourcebook published at irregular intervals detailing information about NIH programs and funding mechanisms.

NSF Bulletin. Washington, DC: National Science Foundation. Issued monthly (except July and August) and provides news about NSF programs, deadlines, publications, meetings, and other sources of information.

Search for Security: The ACCESS Guide to Foundations in Peace, Security and International Relations. Anne Allen, ed. Washington, DC: ACCESS, 1989. A listing of 158 foundations funding peace, security, and international relations issues.

Source Book Profiles, 1990. New York: The Foundation Center, 1989. A listing of profiles and grant disbursement patterns of the 1,000 largest U.S. foundations.

Online Databases

Budgetscope. Washington, DC: Data Resources, Inc. Computer searchable through Data Resources, Inc. Includes federal budget information.

CBD-Online. Silver Springs, MD: United Communications Group. The complete, online equivalent of the *Commerce Business Daily.*

DBD Plus. Greenwich, CT: DMS, Inc. Computer searchable through Data Resources, Inc. Provides contract information of federal government sources.

Federal Assistance Programs Retrieval System. Washington, DC: General Services Administration. Computer searchable through Control Data Corporation Business Information Services. Provides details on federal programs. Corresponds to the *Catalog of Federal Domestic Assistance.*

Federal Research Report. Silver Spring, MD: Business Publishers, Inc. Computer searchable through NewsNet. Includes information on federal contract and grant opportunities. Corresponds to *Federal Research Report* newsletter.

Foundation Directory. New York: The Foundation Center. Computer searchable through Dialog Information Services, Inc. Includes profiles of grantmaking foundations with assets of $1,000,000 or more who have given $100,000 or more in the year of record. *The Foundation Directory* is the corresponding printed source.

Foundation Grants Index. New York: The Foundation Center. Computer searchable through Dialog Information Services, Inc. Details grants of $5,000 and over awarded by major U.S. foundations. *Foundation Grants Index* and *Foundation Grants Bimonthly* are the corresponding printed sources.

GRANTS. Phoenix, AZ: The Oryx Press. Computer searchable through Dialog Information Services, Inc. Includes information on grant sources in support of research and study in all fields. The *Directory of Research Grants, Directory of Biomedical and Health Care Grants,* and *Directory of Grants in the Humanities* are corresponding printed sources.

Grants and Contracts Weekly/Grants and Contracts Alert. Arlington, VA: Capitol Publications, Inc. Computer searchable through NewsNet. Includes federal grant and contract funding information in the social sciences, education, and health. The corresponding printed source is *Federal Grants & Contracts Weekly* and *Health Grants & Contracts Weekly.*

Illinois Researcher Information Service (IRIS). Prepared by Campus-wide Research Services Office. Urbana, IL: University of Illinois at Urbana-Champaign. Contains over 4,000 funding opportunities sponsored by federal agencies, private and corporate foundations, and other organizations which support research and scholarship activities. Identifies potential sponsors for faculty, staff, and graduate students' research, teaching, travel, equipment, advanced study, and other activities.

National Foundations. New York: The Foundation Center. Computer searchable through Dialog Information Services, Inc. Lists 22,500 grantmaking foundations in the United States, including those with total assets less than $1,000,000. The *National Data Book* is the corresponding printed material.

Research Monitor News. Washington, DC: National Information Service. Computer searchable through NewsNet. Includes funding information from the *Commerce Business Daily* and the *Federal Register.*

Sponsored Programs Information Network (SPIN). Albany, NY: The Research Foundation of SUNY. Lists funding opportunities (federal, nonfederal, and corporate) designed to assist faculty and administrators in the identification of external support for research, education, and development projects.

Denise Wallen is research development administrator of the Office of Research Administration at the University of New Mexico, Albuquerque. Karen Cantrell holds a doctorate in anthropology and teaches at the University of New Mexico, Albuquerque. They are coeditors of *Funding for Research, Study and Travel: Latin America and the Caribbean; Funding for Research, Study and Travel: The People's Republic of China; Funding for Anthropological Research;* and *Funding for Museums, Archives and Special Collections,* all published by The Oryx Press.